METAPHORS OF DEATH AND RESURRECTION IN THE QUR'AN

Also Available from Bloomsbury

The Composition of the Qur'an, Michel Cuypers
The Qur'an and Modern Arabic Literary Criticism, Mohammad Salama
Qur'anic Hermeneutics, Abdulla Galadari

METAPHORS OF DEATH AND RESURRECTION IN THE QUR'AN

An Intertextual Approach with Biblical and Rabbinic Literature

Abdulla Galadari

BLOOMSBURY ACADEMIC
LONDON • NEW YORK • OXFORD • NEW DELHI • SYDNEY

BLOOMSBURY ACADEMIC
Bloomsbury Publishing Plc
50 Bedford Square, London, WC1B 3DP, UK
1385 Broadway, New York, NY 10018, USA
29 Earlsfort Terrace, Dublin 2, Ireland

BLOOMSBURY, BLOOMSBURY ACADEMIC and the Diana logo are trademarks of Bloomsbury Publishing Plc

First published in Great Britain 2022
This paperback edition published 2023

Cover images: © Cristina Conti / Alamy Stock Photo and RBD Lewis *O 02 al-Qur'ān.* Folio 88v. Free Library of Philadelphia. Rare Book Department. John Frederick Lewis collection of Oriental Manuscripts.

A catalogue record for this book is available from the British Library.

A catalog record for this book is available from the Library of Congress.

ISBN: HB: 978-1-3502-4452-8
PB: 978-1-3502-4456-6
ePDF: 978-1-3502-4453-5
eBook: 978-1-3502-4454-2

Typeset by RefineCatch Limited, Bungay, Suffolk

To find out more about our authors and books visit www.bloomsbury.com and sign up for our newsletters

To the Living

and all zombies seeking to live

CONTENTS

Preface	viii
Acknowledgements	ix
Notes on Transliteration and Translation	x
INTRODUCTION	1
Chapter 1 CONCEPTS OF THE AFTERLIFE	7
Chapter 2 TERMINOLOGIES OF LIFE	23
Chapter 3 TERMINOLOGIES OF DEATH	37
Chapter 4 DEATH	45
Chapter 5 LIFE	55
Chapter 6 THE VIVID PORTRAYAL OF PHYSICAL RESURRECTION IN QUR'AN 2:259	75
Chapter 7 THE PORTRAYAL OF PHYSICAL RESURRECTION IN QUR'AN 2:260	99
Chapter 8 THE METAPHOR OF PHYSICAL RESURRECTION	119
Chapter 9 THE RED COW AND BRINGING BACK THE DEAD	127
Chapter 10 CONCLUSION: DEATH AND RESURRECTION IN THE QUR'AN	147
Notes	151
Bibliography	189
Index of Biblical and Qur'anic verses	243
General Index	251

PREFACE

With the Qur'an's main theme being the Day of Resurrection, it is only imperative to closely study the topic. The traditional Muslim understanding is that death and resurrection in the Qur'an is physical with resurrection portrayed as bones leaving their graves. One of the problems humanity faces is that once a stimulus is associated with something, they typically take it for granted without questioning the premises. Unquestioned premises kill curiosity, which I think might be the natural pure state of a person that Muslim tradition calls '*fiṭrah*'. In Muslim tradition, every person is born with this pure state, but their surrounding environment feeds them with premises. Humans are born with the thirst for curiosity and, unfortunately, children are usually taught not to question what their parents or teachers tell them. This book attempts to at least resurrect the readers' curiosity and not to push a conclusion on anyone. Once premises are shattered, humans will remove the shackles onto which they chain themselves, and then curiosity may be re-ignited. Curious minds will then attempt to go on a journey in search for truth. Such a journey might be intellectual, spiritual or both. The intention is not to assert what the Qur'an says or means, but it is to make people recognize that no matter how much we think we know, we really do not know anything. A person living in the darkness of a cave for a very long time their eyes become atrophied and, therefore, become blinded. With time living in such darkness, the person would start to hallucinate. After a very long time, that person will be unable to recognize what is reality and what is hallucination. Perhaps this is the state of humanity; our souls are living in the darkness of a cave for a very long time. While this book does not essentially suggest what reality is, it at least attempts to make us recognize that we might be hallucinating. The Qur'an suggests that it endeavours to take people from the darkness to the light. The first step is to make us recognize the darkness that we are in and that we are only hallucinating so that we realize there is more to reality than what we think.

Additionally, inter-religious dialogue is ever-more important. While there are some Muslim theological dialogues with Jews and Christians, meaningful theological dialogues with some Eastern traditions, such as Hinduism, Buddhism, and Sikhism are especially lacking. One of the major differences in the worldview is resurrection vis-à-vis reincarnation. While this book does not claim the Qur'an adheres to a specific worldview that will be fully compatible with another, it does open doors for a humble dialogue.

Let us break ourselves from the shackles of premises, resurrect our curiosity and travel together on a journey of self-discovery and sincere search for truth. It is not easy to leave our comfort zones. The journey is not easy. It is an act of *kenōsis* to reach *theōsis*. I do not even have the answers. I can only make you realize that a journey is important and that we can travel together. Please forgive me for my shortcomings.

ACKNOWLEDGEMENTS

I am very grateful for the Living (*al-Ḥayy*) and the living, for the Living has given the living life. I am also very thankful for the dead, for many who were living are dead.

I am appreciative for my physical life (even if such a physicality is not a reality) and everyone who caused it and sustained it. I am grateful for the First Cause and the chain reaction of causes. I am indebted to my late grandparents (Zainab and Abdulla), my parents (Afaf and Ibrahim) and my siblings (Hassan, Sarah, and Hind). I am also very grateful to the divine for matching me with a partner, Fatma, who would accompany me in my spiritual journeys.

I am indebted to the many mentors, friends and colleagues who have steered and supported the mental exploration without which this work would not have been possible: Reuven Firestone, Gabriel Reynolds, John Kaltner, Walid Saleh, Ulrika Mårtensson, David Penchansky, Zohar Hadromi-Allouche, Ayman Shihadeh, Francis X. Clooney, Kurt Anders Richardson, David Burrell, Gordon Newby, Michael Pregill, Holger Zellentin, Mun'im Sirry, Nicolai Sinai, the late Andrew Rippin, Rick Sopher, Esther-Miriam Wagner, Ahmad al-Khuraibet, Mansour al-Khouri, Ben and Diane Blackwell, and many others who have shared their wisdom over the years. I wish to thank those who supported this project and those who did not. I wish to also thank the anonymous reviewers for their invaluable feedback.

I am truly filled with praise for life and death, light and darkness, vision and blindness, hearing and deafness, noise and silence, friends and enemies, and the unity of all the opposites. I am sincerely grateful for the supreme existence, in which nothing else exists except it.

Notes on Transliteration and Translation

Arabic

ء	ʾ	ر	r	ف	f
ا	a, ā	ز	z	ق	q
ب	b	س	s	ك	k
ت	t	ش	sh	ل	l
ث	th	ص	ṣ	م	m
ج	j	ض	ḍ	ن	n
ح	ḥ	ط	ṭ	ة , ه	h
خ	kh	ظ	ẓ	و	w, ū
د	d	ع	ʿ	ي	y, i, ī
ذ	dh	غ	gh		

The short vowelization at the end of a word is typically omitted.

Other languages

The book uses other languages, mainly Semitic and Greek. For transliterations of the Hebrew Bible (HB) and the Greek New Testament (NT), the *SBL Handbook of Style* (2nd edition) is used. For other Semitic terms, the transliteration follows similar to the Arabic with vowelization sometimes omitted.

Qurʾanic translations used in this book are from *The Study Quran* (*TSQ*),[1] with changes to modernize some English terms or other noted changes. Biblical translations are from the *New Revised Standard Version* (*NRSV*),[2] unless otherwise noted.

Quotes from the Mishnah mostly use Neusner's translation, with some variations.

Quotes from the Jerusalem and Babylonian Talmud mostly use Neusner's translation with some variations.

A note on dates

Throughout the manuscript, two dates of death are given for Muslim individuals: the first date is AH and the second is CE.

INTRODUCTION

Considering all the themes that scholars have explored in combination with the Qurʾan – Jesus in the Qurʾan, women in the Qurʾan, and so forth – the subject of death in the Qurʾan has anchored relatively few modern studies.[1] It is a curious ratio because eschatology and the concept of the Day of Resurrection together constitute a major theme in the Qurʾan,[2] and perhaps the theme to which the text is most devoted.[3]

If the major Qurʾanic discourse is on death and resurrection, then by Socratic definition, it is a book of philosophy. The German philosopher Arthur Schopenhauer (d. 1860 CE) said,

> Death is the real inspiring genius or Musagetes of philosophy, and for this reason Socrates defined philosophy as θανάτου μελέτη [*thanatou meletē*]. Indeed, without death there would hardly have been any philosophizing.[4]

Commenting on Schopenhauer's statement, R. Raj Singh understands from this that, 'Death is described here as not just one among many concerns and issues of philosophy but as *the* business of philosophy.'[5] Some will debate around the edges, but theology and philosophy are closely intertwined. Ingolf U. Dalferth has sketched their relationships in this way:

> Theology is not philosophy, and philosophy is not a substitute for religious convictions. But whereas religion can exist without philosophy, and philosophy without religion, theology cannot exist without recourse to each of the other two.[6]

Plato (d. 347 BCE) narrates that Socrates (d. 399 BCE) defined philosophy as '*meletē thanatou*' (rehearsal for death).[7] The theological arguments of the Qurʾan concentrate greatly on the topic of death and resurrection. Thus, one needs to understand what the Qurʾanic philosophy about death and resurrection is.

One of the scholarly works on death in the Qurʾan in the last century is Thomas O'Shaughnessy's *Muhammad's Thoughts on Death: A Thematic Study of the Qurʾanic Data*.[8] O'Shaughnessy sifts through possible Syriac sources for the concept of death in the Qurʾan.[9] He asserts that the Qurʾan adopts in many instances a biblical view of death, although the earliest references to death in the Qur'an, according to the chronological order he adopts, are metaphoric:

> The subject of death occupies a place of growing frequency and importance in the Qur'ān as one passes from the Meccan to the Medinan period. Its earlier occurrences are more often in figures of speech, but these gradually yield to a greater preoccupation with the reality as Muḥammad advances in years. Even a casual paging through the Qur'ān will show to what extent it reflects the many-faceted Biblical view of death, more evidently as set forth in the Old Testament but as closer inspection will reveal, also as propounded in the figurative language of the New.[10]

One of the great scholarly books written on the topic of death in Islam is *The Islamic Understanding of Death and Resurrection*,[11] in which Jane I. Smith and Yvonne Y. Haddad study how the topic evolved throughout history and through various teachings and theological schools in Muslim traditions. This study, in contrast, does not solely focus on the Muslim tradition, and when it does refer to tradition, it generally uses it as a comparative tool through a critical lens. The aim of this book is to look at the principles of death, life and resurrection in the Qur'an. The intention is not to completely ignore the Muslim tradition but to investigate the definition of death in the Qur'an and any possible subtexts that the Qur'an adopts. The reason for such an approach is simple: investigating the Qur'anic concept; it is not necessarily because Muslim tradition has been viewed by many scholars with a sceptical eye in adequately interpreting the Qur'an, and *sometimes* with good reason; John Wansbrough,[12] Patricia Crone, Michael Cook,[13] Fred Donner,[14] and Gabriel Reynolds[15] have been among the many who point out such inadequacy.[16] However, it is in an attempt to read the Qur'an for what it is without completely ignoring some of the insights that may also be found from the Muslim tradition, which allows us to appreciate the plethora of interpretations that also already exist within it. In other words, it is an attempt to do some form of *ijtihād* (independent reasoning) in Qur'anic hermeneutics and not simply an imitation of it (*taqlīd al-ijtihād*).[17]

Indeed, there are numerous legends in circulation, many of which have been drawn on to fill lacunae in Qur'anic interpretation by traditional exegetes. For example, traditional exegetes have misrepresented and to some extent misinterpreted the *Qiblah* passages in the Qur'an by asserting that they are arguing with Jews and Christians about the prophethood of Muḥammad or the superiority of the Ka'bah, when it seems highly likely that the passages are instead alluding to the *Shema'* in Deuteronomy and its rabbinic commentary.[18] This sometimes calls into question the reliability of Muslim tradition in the interpretation of the Qur'an.[19] Thus, this book treads carefully when comparing Muslim tradition with the Qur'anic text, but still appreciates the diverse and insightful understandings already found from within the tradition.

Patricia Crone is a scholar who has, more recently, discussed resurrection in the Qur'an.[20] She mainly focused on the nonbelievers' attitudes towards the Qur'anic concept, yet, like most scholars, took the Qur'anic understanding of bodily resurrection for granted.[21] She divides the nonbelievers into a spectrum of attitudes, those unconcerned about the resurrection (perhaps because some believe they will be saved) and those who doubt or deny it.[22] Crone identifies Qur'anic passages about those who doubt resurrection using such terms as *rayb* (e.g. Qur'an 22:5), *shakk* (e.g. Qur'an 34:21) or *ẓann* (e.g. Qur'an 28:39).[23]

While Crone upholds that the Qur'an does not much discuss other forms of an afterlife or their nature, she particularly endorses the notion that the Qur'an argues for bodily resurrection:

> In short, the unbelievers in the Meccan suras are depicted now as believing in the resurrection without paying much attention to it, now as doubting it, and now as denying it outright, rejecting the very idea of life after death. Their emphasis on the impossibility of restoring decomposed bodies could be taken to mean that some of them believed in a spiritual afterlife, but there are no polemics against this idea, nor against other forms of afterlife such as reincarnation. In so far as one can tell, the disagreement is never over the form that life after death will take, only about its reality. The choice is between bodily resurrection and no afterlife at all.[24]

She implies two main things: that the Qur'an did not engage with people who believed in different forms of an afterlife, and that it advocates bodily resurrection. However, as is discussed in the first chapter of this book, pre-Islamic Arabia made space for various views of an afterlife, and it is conceivable that Muḥammad might have known many of these views. If the Qur'an did not engage with them, either for or against, it may actually be very telling: the Qur'anic portrayal of what is seemingly a bodily resurrection may not be as literal as one would expect.

Yet one cannot discuss death and resurrection in the Qur'an without also discussing the *nafs*.[25] The meaning of this term, whether in the Qur'an or the Bible, has always daunted scholars of the Near East: is it the soul, an embodied self, or an ethereal spirit? It is said that the concept of a disembodied soul comes from ancient Greek philosophy and is foreign to Semitic people. However, Richard C. Steiner has argued that this is not the case and that the Semitic people from the times of the ancient Near East, including the ancient Israelites, had an understanding of a disembodied *nepeš* even before Hellenistic interaction.[26] Therefore, this book closely investigates the concept of the *nafs* in the Qur'an to understand further the concept of death and life in the Qur'an.

Other issues this study introduces to readers concern reincarnation and resurrection. These two concepts appear to be distinct philosophies that existed in the ancient world. Eastern philosophies, and even ancient Greek philosophy, embraced various concepts of reincarnation or the transmigration of souls. Contrariwise, ancient Egyptians, the Semitic people, and, with the rise of Zoroastrianism, the Persian culture embraced concepts of resurrection instead. These two great philosophies, reincarnation and resurrection, existed in the Near East by the time the Qur'an was formulated. Therefore, it is imperative to understand such notions.

The traditional view, accepted by most scholars, interprets most Qur᾿anic passages concerning resurrection as bodily resurrection. For example, Jane Smith states, 'That resurrection at the time of judgment means a resuscitation of the physical body is an accepted reality in Islam and well attested by the Qur᾿an.'[27] While some studies on death in the Qur᾿an focus on physical death and resurrection, this book analyses the definition of death and resurrection in the Qur᾿an focusing on the metaphorical and spiritual aspects of death, especially in light of some of the intertextual relationships of some Qur᾿anic passages with biblical, extrabiblical and rabbinic literature. It argues that the Qur᾿an portrays two different kinds of death and resurrection, that of the body and that of the *nafs*, which may be understood as the body's soul or life force. Therefore, there needs to be a distinction between what the Qur᾿an describes as the resurrection of the body and what it describes as the resurrection of the *nafs*.

Several passages in the Qur᾿an appear to allude to bodily resurrection, but many of those passages, including some that are very lucid in their description of resurrection, do not necessarily refer to it in a literal way. Throughout Muslim history, several Muslim philosophers and mystics have interpreted resurrection as being completely spiritual, not bodily.[28] Ibn Sīnā (d. 428/1037), for example, rejected the concept of physical resurrection because of its irrationality.[29] In some of his works, such as *Kitāb al-najāh* and *Kitāb al-shifā᾿*, he does concede that it is to be accepted as a doctrine of faith disregarding reason, but in his more esoteric book on metaphysics, *Risālah fil-adwiyah al-qalbiyah*, he completely allegorizes and rejects physical resurrection.

At times, the Qur᾿an appears to be explicitly talking about people who are spiritually dead, who may be described as walking tombs or, in other words, zombies. Certain Muslim schools of thought have very distinct interpretations of an afterlife that mainstream Muslims consider heretical. In some Ismāʿīlī discourse, the resurrection has been understood spiritually, which is the resurrection of the *nafs* (soul) enabling one to understand the esoteric meanings of divine revelation.[30] The *Haft bāb* by Ḥassan-i Maḥmūd-i Kātib (d. *c.* 1242 CE; previously attributed to Ḥassan-i Ṣabbāḥ) depicts the Ismāʿīlī doctrine of resurrection in a spiritual manner when the esoteric understandings of the *sharīʿah* (Islamic law) become manifest.[31]

Setting prophetic traditions (*aḥādīth*) aside and looking mainly at the Qur᾿an, we can identify that physical resurrection is *not* what the Qur᾿an is *always* alluding to in the passages that discuss resurrection. Schools of thought with different interpretations for resurrection do not necessarily need to go out of their way to explain their standpoints.

For the purpose of this book, physical resurrection is defined as dead bodies leaving their graves. The reason this needs to be made explicit is that metaphorical resurrection can also be physical: the resurrection of a city may be metaphorical in the sense of a city being rebuilt and repopulated. Therefore, the main argument this book makes is that passages concerning resurrection in the Qur᾿an are not *always* physical, and when they are physical, they can still be understood metaphorically, without necessarily denoting bodies leaving their graves. However, this argument does not imply that Islam does not teach physical resurrection.[32] Some Muslim doctrines do not necessarily explicitly trace themselves to the Qur'an, such as the expectation of a Messianic figure. Therefore, even if the argument made is that the Qur'an does not *always* denote physical resurrection, I am not at all arguing that the doctrine of physical resurrection is not Islamic.

Another important finding this book tries to understand is the type of audience with whom the Qur'an is in conversation. Understanding the possible subtexts or oral traditions from biblical, extrabiblical and rabbinic traditions open a door in understanding the community with whom the Qur'an engages. It appears that the Jewish community with whom the Qur'an is in dialogue is well-aware of the Torah, rabbinic literature and even Jewish liturgy. This provides us some insights to this community. When analysing Islamic sources about this possible Jewish community, Haggai Mazuz concludes that the Jews, during the earliest years of Islam, were Talmudic-Rabbinic Jews who were observant and held beliefs in accordance with the *midrash* (rabbinic interpretations).[33] While his approach was mainly through Islamic traditional sources and not necessarily the Qur'an, the findings of this book might echo some of his own: the Jewish community with whom the Qur'an is in discussion are well aware of rabbinic tradition, interpretation and liturgy.

Chapter 1

CONCEPTS OF THE AFTERLIFE

Reincarnation and resurrection are both philosophical conceptions of the afterlife, but with apparent contradictions. In general, reincarnation is the broad notion of rebirth, whether the transmigration of conscious souls, as in Hinduism, or the transmigration of fruits of actions (*karma*) taken up by a different, yet related personality, as in Buddhism. Many traditions of ancient Europe, such as Pythagoreanism and Manichaeism, include concepts of reincarnation.[1] Resurrection is also not a concept exclusive to the Abrahamic religions, as it also exists in Zoroastrianism[2] as well as in ancient Egyptian cosmologies.[3] This chapter introduces those different concepts of the afterlife, as they were not foreign to the audience of the Qur'an, though the specifics of their nature have varied across cultures. After introducing these concepts, a section introduces the methodology used in the book in its attempt to focus on the passages of death and resurrection in the Qur'an that are possibly intended to be metaphorical or spiritual or, possibly, effectively have dual meaning.

Reincarnation

The origins of reincarnation are difficult to discern. The notion had some prominence in Indic culture, ancient Greece[4] and even among Celtic Druids.[5] Its attestation among Amerindians and the Inuit led Mircea Eliade and Antonia Mills to argue that such beliefs might also have existed in the shamanic principles of hunter-gatherer tribes.[6] When invoked, ancestors' spirits may sometimes possess the body of the shaman.[7] Such early beliefs might have been the kernel from which the belief in metempsychosis, or transmigration of souls, evolved.

Reincarnation comprises a diversity of beliefs. In ancient Greece, Pythagoras believed in the immortality of the soul[8] and in metempsychosis.[9] Both concepts are prevalent in India, leading some scholars to argue that Pythagorean beliefs might have roots there.[10] Although the ancient Egyptians also believed in the immortality of the soul, the nature of the afterlife and resurrection in Egyptian culture appear to be distinct from the Pythagorean view.

Reincarnation in India underwent a great transformation with the rise of Buddhism. Buddhist teachings do not include the immortality of the soul.

Buddhism denies the existence of a soul or a self in a living being; accordingly, reincarnation does not take the form of metempsychosis, in which a soul is reborn, but in the form of metamorphosis.[11] This was a break from the Hindu understanding of an *ātman* (soul), a term that can be traced back to the Rigveda in the second millennium BCE by the Indo-European tribes that lived in Northern India.[12]

Buddhism teaches non-self (*anattā* or *anātman*), as can be seen in the Nikāya Suttas.[13] In Buddhism, a soul does not migrate to be reborn in another body since there is no concept of an immortal soul.[14] An important tenet of Buddhism is the concept of impermanence (*anicca* or *anitya*), according to which nothing is immortal.[15] Although the concept of impermanence also exists in Hinduism in that everything is constantly changing,[16] the difference is mainly on the existence of a soul (*ātman*).[17] In Buddhism, a soul does not exist.[18] When it comes to paths to liberation (*nirvana* in Buddhism or *moksha* in Hinduism), does the distinction really matter?[19] Is a monk seeking liberation selfish? Buddhist tradition shows that Gautama Buddha tried to teach only what is necessary for liberation. Many Buddhist monks, in some traditions, do not even seek to achieve liberation; rather, the aim is to become a *bodhisattva*, one who wants to become enlightened for the sake of others and not oneself, and who therefore delays *nirvana* out of compassion for all beings.[20]

Whether or not the doctrine of non-self (*anattā*) is a way to teach selflessness,[21] it led to an evolution of the concept of reincarnation – there no longer being a soul to leave a body and be reborn.[22] It was for this reason that some Buddhists prefer the term 'rebirth' over 'reincarnation'.[23]

Concepts of reincarnation can be seen in Kabbalah and in orthodox Hasidic Judaism;[24] in some Muslim schools of thought, such as the Druze (branching from the Isma'īlīs);[25] and among some Christian Gnostics of the past.[26] The various concepts of reincarnation within Judaism, Christianity, and Islam continuously evolved throughout history.[27] Jane Smith writes:

> Metempsychosis [*tanāsukh*] and incarnation of spirits in other bodies [*ḥulūl*] have been upheld by some individuals and some schools in the history of Islam. The doctrine of metempsychosis came originally to Islam from India and gained credence in a number of schools of thought considered outside the orthodox fold. Some persons associated with the Mu'tazila held that God's justice necessitates another opportunity for those whose good and bad deeds are equal and who thus merit neither the Fire nor the Garden. Many of the Shī'a, such as the Ismā'īlia, Bāṭinīya [*sic*] and others, applied the doctrine of metempsychosis both to the Imam and to individual believers. Most Sufis, like most orthodox Muslims, have rejected transmigration, although a few accept it as a means of achieving spiritual perfection.[28]

Despite resurrection being a fundamental theme in the Qur'an, several early Muslim schools of thought accepted reincarnation.[29] Even later Muslim groups, such as Yoruba Muslims, do accept reincarnation; in the Yoruba tradition, reincarnation is believed to occur within the family,[30] as is true of many shamanistic belief systems.[31] Reincarnation's acceptance among Yoruba Muslims suggests that they might have simply been influenced by shamanistic indigenous beliefs that predate Islam in the region. The Druze concept of reincarnation, as another example, is strictly within the faith. That is, a person who is born into a Druze family would not reincarnate as a non-Druze after death.[32] The concept of reincarnation in Islamic thought may have come from the East – in India, as Smith and Haddad state,[33] but it may also have originated with Muslim interaction with the treatises of Greek philosophers, especially among the Druze, many of whom held Pythagoras in high esteem.[34] Delving into various Muslim schools of thought that believed in reincarnation, Patricia Crone found they were from not only esoteric but also exoteric schools.[35] She suggests that influence from followers of the Persian Mazdak (d. 528 CE)[36] – who, though a Zoroastrian, believed in reincarnation[37] – made its way into Muslim thought.[38] While Zoroastrianism espouses a belief in resurrection, it has been suggested that Manichaean influence might have gradually imposed itself during Late Antiquity, including the notion of reincarnation,[39] even though their beliefs and tenets diverged in other aspects.

Although the Qur'an appears to have emerged within a milieu of resurrection surrounded by Judaism, Christianity and even Zoroastrianism, some pre-Islamic Arabs might have believed in some sort of reincarnation called 'the return' (*al-raj'ah*), in which a person returns to this life after physical death.[40] Some Muslim exegetes even interpret the following Qur'anic passages as the *raj'ah* that some pre-Islamic Arabs believed in:[41]

> There is nothing but our life in this world: we die and we live, and we will not be resurrected.
>
> Qur'an 23:37

> They say, 'There is nothing but our life in this world. We die and we live, and none destroys us except time [*al-dahr*].' But they have no knowledge thereof. They are but deluded.[42]
>
> Qur'an 45:24

However, we have no details of the nature of this *raj'ah* or whether, indeed, some pre-Islamic Arabs believed in it. Perhaps it was influenced by Greek, Gnostic, or even Manichaean doctrines of metempsychosis. It could also have been only speculations by some Qur'anic exegetes many centuries after the emergence of the Qur'an to make sense of some of its passages that might point to some people asking for a *raj'ah* (return) to this life (e.g. Qur'an 23:99). Patricia Crone did suggest the possibility of various views on an afterlife existing within the Qur'anic milieu. She argued that the Qur'an particularly engages with those who denied or doubted the reality of it.[43] When commenting on the word order of 'we die and we live', she does, however, assume that the nonbelievers are using a biblical formula, in which God is shown to have the power to bring forth death and life in that order (e.g. Deut. 32:39, 1 Sam. 2:6, 2 Kgs. 5:7).[44] It is likely that the Qur'an is aware of some biblical formulae, but Crone suggests that the nonbelievers, in this case, are also fully aware of the Bible or more so parabiblical literature, and, therefore, know the biblical formula.[45] She is convinced that the Qur'anic nonbelievers (*mushrikūn*) have some Judaeo-Christian roots.[46]

Some later Muslim communities, such as some Shīʿī schools of thought, do believe in the *rajʿah* (return) of their *imāms*, meaning they will return to this life to lead their followers.[47] This kind of return to this life may not be strange within the early Islamic milieu, as resurrection in some Jewish thought is the return of the righteous to this life during the Messianic Age.[48] These conceptions of a select group who would return to life was part of Near Eastern beliefs, as will be discussed in the next section. Abū al-ʿAlāʾ al-Maʿarrī (d. 449/1057) is known to have denied resurrection, and some think he might have subscribed to the *rajʿah*.[49]

Some traditional Muslim scholars interpret the *dahr* (time) in Qur'an 45:24 – 'We die and we live, and none destroys us except time (*al-dahr*)' – as a form of reincarnation.[50] Some scholars hold that some pre-Islamic Arabs believed in this form of reincarnation, and think that it perhaps had Persian influence from Zurvanism, whose name in Middle Persian, *zurvān*, actually means time.[51] After all, Zurvān, who is the god of time, is also the god of life and death.[52] Aida Gasimova argued of Zurvanite influence on pre-Islamic Arabian doctrines,[53] which makes the connection between Zurvān with the concept of *dahr* a possibility,[54] even though W. Montgomery Watt hesitated to assert such relationship.[55] In pre-Islamic Arabian poetry, *dahr* is presented fatalistically.[56]

Acknowledging Manichaeism, Mazdakism within Zoroastrianism, and other traditions, Patricia Crone states, 'Reincarnation of the soul and periodic incarnation of the deity were ideas with a wide diffusion in the pre-Islamic Near East, and the concept of the moon as a carrier of souls is likely to have been widely diffused too.'[57] Within the Islamic milieu of the Near East, reincarnation was not a foreign concept. Moreover, if Hinduism, which has a highly developed concept of reincarnation,[58] emerged from a religion of some Indo-European tribes[59] that migrated to India from Iran or other places within the Eurasian steppes,[60] then the Indian branch may not necessarily be the prime influencer of transmigration of souls among the ancient Greeks or other places like Persia. These traditions might have shared a similar heritage for such belief,[61] or this belief could have emerged in these cultures independently.

One should not assume, as Margaret Smith suggests, that the concept of reincarnation has only entered Muslim thought directly from India, or perhaps to a lesser extent from Greek philosophy on the transmigration of souls,[62] but that such concepts were known to pre-Islamic Arabs through the Persians, within the Qur'anic milieu. Nonetheless, this does not necessarily mean that all Muslim schools of thought that have espoused the doctrine of reincarnation of some sort throughout history have all taken it from either pre-Islamic Arab concepts or Persian; indeed, perhaps some were influenced by other cultures, such as Greek or Indian.[63]

Resurrection

Although the concept of resurrection is found today in religions as varied as Judaism, Zoroastrianism, Christianity and Islam, in the ancient Near East it especially took the form of dying-and-rising deities.[64] In ancient Mesopotamia, the deity Tammuz dies and is resurrected;[65] in ancient Egypt, Osiris goes through a similar cycle.[66] These early concepts of resurrection seem to have evolved into later cultures within the ancient Near East.[67] Although reincarnation in its various forms was a major belief in diverse ancient Greek traditions, the idea of resurrection was also familiar, especially in the sense of mortals killed only to be resurrected as gods, such as Asclepius, Achilles and Memnon.[68]

As reincarnation may have risen from the shamanistic beliefs of hunter-gatherer societies,[69] resurrection may have risen among farming societies.[70] Agricultural communities see the seasons change and understand the dynamic mechanisms of cultivation: plants sprout, give fruit, are harvested and wither away. This, they understood, was an ongoing cycle. After trees shed all their leaves and appear as if dead, they will spring to life again. Therefore, it would make sense to imagine that the same occurs with people: they die only to be raised again.[71] One might thus imagine that the Neolithic Revolution, the long transition period when hunter-gatherer culture changed into agricultural settlements,[72] planted the first seeds for the resurrection of the dead as a concept. Erich Isaac hypothesized that death-and-resurrection myths were first introduced in this period,[73] but Brian Spooner suggests that the reason might have been the high mortality rate in populated settlements during the Neolithic Revolution, occurring due to infectious diseases and a lack of sanitation. As a result, humans developed greater curiosity about and searched for the meaning of death and afterlife;[74] this may also have functioned as a psychosocial tool for grieving.[75] In any case, it seems natural for people who understand the cycle of agriculture to see an analogue in human life and death.[76]

Ancient Egyptian culture was very much dependent on the Nile for its crops.[77] Because of the rise of agriculture, the sun became the centrepiece of human society. The sun was very important for identifying the seasons,[78] upon which holy days and feasts relied (and along with them came the birth of calendars).[79] Even the cycle of the sun itself, which rises and sets only to rise again the next day, is analogous to death and resurrection.[80] In ancient Egypt, the Sun-god, Ra, grew to great prominence.[81] Ra travels on a boat through the sky, and when the sun sets every evening on the horizon (*Akhet*), he travels into the underworld (*Duat*).[82] Ronald A. Wells argues that the concept of an hour, as a measurement of a length of time, is linked to the rising of star patterns in the underworld in ancient Egypt.[83]

The concept of resurrection appears to have evolved later in human history than reincarnation did and is likely to have gained prominence with the invention of agriculture. Nonetheless, the main difference between early and later resurrection myths concerns who dies and who comes back to life. In many ancient societies, it is typically a dying-and-rising god, whereas the concept of a universal resurrection of the dead appears to be a later development.[84] In ancient Egypt, rules and rituals were needed to ensure that the dead would survive the journey in the underworld and rise back to life.[85] Without such rituals, the dead might have no chance of living again.

Whether early Israelites believed in the resurrection of the dead or not is difficult to discern.[86] The early books of the Hebrew Bible do not delve much into ideas about the afterlife. Alan Segal suggests that the reason the Israelites did not emphasize the afterlife is because they wanted to distinguish themselves from the pagans, who did;[87] in the case of the Qur'an, the motivation appears to be reversed. By the time of the Gospels' composition, the Israelites apparently did not agree on the resurrection of the dead, and there were possible debates among the Sadducees and the Pharisees on this issue.[88] It is possible that the concepts of resurrection spilled into Israelite culture during the Babylonian exile, when Zoroastrian ideas were popular.[89] Mary Boyce identifies Zoroastrian influence on Isa. 25:8 and 26:19 that would shape the concept of Jewish resurrection:[90]

> Your dead shall live, their corpses shall rise. O dwellers in the dust, awake and sing for joy! For your dew is a radiant dew, and the earth will give birth to those long dead.
>
> Isa. 26:19

If these passages in Isaiah were shaped by Zoroastrian beliefs on resurrection, it would mean that such influence entered Israelite thought even prior to the Babylonian exile or the Maccabean Revolt.[91] Nonetheless, Boyce makes clear that the Israelites did not simply borrow Zoroastrian concepts but reinterpreted and reconciled them with traditional Jewish beliefs. Yet she claims that the Israelite elite did not accept these concepts, and perhaps that is the reason why the priests, and eventually the Sadducees, denied resurrection.[92] It must, however, be noted that not much is understood and known regarding the Sadducees, and recent biblical scholars attempt to tread carefully through our understanding of their practice and beliefs. Beyond that, it has also been argued that the dualistic nature of the Qumran community's Dead Sea Scrolls is evidence of the Zoroastrian influence on Judaism.[93]

Depictions of resurrection can be found in the books of Ezekiel (e.g. Ezek. 37:1–14) and Daniel (e.g. Dan. 12:1–13), which themselves may have certain Zoroastrian connections.[94] However, the Samaritans also believe in resurrection, though they do not accept any books of the Hebrew Bible besides the books of Moses, and therefore may not have been influenced by exilic and postexilic Jewish books; nonetheless, a scholarly debate exists with some suggesting that the doctrine of resurrection among Samaritans remains relatively late.[95] Some evidence from early rabbinic and early Christian texts suggest that Samaritans did not always hold this belief.[96] On the other hand, there is a possibility that the concept of resurrection did exist during the pre-exilic period.[97] After all, some Semitic tribes may have even been influenced by ancient Egyptian cultures,[98] who did have concepts of resurrection; it would be possible for the Israelites to have understood and perhaps accepted this notion without any Zoroastrian influence during the Babylonian exile.[99]

Jon Levenson, in *Resurrection and the Restoration of Israel*, argues that the Israelites already had the concept of a realm of the dead, which the Hebrew Bible calls Sheol,[100] even prior to the Babylonian exile.[101] However, he claims that the Hebrew Bible is uninterested in the concept of an afterlife.[102]

Christopher Hays argues that First Isaiah[103] and Job seem to show awareness of Egyptian concepts of the afterlife.[104] The ancient Egyptian culture was known to the Canaanites, at least around the fourteenth century BCE.[105] During that time, the Amarna letters, which were diplomatic messages between Canaanite and Egyptian rulers, were written, suggesting that there was contact at least as far back between the eastern and western sides of Sinai.[106] Accordingly, it would not be unusual for the ancient Israelites to have known about Egyptian culture,[107] religion and traditions, including the concept of resurrection.[108] The interaction between the ancient Israelites and the Egyptians appears to have taken place at the turn of the early first millennium BCE as well,[109] which could have further brought in the concept of resurrection in the minds of the ancient Israelites.

The ancient Canaanites did have beliefs of dying-and-rising gods.[110] The Canaanites might have themselves influenced ancient Israelite beliefs on resurrection, as suggested by some scholars.[111] However, others find it unlikely.[112] Most importantly, resurrection was reserved for a select few, a concept that is somewhat echoed in Judaism that only the righteous will be resurrected and will have a share in the Messianic age.[113] Because Canaanite and other Mesopotamian cults also held that most people will never be resurrected, except for a few,[114] some scholars have argued a non-Zoroastrian influence in Jewish eschatology.[115] Although concepts of resurrection exist in ancient Egyptian, Zoroastrian and Canaanite thoughts, some early scholars argue that the Jewish origin of this concept may stem from the Greek metempsychosis, which gradually changed.[116] No strong evidence necessarily suggests this, and in fact David Russell argues that foreign influence on Jewish concepts of the afterlife is drastically overstated and that the concept arose within the Israelite community's conviction of their special relationship with God that would survive death.[117]

During the Second Temple period, Israelite eschatology started to develop further.[118] The development of the doctrine of resurrection in Judaism has drawn significant interest, and at the turn of the last century one of the few who probed this was Arthur Marmorstein.[119] But the research on the topic has long since developed in the field, given newer textual and archaeological discoveries. In a comprehensive review, Harry Sysling has shown how the *targumim*[120] interpreted the resurrection of the dead in its own ambiguities or evidence of its physicality.[121] Expounding further, Casey Elledge proposes three existing concepts on death and the afterlife: (1) bodily resurrection with no specificity on the condition of the human soul; (2) belief in immortality of the soul without bodily resurrection; and (3) belief in bodily resurrection and immortality of the soul.[122] Jason von Ehrenkrook adds a fourth concept that existed at the time, which is the complete rejection of any sort of afterlife.[123]

The rabbinic tradition seems to have been an evolved great-grandchild of Second Temple Judaism.[124] The Mishnah recounts a saying by R. Pinhas b. Yair that the Holy Spirit leads to the resurrection of the dead, which comes through Elijah:

> R. Pinhas b. Yair says, 'Heedfulness leads to cleanliness, cleanliness leads to cleanness, cleanness leads to abstinence, abstinence leads to holiness, holiness leads to modesty, modesty leads to the fear of sin, the fear of sin leads to piety, piety leads to the Holy Spirit, the Holy Spirit leads to the resurrection of the dead, and the resurrection of the dead comes through Elijah, blessed be his memory, Amen.'[125]

Further developing from the Mishnah, the Talmud recounts a debate among the rabbis on who is resurrected, suggesting that only the righteous will be resurrected, while the wicked would never have life, citing Jer. 51:39.[126] Denying the resurrection of the dead is a sin.[127] Yet there is evidence from Jewish inscriptions that proves that such a faith of an afterlife was not a universal view.[128] The Mishnah recounts a tradition that all Israelites will have a share in *ʿolam ha-ba* (the world to come) except for a person who says the resurrection of the dead is a teaching that does not derive from the Torah, a person who says the Torah does not come from Heaven, and an Epicurean.[129] Here, it is interesting that this tradition in the Mishnah abhors not only those who do not believe in resurrection but also those who deny that resurrection is in the Torah.[130] According to some rabbinic traditions in the Babylonian Talmud, Deut. 32:39 implies resurrection of the dead, which states that God causes death and life, and causes wounds and heals.[131] Another tradition to argue for resurrection suggested in the Babylonian Talmud is based on Num. 18:28, which describes giving the heave-offering[132] to Aaron, Moses's priest brother.[133] Aaron died before ever entering the land of Israel, so it is interpreted in the Talmud as Aaron being destined to live once more and the Israelites giving him heave-offering.[134] Another tradition by R. Simai recounted in the Babylonian Talmud suggests that a covenant was made between God and the patriarchs to give them the land of Canaan (i.e. Exod. 6:4), a promise whose fulfilment requires that the patriarchs be resurrected.[135] According to the Babylonian Talmud, R. Eliezer b. R. Yosé also uses the following passage to argue for resurrection: 'such a person [soul/*nepeš*] shall be utterly cut off and bear the guilt' (Num. 15:31).[136] However, this specific passage talks of the *nepeš*, which may involve a point of debate about whether it is the soul with or without a body. Rabbinic traditions in the Babylonian Talmud further explain how the dead will rise and that the body and soul will be judged together.[137]

Several traditions in the Talmud talk of the resurrection of the dead and overcoming death,[138] and provide references from the Hebrew Bible suggesting resurrection (e.g. 1 Sam. 2:6).[139] Commenting on Prov. 30:15–16, a tradition attributed to R. Yoshiya in the Babylonian Talmud compares a barren womb to a grave and relating it to resurrection:

> 'What is the connection between the grave and the womb?'
> 'It is to tell you, just as the womb receives and gives forth, so Sheol receives and gives forth.'

> 'And that moreover yields an argument a fortiori: If the womb receives in secret but gives forth with loud cries. Sheol, which receives with loud cries [of mourning] surely should give forth [the dead] with great noise indeed!'
>
> 'On the basis of that argument there is an answer to those who say that, on the basis of the teachings of the Torah in particular, there is no basis for expecting the resurrection of the dead.'[140]

Nonetheless, the Hebrew Bible generally emphasizes procreation as a norm for allowing one to become immortal by keeping one's name alive through descendants, as in other Near Eastern traditions, such as the *Epic of Gilgamesh*.[141] Accordingly, the rabbis may not have fully conveyed the intention of the authors of Proverbs. Jacob L. Wright states:

> The rabbis of the Tannaitic and Amoraic periods are even more deliberate in their repudiation of heroic death. Thus, they did not transmit 1 Maccabees, with its statist ideals of noble death.[142]

Apart from the Pentateuch, some other parts of the Hebrew Bible speak of what happens after death: 'and the dust returns to the earth as it was, and the breath [spirit/*rûaḥ*] returns to God who gave it' (Qoh. 12:7).[143] Also, Ezek. 37:1–14 explains that dry bones are given life when God gives them the spirit (*rûaḥ*) of life. In it, God promises that He will open the graves of the Israelites and bring them to their land. The rabbis cite this passage in their Talmudic deliberations about resurrection.[144] Ezek. 37:11 makes it explicit that the symbolism refers to the whole house of Israel.[145] Accordingly, even the Talmud portrays the debate on whether this is a metaphor or literal with many theological repercussions:[146] these passages have been understood as a symbolic return of the Israelites from exile,[147] an interpretation also espoused by the Qumran community.[148] During the time of the Bar-Kokhba revolt, this passage continued to be ambiguous in terms of what the community understood – whether they thought it expressed a literal resurrection of those who died for the cause or the resurrection of the cause itself.[149]

The Dura-Europos synagogue paintings of the Ezekiel panel date to the third century CE, and even there it is difficult to assert whether the paintings depict the prophet's vision as the restoration of the nation of Israel or as the Talmudic understanding of the resurrection of the righteous during the Messianic age.[150] Regardless, the Talmud narrates the debate and concludes that Ezekiel's vision is to be interpreted not only metaphorically but also literally.[151]

According to a tradition in the Babylonian Talmud, Ps. 116:9 is also a reference to the resurrection of the dead.[152] Another tradition in the Babylonian Talmud suggests that God has three keys that are not handed over to the hand of an agent: the key to rain, the key to childbirth, and the key to the resurrection of the dead.[153] A different tradition suggests that Job denied the resurrection of the dead, according to Job 7:9.[154] The rabbis in the Talmud not only take it for granted that the resurrection of the dead will occur but also discuss other things about the world-to-come.[155]

Perhaps, in the rabbinic tradition, it had been important to interpret the Hebrew Bible to foster the idea of the resurrection of the dead. For example, when Jon Levenson suggests that the concept of an afterlife existed even during pre-Second Temple Judaism,[156] this in no way suggests that the concept of an afterlife was necessarily a belief in the resurrection of the body.

The Jews at the time of Christ, which included the Pharisees and the Sadducees, were divided between different schools of thought.[157] According to Acts 23:8, the Sadducees did not believe in the resurrection. Benedict Viviano and Justin Taylor state that Acts 23:8 should be translated as, 'the Sadducees say that there is no resurrection either as an angel [i.e. in the form of an angel] or as a spirit [i.e. in the form of a spirit], but the Pharisees acknowledge them both'.[158] However, evidence from the Synoptic Gospels, as well as the writings of Josephus, suggest that the Sadducees did not generally believe in the resurrection of the dead (i.e. Mt. 22:23–33, Mk. 12:18–27, Lk. 20:27–38).[159] Jesus's answer to the Sadducees in the Synoptic Gospels concerning levirate marriage is an argument not necessarily for resurrection but for the existence of an afterlife. If Abraham, Isaac and Jacob are physically resurrected, in which sphere or realm are they resurrected? John Kilgallen argued that, at least in the Lukan account, Jesus's response does not necessarily suggest the patriarchs being currently alive.[160] Moreover, in the Matthean and Lukan accounts, Jesus justifies his response that in heaven people will become like angels. If the Sadducees did not believe in angels, then they might have had a different reaction to Jesus's response. In the Markan account, this particular justification is omitted, suggesting the possibility of a stronger allusion to the Pentateuch.[161] Adelbert Denaux argues that Jesus's answer to the Sadducees in the Synoptics is evidence of Jesus arguing in favour of a general resurrection.[162] Humbly, we might disagree, since the Pharisees did not necessarily believe in a universal resurrection[163] yet seemed satisfied with Jesus's answer.[164]

Bradley Trick argues that for God to fulfil his covenant to the patriarchs by giving them the land of Canaan implies resurrection, as death would mean that the covenant would cease, just as marriage ceases with death.[165] He proposes that the death of the body does not mean that the patriarchs have actually died and the covenant with God is therefore annulled, but rather that they would be alive in an interim state before their bodily resurrection.[166]

The Pharisees may not have believed in a universal resurrection of all the dead, but in the resurrection of the righteous.[167] Evildoers are not understood to be resurrected into eternal damnation and are instead annihilated.[168] It remains unclear whether pre-Christian Judaism defined resurrection to be the rising of the same dead body or the rising of the dead in a different body.[169] Jonathan Draper states that, in rabbinic and early Christian exegesis, resurrection is a reward for those who suffered, such as martyrs.[170] He circumnavigates his argument based on the citation of Zech. 14:5 in the *Didache*:[171] since it is a reward, it is not shared with anyone but the righteous and especially martyrs.[172]

James H. Charlesworth divides resurrection by authors of early Israelite and Christian texts into different categories: (1) resurrecting a nation (e.g. Ezekiel 37);

(2) raising a group from disenfranchisement; (3) raising of the individual from social disenfranchisement; (4) raising of the individual from personal embarrassment; (5) raising of the individual from the sickbed to health (e.g. Mk. 5:21–43); (6) raising of the individual from inactivity to do God's will; (7) raising of the individual from despondency due to consciousness of sin; (8) raising of the individual from ignorance to divinely revealed knowledge; (9) raising of the individual from meaninglessness in this world to a realising eschatology (i.e. experiencing the End Time in the present); (10) Both-And, where the author may intentionally collapse any distinction between the present age and the future age; (11) raising of Christ from Sheol; (12) raising an apocalyptist into heaven; (13) a spiritual rising up or awakening of an individual (14) raising of the individual from death to mortal life (e.g. Lazarus in John 11); (15) raising of the individual from death to eternal life; and (16) intentional ambiguity (i.e. the author intentionally not asserting what happens in the future).[173]

In that light, Outi Lehtipuu ardently argues that even the term resurrection in many Jewish, Christian, and Greco-Roman texts are hopelessly ambiguous, which may even shed light to how it would not be surprising in its ambiguity in the Qur'an:

> resurrection is an ambiguous category in ancient Jewish, Christian, and other Greco-Roman sources. It is not possible to restrict its meaning only to expressing bodily resurrection. Because of the prevalence of the Greek words that are used to denote resurrection, resurrection terminology is hopelessly ambiguous. It is not always obvious whether a word is used for the revival of a dead body without the idea of immortality or whether it means overcoming death permanently, either acquiring a new life after death or as a spiritual process during earthly life ... Resurrection was never a simple, clearly defined symbol, but, from the beginning, it was interpreted in various ways.[174]

Alan Segal suggests that perhaps the Israelites adopted the concept of the immortality of the soul from the Greeks and from the Persians (i.e. Zoroastrians) the concept of resurrection,[175] as some rabbinic literature shows evidence of a conjoined belief.[176] Crone has also pointed to the Zoroastrian belief in resurrection and its possible influence in pre-Islamic Arabia at the time of Muḥammad.[177] In that case, one might also infer that the Qur'an was perhaps not solely under a Judaeo-Christian sphere of influence and understood Zoroastrian doctrines only as mediated through Judaeo-Christian beliefs and literature but could have had first-hand knowledge of Zoroastrian sources. The Qur'an appears, at least once, explicit in its awareness of Zoroastrianism or some form thereof (i.e. Qur'an 22:17).[178] Resurrection being a known concept in pre-Islamic Arabia is even attested in the Qur'an, emphasizing that the Qur'an is not bringing a concept that is foreign to its audience, even when the audience is made up of neither Jews nor Christians; Patricia Crone even made a note of that in an article published posthumously.[179] The following passage demonstrates that the Qur'an's audience is aware of resurrection and believe in God.

> [79]He it is Who created you on the earth, and unto Him shall you be gathered. [80]And He it is Who gives life and causes death, and unto Him belongs the variation of the night and the day. Will you not, then, understand? [81]Nay, but they say the like of that which was said by those of old. [82]They say, 'What, when we have died and are dust and bones, are we to be resurrected? [83]We and our fathers were certainly warned of this before. These are nothing but stories [*asāṭīr*][180] of those of old.' [84]Say, 'Whose is the earth and whosoever is upon it, if you know?' [85]They will say, 'God's.' Say, 'Will you not, then, take heed?'
>
> Qur'an 23:79–85

The logical question the passage poses is that since the audience believes in God, who owns the earth and those upon it, then in what sense would they be surprised if God is capable of resurrecting the dead? Additionally, the Qur'an uses the term *asāṭīr* for stories; often a neglected fact, the term implies that those stories are written down and not simply oral traditions.[181] The root *s-ṭ-r* is even used by the Qur'an to define writing: 'Nūn. By the pen and that which they inscribe [*yasṭurūn*]' (Qur'an 68:1).

Crone writes, 'three positions are described in the Qur'ān: belief in the resurrection, scepticism about it, and outright denial of it'.[182] She assumes the possibility that the audience of the Qur'an might actually have some biblical background. Regardless, the Qur'an does suggest that the message it is bringing them, even when the audience is assumed to be pre-Islamic Arabs (neither Jews nor Christians), is not new and is not something of which their forefathers were unaware (e.g. Qur'an 23:68, 46:17).[183]

With various concepts of an afterlife or lack thereof in Near Eastern cultures, it would be important to understand how and what the Qur'an refers to in its passages about death and resurrection. The next chapters focus on some Semitic terms that denote life and death. Then, a closer reading will analyse the Qur'anic passages on resurrection, while comparing them with biblical, extrabiblical, and rabbinic literature. The comparisons are made to understand the possible subtexts alluded to by the Qur'an and to shed light on the Qur'anic interpretation of some of the passages on death and resurrection.

Methodology

The method used in the analysis and arguments of this book is an intra- and inter-textual analysis of the Qur'an within itself and biblical, extrabiblical and rabbinic literature. In recent scholarship, this method has been used by various scholars, such as Reuven Firestone,[184] John Reeves,[185] Nicolai Sinai,[186] Gabriel Reynolds,[187] Emran El-Badawi,[188] Holger Zellentin[189] and many others. Obviously, this trend has existed even longer than that list suggests; however, some earlier Western scholarship was more polemical in their approach than the more recent scholarship on the matter.[190]

The Qur'an and biblical literature enjoy an intertextual relationship. In Reuven Firestone's words, the Qur'an 'contains so many parallels with the Hebrew Bible and New Testament that it could not possibly exist without its scriptural predecessors as subtexts. The Qur'ān itself recognizes this in its extremely referential nature'.[191] The intra- and inter-textual approach employed in this book mirrors that of the hermeneutical method demonstrated in my previous book *Qur'anic Hermeneutics: Between Science, History, and the Bible*.[192] Accordingly, Arabic terms of the Qur'an are compared to identify how their definitions are attested in other Semitic languages with the possible use of wordplay.

Like *Qur'anic Hermeneutics*, this book attempts to transcend any agenda. It is neither attempting to suggest, for example, that physical resurrection in the sense of bones leaving their graves literally exists in the Qur'an in a clear, uncontested description nor is the goal to frame such a notion as completely alien to the Qur'an. It only suggests that *some* verses in the Qur'an that have traditionally been viewed as clear examples of literal resurrection are perhaps not quite so, when sufficiently intertextualized with biblical, extrabiblical and rabbinic literature.

Some believers of certain religious traditions feel threatened by epistemic humility. However, Katherine Dormandy has demonstrated that epistemic humility serves religious beliefs more than dogmatic beliefs for the very simple reason that when counterevidence is received by a dogmatic believer, their whole worldview may be shattered.[193] She argues that even if someone holds a *dogmatic-but-true* belief, they would still be under the sin of epistemic vices like intellectual arrogance:

> We cannot deny that it [epistemic humility] comes with epistemic risks, but the epistemic gains that it promises, including religious truth, understanding, and epistemic agency, are better than any gains there may be eschewing it. Moreover, eschewing epistemic humility poses a far greater epistemic risk to her religious beliefs than the dogmatic-but-true believer seems to realize.[194]

Since Dormandy considers that if *dogmatic-but-true* belief gives birth to an epistemic vice of intellectual arrogance, epistemic humility, in contrast, is a virtue.[195] She even argues,

> . . . it [religious disagreement] can promote the improvement of religious belief systems by delivering outside criticism, additional evidence, epistemic alternatives, and counterinstances to one's biases. Far from being otiose or distracting when your religious belief system is largely accurate already, religious disagreement can help safeguard it against creeping inaccuracy and promote new insights.[196]

Therefore, as much as possible – and forgive any lapses – the method used attempts to maintain epistemic humility by being as objective as possible without necessarily strongly contradicting existing scholarship. For example, while I do not disagree with much current research, such as that by Gabriel Reynolds[197] and Emran El-Badawi,[198] who have argued the close contact between the Qur'an and the Syriac traditions, I think that, in at least some parts, the Qur'an is still aware of and engaging with other traditions, including perhaps the Greek New Testament. I have argued that the Qur'an is probably aware of the Gospel of John and possibly attempts to interpret the Gospel's Christology based on its Greek text.[199] Even within the Syriac tradition, the Qur'an is possibly aware of traditions beyond just the Peshitta, such as Tatian's rendition of the Gospels.[200] Accordingly, though the Qur'an is aware of the Syriac traditions, it might also be aware of the Hebrew, Aramaic and Greek texts of the Hebrew Bible and the New Testament, or at least in certain hybrid texts. Thus, the engagement of the Qur'an lies not exclusively with the Syriac traditions, and the philological method used in this book reflects that.

Additionally, considerable intratextuality and intertextuality are analysed from within the Qur'an and between the Qur'an and the biblical, extrabiblical and rabbinic traditions. The intra- and inter-connectedness in the text are similar to those outlined by Michael Fishbane on inner-biblical exegesis, in his *Biblical Interpretation in Ancient Israel*.[201] As Fishbane demonstrates, parallelism in vocabulary, phraseology, theme, motif and other linguistic and formulaic markers may provide good cases for candidacy towards intertextual allusions. Within Qur'anic studies, a method similar to that of Fishbane, defined as intertextual polysemy, has also been used to demonstrate how points of intertextuality may be determined to identify inner-Qur'anic and Qur'anic-biblical allusions.[202] As to the use of rabbinic literature, ever more scholarly work suggests that parts of the Qur'an are very well aware of rabbinic tradition,[203] and the findings in this book continue to demonstrate and validate this concept even further.

Much research in Qur'anic studies today discusses the composition of the Qur'an within its Late Antique context. While the earlier Orientalist approach was to show the influence of either Jewish or Christian traditions on the Qur'an, that was much too simplistic and awkwardly biased.[204] However, scholarship in the past few decades has come to appreciate the intricate relationship between the Qur'an and the traditions around it, preferring to call it engagement instead of influence.[205] Regardless of the nomenclature or definitions one prefers to use, there is no doubt that many parts of the Qur'an appear to be aware of many of these traditions. As Michael Graves puts it, the reception history of the Qur'an is not very different from the New Testament, which did not necessarily always directly receive the traditions from the Hebrew Bible, but through a transmission process that elaborated on earlier traditions.[206] Many of the examples made in this book directly reflect the Qur'anic engagement with biblical, extrabiblical and rabbinic traditions, especially when analysing the Qur'anic passages that appear to allude to these literature while discussing the theme of resurrection.

This book begins to look into the terminologies used by the Qur'an on life and death, comparing it with the Near Eastern and biblical traditions. It then looks into the concepts of death and life, doing the same comparison with those traditions. It later engages with the Qur'anic texts that appear to portray vividly and undoubtedly physical resurrection and how these portrayals are compared with biblical, extrabiblical and rabbinic traditions. The examples analysed in detail include (1) the man in the desolate town who dies and is later resurrected (i.e. Qur'an 2:259); (2) Abraham's ritual with the birds, which God asks him to perform as a sign of resurrection (i.e. Qur'an 2:260); (3) the portrayal of people leaving their graves; and (4) the red/yellow cow, which depicts bringing the dead back to life (i.e. Qur'an 2:67–73).

When dealing with biblical texts, scholars have looked into various textual studies that discuss dating, authorship, composition, redaction and so forth. However, since this study looks into the possible relationship between the Qur'an and biblical, extrabiblical and rabbinic traditions, it is looking into the traditions that perhaps existed in Late Antiquity with which the Qur'an is possibly alluding to or drawing its arguments or engagements. For example, while scholars divide the Book of Zechariah, of which chapters 9–14 are considered apocalyptic and composed later than the beginning of the book,[207] during Late Antiquity, the book was already taken as a whole by the community. As the Qur'an is part of the reception history of the biblical traditions within Late Antiquity, this study would not delve into details of these biblical texts and their composition or authorship much earlier during Antiquity: it would be irrelevant to how the Qur'an might have viewed such traditions, except where it may be necessary to note such authorship and composition. For example, when dealing with some rabbinic literature, such questions may become important as some of that literature could be late *midrash* (rabbinic commentaries), which will be an issue, especially when dealing with the red cow ritual in Chapter 9.

Consequently, even when looking at *midrash* works and their interpretations of biblical literature, it is not to suggest that this is what the Hebrew Bible specifically meant by it, but at least, it outlines a reception community with an interpretation that perhaps existed in the Qur'anic milieu. For example, when this book looks into the interpretations in *Genesis Rabbah*, it is not necessarily suggesting that this is what the Hebrew Bible specifically means, but that some of these interpretations might have been available as oral or written traditions that were circulating among the Jewish community in the Qur'anic milieu.

Notably, the limitations of this study must be made explicit.[208] Accordingly, this book will attempt to avoid making assertions and keep its hypotheses in the realm of possibility. There is no way, at least not yet, to go back into history and explicitly manage to ask what the authorial intent is of any piece of literature. Moreover, even with a living author, it is difficult to explicitly understand their intent on the meaning of their narrative, whether oral or literary. Narratives are an art, and like any art, sometimes an author might purposely even allow the listener or reader to develop an independent aesthetical reception, a concept that Wolfgang Iser has argued.[209] Therefore, to pinpoint an exact interpretation of any narrative is not possible. Understanding the humility that comes from dealing with unknowns and uncertainties, one should accept as a natural limitation that no interpretation can be absolute.[210]

The Qur'an is part of the reception history of biblical, extrabiblical and rabbinic literature. As part of this reception history, it is not entirely evident how and why the Qur'an re-articulates some of that literature. For example, even though the earliest intentions of Ezekiel 37 point to the resurrection of a nation and not some eschatological resurrection of bones literally leaving their graves, it does not assume that some later traditions which received Ezekiel 37 did not interpret it in such a way, as well. Therefore, even if we connect some Qur'anic narratives about resurrection with biblical, extrabiblical and rabbinic subtexts that do not necessarily discuss resurrection in a literal sense of bones leaving their graves, it would be difficult to recognize whether the Qur'an is more committed perhaps to the earliest intentions of those texts/traditions or if it is repurposing them.

Timothy Beal argues that reception history of the Bible carries with it such limitations and for that reason he suggests that one needs to shift more towards the cultural history of scriptures.[211] In this he is inspired by Wilfred Cantwell Smith, a Qur'anic scholar, who wanted to introduce the cultural studies applied in the reception of the Qur'an into biblical studies.[212] Since there is no way to know anything definitively – apart from knowing that we do not know, as Socrates put it, according to Plato – the best way to avoid limitations and to maintain intellectual humility is by suggesting possibilities, not closing off avenues of thought by overconfident assertions.

Chapter 2

TERMINOLOGIES OF LIFE

To explore the Qur'an's death and resurrection, it is imperative to ascertain the Qur'anic concept of the *nafs*, or self. Is the *nafs* a disembodied soul or a monistic self (i.e. individual: literally an indivisible persona), in which the soul and body are indistinct? The Qur'an was born out of the Near East and its initial audience comprised direct members of that context; *nafs* evolved with ancient Near Eastern societies before its appearance in the Qur'an in Late Antiquity. One of the largest bodies of literature available from ancient Semites comes from the ancient Israelites, a starting point for defining both *nafs* and 'life' in the ancient Near East. In a book that seeks to understand the concept of death in the Qur'an, then there is no escape from trying to define its concept of life.

Monism/dualism of the soul debate

Due to the rising scholarly debate on bioethics, when Mohammad Rakesh and S.M.R. Ayati looked into the possible understanding of the *nafs* from the Qur'an and its relationship to the so-called mind-body problem and what a soul or personhood means,[1] they concluded that death constitutes the loss of personhood, which is consciousness or mind that is located in the physical brain. The mind-body problem, which exists of course outside Islam and the Qur'an, prompts several theological questions on whether a disembodied soul exists, and if it does, what relationship it has with the body.[2] In the world of cognitive science of religion, what the soul is and how it is related to the mind is unknown.[3] From a scientific perspective, we do not know the nature of the soul and if it even exists.[4] While science appears to be closing down the gap between the mind and the brain, and with it the concept of a dualistic soul,[5] some scholars and theologians have attempted to discredit that science,[6] while others attempt to harmonize their theology with such science.[7]

The definition of *life* similarly enjoys no consensus across various disciplines. Whether it is definable is even up for debate,[8] as Edouard Machery concludes:

> Life definitionists have too often been careless: They have constantly mixed folk intuitions with scientific considerations. However, they have to decide whether

> the notion of life at stake is the folk concept of life or a scientific concept. In the first case, there is little hope of finding a definition of life since, like most folk concepts, the folk concept of life is not a definition, and it is unlikely to yield a set of intuitive judgments about what is alive that can be captured by a definition non-arbitrarily. In the second case, life can perhaps be defined. However, because the study of life spreads over several disciplines, life definitionists are likely to end up with several, intensionally and extensionally different definitions of life without having any means to choose between them. Defining life is then likely to be pointless.[9]

This issue becomes interesting because some scholars have argued that the *nafs* (lit.: breath), according to some ancient Semitic sources, including parts of the Hebrew Bible, is just the life force in the body and not necessarily a disembodied soul. Further exploration shows that the ancient Semites were able to comprehend a dualistic nature of the soul and body, yet it still raises a bedrock question: if the *nafs* is, at least sometimes, understood as a life force in the body as some form of a materialistic monistic view, what exactly is the definition of such a life force, if we cannot even define what life is. The definition of life is unknown and, perhaps, as Machery suggests, pointless.[10] However, without a definition of *life*, can we even define *death*?

There always had been various views about the relationship of the *nafs* and the body in the ancient Near East that varied between a monistic view, which takes the *nafs* as a holistic self of body and soul, and a dualistic view that there is an incorporeal entity – the soul, which is distinct from the body.[11] Although most scholars of ancient Israel claim that the Israelites did not have a dualistic understanding, Richard Steiner and others have argued otherwise.[12] John Cooper even argues that the Hebrew Bible is not only implicit or vaguely points to such a direction, but explicitly forwards the notion when stating, 'and the dust returns to the earth as it was, and the breath [spirit/*rûaḥ*] returns to God who gave it' (Qoh. 12:7).[13]

Nonetheless, some traditional biblical scholars caution that the purpose behind this verse is not to provide a theological understanding of the afterlife but simply to confirm the existence of one,[14] and some insist that it is not necessarily describing a dualistic nature of human beings.[15] According to Howard Bream, this passage is open-ended, providing no definitive answer as to the concept of an afterlife or resurrection.[16] Whether or not the passage ignores the existence of an afterlife and simply suggests that a person might be annihilated,[17] it would be untenable to argue that this verse states the necessary existence of an afterlife or the immortality of the soul.[18] If anything, it seems to negate some sort of physical and bodily resurrection.[19] It is closer to a portrayal of the dualistic nature of a human person than the portrayal of the existence of an afterlife. One might even argue that this passage speaks of the spirit (*rûaḥ*) and not the soul/self (*nepeš*), which may or may not be distinct.[20]

There is no consensus among biblical scholars on the soul-body debate where, one side of the spectrum holds a monistic understanding and the other favours a dualistic nature. This has been especially the case since the discovery of the Dead Sea Scrolls, in which the *nepeš* is sometimes seen holistically,[21] but at times distinctively dualistically[22] – arguably due to Qumran having been associated with a postexilic community.[23]

The medieval Muslim philosophers, Muʿtazilīs and Ashʿarīs, debated the soul-body question, especially whether the soul is a rational entity or just a life force.[24] Ayman Shihadeh, a scholar of Muslim philosophy, shows that throughout medieval times, there was no real consensus, and even while al-Ghazālī (d. 505/1111) stood against many philosophical attitudes,[25] he and al-Rāghib al-Iṣfahānī (d. 502/1108) were influenced by philosophers and had accepted a dual nature of the soul-body problem. Nonetheless, it did not stop the debate amongst Muslim philosophers lasting to the time of Fakhr al-Dīn al-Rāzī (d. 606/1209) and beyond.

As a comparison, most of the Qurʾanic usage for heart(s) (*qalb* or *albāb*) is metaphorical. Scholarly attempts to unravel a physical sense have been admittedly unsuccessful.[26] Since there is no debate that the usage of 'heart' terms in the Qurʾan are typically understood figuratively, it would not be surprising if the *nafs*, even were it as corporeal as the heart, did not hold a metaphorical meaning.

It should not be surprising if we cannot pinpoint the exact definition of *nafs* or life according to the communities of the Near East during Late Antiquity or the medieval period. Since even in modern times there is no consensus and defining it might be futile, perhaps the same can be said of attempts to do so historically. Evidence points to different positions on the matter because even historically, it was unlikely there was any one consensus.

Life

Gen. 1:20 uses *nepeš ḥayyâ* (living breath/soul?), which is typically understood to refer to creatures or animals.[27] Analysing these two terms, *nepeš* and *ḥayyâ*, closely, we may approach what Genesis is trying to convey. Sometimes *nepeš* is used to mean life, but it is clear from the passage that it is not always so. Using the adjective *ḥayyâ* with *nepeš* implies that a *nepeš* may exist without being alive (*ḥay*) – in other words, that there can be a dead *nepeš*, which the Hebrew Bible (e.g. Lev. 21:11) does attest to,[28] as does the Talmud.[29]

The root *ḥ-y-h*, or *ḥ-y-y*, appears in Western Semitic but not Eastern Semitic; it also exists in some other Western Afroasiatic languages.[30] The Ugaritic cognate has its root in *ḥ-w-y*,[31] which would not be strange within weak verb roots, where the *waw* and *yod* are sometimes transposed. Akkadian uses the term *balāṭu* for 'life', which is etymologically related to the root *p-l-ṭ* in Hebrew and Aramaic.[32] There seems to be no cognate for the root *b-l-ṭ* in Arabic, as most likely the definition of *b-l-ṭ* in Arabic that means a hard surface[33] is a loanword from the Latin *palatium*, meaning palace,[34] or from the Greek *platys*, meaning flat and broad,[35] which is in turn from the Proto-Indian-European (PIE) root *plat*, meaning to spread out, to flatten or an expanse,[36] which evolved into 'place' in English. There is some evidence of an early use of the root *b-l-ṭ* in pre-Islamic Arabic poetry dated to the sixth century, if one would accept their authenticity,[37] but the root *b-l-d* is possibly earlier[38] and is used in the Qur'an to mean 'land' (e.g. Qur'an 16:7, 90:1–2).[39] The Arabic root *b-l-d* does not appear to have a cognate in other Western Semitic languages.

The Arabic term *ʿumur* can mean life or lifespan[40] (e.g. Qur'an 2:96, 10:16, 16:70, 21:44, 22:5, 26:18, 28:45, 35:11, 35:37, 36:68), while, from the same root, *ʿamara, maʿmar,*[41] or *maʿmūrah* means a place where people live[42] (e.g. Qur'an 9:17–18, 11:61, 30:9). Similarly, in Arabic, the term *ḥayy*, which means living, is also used to mean a place where people live,[43] and used accordingly in pre-Islamic poetry.[44] The common denominator between those roots is life.

In Western Semitic, such as Ugaritic, the term used to mean life is also *ḥyh*, while the term *blmt*, which is from *bl mt* (without death), is an allusion to immortality, as used in 2 Aqhat 6:26–29.[45] In an earlier passage of the same Ugaritic text, the term *npš* is used with *ḥy* to also note a relationship between the two terms.[46] Phoenician and Punic languages also use the term *ḥym* to mean life.[47] This suggests that the root *ḥ-y-y* for life is well attested in Western Semitic languages sharing the same semantic range.

The Qur'an specifically uses the root *ḥ-y-y* in opposition to *m-w-t*, which means death (e.g. Qur'an 2:154, 3:169, 16:21, 35:22, 77:26). The term *ḥayy* in the Qur'an seems to be very specific to life, and it is distinct from the term *nafs*, since the Qur'an notes that the *nafs* could be dead (e.g. Qur'an 3:185, 29:57, 31:34).[48] Therefore, *ḥ-y-y* may be viewed as very specifically meaning life, unlike *nafs*, which can be described as an entity that can die.

The nature of the nepeš *among the ancient Semites*

The root *ḥ-y-h* in Gen. 1:30, which portrays animals (*kol ḥayyat haʾāreṣ*) as living (*ḥayyâ*) *nepeš*, operates similarly in Gen. 1:20. In the description of the formation of man in Gen. 2:7, God blew into the man's nostrils the breath of life (*nišmat ḥayyîm*) and the man became (*yĕhî*) a living soul/self (*nepeš ḥayyâ*). With life modifying both breath and self, a closer analysis of *nĕšāmā* and *nepeš* is necessary to better recognize their distinction with life (*ḥ-y-h*).

The term *nĕšāmâ* means breath or wind,[49] giving it meanings similar to *nepeš*[50] and *rûaḥ*.[51] In the Hebrew Bible, *nĕšāmâ* seems to be used solely to refer to something coming out of God (e.g. Gen. 2:7, 7:22; Job 4:9, 32:8, 33:4, 37:10). Usually, though not necessarily always, it gives life to living creatures (e.g. Gen. 7:22; Deut. 20:16; Job 27:3; Isa. 2:22; Prov. 20:27; Dan. 5:23, 10:17).[52] In some contexts, *nišmat rûaḥ* denotes a blast of a wrathful breath (e.g. 2 Sam. 22:16, and repeated in Ps. 18:15).[53] Thus, *nĕšāmâ* appears to be breath from God, which sometimes gives life to a creature, making it alive.[54] While this term has an Arabic cognate (*n-s-m*), the Qur'an does not use it.

Nepeš appears to have an overlapping connotation, and it is important to look at it closely. Gen. 1:20–21 states that God made swarms of living *nepeš* in the waters, and in verse 24, the same were created on land. Gen. 2:7 relates that after *nišmat ḥayyîm* was blown into man, the man became a living *nepeš*. This brings us to different interpretations – that *nišmat ḥayyîm* transformed to *nepeš ḥayyâ* or that *nišmat ḥayyîm* is itself *nepeš ḥayyâ*, making *nišmat* and *nepeš* synonymous.[55] Al-Farāhīdī (d. 170/786) has considered the Arabic usage of *nasam*, although not used by the Qur'an, to be synonymous with *nafas*,[56] although there is evidence from poetry contemporary to the Qur'an that show a distinction between those two terms.[57]

In ancient Egypt, the concept of life and its transfiguration in death are multifaceted. A person is made of the *ka*[58] and the *ba*.[59] The *ka* is energy,[60] and the *ba* is the embodiment of power sometimes referred to as the soul[61] – personality and all the characteristics that make an individual unique. The *ba* survives after death; though it is considered physical, it is distinct from the body (*khat*). At the time of death, the *ka* leaves the body.[62] After funerary rites, the dead person transforms into the *akh*, when the *ba* and *ka* are reunited.[63] If the reunification transforms into the *akh*, and the *ba* is considered corporeal, then it is perhaps possible to imagine the *akh* as a resurrected body, but one that it is distinct from the original body (*khat*). Even though ancient Egyptian understanding of the composition of human beings is distinct, it is not completely alien: parts of it are comparable to other ancient Near Eastern cultures, especially when it comes to the life force that animates the body.[64]

In Akkadian, *napishtu* and *napshu* mean life, person, self or breath.[65] As familiar as that may now sound, their use in Akkadian as person or self is less common than it is in Western Semitic: the term more frequently used for self in Akkadian is *ramānu*.[66] The Old Akkadian term *ramanu*, meaning self,[67] does not seem to have a cognate in Western Semitic. Because living creatures breathe, *napshu* may have received the connotation of self over time. Nonetheless, even though there are different terms for breath or life force of the self in Akkadian, there is a distinct word for the soul of the dead, which is *eṭemmu*,[68] although it may have sometimes been used for an embodied soul. In the Akkadian *Epic of Atrahasis*,[69] the *eṭemmu* (human soul)[70] comes from the god's flesh, while the human *ṭēmu* (intellect)[71] is from the *damu* (blood)[72] of the god.[73] Considering these philological relationships and distinctions, ancient Semites do seem to have been aware of some sort of dualist nature of humans (body and soul); the unique term for a disembodied soul can be traced as far back as Sumerian and Old Akkadian writings.[74]

Scholars of Semitic languages, Jonas Greenfield and Richard Steiner suggest that the Hebrew *nepeš* may be compared to the semantic range of the Akkadian *eṭemmu*,[75] as even in Akkadian, the difference between *napishtu* and *eṭemmu*, though once thought to be the difference between an embodied or disembodied soul after death[76] may not necessarily be the case.[77]

The Qur'an uses the root *ṭ-m-m*, which is a *hapax legomenon* in the Qur'an, as a possible reference to the Day of Resurrection (i.e. Qur'an 79:34). It is of obscure meaning. The Arabic lexicographer, al-Farāhīdī, states that in Arabic the root could mean to bury in the soil.[78] He also states that the Arabs used to say, 'They brought with *al-ṭimm* and *al-rimm*', which means they brought a 'great issue'.[79] However, they are unlikely to be related to the Akkadian *eṭemmu* or *ramānu*.

The root *n-f-s* is shared among the greater Afroasiatic languages to mean breath or soul.[80] The Akkadian term *napishtu* can also mean throat, from its use for breathing;[81] however, it also means abundant or carded wool.[82] The term *nepeshtu* or *nepeshu* also means performance, construction or ritual, which is an execution of something.[83] The term can also mean tools or utensils, especially those used in ritual.[84] The term *nepishu* also means a package of gold or silver.[85] As a comparison, in Arabic the term *nafīs* means something desired, of great value or rare, especially money.[86] The use of *nepeš* to mean desire and appetite is also found in Ugaritic,[87] Hebrew and Aramaic.[88] The etymology of this meaning may be due to people competing for or craving (*yatanāfasūn*) it;[89] the semantic definition for competition or craving is used in Qur'an 83:26. The etymology of competition (*munāfasah*) might be due to people competing with exertion and therefore breathing (*yatanaffasūn*) heavily. The term *tanaffas* can also mean to be relieved in Arabic,[90] with Hebrew (e.g. Exod. 31:17), Aramaic and Ethiopic cognates as well.[91]

In Gen. 2:7, it is not clear whether *nepeš* is the same as the *nišmat*. Later rabbis, according to *Genesis Rabbah*, considered *nepeš*, *nišmat* and *rûaḥ* to be all analogous to life.[92] Gen. 2:7 says that God formed man from dust and breathed into his nostrils the breath of life. Then, the man became a living *nepeš*. The question here is what was made alive – the body, which is from dust, or the *nepeš* itself? The rabbis interpreted this passage, according to *Genesis Rabbah*, to mean that when God breathed into the man's nostrils, the man was infused with a soul (*nepeš*).[93] In an attempt to understand the soul in light of biology and psychology in the turn of the twentieth century, H. Wheeler Robinson in *The Christian Doctrine of Man* argues that the Hebrews considered personality (or soul) as part of an animated body, unlike the Greek dualist approach to the soul and the body, which were held in distinction from each other;[94] an understanding still held by some scholars.[95] Similarly, by the mid-twentieth century, Ludwig Köhler suggests that Gen. 2:7 does not denote that a person has a vital self, but *is* a vital self.[96] However, the man being made of dust (the body) does not necessarily mean it is a *nepeš*. It can be interpreted to mean that the *nepeš* came into being (*hayyâ*) only after *nišmat ḥayyîm* was blown into the man (dust).[97]

Arguing that both dualistic and monistic natures of *nepeš* are compatible,[98] Ed Noort looks into the ancient Near Eastern context of Gen. 2:7. He considers its non-priestly and pre-exilic background, which would correspond neither to Ezekiel 37 (which depicts a form of resurrection) nor to the wisdom text of Qoh. 12:7 (which depicts the dead body returns to the dust of the earth and the spirit returns to God) during the Hellenistic period. Accordingly, Noort feels that Gen. 2:7 does not contain a premise for the dualistic nature of humans, nor does he think the latter examples necessarily imply as much. Yet he reasons that Gen. 2:7 still discerns the human body from the life force that animates it. Nonetheless, Noort acknowledges that during the Hellenistic period, various communities understood Gen. 2:7 in a dualistic manner and such understanding continued throughout Late Antiquity, though a non-dualistic understanding of Gen. 2:7 also continued as well.[99]

Ancient Hebrews may have considered the *nepeš* to be the breath of a living creature. At the time of death, this breath (*nepeš*) leaves the body.[100] When the Hebrew Bible speaks of the spirit (*rûaḥ*), the receiving community did not necessarily equate it with the soul (*nepeš*).[101] To some, a person does not have to die for his spirit (*rûaḥ*) to go into someone else, and this is especially the case with Moses and the seventy elders of Israel: God takes part of the spirit in Moses and places it on the seventy (i.e. Num. 11:17). The two also remain distinct when Elisha requests a double portion of Elijah's spirit (i.e. 2 Kgs. 2:9).[102] This seems to suggest strongly that the Hebrew definition of spirit (*rûaḥ*) was usually different from self or soul (*nepeš*), at least to some of the author-editors of the Hebrew Bible.[103]

The Hebrew Bible uses *nepeš* in various contexts to mean soul, living being, life, person, desire, appetite, emotion and passion.[104] In a survey of various biblical dictionaries, Nancey Murphy locates translations for *nepeš* ranging from 'soul' to 'self'.[105] However, looking at the term from a semantic perspective does not always provide us with enough evidence of what it might have meant to the ancient Hebrews, since language evolves through different times and geographic locations. Hans Walter Wolff suggests that the root meaning of *nepeš* may have originated from the Proto-Semitic (PSem) root *peš*, related onomatopoetically to the hissing sound of breath.[106] The same root also exists in Sumerian, and possibly Proto-Sumerian, meaning breath.[107] Gerald Schroeder suggests that the *nepeš* in the creation story of Genesis is a clue that suggests some sort of spiritual creation of the soul and not the body.[108]

It is difficult to discern with any certainty in the Hebrew Bible whether *nepeš* is an immortal soul that survives after bodily death or if it ceases to exist with the death of the body, especially since the type of literature and the period spans a large swathe of time and diverse reception communities. We may derive some clues that the *nepeš* may be delivered from death (e.g. Josh. 2:13; Ps. 33:19, 56:13). However, is the *nepeš* in these instances a matter of a dead soul going into life, or is it a dead body granted life (i.e. the resurrection of the body)? Ps. 56:13 seems to suggest a spiritual death. The psalmist is not necessarily talking of God delivering his body from death but, perhaps, his soul. However, Num. 6:6 prohibits those who vow a separation (dedication) to God to go near a dead *nepeš* – the term is in most instances understood as 'body'. The Septuagint translates *nepeš* mainly as *psychē* (soul), even in Num. 6:6. This leads us to the conclusion that the translators of the Septuagint seem to have understood *nepeš* as the soul.[109] In contrast, the Masoretic text of Ezek. 44:25, which speaks of not going near a dead body, uses the term *ʾādām*, which might infer a physical body. However, the Septuagint still translates this as *psychē*, implying the soul (*nepeš*). Overall, the Septuagint is not always consistent when using *psychē*, when compared with the Masoretic. Thus, it is difficult to understand whether the *nepeš* in Num. 6:6 is to be understood as 'soul' or 'body', at least to the translators of the Septuagint and what the original Hebrew term used from the translated text. Nonetheless, it seems that Ezek. 44:25 is the only instance where the Greek *psychē* is used for a corpse (dead *ʾādām*).[110] Perhaps its use in this passage could have had a different Hebrew term from the translated text (*nepeš* instead of *ʾādām* as in Lev. 21:1),[111] an error, or an interpretation by the translator(s) of this passage.[112]

Steiner suggests that the Hebrew *nepeš* is similar to the Samʾalian[113] *n-b-š*.[114] The transformation of the *pe*ʾ to *bet* may be found in various Northwestern Semitic inscriptions, including Samʾalian.[115] Some scholars have suggested that *n-b-š* and *n-p-š* were indistinguishable in the local dialects, and are both pronounced as *napš*.[116] If *n-b-š* is equivalent to the Akkadian *eṭemmu*, in that it is perhaps a disembodied soul, and *n-b-š* is equivalent to *n-p-š*, Steiner suggests that this should mean that a *nepeš* could also contain the meaning of a disembodied soul (the Akkadian *eṭemmu*).[117]

The root *n-f-s* can also mean a funerary monument in Northwestern Semitic, Phoenician, Syriac Aramaic and South Arabian. In Nabatean, it can even distinctly mean a tomb, which assumes that it is not necessarily life in itself.[118] In ancient Mesopotamian texts, there are two words used to mean a wind-like entity that exists in living bodies and survives death: *zaqīqu* (a dream soul)[119] and an *eṭemmu*.[120] Both souls depart a dead body and go to the netherworld, where they were expected to receive funerary rites and sacrifice from the living,[121] which is not too different from ancient Egyptian concepts.[122] Steiner considers these concepts of the soul to be common in the ancient Near East and believes that if there is any Hittite influence, the Hittite traditions are themselves derived from Syro-Mesopotamian.[123] Steiner even uses Qurʾan 39:42 to describe the concept of *nafs* as a soul that departs a body in his argument that such a concept of '*nepeš*' would have existed in the ancient Near East with the term having a semantic capacity inherited from the speakers of PSem.[124]

If the ancient Hebrews considered *nepeš* the holistic entire being,[125] the physical and the animated living body, then one might consider the psalmists of Ps. 56:13 or 116:8–9, for example, to be referring to a metaphoric spiritual death, when talking of delivering the soul (*nepeš*) from death,[126] which is what Augustine (d. 430 CE) had also suggested:

> For I was what? Dead. Through myself I was dead: through You I am what? Alive. Therefore 'in me, O God, are Your vows, which I will render of praise to You.' Behold I love my God: no one doth tear Him from me: that which to Him I may give, no one doth tear front me, because in the heart it is shut up. With reason is said with that former confidence, 'What should man do unto me?'[127]

Since the psalmists use the death of the *nepeš* as a metaphor for spiritual death,[128] which Michael Fishbane argues is not unusual in the Hebrew Bible,[129] then perhaps the ancient Hebrews had two definitions for *nepeš*. One would imply a holistic view of the physical body and the life force that embodies it, and the other would mean the soul within the body. The latter can be seen in Jonah 4:3 when the titular prophet asks God to take his *nepeš*, as it is better for him to die. It seems unlikely that Jonah asked his holistic self (body and soul) to be taken by God;[130] it is more likely he meant the living force in that body (assuming the soul was separate).

Looking at further clues of what *nepeš* means brings us to the following passage in Deuteronomy:

> Only be sure that you do not eat the blood; for the blood is the life [*nepeš*], and you shall not eat the life [*nepeš*] with the flesh.[131]
>
> Deut. 12:23

Here we see that the *nepeš* is the life force, defined by the blood itself, which is similar to its portrayal in Lev. 17:11. Indeed, in Arabic the term *nifās* is used to mean blood, especially after childbirth or menstrual blood,[132] which might be due to this type of blood specifically related to making life. If the blood is understood to be physical, then the *nepeš* is being described as a physical force of life – another example of the ancient Hebrews holding two possible definitions for *nepeš*.

According to James Barr, *nepeš* in Gen. 2:7 might hold a dualistic nature, in which man is made of two substances, the physical flesh and a disembodied soul or breath.[133] First, Gen. 2:7 states that God created man from the dust of the ground – but the physical body made of dust is not called *nepeš*.[134] Second, it states that God breathed into this dust the breath of life. Only when the breath of life is breathed into the dust does the man become a living *nepeš*.[135] In the context of this passage, the term *nepeš* does not denote a non-living body;[136] it can mean either the soul or, holistically, the living body.[137] Gen. 2:7 seems to describe *nepeš* as living (*ḥayyâ*), as opposed to dead. The verse is perhaps casting the *nepeš* that way because there could, by contrast, be a dead *nepeš*, as has been established. Roger Uitti says as much too, but interprets a dead *nepeš* not as spiritual death but complete annihilation.[138]

When Gen. 2:17 warns of eating from the tree of knowledge of good and evil, the statement that the consequence will be certain death has prompted much scholarly debate as to the nature of that death, with some suggesting that it does not imply the death of the body but more precisely that of the *nepeš*.[139] Later in history, this is how Philo (d. 50 CE) understood it:

> [105]Accordingly God says, 'In the day in which ye eat of it ye shall die the death.' And yet, though they have eaten of it, they not only do not die, but they even beget children, and are the causes of life to other beings besides themselves. What, then, are we to say? Surely that death is of two kinds; the one being the death of the man, the other the peculiar death of the soul – now the death of the man is the separation of his soul from his body, but the death of the soul is the destruction of virtue and the admission of vice; [106]and consequently God calls that not merely 'to die,' but 'to die the death'; showing that he is speaking not of common death, but of that peculiar and especial death which is the death of the soul, buried in its passions and in all kinds of evil. And we may almost say that one kind of death is opposed to the other kind. For the one is the separation of what was previously existing in combination, namely, of body and soul. But this other death, on the contrary, is a combination of them both, the inferior one, the body, having the predominance, and the superior one, the soul, being made

> subject to it. [107]When, therefore, God says, 'to die the death,' you must remark that he is speaking of that death which is inflicted as punishment, and not of that which exists by the original ordinance of nature. The natural death is that one by which the soul is separated from the body. But the one which is inflicted as a punishment, is when the soul dies according to the life of virtue, and lives only according to the life of vice.[140]

The living *nepeš* of Gen. 2:7 is perhaps what would die, according to verse 17. As Steiner points out, when Gen. 35:18 narrates Rachel's death, it states that her *nepeš* was departing, as an allusion to her death.[141] It seems that Gen. 35:18 is referring not to Rachel's body and soul departing, but rather to the life force within her body,[142] possibly something like the soul, which supports the dualistic notion of body and soul. When Elijah raises the widow's son in 1 Kgs. 17:21–22, he stretches his hand over the boy's body and supplicates God asking that his *nepeš* will come into him again. Indeed, his *nepeš* does come, giving him life. Steiner emphasizes that *nepeš* is not life, because life is not a spatial entity that can enter or leave a body.[143] This further indicates that the ancient Israelites were able to conceptualize a dualistic notion of body and soul.

The early Christians also seem to have conceptualized a sort of a disembodied soul, although there are scholars who have argued otherwise.[144] Some Christian theologians assume that the departed soul is embodied with a body in heaven (as opposed to an earthly body) at the time of death to conform to the biblical concept of having no such thing as an intermediate state after death.[145]

Paul states, 'I know a person in Christ who fourteen years ago was caught up to the third heaven – whether in the body or out of the body I do not know; God knows' (2 Cor. 12:2).[146] In this passage, Paul appears to be unsure whether a bodily assumption to heaven had occurred, or one without the body.[147] He grants equal possibility to either. In Walter Schmithals' view, Paul might have had Gnostic opponents with whom he is showing an affinity by proposing a possible disembodied journey.[148] However, this is not necessarily the case.[149] Jewish traditions at the time of Paul do point to both types of assumption as a possibility. According to some Jewish traditions, Enoch and Elijah appear to have been assumed into heaven corporeally.[150] Other Jewish traditions also appear to include a spiritual assumption into heaven as a possibility, where the soul departs the body and enters (or 'is assumed') into heaven. For example, Philo states that when Moses went up to Sinai, his soul left his body: 'To such strains it is said that Moses was listening, when, having laid aside his body, for forty days and as many nights he touched neither bread nor water at all.'[151] Therefore, it would not be unusual for Paul to think that either a bodily or spiritual assumption into heaven was possible. That his audience would be able to entertain the prospect of either does not necessarily mean that Paul was appealing to a certain group, though such a hypothesis also cannot be rejected. Some scholars, such as Jörg Baumgarten, have attempted to push the idea that ancient Israelites would not have been able to fathom a disembodied soul.[152] While one cannot be too sure about the earliest Israelite accounts, at least during the time of Paul the Jews were able to conceptualize a disembodied soul, for even Josephus (d. *c.* 100 CE) also writes of the immortality of the soul and its disembodiment.[153]

Overall, it is apparent that from the ancient times and through Late Antiquity in the Near East, Semites have been able to have different understandings of the *nafs*, sometimes even simultaneously. While the concept of dualism possibly evolved over time amongst the ancient Semites, it still does not mean that a dualistic concept was foreign to them from the very beginning. The purpose behind this analysis is to understand what possible context existed in the Qurʾanic milieu during Late Antiquity, both monistic and dualistic natures of humans pervaded the Near East, perhaps even simultaneously within the same communities.

Nafs *in the Qurʾan*

The Islamic tradition harbours a belief in an intermediate state between death and resurrection.[154] During the intermediate state, the *nafs* (soul) exists, although disembodied, as argued by prominent traditional Muslim scholars such as Ibn Ḥazm (d. 456/1064).[155] The disembodied *nafs* was therefore not foreign to traditional and medieval Muslim scholars, including Ibn Qayyim al-Jawziyyah (d. 751/1350).[156] During the resurrection of the dead, it is assumed that the *nafs* is re-embodied. Yet even in many Muslim traditions, when people are resurrected, they do not necessarily take on their original bodies. Some prophetic traditions suggest that people are resurrected in the form of Adam (sixty cubits tall and thirty-three years of age);[157] according to other traditions, people are resurrected in the beauty of Joseph.[158]

If traditionally the bodies of resurrected people are different from their original bodies, this suggests some form of re-creation, and not pure resurrection as one might infer from the usual understanding of the same earthly body and bones are resurrected and leave their graves. This would also suggest that the *nafs* is a disembodied soul that would be re-embodied into a different physical body (or frame) in the form of Adam, according to some traditions.

Perhaps one of the main differences between the concepts of resurrection and reincarnation is this question of same or different body.[159] However, if some Muslim traditions hint that on the Day of Resurrection, the bodies are different, then it may have more affinity with some form of re-creation than the same bodies leaving their graves, although alternate traditions do assume that as well.

Lisān al-ʿarab states that *nafs* is spirit (*rūḥ*), but also states that there is a difference between them that is not within the lexicon's scope to discuss.[160] The Qurʾan, on the other hand, appears to distinguish between the two. Take Qurʾan 17:85, for example: 'They ask you about the Spirit (*al-rūḥ*). Say, "The Spirit [*al-rūḥ*] is from the Command [*amr*] of my Lord, and you have not been given knowledge, except a little."' Since people were asking about the Spirit, the implication is that they do not know what it is; however, when discussing *nafs*, the Qurʾan apparently assumes its audience will understand what it is. Jane Smith writes, 'It is a matter of general agreement that *nafs* and *rūḥ* are each used in different ways in the

Qur'an, and that these usages can be classified and quite clearly distinguished from each other. Nonetheless from early on the terms came to be used more or less interchangeably by Muslim scholars.'[161] Medieval Muslim scholars were swamped with contradictions concerning *rūḥ* (spirit),[162] and the reason behind their inconsistencies is that they have used the term interchangeably with *nafs*, even though the Qur'an clearly distinguishes between the two.

Al-Ghazālī states that the *nafs* is the origin of everything corrupt in human behaviour,[163] while the *rūḥ* is godly.[164] Modern scholars, such as ʿAbdulkarīm Yūnus al-Khaṭīb (d. 1390/1970), also discuss the debates concerning *nafs* and *rūḥ*, showing their distinct features in the Qur'an.[165] Aḥmad Shawqī Ibrahīm argues that *nafs* and *rūḥ* are two different things according to the Qur'an, where the *rūḥ* is blown into the body, but not the *nafs*.[166] According to his reading of the Qur'an, it is not the body that dies but the *nafs*.[167]

Typically, what is understood from the reference to killing a *nafs* in the Qur'an is killing a person, but did that mean a human, a soul or some other form of life force? To begin the investigation, take Qur'an 5:32, which alludes to a tradition found in the Mishnah and Talmud that killing a *nafs* is like killing all people.[168] The Qur'an, like the Talmud, refers to Cain and Abel's story when making this moral equivalence. The Talmud states that by killing his innocent brother, Cain has killed not only Abel but also an entire people because he has, in effect, killed an entire potential line of descent.[169] The Talmud expands this by repeating Gen. 4:10: 'The bloods of your brother cry', where 'bloods' refers to the descendants.[170] By killing the body, blood comes out and with it the soul, but the Talmud explains bloods metaphorically, extending even to those who were not yet physical beings. Accordingly, should the Hebrew term *nepeš*, cognate to the Arabic *nafs*, be understood as 'soul' or as the physical person and his blood?

Although Alan Segal suggests that the *nafs* in Arabic is the self and not necessarily the soul,[171] this self personification does not necessarily need a body, according to the Qur'an. Perhaps it is even consciousness. The Qur'an appears to state that even God has a *nafs* (e.g. Qur'an 20:41, 5:116), but it is unknown whether the Qur'an means it literally or simply using anthropomorphic descriptions for God. The concept of God having a *nafs* is not unique to the Qur'an. The disembodiment of the *nepeš* may also be seen in the Hebrew Bible's insinuation that God has one (e.g. Lev. 26:11, 26:30; 1 Sam. 2:35; Job 23:13; Isa. 1:14, 42:1; Jer. 31:14; Amos 6:8),[172] as well.[173] The question remains: where the Qur'an explicitly discusses its death and resurrection (e.g. Qur'an 3:185, 21:35, 29:57), is the *nafs* necessarily physical?

Gavin Picken arrived at five meanings in the Qur'an for *nafs*: (1) signifying the soul (e.g. Qur'an 6:93); (2) signifying the human being (e.g. Qur'an 31:28); (3) signifying the human being's power of understanding (e.g. Qur'an 27:14); (4) signifying the heart (e.g. Qur'an 7:205, 12:77); and (5) signifying the inclination to good and evil (e.g. Qur'an 50:16, 75:2, 79:37–41).[174] Picken suggests that the Qur'an provides certain faculties to the *nafs*:[175] it has desires (*hawa*) (e.g. Qur'an 79:40–41), appetites (*shahwah*) (e.g. Qur'an 21:102) and needs (*ḥājah*) (e.g. Qur'an 12:68).[176] The *nafs* also experiences hardship (*mashaqqah*) (e.g. Qur'an 16:7).[177]

The *nafs* can also endure patiently (*ṣabr*) (e.g. Qur'an 18:28).[178] The *nafs* has the qualities of miserliness (*shuḥḥ*) (e.g. Qur'an 4:128), envy (*ḥasad*) (e.g. Quran 2:109), fear (*khawf*) (e.g. Qur'an 20:67–68), anxiety (*ḍīq*) (e.g. Qur'an 9:118), distress (*ḥaraj*) (e.g. Qur'an 4:65), pride (*kibr*) (e.g. Qur'an 25:21) and grief (*ḥasrah*) (e.g. Qur'an 35:8, 39:56).[179] The *nafs* also has certain other cognitive characteristics, such as being affected by eloquent speech (e.g. Qur'an 4:63), the ability to comprehend (*idrāk*) (e.g. Qur'an 31:34) in contrast to conjecture (*ẓann*) (e.g. Qur'an 3:154)[180] and the ability to conceal feelings (e.g. Qur'an 2:284), and take responsibility (e.g. Qur'an 2:286, 14:51).[181]

According to the Qur'an, the *nafs* is associated with three distinct attributes: (1) inclining to evil (*ammāratun bil-sū'*) (e.g. Qur'an 12:53), enticing (*sawwalat*) (e.g. Qur'an 12:18, 20:96), subjecting (*ṭawwa'at*) (e.g. Qur'an 5:30) and tempting (*tuwaswis*) (e.g. Qur'an 50:16); (2) self-reproaching (*lawwāmah*) (e.g. Qur'an 75:1–2);[182] and (3) tranquil (*muṭma'innah*) (e.g. Qur'an 89:27–30).[183]

The philosopher that he was, al-Rāzī felt the need to clarify that the *nafs* is self (*al-dhāt*) and that physical objects (*jamādāt*) also have a *nafs* but do not die.[184] Philosophers suggest that death is certain in this physical life and that the soul (*nafs*) is different from the body (*badan*),[185] but, al-Rāzī states, they do not consider the death of the soul (*nafs*), because when the Qur'an says, 'every soul tastes death', the meaning is that the soul (*nafs*) needs to be alive to taste death.[186] The soul tastes the death of the body but itself continues to survive.[187] It has been suggested that al-Rāzī endorses a materialistic doctrine of the soul (*nafs*).[188] However, suggesting that the Qur'an does not also state that the *nafs* dies might contradict the following:

> [41]Truly We have sent down unto you the Book for humankind in truth. Whosoever is rightly guided, it is for the sake of his own soul. And whosoever goes astray only goes astray to the detriment thereof. And you are not a guardian over them. [42]God takes the souls [*al-anfus*] at the moment of their death, and those who die not, during their sleep. He withholds those for whom He has decreed death, and sends forth the others till a term appointed. Truly in that are signs for a people who reflect.
>
> Qur'an 39:41–42

> Truly with God lies knowledge of the Hour, and He sends down the rain and knows what lies in wombs. And no soul [*nafs*] knows what it will earn on the morrow, and no soul [*nafs*] knows in what land it will die. Truly God is Knowing, Aware.
>
> Qur'an 31:34

These passages seem to suggest the death of the *nafs*. Perhaps connecting Qur'an 39:41–42 with a preceding passage, 'Surely you are dead and surely they are dead' (Qur'an 39:30),[189] might suggest that they are perhaps an allusion to death and eternal life. Qur'an 39:42 goes on to state that the *nafs* also sleeps; al-Ṭabarī (d. 310/923) and al-Rāzī suggest that the passage refers to souls taken away from their sleeping bodies and later return to them.[190] Nonetheless, al-Rāzī does suggest that the soul's death or sleep in this passage is perhaps an allusion to a person being 'spiritually' dead. He suggests that God is the source of guidance and misguidance, where a guided *nafs* is like life and a waking state, while a misguided *nafs* is like death and a sleeping state.[191] This interpretation is an attempt to contextualize the passage, since the preceding passages refer to guidance and misguidance (e.g. Qur'an 39:36–37, 39:41). Al-Ṭabarsī (d. 548/1153), nonetheless, does not interpret death in Qur'an 39:42 as the death of the soul but of its body.[192] Sahl al-Tustarī (d. 283/896), a Sufi, interprets this passage as the death of the soul by taking its spirit,[193] suggesting the soul has a spirit, further suggesting the multifaceted meaning of this passage by various exegetes from different schools of thought.

In Muslim traditions, an intermediate state between death and resurrection exists.[194] During the intermediate state (known as *barzakh*), the *nafs* exists, yet is probably disembodied.[195] During the resurrection of the dead, it is assumed that the *nafs* is re-embodied.

Conclusion

As in the Hebrew Bible, the concept of the *nafs* in the Qur'an has a range of conceptual definitions, including the soul, self, and person (individual). The *nafs* can be disembodied and it can be dead. There is evidence from the Qur'an to suggest that the *nafs* can, but will not necessarily, denote a physical self, which is also supported by ancient Semites' use of this term. However, defining *nafs* definitively is like drawing water from a mirage. Pre-Islamic Arabs defined *qalb* or *lubb* as the physical heart, but they also defined it metaphorically, as it is also most frequently used in the Qur'an. Therefore, even if the *nafs* is physical, it would not mean that the Qur'an may not use it metaphorically. I am not arguing that the Qur'an adopts either a monistic or a dualistic nature of the mind-body paradigm, as it is inconclusive. Evidence from both the Near Eastern context of the Qur'anic milieu during Late Antiquity as well as the understanding of post-Qur'anic traditional Muslim literature suggests that there was never a consensus on defining the *nafs*. For that reason, it is important to investigate the concept of death and resurrection in the Qur'an itself. Is resurrection physical in the sense of people coming out of their graves? Could it refer to a soul that is re-embodied or re-created with a different body, or does it carry a metaphorical or even spiritual sense?

Chapter 3

TERMINOLOGIES OF DEATH

The Qur'an uses many terms for nonbelievers, such as *fujjār*, *kuffār*, *munāfiqūn* and *mujrimūn*. It also uses the verb *yulḥidūn* (usually understood as 'distort') as an action that some nonbelievers do. A brief (noncomprehensive) lexicographic inquiry aims to show that many Qur'anic terms denoting nonbelievers, evildoers, and hypocrites have a common denominator in their polysemous spectrum: they are associated with death. By using terms associated with death to refer to nonbelievers, the Qur'an appears to subtly suggest these nonbelievers are in a state of death, albeit spiritually. Having looked into the concept of life in the previous chapter, it is a natural progression to move on to the concept of death in the Qur'an.

Defining death

As already stated, there is no consensus on the definition of life; consequently, there is no consensus on the definition of death, either. For that reason, many bioethical debates revolve around attempting to define what death is – when comparing a vegetative state, brain death and the like.[1] This is even an issue with organ transplants: when an individual's brain dies, are their body's organs dead, especially if they can be transplanted into someone else's body and continue to function?[2] The controversy over the definition of death has touched religious communities,[3] even inciting Muslim religious edicts.[4] Contemporary Muslim scholars appear to have difficulty defining what death is no less than medical experts and biologists do. Perhaps this a clue that a precise definition in the Qur'an is vague, at best, especially in light of modern science and medicine.[5]

Presumably, humans have always been pondering what constitutes death;[6] what has evolved in human thought is the concept of an afterlife, regardless of its nature.[7] In some longstanding shamanistic beliefs, the spirits of the ancestors were believed to hover around and guide people through the means of a communicator – the shaman.[8] Burial rites and funerary offerings[9] provide some clues as to when the concept of an afterlife took hold in human societies, but they do not provide concrete evidence.[10]

The terminologies of death and darkness in the Qur'an is philologically set in its Near Eastern background. In ancient Egypt,[11] belief in an afterlife is well attested.[12] The ancient Egyptian term for death is rooted in *mt*.[13] After a person dies, they are judged in the court of the god Osiris, where their heart is weighed against a feather using a principle known as *ma'at*, which is truth and justice.[14] If the heart of the person is heavier than the feather, they are considered unjust.[15] To enjoy life with the gods in the hereafter, a person's heart must be unburdened by dishonourable qualities.[16]

Historically, Israelite groups were situated along the land bridge between the centres of ancient Near Eastern civilizations: ancient Egypt and Mesopotamia. These two civilizations had some influence on each other,[17] and therefore exerted a possible influence on the ancient Israelites, who lived along the way between them.[18] Egypt periodically controlled parts of the Levant and had relations with the inhabitants there,[19] putting them in direct or indirect contact with the Israelites.[20] Mesopotamian civilization also had a rich afterlife culture,[21] though arguably less developed than the ancient Egyptians did.[22]

Death and darkness

Resurrection being a major theme in the Qur'an makes the concept of death relevant to Qur'anic study. The root *m-w-t*, defining death, is common in many Semitic languages, such as Akkadian,[23] Hebrew, Aramaic, Ugaritic,[24] Nabatean,[25] Canaanite,[26] Punic, Ethiopic, Arabic and Old South Arabic.[27] It also defines death in Egyptian,[28] as well as in many of the greater Afroasiatic languages.[29]

The Akkadian *mātu* means to die, and it can refer to the actual death of a living creature or a metaphorical death: a tablet whose contents are rendered invalid might be said to be dead.[30] The Akkadian *ṣalālu* means to fall asleep and sometimes used to describe death.[31] This may be compared with the now-familiar Qur'an 39:42, which shows the close relationship between sleep and death.[32] The root *ṣ-l-l* has a wide semantic field within Semitic languages: its Akkadian meaning, to sleep or to lie down, compares with the Hebrew term *ṣ-l-l*, meaning to sink, and the Arabic term *ḍ-l-l*, meaning to disappear or to be hidden.[33] In Akkadian, *ṣalīlu* means not only sleeping but also covering,[34] similar to one meaning of the Arabic term *ẓ-l-l*. The relationship between the Arabic *ḍ-l-l* and *ẓ-l-l* is disputed, although they share the Akkadian and Hebrew semantic range of *ṣ-l-l*.[35] The interchangeability between {/ṣ/ or /ḍ/} and {/ṭ/ or /ẓ/} among Semitic languages and between their dialects, including Arabic, is very common.[36] Many early and medieval Arab philologists have written treatises concerning specifically the fluidity of /ḍ/ and /ẓ/.[37] The free variation between /ḍ/ and /ẓ/ is archaic in the Arabic language, even though some early Arab philologists attempted to prove a subtle distinction between roots that contain them.[38]

In the ancient Near East, the shadow, from the root *ṣ-l-l*, sometimes connotes blackness or darkness. The Akkadian *ṣillu* means shade or cover,[39] and it is a shared definition of the root *ṣ-l-l* among many Semitic languages, including Ethiopic,[40] as well as in several Afroasiatic languages.[41] The Hebrew Bible sometimes uses the term shadow of death (*ṣalmāwet*) (e.g. Ps. 23:4, 44:19, 107:10, 107:14; Job 10:21–

22). It is difficult to tell whether the term *ṣalmāwet* is a construct of *ṣēl* (shadow) and *môt* (death) or if it was simply derived from *ṣelem*, meaning darkness. The *Theological Dictionary of the Old Testament* (*TDOT*) suggests that the concept of the shadow of death in the Hebrew Bible is folk etymology.[42] The Akkadian *ṣalāmu* means darkness or blackness[43] and is cognate to Ethiopic *ṣalama* and the Arabic *ẓalām*.[44] Ethiopic also has the form *ṣalamta* for darkness,[45] so the *TDOT* suggests that *ṣalmāwet* etymology is simply darkness.[46] David van Acker argues that the preferred etymology for *ṣalmāwet* is shadow of death (*ṣēl môt*) and not from the root *ṣ-l-m*, but continues to hold the semantic meaning of darkness.[47] This is no different from the hypothesis proposed by D. Winston Thomas,[48] but the evidence that *ẓlmt* or *ṣlmt* exists in various Semitic languages suggests that it is more likely not a construct of two separate terms.

Besides meaning blackness or darkness, the Akkadian *ṣalmu* also means an image, statue, or figure[49] – a meaning also found in Hebrew.[50] It has been debated whether the meanings of blackness/darkness and an image are associated with each other in some Semitic languages;[51] nonetheless, it is attested in Akkadian, where *ṣillu* (shadow) can also mean likeness.[52]

The following semantic analysis of the root *ẓ-l-m* further corroborates the findings of Johanne Christiansen, who has written an extensive analysis of its relation with darkness in the Qur'an, showing its main metaphorical use, especially in the description of the mental state of nonbelievers.[53] The Qur'an frequently uses the term *ẓulumāt* to mean darkness (e.g. Qur'an 2:257, 5:16), and it is usually used in opposition to light.[54] While in Arabic, the root *ẓ-l-m* means darkness,[55] it also means unfairness or injustice.[56] In Aramaic and Ethiopic, the root *ṭ-l-m* is equivalent to the meaning of unfairness.[57]

The Qur'an uses the term *ḍ-l-l* in opposition to light, connoting darkness, albeit metaphorically (e.g. Qur'an 39:22). The Qur'an also uses the term *ḍ-l-l* in opposition to *h-d-y*, which means to guide or to lead (e.g. Qur'an 2:16, 2:175, 7:30, 28:85, 34:24). Accordingly, the term *ḍ-l-l* would mean to be lost or misguided.[58] The Qur'an also sometimes brings forth the root terms *ẓ-l-m* and *ḍ-l-l* together, suggesting that those causing darkness (*ẓ-l-m*) lead to misguidance (*ḍ-l-l*) (e.g. Qur'an 19:38, 31:11, 71:24). Additionally, Qur'an 27:80–81 and 30:52–53 describe how those who are blind are lost (*ḍalāl*), but also that they are deaf, describing them as if they were dead (e.g. Qur'an 43:40). All these related meanings suggest the close relationship between those roots and their metaphorical uses beyond simply meaning darkness.

Evildoers (fujjār)

In Akkadian, the term *pagru* means a corpse, a body, a self or a person,[59] and its Hebrew and Aramaic cognates share the same meaning, while in Ugaritic, it means stone or altar.[60] In Akkadian, it is frequently used in curses,[61] while the Qur'anic use is a denunciation. The Qur'an uses *fājir* or the plural *fujjār* to describe nonbelievers (e.g. Qur'an 38:28, 71:27, 82:14, 83:7). The Arabic meaning of the term as immoral or sinner[62] is also attested in Jewish Aramaic and Middle Hebrew.[63] The relationship between the Ugaritic and Arabic roots *p(f)-g-r* has long been studied,[64] although none have provided a fully convincing argument of the difference in semantic range. The Ethiopic meaning of *f-g-r* is to strive and to work hard.[65] While the Arabic definition may include such meaning in the sense of evil work, the Ethiopic term is used generally for any work.

The *Theological Dictionary of the Old Testament* suggests that the root meaning is to cleave or to break, which explains why it also means daybreak and came to mean immoral or sinner, as in a breach of morality.[66] The Hebrew Bible uses the term to mean corpse, or a dead body broken off (e.g. Gen. 15:11; Num. 14:29, 14:32; Lev. 26:30; Isa. 34:3; Jer. 41:9; Ezek. 6:5; Amos 8:3).

A tradition in the biography of Muḥammad holds that when he was young he participated in a day known as *yawm al-fijār*.[67] Several wars in pre-Islamic Arabia and reported in Muslim traditions have been called *fijār*.[68] Among the different proposals for why those wars were called *fijār*, one hypothesis is that they happened during the sacred months (*ashhur al-ḥurum*) when wars were prohibited.[69] However, the reports by Ibn al-Jawzī (d. 597/1201) about the Second Fijār War is that it was during the Arabic month Shawwāl, which is not during a sacred month,[70] calling into question the reason behind the naming. It may be possible, however, that the war continued to the next month, Dhul-Qiʿdah, which is a sacred month, and at the time a pact known as *Ḥilf al-Fuḍūl* (League of the Virtuous) was signed.[71] Another hypothesis behind the *fijār* naming reported by Ibn al-Athīr (d. 630/1232) is that it is due to killing the young during those wars,[72] which would fix the meaning of *fijār* as those committing heinous crimes.

Qurʾan 75:1–6 speaks of the Day of Resurrection and offers the imagery of bones. The Qurʾan uses the verb *yafjur* for the person asking when that Day of Resurrection is. The typical understanding of this term is a person who delays repentance and brings forward evil work.[73] If alternatively the term *yafjur* were understood as to be a dead corpse, then the passage would show that the person asking about the Day of Resurrection desires to be a dead corpse not to be resurrected. Ibn ʿArabī (d. 638/1240) states in his *Tafsīr* that the person wants to continue in ignorance, seeking corporal and animalistic desires instead of spiritual.[74]

The Qurʾan sometimes contrasts the term *fujjār* with *abrār* (e.g. Qurʾan 82:13–14, 83:7, 83:18);[75] the latter is typically understood as the righteous, the elect, or the pure.[76]

Nonbelievers (kuffār)

One of the most common descriptions of nonbelievers in the Qurʾan comes from the root *k-f-r*, 'to cover'.[77] In a wonderful and extensive linguistic analysis of *k-f-r* and its polysemous use in the Qurʾan,[78] Juan Cole argues that the term *kāfir* in the Qurʾan should not be understood as 'infidel' or 'nonbeliever', but rather as having a wide semantic range, from 'peasant' and 'pagan' to 'libertine', 'rebel', and 'blasphemer'. He also concludes 'that limiting the meaning of the root so severely causes us to miss a rich set of other connotations that give us a rounder idea of the Quran's intent'.[79]

A village shares the same root *k-f-r*, and a sermon during the battle of Yarmūk (15/636) attributed to ʿAmr b. al-ʿĀṣ (d. 43/664), a companion of Muḥammad, uses it in that definition.[80] Al-Farāhīdī suggests that the reason for the meaning of village is that to city dwellers, villagers are like the dead.[81] Nonetheless, *Lisān al-ʿarab* also states that the meaning of village is a loanword from Syriac, as the people of the Levant use this term for village,[82] which is an ancient meaning also attested in Akkadian.[83] The term *kuffār* also means farmers, and this definition is attested in the Qurʾan:

> Know that the life of this world is but play, diversion, ornament, mutual boasting among you, and vying for increase in property and children – the likeness of a rain whose vegetation impresses the farmers [*al-kuffār*]; then it withers such that you see it turn yellow; then it becomes chaff. And in the Hereafter there shall be severe punishment, forgiveness from God, and contentment, and the life of this world is nothing but the enjoyment of delusion.
>
> Qurʾan 57:20

The term *al-kuffār* in this passage is defined (or 'understood') as *al-zurrā*ʿ (farmers) by the majority of traditional exegetes, such as al-Zamakhsharī (d. 538/1144),[84] al-Rāzī,[85] Ibn Kathīr (d. 774/1373),[86] and others. The reason behind this meaning is that farmers cover seeds with dust (earth) in the process of planting.[87] Al-Rāzī also explicitly states that Arabs have used the term *kāfir* for a farmer due to covering seeds into the dust.[88] The Arabs might have rarely used this term to mean village because of the rarity of farming in the desert of Arabia when compared to Aramaic-speaking people. According to al-Farāhīdī, the root *k-f-r* means to cover anything, and by extension, it has been used for farming villages.[89]

In *Lisān al-ʿarab*, a nonbeliever is called *kāfir* because his heart is veiled (covered) from knowing God.[90] The term *kaffārah* means to purify, atone, or forgive sins based on the definition of covering the sin. This usage is attested in Akkadian,[91] Hebrew (e.g. Deut. 21:8), Aramaic[92] and Arabic (e.g. Qurʾan 5:45, 5:89, 5:95). The Qurʾanic description of a nonbeliever as a *kāfir* parallels the use in Hebrew (*kôper*).[93] It is difficult to discern the reason behind defining *kāfir* as a nonbeliever. According to *Kitāb al-ʿayn*[94] and *Lisān al-ʿarab*,[95] a nonbeliever's heart is covered from faith; Arabic term *kafr* also means a grave, since a grave is covered with dust.[96] The meaning of grave is also attested in Ethiopic.[97]

Some scholars argue that *k-p-r* and *q-b-r* are also synonymous in Nabataean denoting a tomb or burial,[98] and the relationship of those two roots in Arabic has been suggested.[99] Several scholars have suggested that the term *k-p-r* for tomb in Nabataean is possibly of Lihyanite origin,[100] but it seems likely due to its broad Semitic meaning of burial. The Qurʾan also combines both terms *fājir* and *kaffār* into a single passage: 'Truly if You leave them, they will mislead Your servants and will beget nothing but disbelieving profligates [a corpse burial?] [*fājiran kaffārā*]' (Qurʾan 71:27).

The Qur'an even provides a contrast between those who are alive and those who are *kāfirīn*, which further gives the Qur'anic understanding of its metaphoric use of the term *kuffār* for those who are spiritually dead: 'to warn whosoever is alive [*ḥayyan*], and so that the Word may come due for the disbelievers [*al-kāfirīn*]' (Qur'an 36:70). Unlike the root *f-j-r* in Arabic, *k-f-r* clearly holds the connotation of covering, and by extension, a grave.

Hypocrites (munāfiqūn)

The Qur'an uses the term *munāfiqūn* for hypocrites (e.g. Qur'an 4:61, 8:49, 9:68, 29:11, 33:1). The root *n-p-q* is found in Aramaic, where it means to go out or to give, including expenses.[101] The Arabic cognate has a similar semantic range as the Aramaic,[102] and is used by the Qur'an to mean giving out money (expenditure) (e.g. Qur'an 2:3, 2:215, 8:3, 16:75).[103] The sense of separation is also attested in Ethiopic.[104] Going out, giving up or separating is perhaps the root meaning of this term from which all others stem, including the Qur'anic 'hypocrites' (those who give up or leave the faith).[105]

The root *n-f-q* also means a tunnel in the ground (e.g. Qur'an 6:35) and is used in reference to some animal holes.[106] The reason for this meaning is that animals that bore holes in the ground also come out (*naffaqat*) from these holes.[107] The term *n-f-q* can mean dead corpse,[108] perhaps because it is the *nafs* being given up at the point of death. A prophetic tradition (*ḥadīth*) uses *tanfuq* for a dying corpse,[109] as a contampraneous poem attributed to Labīd b. Rabī'ah al-'Āmrī (d. 41/661) also uses *al-nawāfiq* to mean dead corpses.[110] In South Arabic and Ethiopic, it also means a coffin.[111]

In Akkadian, the term *napāqu* is some sort of internal disease or illness or the cause of blockage to the throat or windpipe.[112] The Qur'an sometimes describes the hypocrites as those with sickness in their hearts (e.g. Qur'an 2:8–10, 5:52–54, 8:49, 33:12, 33:60, 47:20–34). According to Absar Ahmad, the Qur'anic concept of spiritual death is associated with the Qur'anic concept of the sealing of the heart and the concept of *fī qulūbihim maraḍ* (in their hearts a sickness) (e.g. Qur'an 2:10, 5:52, 8:49, 9:125), which is usually used for the *munāfiqūn*.[113]

The Qur'an defines the *munāfiqūn* as ones who *kafarū*, which, as established above, holds the meaning of buried: 'That is because they believed, and then disbelieved [*kafarū*]; so a seal was set upon their hearts such that they comprehend not' (Qur'an 63:3).

Sinners (mujrimūn)

The term *mujrimūn* and its morphological permutations are often used by the Qur'an to describe sinners (e.g. Qur'an 8:8, 15:58, 43:74). The root *j-r-m* means to cut off in Arabic,[114] as it does in Hebrew and Aramaic,[115] which has been argued by Bernice Hecker in the course of a greater Semitic etymology.[116] The same root also yields the meaning of bones stripped of flesh, a corpse, or a body.[117] The Hebrew Bible uses this term in these ways (e.g. Dan. 6:24). In archaeological finds along the Levant, the inscription of the root *g-r-m* has been read as denoting ossuaries, where bones are kept.[118]

Though the term *jurm* may hold the meaning of sin in Arabic,[119] it also stands in for an imperfection or a cut, or for an outcast – they all share the root meaning of cut off. It also means body, as attested in the pre-Islamic poem attributed to Muhalhal b. Rabīʿah al-Taghlibī (d. 530).[120] The Hebrew Bible sometimes uses this root to mean strength (e.g. Gen. 49:14) as an allusion of having strong bones (bony) similar to how the root *ʿ-ẓ-m*, which means bone, also contains the morphological permutation of strength (*ʿaẓīm*).[121] The Arab poet, Muzāḥim al-ʿUqaylī (d. 120/738) even specifically says '*al-ʿiẓām jarīm*' (bony body).[122] This might further provide the relationships of the semantic fields for *g-r-m* and *ʿ-ẓ-m* with the commonality in the bone definition. Like many other polysemous terms studied that are being used to denote nonbelievers by the Qurʾan, the term *mujrimūn* could also hold an allusion to a dead corpse.

In Jacob's blessing on his deathbed, Gen. 49:14 narrates him saying, 'Issachar is a strong donkey [*ḥămōr gārem*]', using the root *g-r-m*. It has been suggested by Samuel Feigin that *ḥămōr gārem* means 'castrated ass',[123] but Paul Forchheimer insists it simply means a strong donkey from the etymological root meaning bony donkey;[124] thus further relating together the roots *g-r-m* and *ʿ-ẓ-m*.

The root *j-s-m* meaning body, bulky, or strong,[125] is also found in Aramaic (e.g. Dan. 3:27–28).[126] There is a possibility, as is typical in the evolution of the Semitic languages,[127] of a consonantal shift between various dialects between /*r*/ and /*s*, *sh*/,[128] which created a similar semantic field between *j-r-m* and *j-s-m*. However, regardless of whether *j-r-m* and *j-s-m* are related, the root *j-r-m* on its own holds the meaning of body, bones, and tomb.

Incline (yulḥidūn)

The Qurʾan uses the term *l-ḥ-d* to describe those who veer away (e.g. Qurʾan 7:180, 16:103, 41:40). This term has no known cognates in most Semitic languages.[129] Although the root does exist in Akkadian, it is of unknown meaning.[130] For this reason, finding the root meaning is difficult. The Qurʾan also uses it to mean some sort of refuge (*multaḥadā*) (i.e. Qurʾan 18:27, 72:22).[131]

Nonetheless, one of the meanings of *l-ḥ-d* is the opening of a grave,[132] where the dead are placed on the side (*mayl*) as they are laid to rest.[133] This would keep the root meaning as inclining, and perhaps the Qurʾanic use of *multaḥadā* is that there is no one besides God to incline to,[134] as al-Rāzī suggests.[135] Al-Ṭabarī even suggests *mawʾilā* as a synonym to *multaḥadā*, suggesting the root meaning *mayl* (inclination).[136]

The earliest attested use of *l-ḥ-d* in various pre-Islamic poetry is the meaning of one who is buried, such as in poems attributed to Ṭarafah b. al-ʿAbd[137] and ʿAdī b. Zayd al-ʿIbādī (d. 588).[138] Therefore, its association with death in Arabic is evident.

Conclusion

Many of the terms the Qur'an uses to describe nonbelievers are associated with death. Although those terms are polysemous, with various meanings, the lowest common denominator they all share has to do with death. The *fujjār* are dead corpses; the *kuffār* are covered in a grave. The *mujrimūn* are corpses; the *munāfiqūn* are dead. The *yulḥidūn* are placed in graves. After all, the Qur'an does say of those who are nonbelievers that God places upon their hearts veils and upon their ears deafness, such that they do not understand (e.g. Qur'an 6:25, 17:46, 18:57, 41:5). Since nonbelievers are covered, calling them *kuffār* is natural and faithful to the root meaning of the word.

Qur'an 7:176–180 gives an interesting summary of some of the terms discussed in this chapter. Since the term *nafaq* could mean a hole in the ground or a tunnel, Qur'an 7:176 does state that the nonbeliever penetrates the earth (*akhlad ila al-arḍ*), as if going through it in a hole.[139] Qur'an 7:177 continues to state that these people are the ones who darken (*yaẓlimūn*) their *nafs*. Qur'an 7:178 goes on to state that whoever God guides is guided, but whoever God keeps in the dark (*yuḍlil*) is lost. Qur'an 7:179 continues to describe these people as those whose hearts do not understand (like the ones God covers with veils), who have eyes that do not see and ears that do not hear (as those in their graves, e.g. Qur'an 35:19–22; or those in darkness, e.g. Qur'an 6:39), and that they are like animals, but in even deeper darkness (*aḍall*). Finally, Qur'an 7:180 continues to describe them as *yulḥidūn* (those placed in a grave penetrating the earth). Accordingly, it can be seen that the Qur'an can be consistent in its description using terms describing death and darkness for nonbelievers.

As is seen in the next chapter, the Qur'an frequently describes nonbelievers as spiritually dead. Therefore, it might be possible that – consciously, through wordplay – the Qur'an uses terms associated with death, as presented in this chapter, to describe nonbelievers.

Chapter 4

DEATH

In many instances, the Qur'an invokes death metaphorically, not as a physical state but as some form of spiritual condition. The metaphor sometimes also infers spiritual resurrection, as Rakesh and Ayati argue, referring to Qur'an 6:122 and 3:169 as examples. They look into the metaphorical use of 'light and life' with 'darkness and death' for guidance and misguidance respectively.[1] They have suggested that the Qur'an seems to fit death into three categories: (1) nonhuman death, such as dead earth as a metaphor of barren land; (2) spiritual death that requires spiritual resurrection; and (3) death in a strict, physical sense, such as a dying person writing a will (i.e. Qur'an 2:180) or Jacob on his deathbed (e.g. Qur'an 2:133).[2] When we look at the possible definitions of death contained therein, the Qur'an appears to truly have a specific focus on spiritual death and resurrection, and not only physical.

Definition of death in the Qur'an

In the Qur'an, death is discussed many times, but most instances do not explicitly mention the death of the body (*badan* or *jasad*);[3] rather, they have to do with the death of the *nafs*:

> Every *nafs* shall taste death, and you will indeed be paid [*tuwaffawn*] your reward in full on the Day of Resurrection. And whosoever is distanced from the Fire and made to enter the Garden has certainly triumphed. And the life of this world is nothing but the enjoyment of delusion.
>
> Qur'an 3:185

> 34We have not ordained perpetual life for any flesh [*bashar*] before you. So if you die, will they abide forever? 35Every *nafs* shall taste death. We try you with evil and with good, as a test, and unto Us shall you be returned.[4]
>
> Qur'an 21:34–35

> Every *nafs* shall taste death. Then unto Us shall you be returned.
>
> Qur'an 29:57

Although the Qur'an speaks about death and resurrection in these passages, textually and linguistically it refers not necessarily to the death of the body but, more precisely, to the death of the *nafs*, which, as argued in Chapter 2, might be a monistic soul/body (an individual) or dualistic. These passages are seemingly an attempt by the Qur'an to discuss immortality, which may be seen explicitly in Qur'an 21:34. There, I translate *bashar* as flesh since it appears to be meant in the physical sense, as opposed to the ambiguous nature of the *nafs*.

O'Shaughnessy states that the earliest (based on an assumed chronology) uses of death in the Qur'an are metaphorical.[5] Nonetheless, he states that the Qur'an employs two types of death, the *first death*, which is spiritual, while a person is still physically alive, and the *second death*, which occurs after the physical death of the body:

> Besides the spiritual death the disbeliever suffers even while he is physically alive, there is in the Qur'ān another analogy based on the notion of death, the 'second death' of Hell by which disbelievers are deprived eternal life in the world to come. In such an analogy the state of those in Paradise would stand in relation to that of the damned in Hell somewhat as life as a state does to death.[6]

O'Shaughnessy also identifies the following three Qur'anic passages as portrayals of hell as a living death:[7]

> [12]he who enters into the greatest Fire, [13]then neither dies therein nor lives.
>
> Qur'an 87:12–13

> [16]Beyond him lies Hell; and he shall be given to drink of oozing pus,[17]which he will gulp down, but can scarcely swallow. Death shall come upon him from every side; yet he will not die, and before him lies a grave punishment.
>
> Qur'an 14:16–17

> Verily, whosoever comes unto his Lord guilty, surely his shall be Hell, wherein he neither dies nor lives.
>
> Qur'an 20:74

Despite his thoroughness, O'Shaughnessy appears to have missed the following passage, which also resembles the other three, in which people in hell are portrayed as non-dying:

> [36]As for those who disbelieve, theirs shall be the Fire of Hell. They will neither be done away with so as to die; nor will its punishment be lightened for them. Thus do We requite every disbeliever. [37]They will cry out therein, 'Our Lord! Remove us, that we may work righteousness other than that which we used to do.' 'Did We not give you long life, enough for whosoever would reflect to reflect therein? And the warner came unto you, so taste [the punishment]! The wrongdoers shall have no helpers.'
>
> Qur'an 35:36–37

A conceivable interpretation of a non-dying person in hell is the Qur'anic supposition that the skin of those in hell will be changed every time it roasts in the fires, such that people in it continue to taste pain (i.e. Qur'an 4:56).[8] Nonetheless, Qur'an 87:13 and 20:74 suppose that those in hell neither live nor die. What it means to neither live nor die is peculiar, as it appears to reference zombies, who may be described as neither dead (because they move) nor truly alive. It would appear here that the Qur'an is giving a clue in that life and death are not always to be taken and understood literally. There must be some figurative sense in such a statement that the Qur'an intends to convey. To make literal sense of it, al-Ṭabarī assumed that the soul reaches the throat, where it neither leaves the body nor rests in it,[9] which therefore does assume a disembodied soul. Yet al-Ṭabarī assumes that when a soul reaches the throat, the body is in a suspended state neither dead nor alive – an assumption without attestation in the Qur'an. Alternatively, Ibn ʿArabī resorted to the idea that a person in hell never dies forever, because they never cease to exist. Nor are they alive, because they are spiritually dead.[10]

O'Shaughnessy categorizes death in the Qur'an into four classifications: (1) death of a land (figurative and earliest references of death in the Qur'an);[11] (2) mortal disbelief (spiritual death);[12] (3) bodily death in this world;[13] and (4) death as punishment in hell, which he considers the *second death*.[14] While Patricia Crone does not cite O'Shaughnessy, she accepts the possible definition of *second* death as eternal damnation, stating,

> So what is the second death? This expression is not actually used in the Qur'ān, and for this reason the exegetes had trouble with it. However, it does appear in the Jewish targums, the Talmud, the Apocalypse of John, Syriac texts, a Greek work preserved only in Ethiopic, and Manichaean literature. In this literature, the 'second death' stands for eternal damnation.[15]

Smith and Haddad state, 'The issue of immortality of the soul was generally of less concern to orthodox Islam than the affirmation of the resurrection of the body'.[16] It, thus, assumes that bodily resurrection is a major Qur'anic theme against nonbelievers. In her discussion about the nonbelievers (*mushrikūn*), Crone also assumes that the Qur'an emphasizes a bodily resurrection:

> Their emphasis on the impossibility of restoring decomposed bodies could be taken to mean that some of them believed in a spiritual afterlife, but there are no polemics against this idea, nor against other forms of afterlife such as reincarnation. In so far as one can tell, the disagreement is never over the form that life after death will take, only about its reality. The choice is between bodily resurrection and no afterlife at all.[17]

The human attributes that the Qur'an uses to personify death have been looked into by Ferdows Agha Golzadeh and Shirin Pourebrahim[18] – work that Khan Sardaraz and Roslan bin Ali have extended, depicting how the Qur'an metaphorizes death and resurrection, for instance by attributing human behaviour to them.[19] Yet, while these studies show how metaphor is used in the Qur'an to describe death and resurrection,[20] they do not define death and resurrection themselves as possible metaphors. It is typical for many scholars of Qur'anic studies to take the literality of death and resurrection for granted in most Qur'anic passages.

The Qur'anic contrast between light and darkness, on the other hand, is rarely taken literally. In his analysis of such metaphors, Khaled Berrada states,[21]

> Moreover, in the Holy Qur'an, it is worth emphasizing, there is a recurrent metaphorical use of light to stand for faith, the truth, knowledge, conviction, peace of mind, tranquillity and blessing as opposed to darkness, which is symbolic of the opposed negative qualities: disbelief and heresy, falsehood, ignorance, hesitation, doubt, apprehension, damnation and curse.[22]

Berrada's analysis moves parallel to the traditional Muslim accounts, both orthodox and Sufi, continuing:[23]

> In sum, light in the Qur'an stands for divine, submission to Allah's guidance, Allah's grace and bounty, spiritual progress, faith, the truth, knowledge, joy and felicity and other positive qualities. However, darkness stands for evil, contumacy and misguidance, spiritual retrogression, atheism, falsehood, ignorance, disquietude, grief and poignant doubt, damnation and other vices and negative qualities.[24]

He even identifies how the Qur'anic contrast of light and darkness is also used as an analogy for those who see and those who are blind, which the Qur'an does not identify in a literal sense.[25] This is emphasized more explicitly in the following Qur'anic passage:

> Have they not journeyed upon the earth, that they might have hearts by which to understand or ears by which to hear? Truly it is not the eyes that go blind, but it is hearts within breasts that go blind.
>
> Qur'an 22:46

Because the Qur'an makes an equivalent analogy between light and darkness, seeing and blindness, and life and death, Berrada also avers that life and death are used metaphorically in various passages of the Qur'an: 'Finally, it is worth stressing that the source domain of death and its darkness is mapped unto the target domain of misguidance and ignorance'.[26] Not only in Qur'anic discourse but also in prophetic tradition (*ḥadīth*), the contrasting themes of light and darkness are usually used in a metaphorical sense.[27]

Since the Qur'an uses light and darkness mostly in a metaphorical sense,[28] and invokes sight and blindness figuratively as well, it likewise would not at all be peculiar for it to employ life and death nonliterally, especially when these contrasting pairs appear together (e.g. Qur'an 35:19–22). To create a metaphor, the Qur'an uses terms that people may be able to relate to in order to perceive unknown issues that would otherwise be more abstract.[29] The difference is that scholars have usually understood light and darkness as metaphorical, while the same cannot be said for life and death, which had been mostly understood literally by early Muslim scholars. Some Sufi traditions do not share the same literalism. Sufi tradition has a concept of ego-death that stems from an alleged prophetic tradition (*ḥadīth*) stating, 'Die before you die.'[30] In Sufi tradition, the notion of Qur'anic death is sometimes also understood spiritually.[31]

If the death of the *nafs* is assumed as a metaphor describing someone who is spiritually dead, there are other examples from the Qur'an that point towards spiritual death.

> [20]And those whom they call upon apart from God create nothing, and are themselves created. [21][They are] dead, not living, and they are not aware of when they will be resurrected. [22]Your God is one God. And those who believe not in the Hereafter, their hearts deny and they are arrogant [*mustakbirūn*].
>
> Qur'an 16:20–22

These verses also talk about death and resurrection, but the Qur'an describes those who invoke something other than God as truly dead, not living and in need of resurrection. They are described as being arrogant, using the same term for arrogance that the Qur'an uses to describe Satan's arrogance (e.g. Qur'an 2:34, 7:12–13, 38:73–78). Yūsuf b. Sa'īd al-Fulānī, a Sufi master in the seventeenth-century CE, left a commentary on Qur'an 16 discussing the arrogance of Satan and the relationship between arrogance and the death of the human *nafs*.[32] His works can be compared with the likes of al-Ghazālī on how Satan veils a human heart through the arrogance of the *nafs*.[33] According to al-Ghazālī, the heart can commit two of the following sins, arrogance (*kibr*) and self-pride (*'izzah al-nafs*).[34] From the Qur'an, Munawar Anees extrapolates that arrogance leads to tyranny (*ẓulm*).[35]

There is a debate among commentators regarding the second of the preceding verses (i.e. Qur'an 16:21), with some claiming that people who seem to be alive are actually dead.[36] Al-Ṭabarī refers to idols as the ones that are dead but also shows that it could be a reference to the nonbelievers.[37] The second part of the verse would not make sense if the idols were the ones that did not perceive that they will be resurrected. There is no concept of idols resurrecting; it is only people who are resurrected. If the second part refers to people, then there is no reason to assume that the first part refers to anything other than people as well. Although al-Tha'labī (d. 427/1035)[38] and al-Rāzī also refer to idols as those who are dead, they recognize that the second part of the verse might be referring to the nonbelievers.[39] Al-Rāzī also refers to a tradition by Ibn 'Abbās, who suggests that the verse refers to idols coming to life and speaking. Al-Ṭūsī (d. 460/1067)[40] and al-Ṭabarsī, on the other hand, suggest that it is very possible that it is the people and not necessarily the idols who are dead, which, for the reasons already given, seems more rational.[41] Consequently, the ones who are dead could be understood to mean that people are spiritually dead.

Abul-Qāsim al-Suhaylī (d. 581/1185) associates Qur'an 16:21 with 6:122, understanding it as a description of the spiritual death of nonbelievers.[42] Ibn Qayyim al-Jawziyyah (d. 751/1350) also takes Qur'an 16:21 to describe the spiritual death of the nonbelievers; he emphasizes that the real life is the life of the heart and that the real age of a person is how long they lived with God in their hearts.[43] According to him, any time a person's heart is not with God, they are dead and their life is invalidated – or in other words, it is as though he is calling them zombies.

Sufi interpretations – such as the one transmitted by Sahl al-Tustarī (d. 283/896) in his *tafsīr*,[44] Abū ʿAbdulraḥmān al-Sulamī (d. 412/1021) in *Ḥaqāʾiq al-tafsīr*,[45] Rūzbihān Baqlī (d. 606/1209) in *ʿArāʾis al-bayān fī ḥaqāʾiq al-Qurʾān*,[46] and Ibn al-Ḥāj al-Fāsī (d. 737/1336) in his *Madkhal* – ascribe spiritual death to the meaning of this passage.[47] The Qur'an may indeed be talking about zombies – people walking the earth who think they are alive while in fact they are spiritually dead. In another verse, the Qur'an explicitly states that those who do not listen to the message are dead in their graves:

> And not equal are the living and the dead. Truly God causes whomsoever He wills to hear, but you cannot cause those in graves to hear.
>
> Qur'an 35:22[48]

Some recent Salafi scholars associate this passage with Qur'an 16:21 and understand both not as contentions against the idolatry of worshipping sticks and stones, as they recognize that sticks and stones do not experience resurrection.[49] Those scholars understand this passage against the worship of saints (who died and would be resurrected), with the saints exonerating themselves from those who sought their intercession.[50] Independently arriving at the same conclusion, Patricia Crone also argued that the Qur'anic arguments in this passage against the nonbelievers are mainly impugning a practice similar to (dead) saints that developed later in some Muslim communities.[51] Some of the same Salafi scholars also accept the Qur'anic metaphor of spiritual death when describing nonbelievers in this passage.[52]

There seems to be an inner-Qur'anic allusion between Qur'an 35:22 and Qur'an 3:185, which talks about every soul tasting death. The allusion appears to be based on the verse preceding Qur'an 3:185 and one a few verses after Qur'an 35:22:

> So if they deny you, they certainly did deny messengers before you, who came with clear proofs, scriptures, and the luminous Book.
>
> Qur'an 3:184

> If they deny you, those before them also denied: their messengers brought them clear proofs, scriptures, and the luminous Book.
>
> Qur'an 35:25

This possible inner-Qur'anic allusion perhaps suggests that the living and the dead of Qur'an 35:22 might be related to every *nafs* tasting death in Qur'an 3:185.

Al-Ṭabarī states that the living and the dead in Qurʾan 35:22 are a metaphor for those whose hearts are alive with belief and those whose hearts are dead with disbelief.[53] There is some sort of consensus among traditional Muslim scholars that Qurʾan 35:22 is a metaphor, in which nonbelievers are viewed as dead. Al-Ṭabarī refers to the following passage, which also considers death and darkness as a metaphor for spiritual death, while life and light are a metaphor for spiritual life:

> Is he who was dead, and to whom We give life, making for him a light by which to walk among humankind, like unto one who is in darkness from which he does not emerge? Thus for the disbelievers, what they used to do was made to seem fair unto them.
>
> Qurʾan 6:122

Additionally, three verses later, we have

> Whomsoever God wishes to guide, He expands his breast for submission [*islām*]. And whomsoever He wishes to lead astray, He makes his breast narrow and constricted, as if he were climbing to the sky. Thus does God place defilement upon those who do not believe.
>
> Qurʾan 6:125

Since this passage discusses the guided and misguided, it might be related to Qurʾan 39:41–42, which also talks about guidance and misguidance and deliberates about the death and slumber of souls. There might also be an inner-Qurʾanic allusion connecting these passages, distinguishing those who are spiritually dead from those who are spiritually alive. Regarding Qurʾan 6:122, al-Ṭabarī[54] and al-Rāzī suggest that life and light refer to the divine's guidance, while death and darkness refer to misguidance.[55] Al-Rāzī specifically refers to similar allusions in the Qurʾan, such as the following:

> [They are] dead, not living, and they are not aware of when they will be resurrected.
>
> [Qurʾan 16:21]

> 80 Surely you do not make the dead hear; nor do you make the deaf hear the call when they turn their backs; 81 nor can you guide the blind away from their error. You can only make hear those who believe in Our signs and are submitters (*muslimūn*).
>
> Qurʾan 27:80–81, 30:52–53

> 69 And We have not taught him poetry; nor would it befit him. It is but a reminder and a clear Quran, 70 to warn whosoever is alive, and so that the Word may come due for the disbelievers.
>
> Qurʾan 36:69–70

Earlier scholars, such as al-Zajjāj (d. 311/925),[56] and later scholars, such as Ibn al-Ḥāj al-Fāsī,[57] have also associated Qur'an 6:122 with Qur'an 16:21 as al-Rāzī has. When associating those two passages, al-Zajjāj states in simile, 'every [person] guided is alive and every misguided is like the dead'.[58] Putting the two verses together with Qur'an 36:70, Abū 'Alī al-Fārsī (d. 377/987) wrote, 'The meaning of whoever is alive: from the believers because the nonbelievers are dead'.[59] Ibn 'Arabī interprets Qur'an 6:122 as referring to the death of the soul in its ignorance, and the soul's life in its knowledge of the truth.[60]

With respect to the preceding passages in deliberations, the topic of death seems to refer to the death of the *nafs* and not necessarily the death of bodies, depending on the definition of monistic/dualistic *nafs*. In contrast, the Qur'an states that those who are killed for the sake of God are not dead but alive (i.e. Qur'an 2:154, 3:169).

> And say not of those who are slain in the way of God, 'They are dead.' Nay, they are alive, but you are unaware [*tash'urūn*].
>
> Qur'an 2:154; cf. Qur'an 3:169

This verse itself emphasizes that the Qur'an, when defining life and death, does not necessarily denote it physically. It is obviously not the dead bodies of martyrs that this passage is stating are alive. It is something that is not perceived, which seems more likely to be a reference to some soul (*nafs*) – and that is indeed the understanding of many exegetes, some of whom also suggest that the soul of a martyr is given a body in heaven (as opposed to an earthly body) in the form of a bird.[61] Although Ibn 'Arabī explains this verse not of physical martyrs but spiritual martyrs who kill the ego,[62] even if we do take the traditional understanding of this verse as a reference to physical martyrs, the part that is alive is obviously not their physical bodies.

The Qur'an distinguishes between definitions of death and life. This can be further identified in the Qur'anic intention when describing graves, as in Qur'an 35:22, which states that God causes whomever He wills to hear but that we cannot make those in graves hear. Elsewhere, it is made clear that the Qur'an may be understood only by those who are alive. Again, this alludes to those who are spiritually alive:

> 69 And We have not taught him poetry [*al-shi'r*]; nor would it befit him. It is but a reminder and a clear Quran, 70 to warn whosoever is alive, and so that the Word may come due for the disbelievers.
>
> Qur'an 36:69–70

Traditional commentators, such as al-Ṭabarī, attest that this passage refers to those who are spiritually alive.[63] If we relate the above passages to Qur'an 35:22, we may identify that the dead and the people in the graves who cannot hear are a metaphor for people who are spiritually dead and cannot understand the message of the Qur'an, in accordance with Qur'an 36:69–70. Within the same chapter, another verse makes a claim similar to Qur'an 6:122:

> [33]We know well that what they say grieves you. Yet, it is not you that they deny. Rather, it is the signs of God that the wrongdoers reject. [34]Surely messengers were denied before you, and they bore patiently their being denied and persecuted till Our help came to them. None alters the Words of God, and there has already come unto you some tidings of the messengers. [35]And if their turning away is distressing to you, then seek, if you can, a tunnel into the earth, or a ladder unto the sky, that you might bring them a sign. Had God willed, He would have gathered them all to guidance – so be not among the ignorant. [36]Only those who hear will respond. As for the dead, God will resurrect them, and unto Him they shall be returned.
>
> Qur'an 6:33–36

A few passages later, the Qur'an states, 'Those who deny Our signs are deaf and dumb, in darkness. Whomsoever God will, He leads astray, and whomsoever He will, He places him upon a straight path' (Qur'an 6:39). Those verses also resemble Qur'an 3:184 and Qur'an 35:25, assuring that even previous messengers were not believed. Yet the verses attempt to comfort the recipient of the Qur'an by suggesting that only those who hear will respond to the message. Echoes reverberate in Qur'an 36:70, as also noted by Ibn al-Zubayr al-Ghirnāṭī (d. 708/1308).[64] For those who are described as dead, on the other hand, Qur'an 6:36 confirms that it is God who will resurrect them, suggesting that they would not hear the message due to their state. This mirrors Qur'an 35:22, in which the messenger cannot cause those in their graves to hear, for God will make whomever God wills to hear. Those who do not adhere to the message are symbolized as dead whom God will resurrect according to Qur'an 6:36, whereas Qur'an 6:122 elaborates perhaps on how God spiritually resurrects dead people into life.[65]

Conclusion

The Qur'anic usage for death is sometimes metaphorical, describing spiritual death. Through inner-Qur'anic allusions regarding death and resurrection, the Qur'an does not refer always to bodily death. Even the Qur'anic concept of every *nafs* tasting death seems not to be a matter of bodily death, according to the intratextual relationships with other passages. Nevertheless, at best, the term *nafs* remains ambiguous and cannot be used as a sole evidence to the reference of bodily death either. Therefore, some of the Sufi interpretations, such as that of Ibn ʿArabī, on the nature of spiritual death in the Qur'an are not to be understood simply as esoteric, but philological and textual analysis of the Qur'an may provide some support to that notion. If the concept of death in the Qur'an is mainly metaphorical for some sort of spiritual death, an analysis of the definition of life and resurrection in the Qur'an becomes a natural next step in the inquiry.

Chapter 5

LIFE

In Qur'anic perspective, the concept of death operates in relation to that of life. To distinguish those granted life from those who are not, the biblical tradition used the motif of the book written in heaven (of the living) and the book written on the earth. After touching on this biblical precursor only briefly – for comparative purposes, since a similar concept is also found in the Qur'an, suggesting a possible adoption of a Near Eastern concept of life into the Qur'anic discourse – this chapter delves into how the Qur'an compares this worldly life (*al-ḥayāt al-dunyā*) and the other (*al-ākhirah*) to understand further what the Qur'an means by 'life', which is also compared with biblical literature identifying how the Qur'an might adopt these concepts from within its Near Eastern background. In the analogies it uses for resurrection, the Qur'an constructs an argument of how the human was created the first time through natural birth. Whether birth or even rain that allows plants to grow, the analogues used in the Qur'an situate resurrection as a natural phenomenon and not some supernatural force. It seems that the Qur'an makes analogies for resurrection that would constitute resurrection more as a form of re-creation.

The book of life

The Qur'an developed in a place where the notion of the resurrection of the dead was well known to some of its audience, such as Jews and Christians, and it does not shy away from emphasizing the resurrection of the dead throughout its text. However, the question is, what exactly does the Qur'an suggest is resurrected: is it a monist or dualist *nafs*? Or, in other words, is resurrection spiritual, physical, or both?

In a few instances, the Qur'an makes the analogy that just as rain pouring down brings the dead earth to life, so would the resurrection of the dead occur (e.g. Qur'an 43:11). This analogy is not unique to the Qur'an. Of the core Eighteen Benedictions (now nineteen) of Rabbinic prayer,[1] it is written in the Mishnah, 'They mention [God's] power to bring rain in [the blessing for] the resurrection of the dead, [the second blessing in the *Eighteen Benedictions*].'[2] Written in the Babylonian Talmud, 'Rain is the same thing as making a living.'[3] The rabbis, in Talmudic tradition, also make a connection between the resurrection of the dead and rain, referring to 1 Sam. 12:17, in which God sends rain and thunder.[4]

Referencing rain and lightning (instead of thunder) with the resurrection of the dead can also be seen in the Qur'an:

> 24 And among His signs is that He shows you lightning, arousing fear and hope, and that He sends down water from the sky, then revives thereby the earth after its death. Truly in that are signs for a people who understand. 25 And among His signs is that the sky and the earth stand fast by His Command. Then, when He calls you forth from the earth with a single call, behold, you will come forth.
>
> Qur'an 30:24–25

The image of a resurrection at Judgement Day and the books of deeds that are opened to determine who enters heaven and who enters hell (e.g. Qur'an 83:4–36) is also not unique to the Qur'an. The book of deeds in heaven has roots going far back, from Sumerian to Talmudic times,[5] before finding itself situated within the Qur'an; Shalom Paul gives a brief overview of the various Near Eastern texts that refer to the book of life starting with Mesopotamian myths and its usage in the Hebrew Bible, Pseudepigrapha, Dead Sea Scrolls, and other Near Eastern literature.[6] The book of life is an ancient Near Eastern motif that continued to develop.

In the Talmud, Rabbi Naḥman b. Yitzḥak suggests that the book referred to in Exod. 32:32 are the books of the thoroughly wicked, the thoroughly righteous, and the middling.[7]

> 32 'But now, if you will only forgive their sin—but if not, blot me out of the book that you have written.' 33 But the LORD said to Moses, 'Whoever has sinned against me I will blot out of my book.'
>
> Exod. 32:32–33

A depiction of three similar groups can also be found in the Qur'an:

> 7 and you shall be of three kinds: 8 the companions of the right; what of the companions of the right? 9 And the companions of the left; what of the companions of the left? 10 And the foremost shall be the foremost.
>
> Qur'an 56:7–10

The book mentioned in the Exodus passage seems to be understood as the book of life or the living (*sēper ḥayyîm*), which is also mentioned in Pss. 56:8, 69:28, and 139:16, Dan. 12:1, Phil. 4:3, and Rev. 3:5.[8] Allusions to this book, as in the writing in heaven (*engegraptai en tois ouranois / apogegrammenōn en ouranois*), are also found in Lk. 10:20 and Heb. 12:23.[9] The writing in heaven is in contrast to the writing on the earth in Jeremiah:[10]

> O hope of Israel! O LORD! All who forsake [*'ōzĕbê*] you shall be put to shame; those who turn away from you shall be recorded in the earth[11] [*yikkātēbû bi-ha-'āreṣ*], for they have forsaken [*'ozbû*] the fountain of living water [*mĕqôr mayim ḥayyîm*], the LORD.
>
> Jer. 17:13

Although the contrast between the writing on earth and that of heaven is not seen elsewhere in the Bible, the Milanese church father Ambrose (d. 397 CE)[12] suggests, along with some biblical commentators,[13] that this is what Jn. 8:6–8 demonstrates. This is the story of Jesus saving an adulteress from the hands of those who intended to stone her when he started writing in the earth with his finger.[14]

After writing in the earth, Jesus asks those without sin to cast the first stone and then continues writing on the ground. John never elaborates on what Jesus wrote. However, John describes God and Christ as the fountain of life (e.g. Jn. 4:10, 4:14, 7:38). If the fountain of living waters is compared to those written in heaven described in Jeremiah, then it seems likely that John did not need to elaborate further on the textual context of what Jesus was writing in the earth, in line with Jeremiah; according to Paul Minear, Jesus is depicted as if writing the names of the sinners in the earth.[15] Ambrose proposes that what Jesus is writing in the Gospel of John is a reference to Jer. 22:29–30, where the earth is asked to write the names of those who are disowned.[16] Ambrose contrasts the names of sinners written on the ground and the names of the righteous written in heaven, citing Lk. 10:20.[17]

Some manuscripts of the Gospel of John suggest that Jesus was writing the sins of those present in the ground.[18] Biblical scholar George Aichele argues that one should not pursue what the Gospel of John denotes, due to its wide use of metaphors, and this is also the case in John 8.[19] Instead, he argues that one needs to pursue its connotation. While the canonicity of this passage and its possible insertion in the Gospel of John are brought into question by recent biblical scholars,[20] such a debate may not necessarily have played a role in the seventh century. What matters is not authorship but the possible motif that is being alluded to as part of the Near Eastern background, which the Qur'an might be using.

There is much debate amongst scholars on the intratextuality and intertextuality of what Jesus writes on the ground, according to the Gospel of John. Aichele, for example, argues that Jesus was writing the text of the Gospel of John itself.[21] With the lack of supportive evidence for such an allusion within the Gospel, I find it unconvincing, though I agree with Aichele that Jesus's writing in the Gospel of John might connote Jesus as the Word.

Early Church Fathers, such as Ambrose, Jerome (d. 420 CE), and Augustine have written about this episode in the Gospel of John.[22] Each speculates a different theory about what was written, and their traditions might have been passed down through Late Antiquity to the period when the Qur'an emerged. In these passages from the Gospel of John, the fountain of living water that leads to eternal life is understood to be with Christ, which can thrust from within the body of the believer. This can be compared with the following passage from Jeremiah:[23]

> for my people have committed two evils: they have forsaken me [ʿ*ozbû*], the fountain of living water [*mĕqôr mayim ḥayyîm*], and dug out cisterns for themselves, cracked cisterns that can hold no water.
>
> Jer. 2:13

The fountain of life is also seen in the following passage from the Psalms:

> 8They quench[24] [*yirwĕyun*] on the abundance of your house, and you give them drink [*tašqēm*] from the river [*naḥal*] of your delights. 9For with you is the fountain of life [*mĕqôr ḥayyîm*]; in your light we see light.
>
> Ps. 36:8–9

Additionally, Ps. 69:28 states 'Let them be blotted out of the book of the living; let them not be enrolled among the righteous.' The context of this passage appears to be eschatological, and accordingly, everlasting life is understood as those whose names are written in the book of the living.[25] Ps. 69:28 is the only passage that calls this book *sēper ḥayyîm* (book of the living), and thus, is a *hapax legomenon*.

Giving long life to someone is a topic arising elsewhere in Psalms: 'He asked you for life; you gave it to him—length of days forever and ever' (Ps. 21:4),[26] The following Ugaritic text may be a point of comparison:[27]

> And Virgin Anat replied: 'Ask for life, O hero Aqhat: ask for life [*ḥym*] and I shall give [it] you, immortality [*blmt*] and I shall bestow [it] on you: I shall make you number [your] years with Baal: With the son of El you shall number months, "Like Baal he shall live indeed! Alive, he shall be feasted, he shall be feasted and given to drink. The minstrel shall intone and sing concerning him."'
>
> 2 Aqhat 6:26–32[28]

Ugaritic texts may serve as a possible background to the Book of Isaiah,[29] which describes one of the few instances of the resurrection of the dead in the Hebrew Bible:

> Your dead [*mētêkā*] shall live, my corpse[30] [*nĕbēlātî*] shall rise. O dwellers in the dust, awake and sing for joy! For your dew is a radiant dew, and the earth will give birth to the dead[31] [*rĕpā'îm*].
>
> Isa. 26:19

When this passage of Isaiah is contrasted with verse 14, which shows how other ruling lords besides God are dead and not alive – they are *rĕpā'îm* (dead souls?) that will not arise – one might think that Isa. 26:19 is metaphorical: *your* dead will live, but *their* dead will not.[32] However, it has been proposed that the use of *nĕbēlātî* (my corpse) might suggest a physical resurrection.[33] A problem exists with the use of *nĕbēlātî* in the Masoretic text that scholars continue to debate.[34] The passage seems to use both the plural and singular terms, variously in the first, second, and third person:[35] 'Your [*pl.*] dead shall live; my corpse [*s.*] they [*pl.*] shall rise.' Faced with this obscure grammar,[36] Philip Schmitz suggests that *nĕbēlātî* is not using the first-person pronominal suffix but is a gentilic suffix (a demonym), as found in *'admônî* (red) in Gen. 25:25. He translates the passage as 'Your dead shall live. [As] a corpse they shall rise. Awake and shout for joy, you who dwell in the dust.'[37] The root *n-b-l* has various meanings, including a corpse or a lifeless idol (e.g. Jer. 16:18).[38] The image of a lifeless idol mirrors some of the interpretations of Qur᾿an 16:21, by now familiar.

The last statement in Isa. 26:19 depicts dew that waters the dust of the earth giving birth to the dead. This depiction may be compared with Gen. 2:5–6:[39]

> [5]when no plant of the field was yet in the earth and no herb of the field had yet sprung up for the LORD God had not caused it to rain upon the earth, and there was no one to till the ground; [6]but a stream would rise from the earth, and water the whole face of the ground.
>
> Gen. 2:5–6

In their commentary on this passage in *Genesis Rabbah*, some rabbis interpret that rain is as important as (if not even more important than) resurrection,[40] which is in keeping with the Eighteen Benedictions' connection of the prayer for rain with the resurrection of the dead.

In comparison, Ezekiel gives a detailed depiction of the resurrection of the dead in the valley of dead bones, although the text interprets it as a metaphor for the revival of the nation.[41]

> [1]The hand of the LORD came upon me, and he brought me out by the spirit of the LORD and set me down in the middle of a valley; it was full of bones. [2]He led me all around them; there were very many lying in the valley, and they were very dry. [3]He said to me, 'Mortal, can these bones live?' I answered, 'O Lord GOD, you know.' [4]Then he said to me, 'Prophesy to these bones, and say to them: O dry bones, hear the word of the LORD. [5]Thus says the Lord GOD to these bones: I will cause breath [spirit / *rûaḥ*] to enter you, and you shall live. [6]I will lay sinews on you, and will cause flesh to come upon you, and cover you with skin, and put breath [spirit / *rûaḥ*] in you, and you shall live; and you shall know that I am the LORD.' [7]So I prophesied as I had been commanded; and as I prophesied, suddenly there was a noise, a rattling, and the bones came together, bone to its bone. [8]I looked, and there were sinews on them, and flesh had come upon them, and skin had covered them; but there was no breath [spirit / *rûaḥ*] in them. [9]Then he said to me, 'Prophesy to the breath [spirit / *rûaḥ*], prophesy, mortal, and say to the breath [spirit / *rûaḥ*]: Thus says the Lord GOD: Come from the four winds, O breath [spirit / *rûaḥ*], and breathe upon these slain, that they may live.' [10]I prophesied as he commanded me, and the breath [spirit / *rûaḥ*] came into them, and they lived, and stood on their feet, a vast multitude. [11]Then he said to me, 'Mortal, these bones are the whole house of Israel. They say, 'Our bones are dried up, and our hope is lost; we are cut off completely.' [12]Therefore prophesy, and say to them, Thus says the Lord GOD: I am going to open your graves, and bring you up from your graves, O my people; and I will bring you back to the land of Israel. [13]And you shall know that I am the LORD, when I open your graves, and bring you up from your graves, O my people. [14]I will put my spirit [breath / *rûḥi*] within you, and you shall live, and I will place you on your own soil; then you shall know that I, the LORD, have spoken and will act,' says the LORD.
>
> Ezek. 37:1–14

Ezekiel's depiction parallels Gen. 2:7 on the creation of man through the breath of life.[42] Since a consensus does not appear to have always existed on the doctrine of the resurrection of the dead among early Jewish communities,[43] a literal interpretation of these passages in Ezekiel exists only in the Jewish communities that accept this doctrine.[44] The Talmud depicts an array of rabbinic interpretations of this passage, some of which considered this a parable, while others understood it literally.[45] When in Ezekiel's vision he is asked whether these bones can live, he gives an agnostic response. One may extrapolate two points from this: (1) the doctrine of resurrection may not have been universally espoused by the community during the authorship of Ezekiel, or (2) even if the doctrine did exist, Ezekiel is being respectful in his response to God. If the former were the case, it would mean that even Ezekiel, as a prophet, did not hold the issue of resurrection as a creed. At the very least, he or the author of Ezekiel may not have understood the doctrine of resurrection as dry bones coming back to life in the vivid way described in this vision. There is not much evidence of an eschatological interpretation of this passage in pre-Christian Jewish literature.[46] The medieval Jewish commentator Rashi (d. 1105 CE) did consider Ezekiel's passages to be mostly metaphorical, except for the opening of the graves in Ezek. 37:12, which he considered a reference to the resurrection.[47]

Matthew 27:51–53 suggests that tombs were opened and that many bodies of saints who had died were raised after Jesus's body gave up the spirit. It has been suggested that such a depiction in Matthew might have taken Ezekiel's description as its basis.[48] However, whether Matthew considered this a literal historical account, a preface to a future eschatology, or a depiction of people who were spiritually dead ('asleep') becoming alive is a point for a different discussion.[49] Early church fathers did find the doctrine of the final resurrection present in these passages from Ezekiel,[50] although they might have been aware of the various Jewish views on these passages, ranging from metaphor to literal. Elaborating on the significant parallelism between the prophetic text of Ezekiel 37 and the later Epistle to the Ephesians,[51] Robert Suh has said that Eph. 2:1–10 give the message of spiritual death as a separation from God.[52] Yet both Ezek. 37:1–10 and Eph. 2:1–10 portray new creation from death to life.[53] Accordingly, the author of Ephesians 2 appears to understand Ezekiel 37 in its context not as a physical resurrection but the return of the House of Israel from exile.[54] This point is very important, as it will be seen in Chapters 6 and 7 that the Qur'an also uses motifs of resurrection as an allusion to the return from exile. Furthermore, the earliest evidence does not suggest that Ezekiel 37 was understood as stating the doctrine of resurrection.

Some scholars have argued that another allusion to Isa. 26:19 appears in Dan. 12:2,[55] which gives a representation of resurrection:

> [1]'At that time Michael, the great prince, the protector of your people, shall arise. There shall be a time of anguish, such as has never occurred since nations first came into existence. But at that time your people shall be delivered, everyone who is found written in the book [*kātûb ba-sēper*]. [2]Many of those who sleep in

> the dust of the earth shall awake, some to everlasting life [*le-ḥayyê ʿôlām*], and some to shame [*la-ḥărāpôt*] and everlasting contempt [*le-dirʾôn ʿôlām*].'
>
> Dan. 12:1–2

If Dan. 12:2 is alluding to Isa. 26:19, it would be similar to Ezekiel 37, in which resurrection is a metaphor for the restoration of the nation of Israel.[56] Dan. 12:2 appears not only to possibly allude to Isaiah but also to refer to the book of the living, those who are written to enjoy everlasting life.[57] Given Isaiah 24–27, Bernhard Duhm states that it would be easy to misconceive that the same author could have also authored the Book of Daniel – the affinities and allusions common to the texts are considerable.[58]

The Qurʾan also appears to allude to the book of the living. Although it refers several times to a book of deeds (e.g. Qurʾan 17:71, 69:19, 69:25, 84:7, 84:10), it seems at least in one instance to indicate the book written in the depth of the earth and the book in heaven and constructs it as part of an allusion to the resurrection of the dead:

> [4]Do they not think that they will be resurrected [5]unto a tremendous day – [6]a day when humankind shall stand before the Lord of the worlds? [7]Nay! Truly the book of the profligate [*al-fujjār*] is in Sijjīn. [8]And what will explain you of Sijjīn? [9]A book inscribed. [10]Woe that Day to the deniers, [11]who deny the Day of Judgment, [12]which none deny except every sinful transgressor. [13]When Our signs are recited unto him, he says, 'Fables of those of old!' [14]Nay! But that which they used to earn has covered their hearts with rust. [15]Nay! Surely on that Day they will be veiled from their Lord. [16]Then they will burn in Hellfire. [17]Then it is said unto them, 'This is that which you used to deny.' [18]Nay, truly the book of the pious is in ʿIlliyyīn.[59] [19]And what will apprise you of ʿIlliyyūn? [20]A book inscribed, [21]witnessed by those brought nigh [*al-muqarrabūn*]. [22]Truly the pious shall be in bliss, [23]upon couches, gazing. [24]You do recognize in their faces the splendour of bliss. [25]They are given to drink of pure wine sealed, [26]whose seal is musk – so for that let the strivers strive – [*fal-yatanāfas al-mutanāfisūn*] [27]and whose mixture is of Tasnīm, [28]a spring whence drink those brought nigh [*al-muqarrabūn*].
>
> Qurʾan 83:4–28

Qurʾan 83:7 says the book of the *fujjār* is in *sijjīn*. There is a debate on the root of the term *sijjīn*, which appears to be *s-j-n*, the same as 'prison' (*sijn*).[60] The term *sijn* (prison) is used only in Qurʾan 12 in the story of Joseph (e.g. Qurʾan 12:25), but the root *s-j-n* is also found in Aramaic and possibly Akkadian,[61] meaning chief or official.[62] In Ethiopic, *sagannat* holds the meaning of a watchtower.[63] There is also the possibility that the root of this term is the biconsonantal *s-j* or *s-j-j* with the suffix *-īn* being for the plural. If that is the case, its meanings would include being smeared in mud,[64] which is a definition also attested in Syriac,[65] or could also hold the meaning of inscriptions.[66] Devin Stewart dismisses this because it occurs in this form in both the genitive and nominative cases.[67] That is, it does not appear as *sijjūn*, which should be the case if it were plural. Although *sijjīn* in this Qur'anic verse is usually understood as a description of hell as an eternal 'imprisonment' from the meaning of *s-j-n*, O'Shaughnessy argues that the passages that immediately follow (i.e. Qur'an 83:8–9) suggest that the intention is that it is an inscribed register (i.e. a record) and therefore is related to the root *s-j-l*.[68] Accordingly, he suggests that *sijjīn* is not a description of hell[69] but simply a description of a book of register, where the deeds of the wicked are written,[70] a conclusion Devin Stewart also makes.[71]

Nonetheless, those conclusions are not only from modern scholars. Makkī b. Abī Ṭālib (d. 437/1045) also suggested that *sijjīn* is *sijjīl* with the /l/ converted to /n/.[72] Al-Qurṭubī (d. 671/1273) also considers *sijjīn* to derive from *s-j-l*, as a register of deeds,[73] an assumption made by al-Suyūṭī (d. 911/1505) as well. According to al-Suyūṭī, it is called *sijjīn* because it causes the person to be imprisoned in hell.[74] Thus, those various scholarly debates have already existed and been hypothesized by earlier Muslim scholars.

Regardless of their etymologies, *sijjīn* and *sijjīl* may inscribe a royal edict.[75] Daniel Beck suggests the possibility that both *sijjīn* and *sijjīl* are derived from the Greek *sigillon*,[76] from *sigillio* and corresponding to the Latin *sigillum*, meaning seal.[77] Therefore, he particularly emphasizes it as an authoritative seal.[78] The English 'sign' is derived from the Latin *signum*, in which *sigillum* is a possible derivative.[79] The PIE root is *sek-*, 'to cut', and shares the same meaning of the Afroasiatic root *ṣ-k*.[80] The Arabic *ṣakk*, means to press hard on something and, consequently, also means seal or inscription.[81]

Traditional Muslim commentators like al-Ṭabarī, interpret *sijjīn* as the depth of the earth, or the deepest (seventh) level of the earth.[82] Ibn ʿArabī associates *sijjīn* with *sijn* (prison), describing the imprisonment of those who are egotistical, which is what he interprets as the *muṭaffifīn* in Qur'an 83:1.[83] The depiction of the souls of the unrighteous to be in some sort of prison is found in 1 Enoch 69:28, 2 Bar. 56:13, and the First Epistle of Peter:

> [18]For Christ also suffered for sins once for all, the righteous for the unrighteous, in order to bring you to God. He was put to death in the flesh, but made alive in the spirit, [19]in which also he went and made a proclamation to the spirits in prison [*phylakē*].
>
> 1 Pet. 3:18–19

The Greek term used for prison in this passage is *phylakē*, while the Aramaic Peshitta translates it as *sheol*, which is a term used by the Hebrew Bible for the realm of the dead. The understanding of this passage to refer to the realm of the dead was shared by various church traditions, including the Alexandrian and Greek traditions, and not only the Syriac tradition.[84]

The New Testament also portrays sinning angels bound in chains (e.g. 2 Pet. 2:4, Jude 6, Rev. 20:1–4).[85] The depiction of people in hell bound in chains, as in a prison, is a recurring theme in the Qur'an (e.g. Qur'an 14:49,[86] 40:71, 76:4).[87] The Qur'an also shows that those who are bound are not always to be understood as physically in hell. Nonbelievers who are currently physically alive are also depicted bound in chains:

> [6]that you may warn a people whose fathers were not warned; so they were heedless. [7]The Word has indeed come due for most of them, for they do not believe. [8]Truly We have put shackles upon their necks, and they are up to their chins, so that they are forced up. [9]And We placed a barrier before them and a barrier behind them and veiled them; so they see not. [10]It is the same for them whether you warn them or warn them not; they do not believe. [11]You only warn whosoever follows the Reminder and fears the Compassionate unseen. So give such a one glad tidings of forgiveness and a generous reward. [12]Truly We give life to the dead and record that which they have sent forth and that which they have left behind. And We have counted all things in a clear registry [*imām*].
>
> Qurʾan 36:6–12

These passages describe nonbelievers as bound[88] and give the consolation that you (the assumed the recipient of the message) are only a warner. This sort of consolation is also found in Qurʾan 35:22–24, after describing nonbelievers to be dead in graves. Qurʾan 36:12 also states that God gives life to the dead and that it is all recorded in a clear *imām*.[89] Nonetheless, these passages also seem to be alluding to some sort of book of deeds,[90] perhaps the book of the living, according to its context and intertextuality. The term *imām* as some sort of book can also be perceived in Qurʾan 17:71–72. Additionally, as Qurʾan 35:19 differentiates between the blind and the seeing (spiritually speaking) in the context of the nonbelievers as dead (i.e. Qurʾan 35:19–24), so does Qurʾan 17:72.

If O'Shaughnessy is correct that the Qurʾan explicitly defines *sijjīn* as a book of register and not a description of hell,[91] then it appears that the Qurʾan means something *written* in the depths of the earth, which may or may not be a metaphor for hell. This is especially true when compared to the other book of register, *ʿilliyyūn*, which is written in a high place that the Qurʾan mentions later within the same context. Based on the web of intertextualities between these passages, one can deduce a likelihood that the Qurʾan does allude to the books of the dead, which are written in the earth (*sijjīn*) (e.g. Qurʾan 83:7–9), and of the living, which are written up high in heaven (*ʿilliyyīn*) (e.g. Qurʾan 83:18–20). The description's similarities to those found in the Hebrew Bible contextualizes it within Near Eastern traditions, especially in light of the morphological form of the contrasting term *ʿilliyyūn*, which appears to be most likely a loanword.

Qurʾan 83:18–20 appears to call the book of the living *ʿilliyyīn* or *ʿilliyyūn* – a term rooted in *ʿ-l-y*, which means most high. Although the form *ʿilliyyūn* appears peculiar in Arabic, it is a very common term in Hebrew for the Most High (God), as used by the Hebrew Bible (i.e. *ʿelyôn*). The term is a conjunction between *ʿāl* (*ʿ-l-h* or *ʿ-l-y*) and the afformative *-ôn*.[92] Otherwise, the Qurʾan typically calls God the Most High, using the term *al-ʿalyy* in conjunction with *al-ʿaẓīm* or *al-kabīr* (the Great) (e.g. Qurʾan 2:255, 22:62, 31:30, 34:23, 40:12, 42:4). It is noteworthy that in the Hebrew Bible the term *ʿelyôn* occurs only in poetry or blessings and praise that can also be categorized as a form of poetry.[93] The contrast between *ʿelyôn* and death (*mōth*) is found in proto-Hebrew/Phoenician myth that narrates a battle between two rival gods and the death and resurrection of the saving-god.[94]

The descriptions in the Qur'an of those who are in *ʿilliyyūn* being witnessed by those brought near (*al-muqarrabūn*) drinking from a spring may be compared with the following passage:

> [4]There is a river whose streams make glad the city of God, the holy habitation of the Most High [*ʿelyôn*]. [5]God is in the midst of it [*qirbā*]; it shall not be moved; God will help it when the morning dawns.
>
> Ps. 46:4–5

Drinking from a river as the fountain of life (*mĕqōr ḥayyîm*) specifically is also seen in Ps. 36:8–9, discussed earlier, and the broader depiction of the book of the living or the book written in heaven (*ʿilliyyīn*) and the book written in the depth of the earth (*sijjīn*) found in the Qur'an can be compared with that of the Bible and the general motif existing in the Near East.

Worldly life

The term *dunyā* in the Qur'an is used to refer to the current world, and the term *ākhirah* is used to mean the later world (e.g. Qur'an 2:86). Its root, *d-n-y*, means to befall or to be near,[95] meanings which occur in the Qur'an (e.g. Qur'an 53:8, 69:23, 76:14). Among the other Semitic languages, this term is attested in Syriac and Ethiopic.[96] The root *d-n-y* or *d-n-h* is also used as a demonstrative pronoun in Aramaic meaning 'this',[97] from the meaning of near/occurring. Sabean also uses *dhan* as the demonstrative pronoun meaning 'this', while Ethiopic uses *zentu*.[98] Accordingly, *al-ḥayāt al-dunyā* can mean the occurring life, the near life, or simply 'this life'. This definition contrasts perfectly with *al-ākhirah* ('the other', not 'this').

Frequently, the Qur'an refers to this life as *al-ḥayāt al-dunyā* (this/nearer life) (e.g. Qur'an 2:86). The term *ḥayāh* appears sixty-eight times, sixty-four of them using a definite article, and sixty-one of them in reference to *al-ḥayāt al-dunyā*. The Qur'an only uses the term *al-ḥayāh* without associating it with *al-dunyā* in Qur'an 17:75, 20:97, and 67:2; and the only times it is used without a definite article are in Qur'an 2:96, 2:179, 16:97, and 25:3. Overall, the Qur'an therefore mostly refers to this/nearer life (*al-ḥayāt al-dunyā*), and it usually refers to it negatively and criticizes those who seek it. In contrast, the Qur'an asks its audience to strive for a different kind of world, which it sometimes refers to as 'the later' or 'the other' (*al-ākhirah*).

On these terms for nearer and later lives, Toshihiko Izutsu writes:

> From an entirely different point of view, this world as man actually experiences it and lives in it is, as a whole, called *al-dunyā*, lit. 'the Lower' or 'the Nearer' world.

> The Qur᾽an mostly uses the phrase *al-ḥayāt al-dunyā* ('the lower life') in place of the simple word *al-dunyā* . . . the word *al-dunyā* belongs to a particular category of words, which we might call 'correlation' words, that is, those words that stand for correlated concepts, like 'husband' and 'wife', 'brother' and 'sister', etc. : each member of the pair presupposes the other semantically and stands on the very basis of this correlation. A man can be a 'husband' only in reference to 'wife'. The concept of 'husband', in other words, implicitly contains that of 'wife', and vice versa. In just the same way, the concept of *al-dunyā* presupposes the concept of the 'world to come', *f.e.*, the 'Hereafter' (*al-ākhirah*), and stands in contrast to it.[99]

Izutsu suggests that in pre-Islamic literature, the term *al-dunyā* (this/nearer life) occurs frequently, which implies that the concept of *al-ākhirah* (the later or after) is well known and that Umayya b. Abī-l-Ṣalt (d. 626) emphasized it.[100] He proposes that pre-Islamic Arabia had known about such concepts from Jews and Christians. While this might be a possibility, the authenticity of pre-Islamic Arab literature has been disputed by scholars who consider much of it to have been either edited or created by later Muslims.[101]

The root *᾽-kh-r* is attested in Akkadian to mean 'the far end', 'a later time',[102] 'other',[103] or 'the remainder'.[104] Thus, it has also taken the meaning of 'the future' or 'progeny'.[105] The root *᾽-kh-r* also means the one absent or far away.[106] In the Qur᾽an, the term can be understood to indicate the later or future time as well as the other world. Unlike the negative outlook and the critique of this/nearer life (*al-ḥayāt al-dunyā*), the later or other (*al-ākhirah*) is depicted positively as something to which one aspires.[107] This sense is not unique to the Qur᾽an. The Hebrew Bible uses *᾽aḥărît ha-yāmîm* to refer to the latter days (e.g. Gen. 49:1; Num. 24:14; Deut. 4:30, 31:29; Jer. 23:20, 49:39; Ezek. 38:8)[108]. However, it does not necessarily connote a world other than this one, but rather conjures a limited future time in this world, perhaps without an eschatological aspect, although that does occur in some of the later books of the Hebrew Bible.[109]

The Qur᾽an describes this/nearer life as a pathetic game, in which people strive for something that is wasted (e.g. Qur᾽an 3:14, 47:36, 57:20). The recurring message of the Qur᾽an urges individuals to trade the worldly life that expires for the other life.[110] When speaking of this worldly life, the Qur᾽an frequently refers to life in conjunction with its adjective (*al-dunyā*) denoting 'this life' (*al-ḥayāt al-dunyā*). Life (*ḥayāh*) need not mean life in this world; otherwise, if *al-ḥayāh* alone would have meant this/nearer life, the Qur᾽an would not be compelled to specify *al-ḥayāt al-dunyā*. *Ḥayāh* (life) must have multiple aspects and not always denote this/nearer life. This understanding is widespread. It is typically agreed, as Muhammad Abdel Haleem states, that the Qur᾽an speaks of a life-death-life continuum.[111] In Abdel Haleem's view there are two kinds of life in the Qur᾽an, this/nearer life (*al-ḥayāt al-dunyā*) and the later, last, or other (*al-ākhirah*). However, the Qur᾽an also understands death and life in a spiritual or figurative sense, as in the following:

> Is he who was dead, and to whom We give life, making for him a light by which to walk among humankind, like unto one who is in darkness [*al-ẓulumāt*] from

> which he does not emerge? Thus for the disbelievers, what they used to do was made to seem fair unto them.
>
> Qur'an 6:122

This passage, also discussed earlier, clearly uses a spiritual or figurative sense of death and life,[112] about which both traditional Muslim commentators, such as al-Ṭabarī,[113] and Sufi commentators, such as Ibn ʿArabī, agree.[114] It depicts a person who was dead and was given life and walked among humankind, in contrast to those in *ẓulumāt* (darkness). This means that the Qur'an considers those in *ẓulumāt* to be dead and holds that God can bring them out of this darkness and into life and light among people. The depiction is not of two different physical worlds but a single one, where some people are dead (zombies) and, yet others are alive.

Therefore, the Qur'an gives various valences for life as *ḥayāh*. The question to consider is whether the other, *al-ākhirah*, is a physically different life and in a different world, or whether the 'other life' is simply the spiritual life to which the Qur'an sometimes alludes. In other words, is it possible that when the Qur'an is condemning this/nearer life (*al-ḥayāt al-dunyā*) and revelling in the other/later (*al-ākhirah*) life, it is actually condemning the life of one who is spiritually dead and revelling in one who is spiritually alive? This is a difficult question to answer, partly because, though the other/later (*al-ākhirah*) is sometimes contrasted with this/nearer life (*al-ḥayāt al-dunyā*), the Qur'an does not associate the other/later (*al-ākhirah*) with the attribute of 'life'. The formulation *al-ḥayāt al-ākhirah* never appears, although *dunyā* and *ākhirah* seem to be in perfect contrast with one another in the Qur'an.[115] When the Qur'an associates life (*ḥayāh*) with the *ākhirah*, it takes the atypical form (*al-ḥayawān*):

> The life of this world [*al-ḥayāt al-dunyā*] is nothing but diversion and play. And surely the Abode of the Hereafter [*al-dār al-ākhirah*] is the lively [one] [*al-ḥayawān*],[116] if they but knew.
>
> Qur'an 29:64

Notably, this passage is not contrasting this life (*al-ḥayāt al-dunyā*) with the other life (*al-ḥayāt al-ākhirah*). The 'other' that the Qur'an considers is not another life, but another abode (*dār*). It is the 'other abode' (*al-dār al-ākhirah*) that is *al-ḥayawān* (life?). The grammatical form *ḥayawān* is atypical and a *hapax legomenon* in this form in the Qur'an. Various early Arabic grammarians consider this a peculiar form and interpret it as everlasting life; Sībawayh (d. 180/796),[117] for one, suggests that it is in intensive (*mubālaghah*) form.[118] The form ending with *-ān* may be also considered a plural form (*fiʿlān*), as the Qur'anic term *wildān* (e.g. Qur'an 56:17), but the majority of grammarians do not concede such a hypothesis and instead compare it with *raḥmān*. For such a form to be understood as intensive (*mubālaghah*) is itself unusual. The term *raḥmān* is a rabbinic usage for one of God's names in Aramaic – even in Arabic, it is exclusively used for God[119] – so interpreting it as an intensive (*mubālaghah*) form does not seem self-evident.

There are two possible explanations of this feature: proper name and adjective. The proper name would be similar to *ʿAdnān* or *Qaḥṭān*.[120] It is unlikely to be a proper name, since it uses a definite article. The other, more likely situation is that it is an adjective in the form of *faʿlān*,[121] similar to *marḍān* (one who is sick). In this sense, *al-ḥayawān* could be the adjective of the 'other abode' (*al-dār al-ākhirah*), making it the 'lively place' (*dār al-ḥayawān*). The adjective is usually used for a person, so if *al-ḥayawān* is an adjective perhaps it is not for the 'other abode' but the adjective of the *person* in the 'other abode'. The person in the other abode (*al-dār al-ākhirah*) is the lively one (*ḥayawān*). In this case, *al-ḥayawān* would not refer to the place unless one assumes that *al-dār al-ākhirah* is being described as a person and not a place. If that were the case, then *al-dār al-ākhirah la-hiya al-ḥayawān* might mean that the *person* in the 'other abode' is the one who is alive or the 'other abode' itself is alive. The latter might be unusual, but so is the form used to describe it.

Hence, *al-ḥayāt al-dunyā* means 'this/nearer life', and *al-dār al-ākhirah la-hiya al-ḥayawān* means the 'other abode' is the alive one. The Qurʾanic passage could be stating that this life is not even life; it is the other abode that is truly alive. This reading would appear more natural than assuming the passage is using an unusual intensive (*mubālaghah*) form. Interestingly, in this passage, *dunyā* is called *lahuw* (a descriptive name meaning a diversion, but looks like the masculine singular third-person pronoun, *la-huwa*) and *ākhirah* is referred to *la-hiya* (an actual feminine singular third-person pronoun), which could be part of the poetic style of the Qurʾan.

The peculiarity of *ḥayawān* is difficult to interpret, but it does support the hypothesis that the term *ḥayāh* in the Qurʾan encompasses various meanings and that the term connotes not only a physical but also a spiritual or metaphorical sense of life; after all, a lively abode is considered figurative.

Resurrection as re-creation

The Qurʾanic argument for what Patricia Crone assumes is bodily resurrection is partly determined by its discourse with nonbelievers, who do not appear to believe in bodily resurrection because the body decomposes or get cut into pieces (e.g. Qurʾan 34:7).[122] Crone suggests that such an argument resembles those that Greek and Roman pagans lodged against Christians, or even arguments against a Zoroastrian resurrection, and that it appears to have also been used by Christians who argued in favour of resurrection in a spiritual body, instead of the original flesh. In answer to those who argue against a decomposed body coming back to life, the Qurʾan offers God's ability to re-create. However, does this require that the Qurʾan is arguing in favour of physical resurrection, in the sense that a decomposed body would be revived and brought back to life?

According to the Gospel of John, when Jesus speaks of a person needing to be born anew or from above, Nicodemus asks how can a person enter back into his mother's womb and be born again (i.e. Jn. 3:1–15). Nicodemus appears to have interpreted Jesus's words literally, when Jesus appears to have meant it spiritually.

Similarly, if the Qur'an appears to show that the nonbelievers argued against a decomposed body reviving again, that does not prove the Qur'an is necessarily arguing for physical resurrection in a literal sense; it might suggest that the nonbelievers thought that the Qur'an speaks of physical resurrection literally, when perhaps the Qur'an means it spiritually.

According to O'Shaughnessy and Crone, the analogy of physical resurrection as a form of re-creation was common among Christians and others in the Near East.[123] For example, Isa. 26:19 offers birth imagery for resurrection. The author of 4 Ezra appears to use similar imagery, saying those who dwell in the dust of the earth shall arise (7:32). Further, 4 Ezra 4:40–42 describes Sheol (the abode of the dead) in birth pains, where souls are likened to be in a womb,[124] making it more likely that the author is keeping Isa. 26:19 as the subtext of such an image.[125]

Similarly, 2 Macc. 7:22–29 images resurrection as a second creation and likens it to the first birth.[126] Ezekiel 37, discussed earlier for the metaphor of the rebuilding of a nation and not a literal resurrection, also uses the imagery of re-creation.[127] *Pseudo-Ezekiel*[128] also uses Ezekiel 37 as its subtext and further elaborates on resurrection using imagery of re-creation with phrases that allude to Genesis 1.[129] Johannes Tromp argues that *Pseudo-Ezekiel* should not be interpreted in any way that differs from Ezekiel 37 in its reference to the rise of the Israelite nation instead of physical resurrection.[130]

Contextualizing some of the Qur'anic passages pertaining to resurrection with some Syriac arguments against the denial of bodily resurrection,[131] David Bertaina argues that the Qur'an echoes Syriac Christian Miaphysite debates against Tritheism, a theological movement that emerged during the time, on the issue of resurrection. There were, indeed, many different understandings of resurrection, including some form of re-creation with a new spiritual body circulating in the Near East during Late Antiquity, as Bertaina demonstrates. However, he assumes that the Qur'an is specifically advocating the resurrection of the original body, which may not necessarily be the case. While the Qur'an advocates for resurrection, it is difficult to understand what kind of resurrection – spiritual or bodily. And even if it means bodily, is it the original body or a new one? There does exist some tension in defining the exact meaning(s) of resurrection in the Qur'an.

A close examination of some of the passages that discuss resurrection, such as Qur'an 36:70, suggests that the Qur'an is given to those who are spiritually alive, implying that those who are spiritually dead would not understand the message it contains, as is suggested elsewhere in the text as well. To put Qur'an 36:70 in its context of spiritual life, we find a few verses later the following statements about resurrection:

> [77]Has the human[132] not seen that We created him from a drop, and behold, he is a manifest adversary? [78]And he has set forth for Us a parable and forgotten his own creation, saying, 'Who revives these bones, decayed as they are?' [79]Say, 'He will revive them Who brought them forth the first time, and He knows every creation.'
>
> Qur'an 36:77–79

This passage poses the question of who would bring dead bones back to life. The answer given is whoever created them the first time through the process of birth. Hence, resurrection would echo birth. This concept of re-creation can also be inferred from the following passages:

> Unto Him is your return all together; God's Promise is true. Verily He originates creation, then He brings it back, that He may recompense with justice those who believe and perform righteous deeds. As for the disbelievers, theirs shall be a drink of boiling liquid and a painful punishment for having disbelieved.
>
> Qur'an 10:4

> Say, 'Is there, among your partners, one who originates creation and then brings it back?' Say, 'God originates creation, then brings it back. How, then, are you perverted?'
>
> Qur'an 10:34

> That Day We shall roll up the sky like the rolling of scrolls for writings. As We began the first creation, so shall We bring it back – a promise binding upon Us. Surely We shall do it.
>
> Qur'an 21:104

> He, Who brings creation into being, then brings it back, and Who provides for you from Heaven and the earth? Is there a god alongside God? Say, 'Bring your proof, if you are truthful.'
>
> Qur'an 27:64

> 19Have they not considered how God originates creation, then brings it back? Truly that is easy for God. 20Say, 'Journey upon the earth and observe how He originated creation. Then God shall bring the next genesis into being. Truly God is Powerful over all things.'
>
> Qur'an 29:19–20

> God originates creation, then brings it back; then unto Him shall you be returned.
>
> Qur'an 30:11

> He it is Who originates creation, then brings it back, and that is most easy for Him. Unto Him belongs the loftiest description in the heavens and on the earth, and He is the Mighty, the Wise.
>
> Qur'an 30:27

Furthermore, the following passage also discusses the creation of humans discussing their process of birth, death, and resurrection.

> 12And indeed We created the human[133] from a draught of clay. 13Then We made him a drop in a secure dwelling place. 14Then of the drop We created a blood clot,

> then of the blood clot We created a lump of flesh, then of the lump of flesh We created bones and We clothed the bones with flesh; then We brought him into being as another creation. Blessed is God, the best of creators! 15 Then indeed you shall die thereafter. 16 Then surely you shall be raised up on the Day of Resurrection.
>
> Qur'an 23:12–16

If the Qur'an suggests that God can repeat creation as done the first time, then the resurrection in Qur'an 23:16 may also be a repeat process defined in Qur'an 23:12–14. Similarly, Qur'an 22:5–7 states that people should not be in doubt about resurrection when God created them through foetal evolution to birth and kept some alive into old age. Relating resurrection to how the human was initially created might suggest that any physical resurrection may also occur through rebirth. Some traditional Muslim thought does hold a concept of resurrection as a second birth[134] – one might look to al-Rāghib al-Iṣfahānī[135] and al-Ghazālī.[136] Additionally, rebirth or re-creation in the Qur'an has been understood by traditional Muslims as a metaphor of God's power to revive the dead.[137] If the Qur'an's portrayal of resurrection as rebirth or re-creation is understood metaphorically,[138] then is its description of resurrection also metaphorical in general? The possibility is there.

While the Qur'an suggests that human bones and dust will revive, it does not establish explicitly how human resurrection will occur.[139] For that reason, medieval Muslim philosophers put forward many visions of Qur'anic resurrection. Al-Ghazālī, in *Tahāfut al-falāsifah*, argued fervently against philosophers who dismissed resurrection as spiritual instead of physical,[140] especially bearing Ibn Sīnā in mind,[141] who rejected the concept of physical resurrection. Ibn Rushd's (d. 595/1198) response to al-Ghazālī's arguments, in *Tahāfut al-tahāfut*, was that philosophers, including himself, agreed on physical resurrection necessarily, but disagreed on its nature.[142] If the body were reborn somehow, then the new body would not necessarily be identical to the present body.[143] Accordingly, Ibn Rushd also disagrees with Ibn Sīnā's allegorization of the resurrection.

When portraying the revival of bones, the Qur'an depicts some sort of re-creation, and therefore in the human sense, a form of rebirth as initially conceived, which may be inferred from Qur'an 36:77–81. Needless to say, bones emerging from graves is not analogous to the birth of the human being. Additionally, if the analogy is meant to portray the power of God, the natural power of human birth is also not analogous to the supernatural power needed for bones to leave their graves. Similarly, when the Qur'an also uses the analogy of a dead earth being revived with plants, it does not suggest any supernatural power. In fact, all the analogies used by the Qur'an for resurrection, whether vegetation or birth, are all natural phenomena.

The following Qur'anic passages appear to discuss two kinds of death and two kinds of life:

> How can you disbelieve in God, seeing that you were dead and He gave you life; then He causes you to die; then He gives you life; then unto Him shall you be returned?
>
> Qur'an 2:28

> They will say, 'Our Lord, You have caused us to die twice over, and given us life twice over; so we admit our sins. Is there any way out?'
>
> Qur'an 40:11

Traditional commentators like al-Ṭabarī state that the *first death* is nonexistence before creation, the first life is the existence from birth, the *second death* is the physical death, and the second life is resurrection.[144] To analyse this interpretation carefully, it is necessary to understand each phase. The first phase is nonexistence. It is not a dead physical body because the body does not yet exist. If the *first death* is not physical, then is it necessary to interpret the second life as physical?

If the *first death* is not a bodily death and is not interpreted accordingly, there is no reason to interpret the *second life* as bodily death. Even if we are to agree to the first life is physical and, therefore, the *second death* is physical, but since the *first death* was not physical, then there is no reason to understand the final life as physical either.

The Druze actually use Qur'an 2:28 and the following passage as evidence of reincarnation: 'From it We created you, and unto it We shall bring you back, and from it We shall bring you forth another time' (Qur'an 20:55).[145] Qur'an 2:28 is open to interpretation, and further analysis is necessary before one can conclude this issue. If the passage is a kind of ring structure, then the first and last are of the same spiritual nature, while the inner part is physical. This would translate to the *first death* being that of the soul (*nafs*). The first life is bodily life. The *second death* is physical. Finally, the second life is a soul-life. In other words, the dead soul enters a living body, then the body dies, and thereafter the soul lives. Alternatively, it could be speaking of two truly different kinds of death and life, both spiritual and physical.

As discussed, O'Shaughnessy interprets the *second death* as punishment in hell, which he derives from Judaeo-Christian literature.[146] The notion of a living death in hell already exists in the Qur'an.[147] Independently, Crone concurs with this analysis, finding that in Jewish, Christian,[148] Mandaean and Manichaean literature,[149] the *second death* is understood as ultimate damnation, as in Rev. 2:11.[150] The concept of a *second death* is also in a number of the *targumim* (e.g. Targum Neofiti, Targum Isaiah).[151] The Book of Revelation uses *second death* to symbolize hell, and some scholars have argued that the *second death* is used to contrast it with the Hebrew Bible's concept of the *book of life*.[152]

> [12]And I saw the dead, great and small, standing before the throne, and books were opened. Also another book was opened, the book of life. And the dead were judged according to their works, as recorded in the books. [13]And the sea gave up the dead that were in it, Death and Hades gave up the dead that were in them, and all were judged according to what they had done. [14]Then Death and Hades were thrown into the lake of fire. This is the second death, the lake of fire; [15]and anyone whose name was not found written in the book of life was thrown into the lake of fire.
>
> Rev. 20:12–15

Another possible interpretation is to think of the *first death* and life cycle as repeated the second time. Whatever it means, spiritually or physically, it may simply suggest a cycle. As it was, so will it be. When discussing how God has the power to bring things back to life, the Qur'an uses natural analogies.[153] It does not show that resurrection requires some sort of supernatural forces, for example:[154]

> And God sends down water from the sky, and thereby revives the earth after its death. Surely in this is a sign for a people who hear.
>
> Qur'an 16:65

This passage seems a bit unusual in that it does not describe the natural process of reviving the dead earth to people who can see or feel the rain and what it does; rather, their revival is a sign for those who hear. It is an odd notion that someone would *hear* this process – it would be awe-inspiring to those seeing or feeling it, unless what is meant are those who hear this passage. However, the passages directly preceding this one describes nonbelievers and mention that God sent messengers to warn them (i.e. Qur'an 16:60–64). It appears as if it is an inner-Qur'anic allusion to Qur'an 35:14–26, which as discussed, describes how the nonbelievers, who are dead in their graves, would not be able to hear the message of the Qur'an, just as the people before them did not hear the messengers sent to them. Thus, it would not be surprising that this passage portrays death and resurrection in terms of those who hear since the dead (nonbelievers) do not hear. Another example, describes a natural force (rain) resurrecting the dead earth:

> 63 And were you to ask them, 'Who sends down water from the sky and revives thereby the earth after its death?' They would surely say, 'God.' Say, 'Praise be to God!' Nay, but most of them understand not. 64 The life of this world is nothing but diversion and play. And surely the Abode of the Hereafter is the lively [one] [*al-ḥayawān*],[155] if they but knew.
>
> Qur'an 29:63–64

This passage distinguishes between the two different kinds of life, this and the next. Another example of the Qur'an using natural power to bring life to the dead is the following, which is part of a larger context describing natural divine signs:

> 39 Among His signs is that you see the earth diminished; then, when We send down water upon it, it quivers and swells. He Who gives it life is surely the One Who gives life to the dead. Truly He is Powerful over all things. 40 Truly those who deviate [*yulḥidūn*] with regard to Our signs are not hidden from Us. Is one who is cast in the Fire better, or one who comes in security on the Day of Resurrection? Do what you will; truly He sees whatsoever you do.
>
> Qur'an 41:39–40

This passage again makes an analogy for the power of resurrection as God's power through natural forces. Since the Qur'an describes those not believing in its signs as *yulḥidūn*, which can also mean 'entomb', it is as if one is resurrected from this type of death, a spiritual kind of death, through the same powers as natural forces.

In the Qur'an, resurrection is not depicted as a supernatural miracle. It is portrayed as something completely natural, requiring nothing beyond natural forces. Thus, if the Qur'an is representing any kind of physical resurrection, it suggests a process that is no different from the one in which the physical came to life the first time, and that is through natural birth. The only passage in the Qur'an that appears to explicitly describe some sort of physical resurrection supernaturally, albeit nonhuman, is Qur'an 2:259–260, which is analysed closely in the next two chapters.

Conclusion

The Qur'an uses symbolism common to the Bible and Near Eastern heritage for the book in heaven and the book written in the depths of the earth to portray people of the living and the dead, respectively. The Qur'an's typical portrayal of resurrection proceeds in the same way that God created the first time (perhaps physically), which functions more as a kind of rebirth – it is not bones coming out of their graves. It may be that the Qur'an is describing physical resurrection as re-birth or re-creation, and therefore the bones being clothed with flesh is not depicted as coming out of graves but simply an analogue to physical birth, in which the bones of the foetus are also clothed with flesh (e.g. Qur'an 23:14).

This does not mean that the Qur'an is not necessarily discussing physical resurrection. However, if it does, the Qur'an does not depict it as happening through some supernatural forces of bones coming out of their graves, but through natural forces like childbirth, or rejuvenating rain.

Chapter 6

THE VIVID PORTRAYAL OF PHYSICAL RESURRECTION IN QUR'AN 2:259

Two verses in a single passage in the Qur'an portray the resurrection of dead bodies, albeit non-human, that do not go through birth again:

> 259 Or [think of] the like of him who passed by a town as it lay fallen upon its roofs. He said, 'How shall God give life to this after its death?' So God caused him to die for a hundred years, then raised him up. He said, 'How long have you tarried?' He said, 'I tarried a day or part of a day.' He said, 'Nay, you have tarried a hundred years. Look, then, at your food and your drink – they have not spoiled. And look at your donkey. And [this was done] that We may make you a sign for humankind. And look at the bones, how We set them up, then clothe them with flesh.' When it became clear to him he said, 'I know that God has power over all things.' 260 And when Abraham said, 'My Lord, show me how You give life to the dead,' He said, 'Do you not believe?' He said, 'Yea, indeed, but so that my heart may be at peace.' He said, 'Take four birds and make them be drawn to you. Then place a piece of them on every mountain. Then call them: they will come to you in haste. And know that God is Mighty, Wise.'
>
> Qur'an 2:259–260

Although this passage is one in the Qur'an that literally describes the resurrection of dead bones without analogy to first-time creation, its depiction concerns two types of animals: a donkey and birds. It does not depict the resurrection of the human being. Actually, the human being in this passage, who dies, is not resurrected in the same way as his donkey. The Qur'an implies he was revived just as if he were asleep. The man is asked how long he stayed, to which he answers, 'A day or part thereof.' This response parallels that of the Companions of the Cave (Sleepers) – they slept for 309 years (i.e. Qur'an 18:19).[1] Here in Qur'an 2:259 the term *ba'th* is used for the raising of the dead man, just as it is in Qur'an 18:19 when the sleepers in the cave are revived. The link between Qur'an 2:259 and the Companions of the Cave has been argued by Tommaso Tesei[2] and Dorothee Pielow.[3] Tesei argues that sleep and wakefulness in Qur'an 2:259 and the cave sleepers are metaphors of death and resurrection.[4] If Qur'an 18:18 portrays the sleepers moving while they are asleep, then they are not depicted as clinically dead. Qur᾽an 2:259 uses the root *m-w-t* for the man being caused to die. Death equated with sleep, nonetheless, is seen in various pseudepigrapha texts in the Near East: *Pseudo-Philo*, for example, makes this connection liberally (e.g. *Pseudo-Philo* 19:2, 19:6, 28:10, 29:4, 33:6, 35:3).

While Qur᾽an 2:259–260 is the most explicit in its depiction of nonhuman animals resurrected back to life, Sarra Tlili does not mention it in her discussion of the resurrection of nonhuman animals in the Qur᾽an (e.g. Qur᾽an 6:38, 81:5).[5] It appears that her definition of resurrection is what would traditionally occur eschatologically on the Day of Resurrection.[6] The methods she uses in her arguments are heavily dependent on traditional Muslim exegetes, mainly al-Ṭabarī, al-Rāzī, al-Qurṭubī, and Ibn Kathīr.[7] According to these traditional exegetes, the purpose of the nonhuman animal resurrection is accountability.[8] However, in Qur᾽an 2:259–260, that appears not to be the case. It seems that the purpose behind the depiction of an apparent resurrection of the donkey or birds is for the reassurance of humans, who are asking questions about resurrection, to believe in its possibility.

I will divide the close reading of the two Qur᾽anic verses into two chapters: this and the next, devoting one chapter to each verse. In both cases, significant intertextualities between the Qur᾽an and biblical and extrabiblical literature are presented. The Qur᾽an is most likely informed by these subtexts and the traditions that use them, or their proto-traditions, and is rearticulating them. However, the Qur᾽an's rearticulation is not necessarily done in the spirit of arguing polemically against some of the notions propounded by such traditions to advocate its own message. The Qur᾽an rearticulates the same subtext using different terms and themes, in this case resurrection, but only to interpret the same message in its own way. The Qur᾽an does the same in other examples,[9] such as the parable of the camel passing through the eye of the needle, in which – while the Qur᾽an appears to confront arrogance instead of richness as it is in the Synoptic Gospels – it retains and expounds upon the Gospels' message using different terms and themes.[10]

The reader will recognize the Qur᾽an's use of Israelite exilic imagery and redemption in the passages discussed – its engagements with and allusions to texts and traditions of the exile and their return. Undoubtedly, the question that would be raised is why the Qur᾽an would even be interested in engaging on the topic of the Israelite exiles. However puzzling at first, the reason might ultimately be very simple. However, I appeal to the reader's patience: with the intertextualities involved, this overarching question will be answered by the end of the next chapter, after discussing Qur᾽an 2:259–260 in full.

The man in the desolate town

Although most traditional commentators, such as al-Ṭabarī, understand Qur᾽an 2:259 to mean literally that a man is physically caused to die,[11] Ibn ʿArabī interprets the man's death metaphorically, as a spiritual one, namely describing ignorance.[12]

This merely small example demonstrates that Muslim intellectual history contains various opinions concerning this passage.

The man passes through a desolate town and asks how God will revive it. The question of life from death here concerns neither humans nor nonhuman animals but a town, portrayed as desolate. The man simply asks how a dead town, with death symbolizing its emptiness, would become liveable again. Since the man's question is metaphorical, it should not at all be a surprise if what comes next is metaphorical, as well.

Traditional Qur'anic commentators identify the man in this passage mostly with Ezra, but sometimes with Jeremiah.[13] Most commentators arrive at these views based on presumptions, and therefore it is difficult to follow how these identifications have been first made, but Mahmoud Ayoub has argued that a biblical background is perhaps how these exegetes arrived at their opinions, though not always without confusing biblical and hagiographical accounts.[14] In the next chapter, I will suggest the possibility of identifying the man in another way: with Abraham.

This section discusses two similar traditions: Abimelech – who according to 4 Baruch (*Paraleipomena Jeremiou*) was with Jeremiah, who had slept for sixty-six years during the exile (i.e. 4 Bar. 5:1–35)[15] – and Ḥoni ha-M'agel (the Circle-Drawer),[16] who had slept for seventy years, according to the Talmud, both Jerusalem and Babylonian.[17] Both traditions are related to the exile. Both Jeremiah and Ezra are also related to the exile. When early Muslim commentators identified the man in this Qur'anic passage as either Jeremiah or Ezra, it might have been the case because they somehow were able to relate this story with the exilic traditions. There might have been some Jewish traditions that existed in the earlier Muslim history that combined these exilic traditions. It has already been suggested that the Abimelech narrative in 4 Baruch serves as a link between the Ḥoni tradition in the Talmud and the Christian version of the Seven Sleepers of Ephesus,[18] who are sometimes identified as the Companions of the Cave in the Qur'an.[19] The language of Qur'an 2:259 suggests a parallel with the Companions of the Cave, and by extension with perhaps Abimelech or Ḥoni traditions. Robert Hoyland cleverly connects Qur'an 2:259 with the Companions of the Cave narrative, as well as with Abimelech's narrative in 4 Baruch, and strongly concludes that Abimelech's narrative in 4 Baruch is the underlying subtext for Qur'an 2:259.[20] While 4 Baruch might have been the inspiration for Ḥoni's narrative, another version of Abimelech's sleep was also circulating in the seventh century known as the *Apocryphon Jeremiae de captivitate Babylonis*[21] (*History of the Captivity in Babylon*).[22] While the earliest manuscript is dated to the seventh century, the tradition might be dated earlier. In the *History of the Captivity*, Abimelech sleeps for the entire seventy years of the exile and wakes up as Jeremiah returns with the exiles, similar to the time period in Ḥoni's narrative. Thus, Pierluigi Piovanelli hypothesizes that this is based on older traditions than that of 4 Baruch.[23] Moshe Simon-Shoshan also agrees to Piovanelli's hypothesis.[24]

According to the Babylonian Talmud, Ḥoni the Circle-Drawer is said to have slept for seventy years, the same duration as the exile, because he doubted that one could slumber this long:

> R. Yoḥanan said, 'All the days of that righteous man [Ḥoni] he was troubled by this verse: "A song of ascents: when the Lord brought back those who returned to Zion, we were like those who dream' [Ps. 126:1]. He [Ḥoni] said [to himself], "Is there anyone who sleeps and dreams for seventy years?'
>
> One day he was going along the road. He saw a man who was planting a carob tree. He said to him, "This tree, how long does it take to bear fruit?" He said to him, "It takes seventy years." He said to him, "Is it obvious to you that you are going to live another seventy years?" He said to him, "That man [I] found a world full of carobs. Just as my fathers planted for me, so I plant these for my children."
>
> He sat down to wrap a piece of bread. Sleep overtook him. As he slept, a cliff formed around him and hid him from sight, and he slept for seventy years. When he woke up, he saw a certain man gathering carobs from the tree. He said to him, "Are you the one who planted the tree?" He said to him, "I am his grandson." He said to him, "It is to be inferred that I have slept for seventy years." He saw his donkey, who had produced generations of offspring, and he went home.
>
> He said to them, "Is the son of Ḥoni the Circle-Drawer still alive?" They said to him, "His son is no longer, but his grandson is." He said to them, "I am Ḥoni the Circle-Drawer." They did not believe him. He went to the house of study. He heard the rabbis saying, "His traditions are as clear to us as in the days of Ḥoni the Circle-Drawer. For when he would come to the house of study, any question that the rabbis had, he would resolve it for them." He said to them, "I am Ḥoni the Circle-Drawer." They did not believe him or pay him any proper respect. He was very upset, prayed for mercy, and died. Raba said, "This explains what people say: either fellowship or death."'[25]

The similarity between the Qur᾽anic passage and Ḥoni's narrative is that Ḥoni sees a man planting a tree that takes seventy years to grow. It takes a very long time for it to be fruitful. The Qur᾽an sometimes uses the motif of a dead earth for one that has no plants. Additionally, Ḥoni has a donkey, similar to the Qur᾽anic narrative. Not only did Ḥoni see the tree become fruitful after seventy years, but also he saw his donkey bring forth generations of offspring. It is as if the plant-seed and the donkey-seed, though coming from what are now dead, do bring forth life. In his story, Ḥoni understands the motif in 'When the Lord restored the fortunes of Zion, we were like those who dream' (Ps. 126:1) as the Israelites being in a dream state, sure to prosper again.[26] Simon-Shoshan suggests that the dream-state also reflects Ḥoni's state during the exile: 'The "like dreamers" simile refers to his experience during the exile, rather than after it. Unlike those who went into exile, he did not suffer during this period. He quite conveniently slept through it, awaking as if nothing had happened.'[27]

The narrative according to the Jerusalem Talmud differs slightly and concerns the destruction of Jerusalem, the exile, and the rebuilding of the Temple.[28]

> Said R. Yudan Giria, 'This is Ḥoni the Circle-Drawer, the grandson of Ḥoni the Circle-Drawer. Near the time of the destruction of the Temple, he went out to a mountain to his workers. Before he got there, it rained. He went into a cave. Once he sat down there, he became tired and fell asleep. He remained sound asleep for seventy years, until the Temple was destroyed and it was rebuilt a second time. At the end of the seventy years he awoke from his sleep. He went out of the cave, and he saw a world completely changed. An area that had been planted with vineyards now produced olives, and an area planted in olives now produced grain. He asked the people of the district, "What do you hear in the world?" They said to him, "And don't you know what the news is?" He said to them, "No." They said to him, "Who are you?" He said to them, "Ḥoni, the Circle-Drawer." They said to him, "We heard that when he would go into the Temple courtyard, it would be illuminated." He went in and illuminated the place and recited concerning himself the following verse of Scripture: "When the Lord restored the fortune of Zion, we were like those who dream."'
>
> Ps. 126:1[29]

Simon-Shoshan compares the Jerusalem Talmud's account to three earlier traditions that are all connected to the exile and return: *Ben Sira*'s Simon the high priest (i.e. Sirach 50), 2 Maccabees's Nehemiah hiding and restoring the fire of the temple altar, and 4 Baruch's Abimelech.[30]

Commanded by Jeremiah, the priests in 2 Macc. 1:18–2:18 took some of the fire from the temple's altar during the exile and secretly hid it in a waterless cistern next to Moses's tomb, along with the tabernacle, the ark and the golden altar. After a certain number of years decreed by God, Nehemiah, by the authority of the king of Persia, sent the descendants of the priests to retrieve the fire.[31] They found not the fire but a viscous liquid in its place, which was brought in and sprinkled by sacrificial materials. When the sun shone upon it, a great fire lit and burnt the offerings, as part of the celebrations of the temple's purification. Simon-Shoshan considers hiding the fire during the exile and retrieving it is one of the traditions that might have inspired Ḥoni's narrative in the Jerusalem Talmud indirectly.[32] Since he finds it unlikely that the later rabbis were familiar with the text, he suspects an overarching tradition that circulated which proved a continuity of various traditions.

According to 4 Baruch,[33] Jeremiah is told by God of the impending destruction of Jerusalem and the exile of the Israelites to Babylon. The prophet pleads with God to show mercy and shield Abimelech the Ethiopian, who has been kind to Jeremiah, from seeing Jerusalem destroyed and its inhabitants taken captive (i.e. 4 Bar. 3:12–13). Accepting Jeremiah's plea, God tells him to send Abimelech to the vineyard of Agrippa, where he will be divinely hidden in the shadow of the mountain until the people return to the city (i.e. 4 Bar. 3:14). So Jeremiah asks Abimelech to take a basket and go to Agrippa along the mountain road to bring some figs to the sick people. Meanwhile, God informs Jeremiah that he will speak to Baruch, who weeps for the destruction of Jerusalem and sits in a tomb, while the angels explained to him God's revelations (i.e. 4 Bar. 4:12). The text does not identify the tomb nor does it give any hint as to why Baruch was sitting in one.[34] It is possible that the tomb, which is described as being outside Jerusalem, is a metaphor for the Israelite nation, who were in exile outside Jerusalem; such a metaphor is used in Ezekiel 37.[35] Biblical scholar and historian Dale Allison Jr. states,

> Baruch is obviously not sitting there in order to consult the dead. His action is rather a prophetic symbol. He, like the nation, is lifeless. He will no longer participate in everyday life. He is fit only for the company of the dead.[36]

The metaphor of death and resurrection of the nation of Israel through its biblical intertextualities – some of which are portrayed in this chapter – is best developed by closely analysing the symbolism used in the prophetic books of the Hebrew Bible, as demonstrated by biblical scholar and theologian Donald E. Gowan in his biblical study on death and resurrection.[37] This chapter uses only some of the symbolism that appears to be directly related to Qur'an 2:259, but it is an overarching theme that exists within the Hebrew Bible, which has several inner-biblical allusions associated with this symbolism.[38] Gabriel Reynolds speculates that the clothing of bones with flesh in Qur'an 2:259 mirrors Ezekiel 37,[39] further associating this passage with the Babylonian exile.

In 4 Bar. 5:1–35, Abimelech takes a basket and collects figs under the burning sun. Since it is too hot, he decides to rest under the shade of a tree. Between 4 Baruch and the Qur'anic passage we see similarities, but two main differences: (1) the Qur'an narrates that the man died for 100 years, while Abimelech sleeps for sixty-six, and (2) the Qur'an states that the man had a donkey, while no mention of a donkey exists in 4 Baruch (though Ḥoni the Circle-Drawer has one in the Babylonian Talmud). However, in both cases, a man has ripe fruit that continues to be fresh after so many years.

Afterwards, Abimelech is taken to the tomb (i.e. 4 Bar. 6:2) where Baruch had been sitting – apparently staying there all the time that Abimelech was asleep.[40] Allison analogizes Baruch's time in the tomb to exiled Israel itself, which 'has been in mourning for decades', in a kind of 'liminal' state.[41] Baruch looks at the ripe figs and tells his heart that it (along with his flesh) will be filled with joy and that it will come back to life:

> [6]You are the God who gives a reward to those who love you. Prepare yourself, my heart, and rejoice and be glad while you are in your tabernacle, saying to your fleshly house, 'your grief has been changed to joy'; for the Sufficient One is coming and will deliver you in your tabernacle – for there is no sin in you. [7]Revive in your tabernacle, in your virginal faith, and believe that you will live! [8]Look at this basket of figs – for behold, they are 66 years old and have not become shrivelled or rotten, but they are dripping milk. [9]So it will be with you, my flesh, if you do what is commanded you by the angel of righteousness. [10]He who preserved the basket of figs, the same will again preserve you by his power.
>
> 4 Bar. 6:6–10[42]

This passage shows that Baruch interprets the ripe figs he saw to mean that his flesh and heart would be given life and resurrected,[43] if he does what the angel commanded him. One assumes that the angels who came to him in the beginning, when he sat in the tomb (i.e. 4 Bar. 4:12), ordered him to do something, to which he is now referring. Baruch apparently knows that whatever he is seeing is a sign from God that the Israelites will return to Jerusalem. Baruch and Abimelech then pray to God to show them the way to give the news to Jeremiah (i.e. 4 Bar. 6:14). The answer came to Baruch through an angel, informing him that he should write a letter to Jeremiah, which an eagle will deliver (i.e. 4 Bar. 6:15–18).

Then, Baruch ties the letter and fifteen figs from Abimelech's basket to the eagle's neck (i.e. 4 Bar. 7:7). The eagle travels to Babylon and rests on a post outside the city in the desert (i.e. 4 Bar. 7:12). The place is described as a graveyard, another death motif. Jeremiah and the people come to this place to bury the corpse of a dead Israelite (i.e. 4 Bar. 7:13–14); the eagle comes down on the corpse, and the corpse revives (i.e. 4 Bar. 7:15–19).

After the Israelites return to Jerusalem, the text later narrates that Jeremiah appears to have died (i.e. 4 Bar. 9:7). When Baruch and Abimelech wanted to bury his body, a voice commands them not to bury someone who is still alive, because his soul will return to his body (i.e. 4 Bar. 9:11–12). In three days, Jeremiah's soul returns and he is resurrected, prophesying the coming of Jesus (i.e. 4 Bar. 9:14) – which suggests a later Christianized redaction.[44]

While Simon-Shoshan suggests that Ḥoni's narrative shows the continuity of the pre-exilic and postexilic community, Abimelech of 4 Baruch wakes up before the return of the exile, seeing the city's desolation and redemption.[45] Its theme is thus closer to that of the Qur᾽an's narrative than Ḥoni, who never really saw the city desolate.

Simon-Shoshan suggests that 4 Baruch and Ḥoni's narratives are distinct and have evolved separately from traditions linking them to *Ben Sira* and 2 Maccabees. He asserts that Ḥoni's narratives did not develop from 4 Baruch.[46] His main argument is based on the difference between the number of years slept, whether the time of the exile (seventy years) or sixty-six years. The latter would mean that the man saw the desolation of the city before it was rebuilt. The Qur᾽anic narrative clearly shows the amalgamation of both narratives, including the donkey in Ḥoni's version. The number of years cannot be used as a litmus test in the Qur᾽anic narrative, because it is one hundred years, and yet depicts a person who saw the city desolate. In the next chapter, it is proposed that the man in the Qur᾽anic narrative is Abraham, who had Isaac at one hundred years old. This might suggest that there was an interim tradition that takes inspiration from *Ben Sira* and 2 Maccabees or similar proto-traditions, from which both 4 Baruch and Ḥoni's narratives derive independently, while the Qur᾽anic narrative also stemmed from a third, separate branch. That would confirm Simon-Shoshan's conclusion that 'entire complexes of narrative traditions circulated and developed among differing communities'.[47]

The similarities between Ḥoni's narrative in the Talmud and that of Abimelech in 4 Baruch with the Qur᾽anic version, which seemingly has bits and pieces from both versions but more closely resembles 4 Baruch, suggests several theories: (1) both narratives served as a subtext for the Qur'anic narrative; (2) an oral tradition of 4 Baruch that adds a donkey (based on Ḥoni's narrative in the Talmud) served as a subtext for the Qur'anic narrative; (3) the Qur'an is referring to a different tradition that itself evolved from proto-traditions for the Talmud and 4 Baruch or; (4) a post-tradition that combined both. Various similar traditions existed in the Near East during Late Antiquity in Greek, Jewish, and Christian sources.[48] Pieter van der Horst suggests that while 4 Baruch was later Christianized, its origins might have been Jewish and that the Christian author of the Seven Sleepers of Ephesus might have used similar motifs from it.[49] Therefore, it is likely that there were traditions in the Qur'anic milieu that mixed earlier traditions of long-sleepers, which might even suggest the possible reasons with the similarity in some of the language between Qur'an 2:259 and the Qur'anic narrative of the Companions of the Cave.

The man's ṭaʿām *(food or commandment)*

According to Qur'an 2:259, the man had food that did not spoil, similar to the figs of Abimelech in 4 Baruch. What is the significance of mentioning the food not being spoiled in the Qur'an? What does it have to do with resurrection, if anything?

To put this passage in context, perhaps one needs to understand the significance of the figs of Abimelech in 4 Baruch. Some scholars argue that the Hebrew Bible has a pattern of using figs as a metaphor for the nation of Israel,[50] as in Hos. 9:10 (also echoed in Mic. 7:1): 'Like grapes in the wilderness, I found Israel. Like the first fruit on the fig tree in its first season, I saw your ancestors.' The absence or the withering of figs is sometimes also understood as a curse on the nation of Israel or its land:[51] 'When I wanted to gather them, says the LORD, there are no grapes on the vine, nor figs on the fig tree; even the leaves are withered, and what I gave them has passed away from them' (Jer. 8:13). Haggai also has this contrast between barren fig trees and blessing: 'Is there any seed left in the barn? Do the vine, the fig tree, the pomegranate, and the olive tree still yield nothing. From this day on I will bless you' (Hag. 2:19).

Just before recounting the seventy years of captivity, Jeremiah's vision in chapter 24 calls figs to mind:[52]

> [1]The LORD showed me two baskets of figs placed before the temple of the LORD. This was after King Nebuchadrezzar of Babylon had taken into exile from Jerusalem King Jeconiah son of Jehoiakim of Judah, together with the officials of Judah, the artisans, and the smiths, and had brought them to Babylon. [2]One basket had very good figs, like first-ripe figs, but the other basket had very bad figs, so bad that they could not be eaten. [3]And the LORD said to me, 'What do you see, Jeremiah?' I said, 'Figs, the good figs very good, and the bad figs very bad, so bad that they cannot be eaten.'

> [4]Then the word of the LORD came to me: [5]Thus says the LORD, the God of Israel: Like these good figs, so I will regard as good the exiles from Judah, whom I have sent away from this place to the land of the Chaldeans. [6]I will set my eyes upon them for good, and I will bring them back to this land. I will build them up, and not tear them down; I will plant them, and not pluck them up. [7]I will give them a heart to know that I am the LORD; and they shall be my people and I will be their God, for they shall return to me with their whole heart.
>
> [8]But thus says the LORD: Like the bad figs that are so bad they cannot be eaten, so will I treat King Zedekiah of Judah, his officials, the remnant of Jerusalem who remain in this land, and those who live in the land of Egypt. [9]I will make them a horror, an evil thing, to all the kingdoms of the earth – a disgrace, a byword, a taunt, and a curse in all the places where I shall drive them. [10]And I will send sword, famine, and pestilence upon them, until they are utterly destroyed from the land that I gave to them and their ancestors.
>
> Jer. 24:1–10

This passage might contextualize Abimelech's story in 4 Baruch with whom Jeremiah interacted. The figs not spoiled in 4 Baruch might be an allusion to this motif in Jer. 8:13 and Jeremiah 24.[53] In 4 Baruch, the figs were given to sick people and might mirror the figs used to heal and cleanse Hezekiah from the terminal illness he had, and used as a sign to go up (*'e'ĕle*) to the temple (i.e. Isaiah 38). In 4 Baruch, the sick people might symbolize the people of Israel and the figs are a sign of them being healed, as a symbol of their return from exile and for going up to the Temple (perhaps as pilgrims).

Analysing the Gospel of Mark's narrative on Jesus cursing a fig tree (e.g. Mk. 11:12–25), Brent Kinman states,

> Others think that an eschatological emphasis is to be seen. According to this view, the destruction of the Temple and Jerusalem is the real focus of the narrative in which Jesus, by a prophetic act or acted parable (the cursing of the tree), announces impending judgment. The fig tree represents Israel in Jesus' day, and its cursing symbolizes the destruction of the city and Temple by the Romans some years later.[54]

In parallel, New Testament scholar John P. Heil also writes, 'The Marcan audience realizes that the temple, like the fruitless fig tree, is condemned to destruction for failing to attain its purpose to be a house of prayer for all peoples.'[55] Hence, there is a possibility that the non-spoiling figs of Abimelech in 4 Baruch are symbolic of the nation of Israel, which though destroyed and exiled are restored and, indeed, not spoiled.

In the Qur'anic narrative, two terms need to be investigated closely: *ṭa'ām* (food) and *yatasannah* (spoiled). The latter is rooted in *s-n-h*, which can mean sleep, as used in Qur'an 2:255. However, because the same root also means years or growing old (as understood in Qur'an 2:259 as old and decayed),[56] it is difficult to suggest whether or not those two root meanings are related to one another.[57] If the root meaning is sleeping or staying still, then the meaning of passing time and growing old may be a natural evolution of that,[58] in which it decays as something ages. If Qurʾan 2:259 is demonstrating that a man falls into a deep sleep (metaphorically dies), then the term *yatasannah* could show that his food did not sleep. If it means that his food did not grow old, meaning that it did not decay, then the question one must ask is whether the man himself grew old. In the Sleepers of the Cave narrative, the Qurʾan implies that the men grew old because anyone who would see them would be smitten with fear (i.e. Qurʾan 18:18). However, if the men did grow old, they would have realized the changes and would not have thought that they slept only a day or a part thereof. Thus, it is difficult to answer whether in this passage the man grows old or not, but since he did not realize the passage of time, then it is likely that he did not. Similarly, Abimelech in 4 Baruch and Ḥoni the Circle-Drawer of the Talmud show no explicit evidence that they too grew old.

As the Qurʾan might be using *yatasannah* in two definitions, *ṭaʿām* might also be used in two definitions. This term is obviously understood as food and is attested throughout the Semitic languages to have the basic meaning of taste.[59] Nonetheless, Akkadian,[60] Aramaic and Hebrew include another meaning for *ṭĕʿēm*, which is command, discernment or intelligence.[61] The *Theological Dictionary of the Old Testament* (*TDOT*) suggests that since the root meaning is perceiving taste, it evolved to mean discernment or intelligence, which is an act of perception and, by extension, came to mean a decree or command that occurs through discernment and rationale.[62] John Makujina argued for two possible origins of the meaning of decree, either Old Persian or Semitic; in his estimation the evidence leans more towards the former.[63] Could this meaning have also found its way into Arabic, and perhaps become incorporated within the Qurʾan? Or at least could the Qurʾan's audience have understood the wide semantic field of this term? I hypothesize that the answer to both is *yes,* but not that the Arabic language simply borrowed such a definition. However, the Qurʾan sometimes uses specific terms that would resonate with the audience. For example, the Qurʾan uses the term *qiblah* to resonate with the Talmudic *qabbalah* as an allusion to the *Shemaʿ*.[64] The Qurʾan sometimes uses the term *al-ḥaqq*, with the meaning of 'decree' in the *Qiblah* passages to resonate with the *Shemaʿ* passages,[65] as well as in the cow passage to resonate with the rabbinic commentary of the red cow ritual, which is discussed in Chapter 9. Since the context of Qurʾan 2:259 is argued to be that of the Israelite exile, which would correspond to an audience that would be familiar to some of the books of the Hebrew Bible on the exile, such as Ezra-Nehemiah, Jeremiah and others, the use of *ṭĕʿēm* in these texts is sometimes specific to the meaning of 'decree'. Moreover, the Arab poet, al-Farazdaq (d. 730), uses *al-ṭiʿmah*, from the same root, to mean a trait or a conduct,[66] while *ṭaʿm*, in Arabic, also means understanding,[67] similar to its Aramaic definition, which by extension came to mean decree.[68]

The usage of *ṭaʿām* might resonate with Israelite literature pertaining to the exile, which uses *ṭĕʿēm* as 'decree', as the following Qurʾanic passage may contextualize:

> All *al-ṭaʿām* was lawful unto the Children of Israel, except what Israel had forbidden for himself, before the Torah was sent down. Say, 'Bring the Torah and recite it, if you are truthful.'
>
> Qur᾿an 3:93

The context of this verse has nothing to do with food. Nothing preceding nor following this passage has anything to do with food at all. The overarching theme of this passage's context is faith. If this passage were understood to be about food, then it would seem out of its Qur᾿anic contextual flow and completely random. However, if we tweak the meaning of *ṭaʿām* in this passage to commandment or decree, as it can also be defined in Hebrew and Aramaic, we get the following:

> All decree/commandment [*al-ṭaʿām*] was lawful unto the Children of Israel, except what Israel had forbidden for himself, before the Torah was sent down. Say, 'Bring the Torah and recite it, if you are truthful.'
>
> Qur᾿an 3:93

This definition of the term would make more sense. The Qur᾿an is arguing that God's commandments did not exist in the time of Israel (Jacob). God's commandments came later, through the Torah. Consequently, these commandments are not the essence of faith. The Qur᾿anic argument is that the essence is the faith of Abraham (i.e. Qur᾿an 3:95), who came before the Torah and, therefore, before its commandments; and the preceding context, Qur᾿an 3:65 states exactly that:

> 65O People of the Book! Why do you dispute concerning Abraham, as neither the Torah nor the Gospel was sent down until after him? Do you not understand? 66Behold! You are the very same who dispute concerning that of which you have knowledge; so why do you dispute concerning that of which you have no knowledge? God knows, and you know not. 67Abraham was neither Jew nor Christian, but rather was a *ḥanīf*, a submitter, and he was not one of the idolaters.
>
> Qur᾿an 3:65–67

Therefore, understanding *ṭaʿām* in Qur᾿an 3:93 as a decree or commandment makes a lot more sense and flows rather well with the context. Otherwise, understanding *ṭaʿām* as food would isolate this passage from its immediate context. Coming after Qur᾿an 3:93, the text discusses the *first house*, an allusion to the House of God and its dedication to the people.

> 96Truly the first house established for humankind was that at Bakkah, full of blessing and a guidance for the worlds. 97Therein are clear signs: the station [*maqām*] of Abraham, and whosoever enters it shall be secure. Pilgrimage [*ḥajj*] to the House is a duty upon [*ʿala*] humankind before God for those who can find a way. For whosoever disbelieves, truly God is beyond need of the worlds.
>
> Qur᾿an 3:96–97

Several intertextualities are seen between Qur'an 3:93–97 and the Book of Ezra. First, the Book of Ezra frequently uses the Aramaic term *ṭĕ'ēm* for decree, with much of it discussing the decree of rebuilding the Temple of God in Jerusalem (e.g. Ezra 6:1, 6:3, 6:8, 6:11–12). Second, the Book of Ezra continuously discusses the rebuilding of the House of God, the Temple. Third, Ezra-Nehemiah[69] does present the Israelites returning to Jerusalem as pilgrims.[70]

The Qur'an appears to be using wordplay. As in the passage just preceding Qur'an 2:259, it uses the root *ḥ-j-j*, but in a different polysemous meaning of arguing or debating,[71] when also portraying a matter of life and death (or resurrection):

> Have you not considered him who disputed [*ḥājj*] with Abraham about his Lord because God had given him sovereignty? When Abraham said, 'My Lord gives life and causes death,' he said, 'I give life and cause death.' Abraham said, 'Truly God brings the sun from the east. Bring it, then, from the west.' Thus was he who disbelieved confounded. And God guides not wrongdoing people.
>
> Qur'an 2:258

Furthering the relationship between Qur'an 3:93–97 and the Book of Ezra, Ezra 6:18 describes the reinstatement of the priestly functions in the Temple, according to the Book of Moses. The Qur'an appears to argue that all *ṭa'ām* were allowed to the Children of Israel, except what Israel had forbidden to himself before the revelation of the Torah (i.e. before the Book of Moses). When discussing that all *ṭa'ām* were lawful to the Israelites before the Torah, Qur'an 3:93 specifically asks to bring the Torah and to read it as proof. This reading request might be intertextualized with Neh. 8:1–8, which narrates how the Israelites asked Ezra to bring the Book of Law of Moses (i.e. Neh. 8:1) and to read it (i.e. Neh. 8:1–8). After Ezra read before the Israelites the Book of Moses, the narrative states, 'So they read from the book, from the Law [*tôrat*] of God, with interpretation [*mĕpōrāš*].[72] They gave the sense [*śôm śekel*], so that the people understood the reading' (Neh. 8:8). Makujina argues that the term *śôm śekel* in this passage is the same as *śôm ṭĕ'ēm* used in the rest of Ezra-Nehemiah and needs to be understood as to 'give a [divine] order'.[73] Therefore, as it is being argued that the context of Qur'an 3:93 is seemingly engaging with the Second Temple, especially within Ezra-Nehemiah, then it seems highly likely that the *ṭa'ām* of Qur'an 3:93 is divine commandment. In addition, Qur'an 3:93 requests that Jews bring the Torah and read it; the centrality of public recitation of the Torah within the Jewish community is described in the Ezra-Nehemiah narrative.[74]

Brannon Wheeler[75] and Noah Feldman[76] have argued that Qur'an 3:93 is specifically in reference to the prohibition of the sinew of the thigh (*gîd ha-nāše*): 'Therefore to this day the Israelites do not eat the thigh muscle [*gîd ha-nāše*] that is on the hip socket, because he struck Jacob on the hip socket at the thigh muscle [*gîd ha-nāše*]' (Gen. 32:32). Feldman concludes Qur'an 3:93 is anti-Jewish, to prove that Israel (Jacob) forbade something to himself without divine sanction.[77] I humbly disagree with Feldman's conclusion, in light of my own argument on the *Qiblah* passages in the Qur'an, which are viewed by many scholars as anti-Jewish.

However, the *Qiblah* passages only engage with Jews, reminding them of what is truly important, the *Shema'*.[78] Given the overall context of Qur'an 3:93, dietary prohibition would seem out of place. It is more likely that the passage is engaging with Ezra-Nehemiah and the Second Temple. Therefore, dietary laws do not seem like the actual issue in Qur'an 3:93, but – as is typical with the Qur'an – its creative use of polysemy and therefore double meaning is a possibility.[79] Moreover, after Ezra read the Torah to the Israelites, they were asked to stop weeping and rejoice and have a feast and eat and drink (i.e. Neh. 8:9–18).

If the man in the desolate town described in Qur'an 2:259 is understood to be engaging with either Abimelech's narrative in 4 Baruch or Ḥoni the Circle-Drawer in the Talmud – which is about the Israelites return from exile to rebuild Jerusalem and the Temple, as described in Ezra-Nehemiah – then the *ṭa'ām* that did not spoil might be a clever reference to the Torah of Moses, which Ezra was also able to restore. It did not spoil, that is, even after it appeared to have been lost during the time of the exile.[80]

The broader Qur'anic context of this passage is faith and asking the People of the Book to return to the faith of Abraham, who was neither a Jew nor a Christian, because the Torah and the Gospel were revealed after him. Ezra-Nehemiah and the traditions based thereon speak of the House of God rebuilt according to the prophecy of Haggai and priestly functions reinstituted as per the Book of Moses. If this passage is engaging with those traditions, then the Qur'an argues that Abraham, his station (*maqām*), and his call for pilgrimage (*ḥajj*) predate the Torah.

When another chapter of the Qur'an describes the *ḥajj* rituals, it refers to the House as *al-bayt al-'atīq* (the ancient house) echoing Ezra 5:11, which shows that the Jews who were rebuilding the house in Jerusalem stated, 'we are rebuilding the house [*baytā'*] that was built many years ago [*mi-qadmat*]'. As the Qur'anic passage describes pilgrimage, that also echoes Ezra-Nehemiah's portrayal of the Israelites returning to Jerusalem as pilgrims.[81]

Where the pilgrimage portrayal is found in Qur'an 3:96–97, it is within the direct context of the *ṭa'ām* in Qur'an 3:93: the *ṭa'ām* in this passage may very well be meant as decree referring to the Torah. The *ṭa'ām* of the man in the desolate town may refer to the Torah being unspoilt, and function as a metaphor for its restoration, as the figs of Abimelech in biblical literature are understood to represent the Israelite nation, which did not decay but was restored. The rabbis of the Babylonian Talmud explicitly correlate figs with the Torah:

> What is the meaning of this verse of Scripture: 'Whoso keeps the fig tree shall eat the fruit thereof'? [Prov. 27:18] How come words of the Torah were compared to a fig? Just as the fig – the more someone examines it, the more one finds in it, so words of the Torah – the more one meditates on them, the more flavor he finds in them.[82]

> He who in a dream sees a fig will find that his knowledge of Torah will be fully protected within him. For it is said, 'He who keeps the fig tree shall eat the fruit thereof'.
>
> Prov. 27:18[83]

The term used for pilgrimage in the Hebrew Bible is sometimes rooted in *ʿ-l-y* or *ʿ-l-h* (e.g. Exod. 34:24),[84] which is understood from its root meaning as 'going up',[85] much as Hezekiah looks for a sign to go up to the Temple after being healed with figs.

In Ezra this going-up may denote the journey of the Israelites to Jerusalem and further emphasize it as a portrayal of pilgrimage.[86] The Book of Ezra starts its description of the journey with Cyrus's edict to go up (*ya ʿal*) to Jerusalem (i.e. Ezra 1:3); the people were stirred to go up (*la- ʿălôt*) and rebuild the house of the Lord (i.e. Ezra 1:5); the gold and silver are brought up (*he ʿĕlâ*) when the exiles were brought up (*hē ʿālôt*) from Babylonia to Jerusalem (i.e. Ezra 1:11).[87] Knowles further points out that Ezra and the Israelites offering a sacrifice in Jerusalem (i.e. Ezra 8:32–35) further accentuates the journey's portrayal precisely as a pilgrimage.[88]

Indeed, Ezra-Nehemiah recounts the Israelites celebrating, upon their return to Jerusalem, the Festival of Booths (*ḥag ha-sukkôt*) (i.e. Ezra 3:1–4, Neh. 8:13–18).[89] After the first group celebrates the Festival of Booths (*ḥag ha-sukkôt*) (i.e. Ezra 3:1–4), the text discusses the rebuilding of the Temple and its dedication (i.e. Ezra 3–6).[90] Immediately after the dedication of the Temple, Passover, another pilgrimage, is celebrated (i.e. Ezra 6:19–22).[91]

Additionally, the use of the term *maqām* for the station of Abraham in Qur'an 3:97 would resonate with its Jewish audience because of the Hebrew term *māqôm*. Qur'an 3:97 states that anyone who enters it shall be secured. This description parallels that of Hag. 2:9, 'The latter [*hā- ʾaḥărôn*] glory of this house [*ha-bayit*] shall be greater than the former, says the Lord of hosts. And in this place [*māqôm*] I will give peace, declares the Lord of hosts.'[92] In another account,

> But now for a brief moment favor has been shown by the Lord our God, who left us a remnant [*pĕlêṭâ*] and given us a stake in his holy place [*mĕqôm*], in order that our God may brighten our eyes and grant us a little sustenance [revival] in our slavery.
>
> Ezra 9:8

In these accounts, the house is described as a place (*maqām*) and anyone in it is granted security or peace, which is also reflected in the Book of Zechariah, who is mentioned in Ezra 6:14 as one who prophesized the rebuilding of the House of God.

> It is he who shall build the temple of the Lord; he shall bear royal honor, and shall sit and rule on his throne. There shall be a priest by [on] his throne with peaceful understanding between the two of them.
>
> Zech. 6:13

Moreover, the Temple is identified as the place where Abraham wanted to sacrifice his son, on Mount Moriah (i.e. Gen. 22:2, 2 Chron. 3:1),[93] thus becoming a good candidate for the Qur'an's station of Abraham. Haggai encouraged the exiled Jews to return to Jerusalem and rebuild the House of God.[94] One recent study has explored the agricultural theme in Haggai in the rebuilding of the Temple, but mainly looked at it as an economic portrayal of Jerusalem.[95] I am more inclined to deduce that such a portrayal of agriculture in Haggai sheds light on some intertextuality with other biblical texts as a metaphor for the nation of Israel being restored after the exile. Similarly, Zechariah encouraged the exiles to return to God and to repent such that God may bring back their glory.[96] Just prior to its discussion on the *ṭaʿām* and *ḥajj* (pilgrimage), Qurʾan 3:89–90 praises those who repent and return to God and those who work for reform (*aṣlaḥū*), while warning those who increase in their *kufr* (disbelief) that their repentance will not be accepted:

> [89]except those who repent after that, and make amends (*aṣlaḥū*), for truly God is Forgiving, Merciful. [90]Truly those who disbelieve after having believed, then increase in disbelief, their repentance shall not be accepted, and they are the ones who are astray.
>
> Qurʾan 3:89–90

The passage avers that God will forgive those who repent or return (*tābū*) and work for reform (*aṣlaḥū*). The root of the term for repentance has its cognates in Hebrew and Aramaic, as they are used and associated with the rebuilding of the Temple in the Books of Ezra-Nehemiah,[97] Haggai[98] and Zechariah. Yet another important term the Qurʾan uses is *aṣlaḥū*. Its Aramaic cognate is also used in the Book of Ezra, when the exiled Jews returned and worked for reform; for example:

> May it be known to the king that we went to the province of Judah, to the house of the great God. It is being built of hewn stone, and timber is laid in the walls; this work is being done diligently and prospers [*maṣlaḥ*] in their hands.
>
> Ezra 5:8

Accordingly, the account in Ezra shows that the exiled Jews rebuilding the Temple have returned to God and are working for reform. Therefore, if the Qurʾanic context were established with its intertextuality among the Books of Ezra-Nehemiah, Haggai, and Zechariah on the House of God,[99] then this passage would allude to those exiled Jews who are rebuilding the Temple, as recounted in Ezra 6:14 with the term *maṣlĕḥîn*. That being the case, Haggai and Zechariah warn the Jews that they should repent for God to return His favour to them. As the exiles were allowed to return and were allowed to rebuild the Temple, it means that God did, accordingly, grant them favour. After the many warnings the Qurʾan gives to the People of the Book in the context of this passage, it asserts that not all of the People of the Book are equal, and that some are good and reformers or righteous (*ṣāliḥīn*). Therefore, the context of this Qurʾanic passage continues to show parallelism with the books of Ezra-Nehemiah, Haggai, and Zechariah.

> [113]They are not all alike. Among the People of the Book is an upright community who recite God's signs in the watches of the night, while they prostrate. [114]They believe in God and the Last Day, enjoin right and forbid wrong, and hasten unto

good deeds. And they are among the righteous [*al-ṣāliḥīn*]. [115]Whatsoever good they do, they will not be denied it. And God knows the reverent.

Qur'an 3:113–115

Another intertextuality between the Qur'anic passage and the rebuilding of the Temple in Jerusalem is the Qur'anic association of the *first house* with 'Bakkah'. Although traditional Muslim commentators interpret the *first house* as the Ka'bah and the enigmatic 'Bakkah' as a name for Makkah,[100] the following passage from the Book of Ezra might shed some additional light on this.

[12]But many of the priests and Levites and heads of families, old people who had seen the *first house* on its foundation, wept [*bōkîm*] with a loud voice when they saw this house, though many shouted aloud for joy, [13]so that the people could not distinguish the sound of the joyful shout from the sound of the people's weeping [*běkî*], for the people shouted so loudly that the sound was heard far away.

Ezra 3:12–13, *emphasis added*

This passage in Ezra narrates how the people who had seen the *first house* wept, with weeping rooted in *b-k-y* or *b-k-h*. According to Ezra 6:3, it is assumed that the original foundation was repaired and rebuilt.[101] This description of people unable to distinguish between joyful shouts and the sound of weeping is essential here, as this is obviously a great event, which the Qur'an might have taken into consideration when narrating it, since it calls it the *first house* and the place of weeping.

When, during the exile, some Israelites intermarried with foreigners against the Law of Moses (i.e. Exod. 34:16, Deut. 7:3), Ezra pleaded before God confessing the sins of the Israelites and wept.[102] People confessing their sin also wept with him:

While Ezra prayed and made confession, weeping [*bōkeh*] and throwing himself down before the house of God, a very great assembly of men, women, and children gathered to him out of Israel; the people also wept [*bākû*] bitterly.

Ezra 10:1

The image of the Israelites weeping, as they listened to Ezra reading the Torah, is also narrated in Nehemiah 8. Ezra and the people weeping while confessing their sins and prostrating before the house of God also supports Qur'an 3:113–115 in accepting that not all of the People of the Book are alike. Some are truly devout: they prostrate, do good and are considered among those who make reforms (*al-ṣāliḥīn*). This is what was found among those rebuilding the Second Temple in the Books of Ezra, Haggai and Zechariah. An image repeated in Nehemiah also makes the distinction:

[6]Then Ezra blessed the Lord, the great God, and all the people answered, 'Amen, Amen,' lifting up their hands. Then they bowed their heads and worshiped the Lord with their faces to the ground. [7]Also Jeshua, Bani, Sherebiah, Jamin,

> Akkub, Shabbethai, Hodiah, Maaseiah, Kelita, Azariah, Jozabad, Hanan, Pelaiah, the Levites, helped the people to understand the law, while the people remained in their places. 8So they read from the book, from the law [*tôrat*] of God, with interpretation [*mĕpōrāš*].[103] They gave the sense [*śôm śekel*], so that the people understood the reading. 9And Nehemiah, who was the governor, and Ezra the priest and scribe, and the Levites who taught the people said to all the people, 'This day is holy to the LORD your God; do not mourn or weep [*tibkû*].' For all the people wept [*bôkîm*] when they heard the words of the law [*tôrâ*].
>
> Neh. 8:6–9

Ezra-Nehemiah's portrayal of the Israelites returning to Jerusalem as pilgrims[104] might be an inner-biblical allusion between these passages and Psalm 84:

> 4Happy are those who live in your house, ever singing your praise! *Selah* 5Happy are those whose strength is in you, in whose heart are the highways [*mĕsillôt*] to Zion. 6As they go through the valley of Baca [*ha-bākā'*, weeping] they make it a place of springs; the early rain also covers it with pools [blessings / *bĕrākôt*]. 7They go from strength to strength; the God of gods will be seen in Zion.
>
> Ps. 84:4–7

The *first house* in Ezra 3:12 is a reference to the original Temple, where the people wept. In Nehemiah 8, when Ezra brings the Book of Moses to recite, he does so in front of the Water Gate and all the people also wept. Ps. 84:6 describes blessings (*bĕrākôt*), sometimes translated as pools (*bĕrekôt*). The Septuagint translates *bĕrākôt* in this verse into Greek *eulogias* (blessing) instead of pools.[105] Much as Ps. 84:6 does, Qur'an 3:96 uses the terms for weeping (*bakkah*) and also blessed (*mubārakan*). Ezek. 34:25–28 also discusses the security and the blessing of the area,[106] a theme argued to be prominent in Psalm 84[107] and emphasized in Qur'an 3:96–97,

> 25I will make with them a covenant of peace and banish wild animals from the land, so that they may live in the wild and sleep in the woods securely. 26I will make them and the region around my hill a blessing [*bĕrākâ*]; and I will send down the showers in their season; they shall be showers of blessing [*bĕrākâ*]. 27The trees of the field shall yield their fruit, and the earth shall yield its increase. They shall be secure on their soil; and they shall know that I am the LORD, when I break the bars of their yoke, and save them from the hands of those who enslaved them. 28They shall no more be plunder for the nations, nor shall the animals of the land devour them; they shall live in safety, and no one shall make them afraid.
>
> Ezek. 34:25–28

Psalm 84 is understood as a portrayal of pilgrimage to the Temple in Jerusalem.[108] Moreover, Qur'an 3:97 states that people need to go to on pilgrimage to this *first house* in Bakkah whoever is able to find 'a way' (*sabīlā*) to it. This 'way' shows similarity to the highways (*mĕsillôt*) to Zion in Ps. 84:5. The Peshitta translates the Hebrew 'There are highways (*mĕsillôt*) in their heart'[109] to the Aramaic 'Your highways [*šbylyg*] are in his heart.'[110] The intertextuality is that the Qur'an is using the Arabic, *sabīl*, which is the cognate of the term used by the Aramaic text, *šbyl*.[111] There is much intertextuality in the usage of terms and descriptions between this Qur'anic passage and biblical literature; it becomes likely that the Qur'an is engaging with the books of Ezra-Nehemiah, Haggai, and Zechariah or some other text or oral tradition that combines these. Further examples to show the relationship of this Qur'anic passage with the Israelite exile are also proposed in the next section. Therefore, the *ṭaʿām* in Qur'an 3:93 is likely to be understood within such a context as a divine decree or commandment, which would resonate with the audience. The *ṭaʿām* of the man in the desolate town in Qur'an 2:259 holds the dual meaning of food and, metaphorically, the restoration of the Torah, and subsequently, the restoration of the nation of Israel.

The measuring line (ḥebel) *and the fiery furnace*

While biblical scholars divide the Book of Zechariah between chapters 1–8 and 9–14,[112] the partition may not have been apparent to the traditions of the Qur'anic milieu. Therefore, this section does not assume that the Qur'an or existing traditions during Late Antiquity made such a distinction.

Zechariah 2 narrates a vision of a man with a measuring line (*ḥebel*), identified as the line that would measure Jerusalem, and a prophecy that Jerusalem will revive again with a multitude of people, even though it was desolate:[113]

> I looked up and saw a man with a measuring line in his hand [*ḥebel*]. [2]Then I asked, 'Where are you going?' He answered me, 'To measure Jerusalem, to see what is its width and what is its length.' [3]Then the angel who talked with me came forward, and another angel came forward to meet him, [4]and said to him, 'Run, say to that young man: Jerusalem shall be inhabited like villages without walls, because of the multitude of people and animals in it. [5]For I will be a wall of fire all around it, says the Lord, and I will be the glory within it.'
>
> Zech. 2:1–5

This passage in Zechariah of a vision of a man with a measuring line (*ḥebel*) might be a clue to the Qur'anic context of the *first house*. A few verses after the Qur'an states that all *ṭaʿām* was allowed to the Children of Israel, it twice repeats the rope (*ḥabl*) of God, using the same cognate term used in Zechariah for the measuring line.

> And hold fast to the rope [*ḥabl*] of God, all together, and be not divided. Remember the Blessing [*niʿmat*] of God upon you, when you were enemies and He joined your hearts, such that you became brothers [*ikhwānā*] by His Blessing [*bi-niʿmatih*]. You were on the brink of a pit of fire and He delivered you from it.

> Thus does God make clear unto you His signs, that haply you may be rightly guided.
>
> Qur'an 3:103

> They shall be struck with abasement wherever they are come upon, except by means of a rope [*ḥabl*] from God and a rope [*ḥabl*] from people.[114] And they shall earn a burden of wrath from God, and they shall be struck with indigence. That is because they used to disbelieve in God's signs and kill the prophets without right. That is for their having disobeyed and transgressed.
>
> Qur'an 3:112

Immediately following this passage, the Qur'an makes a distinction between the People of the Book, who are not all alike. The use of the term *ḥabl* in these Qur'anic passages is the only time the rope of God is mentioned. Being within the same context with the aforementioned intertextuality on the rebuilding of the Second Temple gives possible credence to further such intertextuality between the rope (*ḥabl*) of God mentioned in these passages and the measuring line (*ḥebel*) of Zechariah to measure Jerusalem and bring it back to life for God to dwell in its midst.

Traditional Qur'anic commentators[115] and also some contemporary scholars interpret the rope (*ḥabl*) of God in the Qur'an as a covenant,[116] which would keep the context of this passage parallel to that of Zechariah. Analysing the term *ḥabl*, Reuven Firestone suggests the possibility – though admittedly not the certainty – that it reflects the notion of a covenant in the Hebrew Bible.[117] Intertextualities between this Qur'anic passage and the idea of a covenant from the Hebrew Bible might actually make such an inference more likely.

Additionally, Qur'an 3:103 speaks of not only a rope (*ḥabl*) but also a brotherhood (*ikhwānā*). This may be compared with the following passage in Zech. 11:14: 'Then I broke my second staff Union [*ha-ḥōbĕlîm*], annulling the brotherhood [*'aḥăwâ*] between Judah and Israel.' The term 'brotherhood' used in this passage in the form *'aḥăwâ* is a *hapax legomenon*. Zech. 11:14 is alluding to the Israelite national unity between the kingdoms of Judah (the southern kingdom) and Israel (the northern kingdom).[118] Solomon, who according to the Israelite tradition built the First Temple, was the last king of the United Monarchy. Traditionally, the division occurred after his death, when the tribes of Judah and Benjamin accepted Rehoboam, the son of Solomon, as their king, while the rest of the Israelite tribes rejected him, leading to what was known as Jeroboam's revolt.[119] After that, the kingdoms of Judah and Israel remained distinct until the destruction of each. According to the biblical account, the kingdom of Israel was destroyed by the Assyrians,[120] and the kingdom of Judah was destroyed by Nebuchadnezzar, the Babylonian, who besieged Jerusalem and destroyed the Temple.[121] Thus, the *ḥōbĕlîm* (union) of *'aḥăwâ* (brotherhood) was broken.[122]

The passage of Zech. 11:14 appears to refer to the Israelites quarrelling amongst themselves after the building of the First Temple, and appears to be an inner-biblical allusion to Ezek. 37:15–28.[123] The significance of this allusion is the broader context of Ezekiel 37, which discusses the valley of dry bones that are resurrected as a reference to the return of the Israelites from exile.

Zech. 11:7 speaks of two different staffs, each one given a name: 'I became the shepherd of the flock doomed to be slaughtered by the sheep traders. And I took two staffs, one I named Favor [*nōʿam*], the other I named Union [*ḥōbĕlîm*]. And I tended the sheep.' God breaks each staff, annulling with it a covenant: 'I took my staff Favor [*nōʿam*], and I broke it, annulling the covenant that I had made with all the peoples' (Zech. 11:10). The first staff, Favor (*nōʿam*), is broken, annulling the covenant made with all the people, and the second staff, Union (*ḥōbĕlîm*), is broken, annulling the covenant made between the brotherhood (*ʾaḥăwâ*) of Judah and Israel. There are three distinct intertextualities between these passages and Qurʾan 3:103: (1) the *ḥabl*, understood as a covenant; (2) the brotherhood (*ikhwānā*); and (3) God's favour (*niʿmatih*). All three terms are found in Zechariah within a single thematic context, the doom of Israel.

While continuing to portray God's wrath against Jerusalem and the Israelites (i.e. Zech. 12:1–3), Zechariah nonetheless continues to provide hope that God's salvation will be at hand.[124] According to Zechariah, God's salvation would come through the tribe of Judah like a blazing fire: 'On that day I will make the clans of Judah like a blazing pot on a pile of wood, like a flaming torch among sheaves; and they shall devour to the right and to the left all the surrounding peoples, while Jerusalem shall again be inhabited in its place, in Jerusalem' (Zech. 12:6).

In showing how the tribe of Judah will be like a blazing fire against its enemies,[125] Zech. 12:6 contrasts with Jer. 5:14, 'Therefore thus says the LORD, the God of hosts: "Because you have spoken this word, I am making my words in your mouth a fire, and this people wood, and the fire shall devour them."'[126] Jeremiah then continues to show how the Israelites will be destroyed by other nations and dispersed (i.e. Jer. 5:15–18, cf. Jer. 8:13).[127] Jer. 5:17 even states that other nations will eat their fig trees, a common theme with Abimelech who saw that his figs were not spoiled, in relation to the similar account in the Qurʾanic narrative. As God's judgement is portrayed as fire against Israel through foreign nations in Jer. 5:14, so is Israel becoming a fire against other nations per Zech. 12:6.

The fire in Zechariah tests the Israelites, which resonates with Ps. 66:10–12,[128] Isa. 48:10[129] and Mal. 3:2–3,[130] as well as many other biblical passages that have been closely analysed by biblical scholar Daniel Frayer-Griggs.[131] In addition, Zechariah continues,

> [8]In the whole land, says the LORD, two-thirds shall be cut off and perish, and one-third shall be left alive. [9]And I will put this third into the fire, refine them as one refines silver, and test them as gold is tested. They will call on my name, and I will answer them. I will say, 'They are my people'; and they will say, 'The LORD is my God.'[132]
>
> Zech. 13:8–9

The portrayal of Israel going through a fiery furnace can also be seen as an allusion to Deut. 4:20:[133] 'But the LORD has taken you and brought you out of the iron furnace, out of Egypt, to become a people of his very own inheritance, as you are this day.'[134] The description of Egypt as having been an iron furnace for the Israelites has parallels in 1 Kgs. 8:51 and Jer. 11:4.[135] Jeremiah 11 depicts the Israelites breaking the covenant, and recounts that though God brought them out of the iron furnace and Egypt, but they still did not hearken to Him or do as commanded. The covenant had established that if they walked in the way of God and did as commanded, they would be given the land flowing with milk and honey that was promised to their fathers.[136]

A representation of God's wrath as a fiery furnace is also seen in Ezekiel:[137]

> 17The word of the LORD came to me: 18Mortal, the house of Israel has become dross to me; all of them, silver,[138] bronze, tin, iron, and lead. In the smelter they have become dross. 19Therefore thus says the Lord GOD: Because you have all become dross, I will gather you into the midst of Jerusalem. 20As one gathers silver, bronze, iron, lead, and tin into a smelter, to blow the fire upon them in order to melt them; so I will gather you in my anger and in my wrath, and I will put you in and melt you. 21I will gather you and blow upon you with the fire of my wrath, and you shall be melted within it. 22As silver is melted in a smelter, so you shall be melted in it; and you shall know that I the LORD have poured out my wrath upon you.
>
> Ezek. 22:17–22

Thus, the Israelites being tested through a fiery furnace, which often alludes to God's covenant, is a recurring theme in the Hebrew Bible.[139] The Hebrew prophets warn the Israelites, asking them to hearken to the words of God, so that they may be saved and will not ignite the wrath of God against them. Similarly, when in Qur'an 3 a warning is made against the People of the Book, notably the Jews, it should not be seen as anti-Jewish, but as the warnings of the Hebrew prophets to the Jews to obey the words of God. This is in contrast to Reynolds's link of Christian anti-Jewish polemic and its relationship with the Qur'an.[140] Reynolds especially discusses the concept that the Qur'an accuses some of the Jews of having falsified their scripture (*taḥrīf*).[141] Yet I have argued that the concept of *taḥrīf* in the Qur'an is an accusation not that some Jews have falsified their scriptures but that they have turned away from them, while the Qur'an calls on Jews to uphold their scriptures instead.[142]

Looking objectively at some of its themes and language, the Hebrew Bible may have elements that, if they appeared in other contexts, would be read as anti-Jewish. However, the denunciations and condemnations are understandably regarded instead as a series of calls for reforms from within the tradition and culture, and when texts such as the New Testament or the Qur'an appear to admonish Jews, it is viewed differently – often as anti-Jewish. The admonitions of Jews within the Qur'an, may in large part (and in detail) be no different from the admonishments of the Israelites by their own prophets as narrated in the Hebrew Bible, but the context colours the reception and opens the door to characterizations of anti-Jewishness. Remember, though, that the Qur'an views itself not as ushering in a new religion but as a call for reform, going back to its Judaeo-Christian roots.[143]

Besides pulling from the Hebrew Bible to reference the covenant and measuring line (*ḥabl*), the staff of unity (*ḥabl*) and favour (*niʿmah*), Qurʾan 3:103 also states that 'You were on the brink of a pit of fire and He delivered you from it.' Given the context established between this passage and the Books of Ezra-Nehemiah, Haggai, and Zechariah, the pit of fire seems to be God's judgement against the Israelites, from which God delivered them. The wrath of God and its association with the breaking of the covenant (*ḥabl*) is clearly seen in Qurʾan 3:112: 'And they shall earn a burden of wrath from God.' This pit of fire in the Qurʾan could be either an allusion to God's judgement against the Israelites while in Egypt and their later salvation through the Exodus, or to the nations fighting against them and the later reestablishment of their nation and the Second Temple once they had repented. 4 Bar. 6:19–25 also references the fiery furnace in the letter Baruch sent to Jeremiah, showing that God delivered the Israelites from the fiery furnaces of Egypt and Babylon, further intertextualizing this imagery with Qurʾan 2:259 and subsequently Qurʾan 3:93.

The divine covenant

The flipside of the fiery furnace is the concept of a divine covenant that also occurs within the context of Qurʾan 2:259 – not just in Qurʾan 3:93–103, which might further suggest a relationship between both Qurʾanic passages. A few verses before Qurʾan 2:259, it discusses some sort of divine covenant calling it *al-ʿurwah al-wuthqā*: 'There is no coercion in religion. Sound judgment has become clear from error. So whosoever disavows false deities and believes in God has grasped the most unfailing handhold [*al-ʿurwah al-wuthqā*], which never breaks. And God is Hearing, Knowing' (Qurʾan 2:256). This unfailing handhold (*al-ʿurwah al-wuthqā*) of Qurʾan 2:256 may be associated with the *ḥabl* (rope) of Qurʾan 3:103 and 3:112.

There are some Muslim traditions, especially expounded by Ibn ʿAsākir (d. 571/1176) suggesting the *ḥabl* (rope) and *al-ʿurwah al-wuthqā* (unfailing handhold) are synonymous,[144] which al-Suyūṭī had referenced in his *al-Durr al-manthūr*.[145] Muḥammad al-Shaʿrāwī (d. 1419/1998) also specifically associates *al-ʿurwah al-wuthqā* (unfailing handhold) of Qurʾan 2:256 with the *ḥabl* (rope) of Qurʾan 3:103.[146] In more recent scholarship, Joseph Lumbard also confirms, 'Discussions of the covenant are also found in the exegetical treatment of Qurʾanic terms such as *ḥabl Allāh* [the rope of God, Q. 3:103, cf. Q. 3:112] and *al-ʿurwah al-wuthqā* [the most unfailing (or the firmest) handhold, Q. 2:256; Q. 31:22], among others.'[147] Some Muslim commentators and modern scholars suggest that this covenant or pact in these Qurʾanic passages specifically denote a pact between God and the Muslims.[148] However, it is apparent that it might be mirroring the concept of the covenant from the Hebrew Bible,[149] suggesting that the Qurʾan is either trying to transpose this concept and repurpose it or suggesting that this pact is perhaps not exclusive between God and the Israelites – and that anyone who chooses to be part of the pact is someone God would choose to forge alliances with.

The Abrahamic covenant or promise made in Genesis 15 includes the promise of both children and land,[150] so the topic of the divine covenant associates the contexts of both Qur'an 2:256–260 and Qur'an 3:93–103. The intertextualities with the covenant in the Hebrew Bible have been shown earlier in this chapter, and will be seen in the next as well. This intertextuality further supports the concept that the Qur'anic text is alluding to these biblical and extrabiblical materials. The man in the desolate town seems an allusion to the destruction of Jerusalem, the exile of the Israelites, and their eventual return and rebuilding.

Conclusion

From the close reading of Qur'an 2:259 and its intertextualities with the Books of Ezra-Nehemiah, Haggai and Jeremiah, along with identifying the narrative to the rich traditions circulating in line with Abimelech of 4 Baruch or Ḥoni the Circle-Drawer of both the Jerusalem and Babylonian Talmud, we may draw certain conclusions from this passage and its allusions. First, we can say that the biblical text, along with the deuterocanonical texts in question, do not identify death with actual death, but with sleep. The intertextualities and intrabiblical allusions portray the death and resurrection as the Israelite return from exile, which further emphasizes its metaphorical sense.[151]

In the Talmud, Ḥoni the Circle-Drawer sees his own grandchild, sees that his donkey had generations of offspring, sees the seeds flowering, and sees his own teachings surviving. It has been suggested that the Talmudic redactor perhaps intended to reflect Ketubot 50 of the Babylonian Talmud, which interprets, 'May you see your children's children! Peace be upon Israel' (Ps. 128:6) in that regeneration through birth guarantees the survivability of Israel.[152] After all, according to Gen. 30:1, a person without children is likened to a dead person, which is also elaborated in the Talmud.[153] Thus, the context of Ḥoni's narrative is that he did not see the dead as truly dead, since they had children and children's children.

In 4 Baruch, death is understood as a metaphor for the destruction of Jerusalem and the Israelites scattered and subdued by other nations due to God's wrath about their iniquity. The resurrection is understood as the Israelites returning to Jerusalem, rebuilding the Temple, and bringing it back to its former glory and beyond, because of a group of Israelites who were diligent in repentance and worked hard for reform.

Since Qur'an 2:259 and its direct context is fully engaging or rearticulating biblical, extrabiblical and rabbinic texts and traditions in regards to the destruction of Jerusalem, the exile and the rebuilding, then the resurrection reference in that passage is also to be understood metaphorically no differently from how it is understood from its subtexts. Additionally, with Qur'an 3:93–103 also making reference to biblical and extrabiblical texts in regards to the Israelite exile, then its association with Qur'an 2:259 is likely – thus building an inner-Qur'anic allusion. Given all this context, the *ṭaʿām* in Qur'an 3:93 becomes more naturally a reference to the Aramaic/Hebrew *ṭeʿem*, meaning decrees and commandments. Accordingly, Qur'an 2:259 perhaps uses it in dual meaning, as food and as a metaphor for the restoration of the Torah and, subsequently, the nation of Israel after the exile. Recall that the figs used as such in Abimelech's story in 4 Baruch and the general metaphorical use of figs in the biblical, extrabiblical, and rabbinic literature.

All this suggests that Qur'an 2:259 does not depict a literal resurrection of bodies leaving their graves, but possibly a physical resurrection of a nation that was destroyed and then rebuilt. The next chapter discusses the subsequent Qur'anic passage (i.e. Qur'an 2:260), which appears to allude to God's covenant with Abraham, promising children and land, and also proposing the identification of the man in Qur'an 2:259 as Abraham, who having no children was as if dead, but at one hundred years of age sired Isaac.

Chapter 7

THE PORTRAYAL OF PHYSICAL RESURRECTION IN QUR᾽AN 2:260

Continuing from the last chapter, this one looks at the second verse of the Qur᾽anic passage (i.e. Qur᾽an 2:260). Closely analysing Qur᾽an 2:259 with its biblical, extrabiblical and rabbinic intertextualities showed that it is highly likely to be a metaphor for the rebuilding of the Israelite nation. It was also shown that the regeneration of the Israelite nation after the exile is part of a prophetic theme about a covenant between God and the Israelites, the breaking of the covenant, and the resurrection (metaphorically speaking) of this covenant, while still keeping open the possibility for a destroyed nation to be rebuilt – physically resurrected.

Qur᾽an 2:260 will also be argued to have a biblical relationship, in particular to the covenant that God makes with Abraham, according to Genesis. Qur᾽an 2:260 narrates Abraham asking God to show him how the dead are resurrected. Then, God asks him to bring four birds, put a piece of them in each hill, and call for them; and they come to Abraham. The act the Qur᾽an depicts that Abraham was supposed to do to prove to him the resurrection of the dead has a relationship with Genesis 15. Abraham, in Genesis 15, appears to complain that he has no children, but God promises him that he will, and makes a covenant with him.[1] This will be a familiar theme, as in Qur᾽an 2:259, resurrection maybe understood as having children, just as the donkey having generations of offspring in Ḥoni the Circle-Drawer's narrative in the Talmud.[2]

Accordingly, the interpretation of Qur᾽an 2:260 continues to be closely associated with Qur᾽an 2:259, in which the topic of resurrection is metaphorical though still physical, but not in the sense of dead bones leaving their graves. In Qur᾽an 2:259, resurrection is the regeneration of the Israelites coming back from exile; in this next verse, it is a promise for Abraham to have children, which is perhaps why the narrative suggests God allowing the Israelite nation to be regenerated after being exiled. Through this promise God has proven to Abraham the power to resurrect, the resurrection of Abraham through his generations of children. Additionally, biblical literature, as will be seen, directly connects the covenant with Abraham, in Genesis 15, with the Israelite exile.

Abraham and the birds

Qurʾan 2:260 recounts the story of Abraham asking about resurrection. The story has similarities to and differences from Genesis 15.[3] In Genesis 15, Abraham complains that he is childless, but God promises Abraham two things: children and land.

In the Qurʾanic account, Abraham wants to know how God gives life to the dead; in Gen. 15:8, Abraham asks to know about the land he will possess. In the Qurʾan, God asks Abraham if he has not believed, and he responds affirmatively that he has; Gen. 15:6 by comparison has Abraham believing God's promise that he will have a son. The centrality of Abraham's belief is paralleled in both narratives. Even though Abraham is said to have believed, he still asked for some sort of sign.

The early church emphasized the role of Abraham's faith in this passage as a way to counter the Jewish emphasis on the law commandments in the rabbinic writings, especially with Abraham's assumed lack of faith in Gen. 15:8.[4] Therefore, as Qurʾan 2:259 is related to Qurʾan 3:93–97, which also emphasizes Abraham's faith, Qurʾan 2:260 might respond to rabbinic writings by emphasizing faith over the law, especially in light of the argued understanding of *ṭaʿām* in Qurʾan 3:93. Later rabbis emphasized Abraham's actions and obedience to commandments over his faith, as rabbinic scholar Norman Cohen states:

> Therefore, even if early traditions did imply that Abraham's righteousness was expressed through his faith alone, it seems that a bit later on the rabbis went out of their way to emphasize that his faith was expressed through action, be it his willingness to sacrifice his son Isaac or, by implication, his fulfilment of the commandment of circumcision. It is in this light that Abraham is brought as the first illustration of R. Nehemiah's principle – he is rewarded because of his faithful action, i.e. his *ʾamanah*.[5]

While later rabbis tried to convey that the meaning of *ʾamanah* as faithful action and not faith alone,[6] the Qurʾanic narrative in Qurʾan 2:259–260 and its conjunction with Qurʾan 3:93–97, appear to interpret it differently. The commandments came later (i.e. Qurʾan 3:93), but faith came first (i.e. Qurʾan 2:260), and it was due to this faith alone that Abraham was counted among the righteous (i.e. Qurʾan 3:95). The Qurʾanic narrative, however, appears to emphasize faith (*īmān*) coming before action, as it also appears in Gen. 15:6, echoing the same concept that Paul stresses in Romans 4,[7] and the early Church Fathers who have argued against the rabbis.[8]

Qurʾan 3:93–97 and Qurʾan 2:259 allude to one another; by extension, Qurʾan 3:93–97 also discusses Abraham's faith, as in Qurʾan 2:260. Qurʾan 3:93 discusses the Torah, arguing that the commandments came later, and within this context, Qur'an 3:64–68 emphasize that Abraham was righteous not because of commandments but because of faith. In this narrative, it appears that the Qurʾan is echoing Romans 4, especially when discussing the promise of the restoration of the nation of Israel and the Temple in Qurʾan 2:259 and Qurʾan 3:93–97,

> [13]For the promise that he would inherit the world did not come to Abraham or to his descendants through the law but through the righteousness of faith. [14]If it is the adherents of the law who are to be the heirs, faith is null and the promise is void. [15]For the law brings wrath; but where there is no law, neither is there violation.
>
> [16]For this reason it depends on faith, in order that the promise may rest on grace and be guaranteed to all his descendants, not only to the adherents of the law but also to those who share the faith of Abraham (for he is the father of all of us, [17]as it is written, 'I have made you the father of many nations') – in the presence of the God in whom he believed, who gives life to the dead [*tou zōopoiountos tous nekrous*] and calls into existence the things that do not exist. [18]Hoping against hope, he believed that he would become 'the father of many nations,' according to what was said, 'So numerous shall your descendants be.' [19]He did not weaken in faith when he considered his own body, which was already as good as dead (for he was about a hundred years old), or when he considered the barrenness [*nekrōsin*/deadness] of Sarah's womb. [20]No distrust made him waver concerning the promise of God, but he grew strong in his faith as he gave glory to God, [21]being fully convinced that God was able to do what he had promised. [22]Therefore it [his faith] 'was reckoned to him as righteousness.' [23]Now the words, 'it was reckoned to him,' were written not for his sake alone, [24]but for ours also. It will be reckoned to us who believe in him who raised Jesus our Lord from the dead, [25]who was handed over to death for our trespasses and was raised for our justification.
>
> Rom. 4:13–25

Evidently, Romans 4 attempts to interpret Genesis 15.[9] Thomas Tobin has argued that Romans 4 fervently asserts the supremacy of the faith of Abraham over the divine commandments that came only through the Torah (Mosaic Law):[10]

> First, righteousness was reckoned to Abraham because of his faith and not because of his observance of the law (Rom 4:1–8); second, righteousness was reckoned to Abraham before Abraham's circumcision (4:9–12); and third, God's promise to Abraham and his 'seed' came through faith, not through the Mosaic Law (4:13–17a). All three points are based on Paul's interpretation of Gen 15:6 and closely related texts. Paul appealed to Abraham in order to show that Abraham was meant to be the father not only of the circumcised but also of the uncircumcised (Rom 4:11–12, 16–17).[11]

The Qur'an very strongly parallels much of the arguments that Romans 4 typically makes, reminding Jews and Christians (the People of the Book) to return and follow the faith of Abraham. Whereas Qur'an 3:93–95 states that divine commandments came through the Torah and not before it, reminding its audience to follow the faith of Abraham, Rom. 4:16 emphasizes that whoever shares the faith of Abraham, even nonadherents of the law, is part of the promise and becomes a spiritual seed of Abraham.[12] With the intertextuality between Romans 4 and both Qur'an 2.259–260 and Qur'an 3:93–95, these passages are strongly contextualized with Genesis 15.

There also seems to be another relationship between Qur'an 2:260 and Rom. 4:17, in which both put Abraham's context of faith with God's power to resurrect the dead. The Qur'anic phraseology echoes that of Rom. 4:17: neither text uses the term for 'resurrection'. Qur'an 2:260 uses the phrase 'show me how you give life to the dead', which parallels Rom. 4:17, 'who gives life to the dead'. The phrase 'and calls into existence the things that do not exist' in Romans has some resemblance with Abraham calling the birds who come forth to him in Qur'an 2:260. The main difference between the Qur'anic narrative and Romans 4 is that though Romans 4 is referring to Genesis 15, it does not discuss the ritual – Qur'an 2:260 does.

Nonetheless, while Genesis 15 does not associate resurrection with Abraham's faith, Rom. 4:17 overtly suggests that the faith of Abraham in Genesis 15 also implicitly includes the belief in resurrection. Nicholas T. Wright states:

> In 4.17 Paul describes Abraham's God in two ways, corresponding exactly to this parallel. Abraham, he says, believed in the God who
>
> (a) raises the dead and
> (b) calls the non-existent things into existence.
>
> I suggest that Paul, in reading Gen. 15, sees these two reflected in Abraham's request and God's promise. Abraham asked God about an actual physical offspring; this is answered by God 'raising the dead', giving life to his and Sarah's 'dead' bodies by giving them a son of their own.[13]

Wright makes a strong case of how Paul's Epistle to the Romans interprets Genesis 15 in view of resurrection, which would resonate with Qur'an 2:260. Even while Genesis 15 is not explicit on death, let alone resurrection, Benjamin Schliesser, in *Abraham's Faith in Romans 4*, emphasizes the metaphorical use of "death" in Romans 4 in light of Genesis 15:

> God's judgement on Abraham's faith has a creative, qualitative-authoritative character already in Gen 15:6 … For Paul now God's judgment encounters Abraham in a state of a fundamental antithesis to God, of ungodliness ([Rom.] 4:5) and nothingness, symbolized through the notion of 'death' (4:17).[14]

Additionally, preceding Romans 4, Rom. 3:30 explicitly states that *God is one* when it speaks of circumcision, which is further deliberated in Rom. 4:9–12. It has been suggested that this appears to be an invocation of the *Shema*ʿ (oneness of God) (i.e. Deut. 6:4).[15] Mark Nanos suggests that the basis of the argument in Romans 3–4 is the supremacy of the *Shema*ʿ over the law, which Abraham believed even before the circumcision,[16] and that the *Shema*ʿ is the overarching theme and argument throughout the Epistle to the Romans.[17] The Qur'an also appears to have invoked the *Shema*ʿ in the throne verse just before Qurʾan 2:259–260, and just prior it discusses the covenant, *al-ʿurwah al-wuthqā*, in Qurʾan 2:256, when stating:

> God, there is no god but He, the Living, the Self-Subsisting [Resurrector] [*al-ḥayy al-qayyūm*]. Neither slumber [*sinah*] overtakes Him nor sleep. Unto Him belongs whatsoever is in the heavens and whatsoever is on the earth. Who is there who may intercede with Him except by His Leave? He knows that which is before them and that which is behind them. And they encompass nothing of His Knowledge, except what He wills. His Seat [throne] embraces the heavens and the earth. Protecting them tires Him not, and He is the Exalted, the Magnificent.
> Qurʾan 2:255

This further acknowledges how Qurʾan 2:260 might be engaging with Romans 4 or a tradition based on it, just as an earlier passage invokes the *Shema*ʿ (oneness of God), similar to Rom. 3:30. The similarity of the opening of Qurʾan 2:255 and Qurʾan 112:1 is also evident, in which the latter has been recognized by some scholars as an indication for the *Shema*ʿ. While most scholars emphasized the use of *aḥad* in Qurʾan 112:1,[18] it must be noted that this verse also defines God as *huwa* (the third person singular masculine pronoun), which resembles the Tetragrammaton *YHWH* of the *Shema*ʿ as well, and is sometimes used in this form in theophoric names.[19] In this case, *huwa* is also defined as God in Qurʾan 2:255. After all, the Peshitta translates the Shemaʿ in Deuteronomy 6:4 as 'Hear O Israel, the Lord our God, the Lord One is He [*hu*].' By introducing God as the Living (*al-ḥayy*) and Self-Subsisting or Resurrector (*al-qayyūm*), Qurʾan 2:255 is put within the context of resurrection; this is itself a phrase frequently found in Jewish liturgy and, perhaps most importantly, in the daily *Shema*ʿ blessing (i.e. *ēl ḥay w-qayām*), which possibly further relates the Throne verse with the *Shema*ʿ.

One of the main themes of the Epistle to the Romans is death and life. Sometimes it speaks of the death and resurrection of Christ, and at other times speaks of it in a metaphorical sense, when contrasting people's death through sin (e.g. Romans 5). Rom. 5:12 elaborates that death came through sin, which is due to the transgression of Adam (i.e. Rom. 5:14). While death came through Adam, life came through Christ (i.e. Rom. 5:17–21). The righteous act of Christ and the faith in Christ in Romans 5 appears to be paralleling Romans 4 on the righteousness and faith of Abraham.[20] The epistle's metaphors are prominent in Rom. 6:1–14, which discusses being dead to sin, but alive to God: 'No longer present your members to sin as instruments of wickedness, but present yourselves to God as those who have been brought from death to life, and present your members to God as instruments of righteousness' (Rom. 6:13). However metaphorical this appears, biblical scholar Menahem Kister suggests that Rom. 5:12–21 appears to parallel some rabbinic texts, specifically the *Sifra*,[21] which appears not to understand this context as spiritual death.[22] Though some scholars have understood death in this context as spiritual death, and while both Hellenistic and Palestinian Judaism have concepts of spiritual death as well,[23] Kister would rather not read spiritual death into Rom.

5:12–21.[24] It is very apparent in the whole context of Romans 5–8 that the notion of death is in tension with various concepts, and not any single concept,[25] as New Testament scholar C. Clifton Black II states:

> Thus in the first fourteen verses of Romans 6 we may detect no fewer than seven related though subtly different conceptions of death: as a physiological event, as associated with sin, as liberation, as a settlement of debt or an atoning sacrifice (according to some exegeses of 6:7), as an occasion for tempered hope, as the impetus for righteous living, and as a tyrannical power.[26]

The metaphorical understanding of death in the Epistle to the Romans is emphasized by the scholar of Christian history Emma Wasserman, in *The Death of the Soul in Romans 7*, where she writes, 'The moral discourse about soul-death is particularly helpful for making sense of Paul's statements to the effect that the believer must "die" to sin, "live" to God, and "put to death" the sinful body.'[27] Wasserman assumes that the Epistle to the Romans was influenced by Hellenistic moral psychology.[28] If the Epistle to the Romans or an exegetical text or oral tradition that uses it was the conduit that passed to Qur᾽an 2:260, then it might not be surprising if the very understanding of a dual natured soul-body was passed along, as well.

Romans 8, for example, is clear that death and resurrection are to be understood in a metaphorical way, where one is spiritually dead in sin and spiritually alive in Christ.[29] Black finds the notion of life and death under great tension in Romans 5–8, between physical and spiritual senses.

> [10]But if Christ is in you, though the body is dead because of sin, the Spirit is life because of righteousness. [11]If the Spirit of him who raised Jesus from the dead dwells in you, he who raised Christ from the dead will give life to your mortal bodies also through his Spirit that dwells in you.
>
> Rom. 8:10–11

The tension in the various meanings of death intended in the Epistle to the Romans has a long history within Christianity. Origen, for example, understands it both figuratively and literally, in which he relates it with the saying in Col. 3:5, 'Put to death, therefore, whatever in you is earthly.'[30] Origen considers the dead in the Epistle to the Romans to be the sinners.[31] Pelagius (d. 418), who after his death was deemed a heretic by the Third Ecumenical Council (Ephesus, 431 ce),[32] interprets 'the dead' in 'life to the dead' in Rom. 4:17 as those who have no children. Giving 'life to the dead [those without children],' in this passage, Pelagius interprets as allowing them to bear children.[33] This meaning may carry some weight for understanding Abraham's situation in seeking to have children in Genesis 15.

Within Muḥammad's own time, his contemporary John Climacus (d. 649 ce), a Christian monk at the Mount Sinai monastery, wrote *The Ladder of Divine Ascent*. His work discusses the monastic and ascetic framework on the art of dying; that is to gift one's mind, soul and body by dying for Christ, to live in Christ.[34] He extensively uses the Epistle to the Romans in his writing when discussing the issue of death.[35] In scholar of early Christianity Jonathan Zecher's reading,

> Climacus, building on traditional ascetic ideas, makes of death a symbolic framework within which to cultivate and communicate the contours of Christian ascetic identity – like the wall of the monastery, it divides by its equivocality those within [the blessed dead] from those without [those perishing]. The *Ladder* highlights the profound importance of understanding practices such as the 'memory of death' and metaphorical deployment of 'death' for interpreting the ideals and tools of Christian asceticism.[36]

Understanding death and life metaphorically in the Epistle to the Romans was customary within the church at the time of Muḥammad. The daily dying exercise, as argued by John Climacus targeting monks at Christian monasteries at the time, resembles the Muslim alleged prophetic tradition (*ḥadīth*) propagated mostly by Sufi scholars that states, 'Die before you die.' If Qur'an 2:255–260 and Qur'an 3:93–103 appear to be engaging with the Epistle to the Romans or a tradition based on it, it would not be unusual for the Qur'an to take life and death from a metaphorical perspective, similar to how some Christian literature and traditions at the time have viewed the text.

As has been argued so far, Qur'an 2:258–260 connects the concept of death and resurrection directly to the exile of the Israelites and the subsequent return from exile. The Qur'an appears to understand it almost exclusively in a metaphorical sense, which makes Qur'an 2:258 clearer in that the topic is not truly about physical death and resurrection of literal bodies from graves. Qur'an 2:258 shows that Abraham tells a person (a supposed king) that God has the power to bring forth death and life, and the person (the supposed king) says that he, too, has such a power. Obviously, it is inconceivable to think that the Qur'an is arguing that the man has the power to resurrect a dead physical body out of its grave. However, from a metaphorical perspective in the context of the destruction of Jerusalem, the exile and the return of the Israelites, and the rebuilding and restoration of Jerusalem, a person can have such power. After all, according to biblical tradition, King Nebuchadnezzar destroyed Jerusalem and exiled the Israelites to Babylon but eventually King Cyrus decreed that the Israelites return and rebuild Jerusalem. Within the context of Qur'an 2:258–260, such an understanding would fit well.

Traditional Muslim exegetes, such as al-Ṭabarī, interpret Qur'an 2:258 as a person (sometimes identified as King Nimrod) arguing with Abraham in that he, also, has the power to bring forth life and death, when Abraham tells him that his God can bring forth life and death.[37] The exegetes claim that the meaning behind it is that if a person intends to kill someone and does not, it is as if he gave them life.[38] However, when taken into the context of the Babylonian exile with the destruction of Jerusalem and its rebuilding in Qur'an 2:259, it would make more sense to understand death and life in such a background, instead.

While Romans 4 associates Genesis 15 with resurrection, the contextual sense of Genesis 15 does not. Though Genesis 15 elaborates on the ritual performed by

Abraham, Romans 4 does not. Qur'an 2:260 contains both resurrection and the ritual, as well as being within the context of the *Shema*ʿ (oneness of God) in Qur'an 2:255, which is evident in Romans 3, but not in the Genesis account. Therefore, it is difficult to discern a subtext for this Qur'anic verse. The Qur'an may be engaging with either, both, or neither. In other words, it might be that the Qur'an understands that Romans 4 engages with Genesis 15 and so it engages and interprets both texts simultaneously. Otherwise, there could be a different text, most likely a Christian text or oral tradition, which is exegetical of Romans 4 and discusses its close relationship with Genesis 15, and this text or oral tradition would be the subtext of the Qur'an.

In the Qur'an, God asks Abraham to bring four birds and to divide them between different hills. In Gen. 15:9–10, God asks Abraham to get a heifer, a she-goat, a ram, a turtledove, and a pigeon. He cut them in half, except for the birds. Although the Qur'anic account seems to provide the reason why Abraham was to divide the birds between different hills – to show how they will come alive – Genesis 15 gives no reason why those animals were required or why such a ritual was to be performed. The term used for cutting is from the Hebrew root *b-t-r*, and is used for a covenant.[39] The only other part of the Hebrew Bible that uses this term for the cut parts of an animal in a similar, covenant-making context is Jer. 34:18–22.

Some scholars have argued that to cut up animals was part of the ancient Near Eastern culture of covenant-making. It symbolizes the curse that would befall any who broke a covenant: they would also be cut in a way similar to the portrayal in Jer. 34:18–22.[40] Yet there is no consensus among scholars that links Genesis 15 with Jeremiah 34, because in Genesis, God is a party to the agreement, and it would be inconceivable to impose a self-curse in the case of God not upholding the terms of the agreement.[41] Nonetheless, whether it is meant as a curse or simply the ratification of a treaty is highly debatable.[42]

Some scholars prefer to divide the passage into two, Gen. 15:1–6 and 15:7–21, which becomes evident due to the mismatch in the day's chronology. Even early Jewish and Christian exegetes[43] tried to explain why it is night in Gen. 15:5 and yet the sun sets in Gen. 15:12.[44] Some have interpreted the former part of the narrative as a promise for a son, while the latter narrative as a promise for land.[45]

Abraham's ritual in Genesis Rabbah

Abraham's ritual in Genesis 15 captured the attention of various rabbis who attempted to explain its symbolism in *Genesis Rabbah*.[46] Redacted sometime around the fifth century,[47] *Genesis Rabbah* cites definitions of certain terms as found in Arabia, suggesting its traditions were in close proximity and some of the rabbis were living there.[48] In the seventh-century milieu of the Qur'an, it is therefore likely that either traditions stemming from *Genesis Rabbah* or the proto-traditions that gave birth to it might have been accessible to the surrounding Jewish communities and perhaps garnered some popularity, as midrashic scholar Burton Visotzky suggests.[49]

Given *Genesis Rabbah*'s wide influence, the way the rabbis have interpreted Genesis 15 might provide us with some insights for why the Qur'an contextualizes the ritual as resurrection from death and how it relates to the Israelite exile, as in Qur'an 2:259. From *Genesis Rabbah*, it is clear that some rabbis understood how this ritual foreshadows later Temple rituals.[50]

The rabbis explain that God shows Abraham three kinds[51] of heifers, three kinds of goats, and three kinds of rams.[52] The three heifers are (1) the one sacrificed on the Day of Atonement, (2) the heifer brought on for unwittingly transgressing any of the precepts (i.e. Lev. 4:13–21), and (3) the heifer whose neck was broken (i.e. Deut. 21:1–9).[53] The three goats are (1) the one sacrificed on festivals, (2) the one sacrificed at New Moon, and (3) the goat brought by an individual as a sin offering for an unintentional sin (i.e. Lev. 4:27–31).[54] The three rams are (1) the guilt-offering of certain obligations (i.e. Lev. 5:15, 14:24, 19:21; Num. 6:12), (2) the guilt-offering of doubt,[55] and (3) the lamb brought by an individual (i.e. Lev. 4:32).[56] The turtledove and the young pigeon are also considered sacrificial but are not divided, because a fowl burnt offering[57] is divided but a fowl sin offering is not.[58] Thus, some rabbis conclude in *Genesis Rabbah* that God shows Abraham all the atoning sacrifices.[59]

Another interpretation offered for the symbolism is that the three heifers allude to Babylonia, which produced three kings, Nebuchadnezzar, Evil-Merodach, and Belshazzar.[60] The three she-goats allude to Media, which produced three kings, as well, Cyrus, Darius, and Ahasuerus.[61] The three rams allude to Greece, which conquered the west, north, and the south except the east.[62] Dan. 8:4 symbolizes a ram charging through these three directions.[63] However, Dan. 8:20–21 explains that the ram with two horns symbolizes the kings of Media and Persia, while the he-goat is the king of Greece.[64] Why some rabbis in *Genesis Rabbah* reverse the symbolism remains unknown. The turtledove and young pigeon refer to Edom, according to this second interpretation.[65] The animals being divided and placed on top of one another shows how the kingdoms will be divided and go against the other, while the birds, symbolizing Israel, are not divided.[66] This interpretation may be the reason why the Qur'anic account implies that the birds were divided: if they symbolize Israel, the Qur'an might consider the nation divided, especially since it is within the context of the exile. Although divided, they did come back together again – and yet the Qur'an is not very explicit as to whether the birds were divided in the sense of being cut. It suggests only that Abraham was to take four birds, bind them together, and leave a part on each hill. These instructions would imply that their bodies are cut, but it leaves open the possibility that each bird was left on a different hill. The Qur'an is even silent as to how many hills there are: two, four, or perhaps even more. If the birds symbolize the nation of Israel, the Qur'an might even be alluding to the four cardinal directions to which the Israelites are scattered in the Diaspora whom God is capable of bringing together.

If one takes Qur'an 2:259–260 as referring to the Jewish Diaspora, then that might also be the reason why there are differences between those verses and their assumed subtexts. Qur'an 2:259 narrates the story of a man who dies for a hundred years, instead of only sixty-six or seventy years, as Abimelech or Ḥoni the Circle-Drawer, respectively, in the extrabibilical and rabbinic traditions. The hundred years might suggest that the man is to be identified with Abraham himself, who had Isaac when he was that age (i.e. Gen. 17:17). After all, the verse immediately preceding it (i.e. Qur'an 2:258) and following it (i.e. Qur'an 2:258) explicitly name Abraham. The rabbis in the Babylonian Talmud also associate the hundred-year-old Abraham with birds:

> 'And it came to pass after these words that God tested Abraham' (Gen. 22:1) What is the meaning of 'after'? Said R. Yohanan in the name of R. Yosé b. Zimra, 'It was after the words of Satan. For it is written "And the child grew and was weaned and Abraham made a great feast the same day that Isaac was weaned" (Gen. 21:8). Said Satan to the Holy One, blessed be He, "Lord of the world, as to this old man, you have shown him grace by giving him the fruit of the womb at *one hundred years*.[67] Now of the entire meal that he has made, he did not have a *single pigeon* or a *single dove* to offer before you."[68] He said to him, "Has he done anything at all except to honor his son? [But] if I were to say to him, 'Sacrifice your son before me,' he would sacrifice him immediately." Forthwith: "And God tested Abraham" (Gen. 22:1).'[69]

Moreover, if Qur'an 2:260 is aware of Romans 4 or some tradition based on it, it is relevant that Rom. 4:19 explicitly mentions Abraham's age when he had Isaac, 'He did not weaken in faith when he considered his own body, which was already as good as dead (for he was about a *hundred years old*),[70] or when he considered the barrenness of Sarah's womb' (Rom. 4:19). Therefore, Abraham is a likely candidate for the man in Qur'an 2:259. Additionally, the Qur'an's discussion in 2:260 of four birds instead of just two, as in Genesis 15, perhaps does not symbolize the two divided nations of Israel but the Jewish Diaspora scattered to the four corners of the earth.

Covenant-making language is also not absent in Qur'an 2:260. Not only is it mentioned within the context of Qur'an 2:256, as cited earlier, but also Qur'an 2:260 uses the phrase *fa-ṣurhunn ilayk* (bind them to you). The root *ṣ-r-r* as binding resonates with covenant-making, giving further support to the possibility that it alludes to Genesis 15. Moreover, the Qur'anic language where Abraham needs to bind them together to him and put a piece on each hill or mountain also resonates with the binding of Isaac (*Akedah*) on Mount Moriah in Genesis 22. The symbolism the Qur'an might be making is how the Israelites are scattered to the four corners of the earth. This would also reverberate with the weekly Torah portion reading for Genesis 15, part of *Parashat Lekh-Lekha* (i.e. Gen. 12:1–17:27), in which the addendum reading (Haftarah) is from Isa. 40:27–41:16, where the chosen offspring of Abraham, Israel, who God calls from the farthest corners of the earth will not be cast off (i.e. Isa. 41:8–9).

Furthermore, the binding of Isaac (*Akedah*) in Genesis 22 is part of the weekly Torah portion reading of *Parashat Vayera* (i.e. Gen. 18:1–22:24), which has an addendum Haftarah of 2 Kgs. 4:1–4:37 that actually narrates how Elisha prophecizes that a childless Shunammite woman will have a son, even though she initially does not believe him, which would resonate with Abraham's promise for a son as well as with Sarah who was barren. However, the Shunammite's son later dies only to be raised up again by Elisha. The binding of Isaac is also about a boy about to be sacrificed only to be saved from death. Thus, the parallelism between the Parashat and the Haftarah are evident, and would possibly bring Qur'an 2:260 in the context of resurrection. This might even suggest that the Qur'an is in conversation with a Jewish community that has a liturgical tradition which includes the weekly Torah portion reading.

A significant part of *Genesis Rabbah*'s interpretation by the rabbis that links Genesis 15 to the Qur'an is the birds of prey that attempt to eat the carcasses. According to R. ʿAzariah, when Abraham drove away the birds of prey which came upon the carcasses, God was hinting to him that when his children become like carcasses without sinews or bones, his virtue will sustain them.[71] The significance of this is that the Qur'anic account has an allusion to some form of resurrection – namely that, even if Abraham's children were corpses, Abraham's merits could still save them, and it is done through their repentance, as symbolized by the offerings discussed earlier.

Nonetheless, the kind of resurrection that *Genesis Rabbah* seems to be writing about is not one that involves bones coming out of their graves. Rather, it is metaphorical for how, though the nations may prey on the sinful Israelites, symbolized as corpses, if the Israelites repent and return to God, God will save them through Abraham, as in resurrecting them. This interpretation by the rabbis is further supported by the following verses in Genesis, in which God tells Abraham that his children will become servants in a stranger's land and that God will bring judgement on the nation whom they served – 'afterward', they will come out with a great possession (i.e. Gen. 15:14).

Genesis 15:17 continues expressing that as the sun set and it became very dark, a smoking furnace and a flaming torch passed through the sacrificial pieces. Speaking in the authority of R. Yoḥanan, Simeon b. Abba interprets this to mean that God shows Abraham hell (*Gehenna*) and the foreign kingdoms which will subdue the Israelites, and shows him the Revelation and the Temple with the promise that if his children dwell with the latter two, they will be saved from the former two.[72] However, if they forgo those, the former two will punish them.[73] Several rabbis in *Genesis Rabbah* continue to portray God as giving Abraham a choice of whether he would rather his children fall into hell (*Gehenna*) or be conquered by foreign kingdoms.[74] Among the rabbis, opinions differed as to what Abraham chose:[75] some say that Abraham chose foreign kingdoms, while others opine that he chose *Gehenna* (hell), but that God chose foreign kingdoms.[76] Others even suggest that Abraham chose that his children would be subdued by foreign kingdoms instead of falling into *Gehenna* (hell), and God approved his choice.[77] Recall the description in the previous chapter of the fiery furnace motif in the different parts of the Hebrew Bible symbolizing the Israelites conquered by foreign kingdoms. Dennis Johnson asserts that the image of trial by fire in the Hebrew Bible starts with Abraham's vision of the torch-furnace in Genesis 15.[78]

After all, Deuteronomy 30 states that if the Israelites repent and keep God's commandments, they will be brought together again after they have been scattered.

It explains (instructs) that God has given them both life and death; if they keep the commandments, they will be granted life. Hence, even if they metaphorically die and their enemies take over, through repentance they may be given life again.

According to R. Joshua, the smoking furnace and the flaming torch passing through these pieces (*gĕzārîm*) also allude to the parting of the Red Sea, a phenomenon for which Ps. 136:13 uses the term *gōzēr*.[79] *Genesis Rabbah* continues by showing the disagreement of the rabbis over the interpretation of God's covenant with Abraham in Gen. 15:18. Some rabbis say that God revealed this world to Abraham but not the next.[80] In other words, God informed Abraham what would happen to the Israelites in this world but not in the next; others opine that God revealed to Abraham both this world and the next.[81] On interpreting *ba-yôm ha-hû* (in that day) in Gen. 15:18, the rabbis disagreed on whether God revealed to Abraham the future *until* that day (i.e. until the Exodus) or *from* that day (i.e. from the Exodus until the Messiah's coming).[82] Either way, the focus of the conclusion is the redemption given to the Israelites.[83]

After God promises Abraham in Genesis 15 that he will bear children, Sarah tells him, 'You see that the lord has prevented me from bearing children; go in to my slave-girl; it may be that I shall obtain children [*ʾibbāne*] by her' (Gen. 16:2). The term *ʾibbāne* used in this passage also means to be built up.[84] On this passage, the following is written in *Genesis Rabbah*:

> It may be that I shall be builded up through her. It was taught: He who has no child is as though he were dead and demolished. As though dead: And she said unto Jacob: Give me children, or else I am dead [Gen. 30:1]. As though demolished: It may be that I shall be builded up through her, and only that which is demolished must be builded up.[85]

When taking Qur'an 2:259–260 together and in context, the first verse speaks of a dead (demolished) city that is revived (built up), and the second verse speaks of a dead man (Abraham) because he has no children given life; thus, the Qur'anic passage discusses the promise of land and children. Rom. 4:17 implies that Genesis 15 has something to do with resurrection and Rom. 4:19 is explicit in interpreting that Abraham's body is as good as dead due to Sarah's womb being dead, which is the term used to symbolize her barrenness.[86] In both instances, the analogy is that they are both demolished and in need of building up.

Additionally, as in Gen. 30:1, where a person without children is described as dead, in this Qur'anic passage Abraham could be entreating to be shown how God will make the dead alive. The response from God is to ask whether Abraham has not yet believed. It appears that God makes a promise to Abraham, but Abraham wants some sort of sign. When intertextualized with the Genesis narrative, Abraham has no children, which is equated with being dead, but God promises him children: he is not dead but alive. Therefore, Abraham asks God for a sign, which is when God asks Abraham to perform the ritual. Thus, once the Qur'anic passage is considered with its possible biblical subtext, it can be seen that the resurrection of the dead implied in the Qur'anic passage is a metaphor for a person with no children having children and not about literal dead bones coming out of their graves. This is emphasized even further in the Talmud:

> 'You shall indeed die'? *The sense of* 'death' *here is* 'poverty,' for a master has said, 'Four classifications of persons are equivalent to corpses, and these are they: the poor man, the blind man, the person afflicted with the skin disease [of Lev. 13], and the person who has no children. The poor man, as it is written: 'for all the men are dead who sought your life' (Ex. 4:19). *Now who were they? This refers to Dathan and Abiram, and they were certainly not then dead*, they had only lost all their money. The blind man, as it is written: 'He has made me dwell in darkness as those that have been long dead' (Lam. 3:6). The person afflicted with the skin disease, as it is written: 'Let her, I pray you, not be as one who is dead' (Num. 12:12). And the person who has no children, as it is written: 'Give me children or else I die' (Gen. 30:1).[87]

The deep sleep (*tardēmâ*) that Abraham undergoes suggests further intertextuality (i.e. Gen. 15:12). Although this deep sleep is not explicitly attested in the Qurʾanic account, it is associated with the Companions of the Cave, which has some phraseology closely related to Qurʾan 2:259. Moreover, this kind of deep sleep is what both Abimelech and Ḥoni the Circle-Drawer undergo for sixty-six and seventy years respectively, as discussed in the previous chapter, further fitting this passage with the whole context.

Israelite exile and restoration in the Qurʾan

Undoubtedly, by now, the reader will wonder why the Qurʾan is interested in engaging with and alluding to materials on the Israelite exile and their return. The answer to this puzzling question might be simpler than it initially seems, which is presented in a list of fourteen points of intertextuality.

First be reminded that Qurʾan 2:259–260 is discussing resurrection. In relation to Jewish understandings of the return of the exiles or the ingathering of the Israelites, the Qurʾan's notion would correspond to the End of Days or, in other words, the Messianic Age. Numerous rabbinic traditions connect the exilic imagery of the Israelites and their ingathering or return with the End of Days; perhaps one of the most prominent is the daily Jewish prayer (ʿAmidah).[88] It would seem very natural for the Qurʾan's Jewish audience to be familiar with the ʿAmidah and its imagery, especially since the same Qurʾanic chapter includes a discourse on the Jewish direction of prayer (*Qiblah* passage), which would have the ʿAmidah in mind, as it is the prayer that the Jews are required to face Jerusalem. The ʿAmidah prayer frequently praises God and God's power to raise the dead (e.g. the second benediction), and frequently petitions for God's forgiveness, mercy, and redemption.[89] This Qurʾanic chapter even ends by glorifying the power of God, reinstating faith, and petitioning God with a prayer for forgiveness, mercy and victory (or redemption) (i.e. Qurʾan 2:284–286).

Second, if Qur᾿an 2:260 uses four birds to symbolize the Israelites scattered to the four corners of the earth and then Abraham calling them to bring them together, then this would also parallel the ʿAmidah's tenth benediction:

> Sound a great Shofar [rams horn of the Messiah], for our freedom, and raise a flag to gather our exiles, and assemble us together quickly from the *four corners* of the earth to our land [of Israel]. Blessed are You, that assembles the displaced of His people, Israel.

The theme of ingathering and redemption is strongly highlighted in both the daily *Shema*ʿ blessings and the ʿAmidah,[90] which would possibly constitute the backdrop of the Qur᾿an's theme in these passages.

Third, if Qur᾿an 2:259 is alluding to the restoration of Jerusalem and the rebuilding of the Temple, then this would parallel the ʿAmidah's fourteenth, fifteenth and seventeenth benedictions, which are prayers for the rebuilding of Jerusalem, the coming of the Messiah, and the restoration of the Temple.[91]

Fourth, if Qur᾿an 2:258–260 uses Abraham as the one who seeks to ensure that the resurrection and restoration of the Israelite nation, then this would parallel the ʿAmidah's first benediction. It recalls the patriarchs, and especially exalting God as the shield (protector) of Abraham, which is an expression only found in Gen. 15:1 in the Hebrew Bible, just before Abraham was asked to make the aforementioned ritual as a sign for God's promise of children and land.[92]

Fifth, it is important to understand that the context of Qur᾿an 2:259–260 is within an overarching imploration of giving charity. This imploration starts before the Throne verse (i.e. Qur᾿an 2:254) urging people to pay charity before a day comes when no business deals would be allowed (implying the Day of Resurrection/Judgement) and it continues in a relatively lengthy discourse immediately after the passage in question (i.e. Qur᾿an 2:261–274). Even Qur᾿an 3:93–115, which has been discussed as alluding to the Israelite exile and the building of the Temple, is preceded with an imploration to give charity (i.e. Qur᾿an 3:91–92) and followed with a warning that riches stored in this world will be worthless (i.e. Qur᾿an 3:116–117). Giving charity is also related to the ʿAmidah in rabbinic traditions. Charity is not only related to prayer in rabbinic literature, but it is also closely related to prayer in the Qur᾿an. Giving alms is almost always associated with prayer in the Qur᾿an.[93]

Qur᾿an 2:261–274 uses the plural term for *ṣadaqah* to refer to charity, which would resonate with its Jewish audience, who also use this term. It might seem a bit strange to discuss resurrection or the return of the Israelite exiles within the context of charity. However, an old Arabic adage says, 'If the reason is known, the strangeness disappears'. If the Qur᾿an expects its audience to keep in mind the ʿAmidah, which is a prayer for resurrection and the return of the Israelite exiles, then its imploration towards charity becomes clear: according to some rabbinic traditions, before one starts to pray, they are to give charity.

For example, the Babylonian Talmud narrates a tradition by R. Dosetai b. R. Yannai, who says that someone who gives a gift to God by giving a coin to the poor will be granted an audience with God, which is what prayer represents.[94] Another narrative from R. Eleazar features his idea of paying a coin to a poor man before praying, in compliance with his interpretation of Ps. 17:15 ('I shall behold your face in righteousness [charity]').[95] Then, the Talmud continues with a tradition by R. Naḥman b. Yitzḥak, who interprets the second half of Ps. 17:15 as a reference to the World-to-Come (Messianic Age / End of Days). Charity is discussed in relation to resurrection.

Sixth, Qurʾan 2:259–260 has been placed within the context of God redeeming the Israelites and returning them from exile within a greater discourse on charity. In the Talmudic discourse on charity, which associates the giving of charity with the ʿAmidah, R. Judah says, 'Great is charity, for it draws redemption nearer', referring to Isa. 56:1.[96] Since charity has the power for redemption,[97] it is perhaps why the Qurʾanic discourse puts it in that context understanding its rabbinic interpretation.

Seventh, while the Israelite redemption seems general, the Qurʾanic passage is very particular about putting it in the context of death and resurrection. The metaphor the Qurʾan uses is death. The Talmud further states that R. Judah was also specific that while ten strong things exist in the world, death is the strongest of all, but charity saves from death, referring to Prov. 10:2. The Qurʾan's emphasis on charity within the context of death and resurrection perhaps alludes to this teaching.

Eighth, on charity, the Talmud then also continues with a tradition by R. Yoḥanan interpreting Prov. 19:17: 'Whoever is kind to the poor lends to the lord.' This passage has some resemblance to a verse in the Qurʾan also preceding the Throne verse: 'Who shall lend unto God a goodly loan, which He will multiply for him many times over? And God withholds and outstretches, and unto Him shall you be returned' (Qurʾan 2:245).

Ninth, this particular tradition's interpretation in the Talmud has parallels with the Qurʾanic passage concerning the day of wrath when riches will be worthless. The interpretation provided by R. Yoḥanan refers to Prov. 10:2 and 11:4, which both have a similar message: that wealth is irrelevant on the day of wrath, but righteousness (charity) delivers from death. Since the phrase on righteousness delivering from death is mentioned twice by both passages, it is interpreted that one of them, which uses the day of wrath (i.e. Prov. 11:4), delivers from hell. According to the tradition, the day of wrath is the day Zeph. 1:15 refers to, which also later states that their silver and gold will not save them on that day (i.e. Zeph. 1:18).[98] This warning is mirrored just before the Throne verse in Qurʾan 2:254, where charity needs to be made before a day comes when no business deal will save anyone. A similar warning is seen in Qurʾan 3:91: even if one would offer the gold that fills the earth, it would not be accepted, a message recurring in Qurʾan 3:116–117.

Tenth, the other righteousness (charity) (i.e. Prov. 10:2) is interpreted as deliverance from unnatural death, which the Talmudic narrative continues to suggest occurs when the giver does not know to whom he is giving and the recipient does not know the giver's identity. Qurʾan 2:264 also warns the uselessness of someone giving charity to boast in front of people, as Qur'an 2:271 is also explicit that while one can give charity in the open, it is still better to do it in secret. Qur'an 2:274, then suggests that both types of charity will be rewarded. As Qur'an 2:264 warns against those who give charity to boast before others, in the Talmud, several rabbis concur that while idolaters may also give charity, they do it for self-aggrandizement and pride instead of sincerity.[99]

Eleventh, Qur'an 2:262–264 emphasizes the importance of not following giving charity with hurtful words. Qur'an 2:263 is specific that saying kind words are even better than giving charity if that generosity is followed by hurtful words. This might also resonate with a Talmudic teaching within the same discourse of giving charity attributed to R. Yitzḥak, who says, 'Anyone who gives a coin to the poor is blessed with six blessings, and anyone who speaks to him in a comforting manner is blessed with eleven.'[100] The emphasis of speaking kindly to the poor is mirrored in both the Talmudic and the Qur'anic discourses, further suggesting the possible Qur'anic engagement with these traditions.

Twelfth, during the relatively lengthy discourse on charity and emphasizing using kind words thereafter, Qur'an 2:269 abruptly speaks of those given wisdom. The logical flow of the passage moves smoothly until one arrives to this sudden change of topic, but then the passage returns to a further discussion of charity immediately thereafter. This does not necessarily suggest that Qur'an 2:269 might have been edited into the passage, as the Babylonian Talmud also includes a similar reference: in the middle of its also relatively lengthy discourse on charity, and also after it emphasizes speaking kindly to the poor, it adds a tradition by R. Yeshua b. Levi saying, 'Whoever is accustomed to do acts of charity gains the merit of having sons who are masters of wisdom, wealth, and lore.'[101] The tradition refers to Prov. 21:21, where wisdom, wealth, and lore correspond to the idea that he who follows after righteousness (charity) and mercy finds life, righteousness, and honour respectively.

Thirteenth, the ʿAmidah emphasizes the power of God as the redeemer of the Israelites. There is no place in its theological construct for a human redeemer. Even in its Messianic motif, God's power is invoked and it is only God who shall provide salvation and redemption. As rabbinic scholar Reuven Kimelman concludes about the ʿAmidah,

> In sum, the Amidah, like the Mishna and the Haggadah, reflects a tannaitic view of redemption that draws upon both prophetic language and perspective in order to present a restorative vision that minimizes human agency while maximizing divine agency.[102]

While this theme is no different in the theological construct of the Qur'an, the Throne verse makes it very clear that no one may even intercede with God without God's own permission (i.e. Qur'an 2:255). More importantly, immediately before Qur'an 2:259–260, the power of God is contrasted with a power of a human king, to emphasize that no power is comparable (i.e. Qur'an 2:258), since God not only gives life to the dead, but also brings the sun from the east.

The Babylonian Talmud narrates a conversation that occurred between Antoninus and the Rabbi redactor, who asks why the sun rises in the east and sets in the west.[103] The response provided is that it does so in obeisance to God, referring to Neh. 9:6. It is worth noting that the referenced verse is a prayer of Ezra's that signifies the power of God, who created everything and gave everything life, and that the host of heaven (including the sun) worship God. Then the passage immediately moves on to discuss God's choosing Abraham and making a covenant with him to give his descendants land. Thereafter, it supplies a brief history of the Israelites from the exodus to the exile and their disobedience, while Ezra beseeches God's forgiveness and redemption. Qur'an 2:258 would therefore be well situated within the broader context of Qur'an 2:259–260, which has been argued to be in conversation with the Israelite exile and their return.

Fourteenth, the Qur'an's engagement on the direction of prayer through the *Qiblah* passages had been shown to emphasize the importance of the *Shema*ʿ and its rabbinic commentary.[104] This would also suggest that the Qur'an might not only be aware of the daily ʿAmidah benedictions recited, but also the daily *Shema*ʿ blessings. Even in the *Shema*ʿ blessings, a prayer for the ingathering of the Israelites from the four corners of the earth and frequent petitions for redemption are made.[105]

Given this web of intertextualities, it would seem very plausible that the Qur'an's reason for using Israelite exilic imagery, their return and redemption to not necessarily simply denote some history but also perhaps a future. As Genesis 15 discusses God's dual promise to Abraham, Qur'an 2:259–260 also presents this promise of land and children. The passage shows that God has the power to bring the dead back to life, which translates into rebuilding a dead and desolate town and for the scattered children of Abraham to strive quickly to return from the four corners of the earth. The passage is within the context of giving charity due to the power of charity in saving people from death.

The use of the ʿAmidah's imagery is not surprising in a chapter aware of the Jewish direction of prayer (*Qiblah* passage). After all, the ʿAmidah, though a prayer for a future, itself is a web of intertextualities that are deeply rooted in the Hebrew Bible, containing passages from Isaiah, Micah, Zephaniah, Jeremiah, Ezekiel, Joel, Malachi and the Psalms.[106] Therefore, it should not be surprising that the Qur'an would be aware not only of the ʿAmidah but also of its content: the resurrection of the dead, the ingathering of the exiles, and perhaps the intertextual style it uses to portray not only a history but also a future. I hope by now the patient reader appreciates that the Qur'anic engagement with the Israelite exile is not as absurd as it might have initially seemed.

Conclusion

The most vivid portrayal of resurrection in the Qur'an (2:259–260) seems to evidently engage with biblical, extrabiblical, and rabbinic material. The context of the biblical, extrabiblical, and rabbinic material in both cases is not a literal understanding of death and resurrection in the sense of bones leaving their graves. The intertextual background of Qur'an 2:260 is seemingly Genesis 15, with its rabbinic commentary and Romans 4. The resonances may not mean that the Qur'an necessarily draws from these texts directly; perhaps it engages them in an indirect manner through secondary texts or oral traditions that in turn concern these materials. The same can be said regarding Qur'an 2:259, in that it does not necessarily engage with the primary sources of either 4 Baruch or the Talmud along with the biblical context of the exile; it may pull from some secondary sources or oral traditions that engage with them or those based on their proto-traditions.

There is a discrepancy of the one hundred years suggested in the Qur'anic account with the years of the exile in the biblical, extrabiblical and rabbinic accounts. It is being proposed that the Qur'an's narrative identifies the man with Abraham, who begat Isaac at one hundred years old. In other words, Qur'an 2:259 signifies the promise of land, and Qur'an 2:260 signifies the promise of children. After all, the passage immediately preceding Qur'an 2:259 and following it explicitly name Abraham. Furthermore, as Qur'an 2:260 shows a possible awareness of Romans 4 or a tradition stemming from it, Rom. 4:19, explicitly mentions Abraham's age of one hundred years when he had Isaac.

Another discrepancy is the four birds instead of two in Genesis 15. The Qur'an appears to use the same motifs of the exile but rearticulates them. Perhaps it even suggests the Israelite Diaspora and the dispersion of the Israelites to all four corners of the earth, especially after the destruction of Jerusalem and the Second Temple in 70 CE, which continued to be the case during the Qur'an's composition. It has been suggested by scholars that the discrepancy of sixty-six years in 4 Baruch might be a reference to the Bar Kokhba revolt in 136 CE, which is sixty-six years after the destruction of the Second Temple.

Furthermore, the Qur'an appears to be aware of Jewish liturgy, such as the daily ʿAmidah prayer and the daily *Shemaʿ* recitation including the possibility of its awareness of the weekly Torah portion readings. This even sheds light on the beliefs and rituals of the Jewish community with whom the Qur'an is in conversation.

Regardless of the exact sources of these stories, the intertextuality between the Qur'anic account with the biblical, extrabiblical, and rabbinic material is palpable. Since the biblical subtext and context are not about physical death and resurrection of bones from their graves but are about the destruction of Jerusalem and the exile along with the return and restoration of Jerusalem and the nation of Israel, then that is how apparently Qur'an 2:259 should be understood. In Qur'an 2:260, the subtext and context both are about Abraham and the ritual he had performed after asking to know about God's promise of bearing children and granting land. While Genesis 15 does not explicitly associate death and life to the context, Romans 4 does so directly. Accordingly, the Qur'an must have been aware either of the Epistle to the Romans or a text or oral tradition that interprets it in its Genesis 15 background.

Given that neither the biblical, extrabiblical and rabbinic subtext nor context is about physical death and resurrection from graves, then the same can be said about Qur'an 2:259–260. The destruction of Jerusalem and its restoration – or even Abraham having children and being gifted land – are not necessarily immaterial, but the death and resurrection described are not imagined as dead bodies leaving their graves in a very vivid manner. The whole concept, though it may have to do with the physical, is a metaphor and, with the given evidence, appears to be distinctively so.

Chapter 8

THE METAPHOR OF PHYSICAL RESURRECTION

This chapter focuses on two other portrayals of death and resurrection in the Qur'an. As the last two chapters concentrated on the most vivid of all portrayals of resurrection in Qur'an 2:259–260, this chapter is devoted to the less intense portrayals of resurrection in the Qur'an, which describe how people shall leave their graves. However, continuing the methodology used throughout, the philological approach and intertextuality with biblical literature are used.

Leaving the grave

The Qur'an explicitly mentions that a dead *nafs* is interred in its grave: '7by the soul and the One Who fashioned it 8and inspired it as to what makes it iniquitous or reverent! 9Indeed, he prospers who purifies it. 10And indeed he fails who buries it [*dassāhā*]'[1] (Qur'an 91:7–10). The root '*d-s-s*' can mean to bury under the ground,[2] as it is also explicitly used in a different verse: 'Shall he keep it in humiliation, or bury it [*yadussuh*] in the dust?' (Qur'an 16:59). The concept of a *nafs* buried in a grave is well attested in the Qur'an. If a *nafs* may be buried in a grave, as in Qur'an 91:10, it may also leave such a grave.

Besides *qubūr*, another term for 'graves' that the Qur'an uses is *ajdāth*, which is cognate to the Hebrew and Aramaic *gedeš*, meaning heap.[3] It is used in the following passage as a reference to a tomb: 'When he[4] is carried to the grave [*qĕbārôt*] a watch is kept over [the] tomb [*gādîš*]' (Job 21:32). Why is the Book of Job referring to a tomb as a *gādîš*? Perhaps because a grave could be described as an earthly mound. However, it might also be due to the Book of Job analogizing a person placed in a grave to a sheaf gathered up in its season, which is attributed to Eliphaz the Temanite:[5]

> 25You shall know also that your descendants will be many, and your offspring like the grass of the earth. 26You shall come to your grave [*qāber*] in ripe old age, like a sheaf [*gādîš*] comes up in its season.[6]
>
> Job 5:25–26

In this passage, a person goes to the grave like a *gādîš* (sheaf) due to having numerous descendants. In the rest of the Hebrew Bible, *gādîš* is used only to mean a stack of sheaves (e.g. Exod. 22:6, Judg. 15:5). This term is rare, appearing only four times in the Hebrew Bible.

The occurrence of the root *j-d-th* in Arabic is also rare, earning it a very short description in *Kitāb al-ʿayn*[7] and *Lisān al-ʿarab* with the definition of grave.[8] It is, however, attested in a pre-Islamic poem attributed to Abū Muzāḥim al-Thumālī (d. 538) as a reference to graves.[9] However, the *Brown-Driver-Briggs Lexicon* (*BDB*) suggests its possible use in Arabic to mean stacking comes from the root *k-d-s*,[10] which means a heap or a stack of things, and it does take on various morphological forms.[11] Accordingly, both *k-d-s* and *j-d-th* might share the same etymology.[12]

The Qur'an uses *j-d-th* three times, in the following contexts:

> [49]They await nothing but a single cry that will seize them while they dispute among themselves, [50]and then they can make no bequest, nor return to their people. [51]And the trumpet will be blown. Then, behold, they will *yansilūn* from their *ajdāth* (tombs) unto their Lord. [52]They will say, 'Oh, woe unto us! Who has raised us [*baʿathnā*] from our place of sleep [*marqadinā*]?' 'This is that which the Compassionate did promise; and the message bearers spoke true.' [53]There shall be but a single cry. Then, behold, they will all be arraigned before Us! [54]This Day no soul [*nafs*] will be wronged in any way, and you will not be recompensed, except for that which you used to do.
>
> Qur'an 36:49–54

> [4]Indeed reports have come to them wherein is a reproof, [5]conclusive wisdom, but the warnings availed not. [6]So turn away from them on the Day wherein the caller will call unto a terrible thing. [7]With their eyes humbled they emerge from the *ajdāth* [tombs] as if they were scattered locusts, [8]scrambling toward the caller. The disbelievers say, 'This is a calamitous day.'
>
> Qur'an 54:4–8

> [42]So leave them to indulge in idle talk and play until they meet the Day that they are promised, [43]a day when they come forth from their *ajdāth* [tombs], hastening as if racing to a goal, [44]their eyes humbled, abasement overcoming them. That is the Day they have been promised.
>
> Qur'an 70:42–44

These passages put the term in the context of what appears to be resurrection. The first passage (i.e. Qur'an 36:49–54) seems to suggest that the *nafs* is resurrected from some sort of soul-sleep, as in sleep/death relationship. Nonetheless, the passage describes how, when leaving the *ajdāth* (tombs), they are *yansilūn*. This term, though traditionally understood as rushing out, also means to produce offspring,[13] and is defined as such in the Qur'an (e.g. Qur'an 2:205, 32:8). Keeping in mind how Job 5:25–26 contextualizes the term *gādîš* with having numerous descendants, Qur'an 36:51 fits right in. Resurrection in Qur'an 2:260 was shown to be an allusion to Abraham having numerous descendants. The Arabic root *n-s-l* is cognate to the Hebrew *n-š-l*, meaning to drop off, to draw off, or to clear away,[14] and is also related to the Arabic *n-sh-l*.[15] The Hebrew Bible sometimes uses this root in the context of driving people out from a land, such as when God promises the Israelites that they will drive away the nations from the land He promised they will possess (e.g. Deut. 7:1, 7:22) or when the Israelites were themselves driven out (i.e. 2 Kgs. 16:6). The root meaning of dropping off is probably what gave rise to the meaning of descendants in the Arabic form of *nasl*.

Both Qur'an 2:259 and 2:260 used death and resurrection as a metaphor for the indirect meanings of the root *n-s-l*, with the former concerning the relationship between death and resurrection with the concept of driving away a nation and bringing them back and the latter associating death and resurrection with the concept of descendants.

Qur'an 32:7–22, uses certain keywords – *n-s-l* (progeny), death, *nafs*, and the comparison between believers and nonbelievers – that also appear in Qur'an 35:19–22. First, Qur'an 32:7–9 seems to talk about human physical creation from earth, his progeny's (*nasl*) physical creation from fluid; only then is the human formed and given a spirit and life. Accordingly, it appears that the human's progeny existed even before the human was formed and given life.[16] This may appear paradoxical, but perhaps the Qur'an distinguishes between creation (*khalq*) and being (*takwīn*), especially when it concerns humans.[17] The passage also moves in parallel with the concept that physical life is not to be equated with a spiritual one, or that of the *nafs*.

Second, Qur'an 32:11, like many others in the Qur'an that concern resurrection, states that people will be returned to their Lord. Returning implies being there in the first place. There is no evidence from the Qur'an that the human was physically present with God before this life. However, there is the assertion that God blows or breathes into the human, as shown in this same passage. Perhaps this breath returns to whence it came. The physical body made from earth or the progeny made from fluid was not with God and thus unable to return to God. Accordingly, it seems more likely that the *nafs* is what returns, perhaps like the biblical passage 'and the dust returns to the earth as it was, and the breath [spirit/*rûaḥ*] returns to God who gave it' (Qoh. 12:7), as discussed in Chapter 2.

Third, the term *nafs* is used twice (i.e. Qur'an 32:13, 32:17), reinforcing its centrality among the passage's concerns; and if the *nafs* is disembodied, then the passage necessarily cannot be describing physical resurrection. As in other passages regarding the *ajdāth* (tombs), and Qur'anic eschatological passages in general, a trumpet, a call or a scream (*ṣayḥah*) is sounded on the Day of Resurrection, which will cause the dead to live. This recalls that the dead do not hear and no one except God would make them hear, as in Qur'an 35:22: 'Not equal are the living and the dead. Truly God causes whomsoever He will to hear, but you can not cause those in graves to hear.' However, those described as dead in Qur'an 35:22 are not physically dead; they are the nonbelievers or the spiritually dead. In this Qur'anic context, they are the ones who cannot hear, just as the Qur'an describes nonbelievers having deafness (*waqr*) in their ears (e.g. Qur'an 6:25, 17:46, 18:57, 31:7, 41:5, 41:44). They are described as spiritually deaf, not physically.

With all these passages placed into one context, God emerges as the one who will cause them to hear the trumpet, the call or the scream (*ṣayḥah*). The *ajdāth* are possibly the bodily graves of the souls, as is further exemplified in the following passage:

> 42 So leave them to indulge in idle talk and play until they meet the Day that they are promised, 43 a day when they come forth from their *ajdāth* [tombs], hastening as if racing to a goal, 44 their eyes humbled, abasement overcoming them. That is the Day they have been promised.
>
> Qur'an 70:42–44

This passage shows that the idle talk and play will continue until the promised day when they emerge from the *ajdāth* (tombs), with a phraseology similar to Qur'an 43:83. It does not say that the idle talk and play will continue until they are interred into the *ajdāth* (tombs), but until they emerge. Since being physically dead in the grave means that they will not be able to have idle talk and play, one could then infer that the idle talk and play will stop with some form of spiritual resurrection; Ibn ʿArabī describes it as when the *nafs* emerges from its bodily grave.[18] Therefore, the Qur'anic passages involving the *ajdāth* (tombs) are possibly no different in their context and intertextuality from those that involve the *qubūr* (graves) discussed earlier, which is possibly spiritual death, not necessarily physical.

Spiritual death

When Ibn ʿArabī interprets Qur'an 2:259–260 spiritually, in that the death it addresses is ignorance,[19] he relates the passage with the following verse:

> How can you disbelieve in God, seeing that you were dead and He gave you life; then He causes you to die; then He gives you life; then unto Him shall you be returned?
>
> Qur'an 2:28

This verse shows that there are two deaths and two lives, also resembling the following passage:

> They will say, 'Our Lord, You have caused us to die twice over, and given us life twice over; so we admit our sins. Is there any way out?'
>
> Qur'an 40:11

Traditional commentators, and even Ibn ʿArabī, interpret the *first death* as the human sperm phase and the first life as a living foetus; the *second death* is the natural death and the second life is resurrection.[20] However, when asked how long he has stayed, the man in Qur'an 2:259 whom God causes to die for a hundred years answers, 'for a day or part of a day'. This specific statement provides allusions to other parts of the Qur'an (e.g. Qur'an 10:45, 23:113, 46:35, 79:46). It is necessary to evaluate them in their context. The context for Qur'an 10:45 is the following:

> [42]And among them are those who listen to you. But do you make the deaf to hear, though they understand not? [43]And among them are those who look at you. But could you guide the blind, though they see not? [44]Truly God does not wrong [*yaẓlim*/darken] human beings in the least, but rather human beings wrong [*yaẓlimūn*/darken] themselves [*anfusahum*]. [45]On the Day when He shall gather them, it will be as if they tarried but an hour of the day, acquainting themselves with one another. Lost indeed are those who denied the meeting with God, and they were not rightly guided. [46]Whether We show you a part of that which We promise them, or We take you [*natawaffayannaka*/cause you to die], their return shall be unto Us. Then God is Witness over that which they do.
>
> Qur'an 10:42–46

There is perhaps an inner-Qur'anic allusion between these passages and Qur'an 27:80–81, 30:52–53, and 35:19–22. The commonality between them is that they seem to show that those who do not believe are spiritually blind, spiritually deaf, and spiritually dead – motifs that are recurrent throughout the Qur'an.[21] The term *ẓulm* in Qur'an 10:44 is used to mean that God does not wrong people; rather, their *nafs* is what wrongs them. *Ẓulm* is polysemous, as it is related to *ẓalām* and *ẓulumāt*, which mean darkness.[22] This may perhaps signify the spiritual darkness that dead souls would be bound, in contrast to those whom God gives life and light (i.e. Qur'an 6:122). Qur'an 10:45 even ends by suggesting those who are spiritually dead are misguided. Nonetheless, if Qur'an 10:41–46 have inner-Qur'anic allusions with passages that speak of spiritual death, then perhaps those verses are themselves referring to spiritual death.

Take Qur'an 46:35 in its context:

> [25]destroying everything by the Command of its Lord. They became such that nothing was seen but their dwellings. Thus do We recompense the guilty people. [26]Indeed We established them in a manner in which We did not establish you, and We endowed them with hearing, sight, and hearts. But their hearing, sight, and hearts availed them nothing, since they rejected God's signs, and that which they used to mock beset them. [27]And indeed We destroyed the towns around you, and We vary the signs that haply they might return. [28]Why, then, did they – whom they had taken as gods apart from God and as a means of drawing nigh [unto God] – not help them? Nay, they forsook them. That was their perversion and that which they used to fabricate. [29]And [remember] when We made a group of jinn incline unto you, listening to the Quran, when in its presence they said, 'Hearken!' Then when it came to an end, they went back to their people as warners. [30]They said, 'O our people! Truly we have heard a Book sent down after Moses, confirming that which came before it, guiding to the truth and to a straight road. [31]O our people! Answer God's caller and believe in him, then He will forgive you some of your sins and protect you from a painful punishment.

> [32]And whosoever does not answer God's caller thwarts not on earth and has no protectors apart from Him – they are in manifest error.' [33]Have they not considered that God, Who created the heavens and the earth and did not weary in their creation, is able to give life to the dead? Yea! He is Powerful over all things. [34]On the day when those who disbelieve are exposed to the Fire: 'Is this not true?' They will say, 'Yea, by our Lord!' He will reply, 'Taste the punishment for having disbelieved.' [35]So be patient, as the resolute among the messengers were patient. And seek not to hasten for them. It shall be for them, on the day when they see that which they are promised, as though they had tarried nothing but an hour of a day. A proclamation! Will any but the iniquitous people be destroyed?
>
> Qur'an 46:25–35

Qur'an 46:25 and 46:27 talk of desolate cities, not unlike the desolate town of Qur'an 2:259. Those who are spiritually deaf and spiritually blind figure in Qur'an 46:26; Qur'an 46:28 and 46:32 speak of misguidance. Then Qur'an 46:33 goes on to speak of God giving life to the dead. Here again, the context refers perhaps to those who are spiritually dead and their resurrection. Najm-ul-dīn al-Kubrā (Aḥmad b. ʿUmar) (d. 618/1221), in his *al-Taʾwīlāt al-najmiyyah fil-tafsīr al-ishārī al-ṣūfī*, interpreted death and resurrection in this passage as spiritual.[23]

Analysis now turns to a contextualized Qur'an 79:46 – 'The Day they see it, it will be as if they had tarried but an evening or the morning thereof' – especially since it uses an analogy similar to the one found in Qur'an 2:259, where people appear to have only remained a part of a day. The *saʿā* (strove) of Qur'an 79:35 can also be related to the *saʿyā* (come) similar to Qur'an 2:260. Taking a look at the inner-Qur'anic allusion between Qur'an 79 and Qur'an 102,

> [36]and Hellfire [*al-jaḥīm*] is made visible for one who sees—[37]as for one who rebels [38]and prefers the life of this world, [39]truly Hellfire [*al-jaḥīm*] is the refuge.
>
> Qur'an 79:36–39

Qur'an 79:36 states that *al-jaḥīm* (hellfire) will be exposed to those who see, which implies the inverse: those who do not see, hellfire would not be displayed to them. Al-Rāzī acknowledged a trivial debate among exegetes of what it means 'for one who sees' in this verse, but none of the interpretations took it metaphorically.[24] However, Ibn ʿArabī interprets it in a way that believers, who will have no veils on their hearts, would see hellfire (*jaḥīm*) and know it, while nonbelievers will burn in it.[25] This suggests that nonbelievers may even be unaware of the hellfire (*jaḥīm*) that consumes them because they do not recognize it.

The question here is who *are* those who see? According to Qur'an 102:5–7, those who know certainty (*ʿilm al-yaqīn*) will see *al-jaḥīm* (hellfire). By associating the *yaqīn* (certainty) in this verse with the one in Qur'an 15:99,[26] al-Rāzī suggests that those who do not know certainty are perhaps those who are spiritually blind and cannot see *al-jaḥīm* (hellfire). Qur'an 102 might be talking of those who are spiritually dead; perhaps Qur'an 79:38–39 suggests that the life of this world is in itself *al-jaḥīm* (hellfire), but people do not see it or recognize it because they are spiritually blind. There is a likelihood that the Qur'an is describing the life of this world as hell (*al-jaḥīm*), but people are spiritually blind, not knowing its true reality (*'ilm al-yaqīn*). Perhaps the Qur'an is describing the soul as dead in hell. This issue of souls veiled from knowing reality is detailed in al-Ghazālī's *Mishkāt al-anwār* (*The Niche of Lights*).[27] The suggestion that there are people who perhaps do not see *al-jaḥīm* (hellfire) appears elsewhere too:

> [51]One among them will say, 'I had a companion [52]who would say, "Are you among those who confirm? [53]What! When we have died and are dust and bones, are we to be requited?"' [54]He will say, 'Will you look?' [55]So he will look and see him in the midst of Hellfire [*al-jaḥīm*].
>
> Qur'an 37:51–55

Qur'an 79:11–14 seems to elaborate further about the bones returning, which is described in Qur'an 37:53.

> [11]'What! When we have become decayed bones?' [12]They say, 'This, then, would be a ruinous return!' [13]Yet it shall be but a single cry, [14]then, behold, they will be upon a wide expanse.
>
> Qur'an 79:11–14

The bones could be returning as God created them initially, through birth. If Qur'an 21:104 suggests that God can duplicate creation, just as it was the first time, then the resurrection of Qur'an 79:11–14 may also take the form of a reprisal.

As there seems to be two kinds of death and two kinds of life in the Qur'an – spiritual and physical – each kind of death perhaps has its own type of resurrection. The physical death of the body is perhaps returned in the same manner as it was created the first time, through rebirth to remain suffering in hell, as described in the following passage:

> Those who disbelieve in Our signs, We shall surely cause them to burn in a Fire. As often as their skins [*julūduhum*] are consumed, We shall replace them with other skins [*julūdan*], that they may taste the punishment. Truly God is Mighty, Wise.
>
> Qur'an 4:56

This passage has frequently been used in some Ismā'īlī and Ahl-i-Ḥaqq *ta'wīl* (interpretation) as proof of metempsychosis.[28] This passage is talking about the physical aspect by referring to skin (*julūd*), and not the *nafs*. When their skins (bodies) wither away, they are given other skins (bodies).

After Qur'an 45:24 describes the '*dahr*', as discussed earlier, the passage later continues with a noteworthy ambiguity that might suggest a concept of karmic reincarnation, where people are judged by their deeds and may be unable to leave this world:

> [34]And it will be said, 'Today We forget you [*nansākum*] just as you forgot [*nasītum*] the meeting with this your Day; your refuge is the Fire and you have no helpers. [35]That is because you took the signs of God in mockery and the life of this world [*al-ḥayāt al-dunyā*] has deluded you.' So today they will not be removed from it [*minhā*]; nor can they make amends.
>
> Qur'an 45:34–35

The main question in this passage is to understand what that final 'it' refers to – the Arabic singular third-person feminine pronominal suffix *-hā* in *minhā*. Typically, it is taken as referring to the fire (*al-nār*) in the preceding verse.[29] However, there is nothing grammatically that would preclude reading 'it' as the worldly life (*al-ḥayāt al-dunyā*) mentioned within the same verse, which might be a description of hell. Since the worldly life (*al-ḥayāt al-dunyā*) appears in the immediate context, one might think this would be the most obvious reference for this pronominal suffix. Considering that possibility, the Qur'an would explicitly be saying that they will not be removed from this worldly life. Accordingly, this could hint as reincarnation, and perhaps the Qur'an is alluding to this life as the fire (*al-nār*) – or, in other words, hell. This is especially the case when one contextualizes this passage with *al-dahr* in Qur'an 45:24, which, as discussed in Chapter 1, some Muslim scholars have interpreted as a reference to some form of reincarnation.[30]

Conclusion

The Qur'anic portrayal of people leaving their tombs has been shown to have a possible spiritual connotation rather than simply physical. Qur'an 70:42–44 appears to be the most explicit in the sense that it leaves nonbelievers to their idle talk and play until the day they emerge from their tombs (*ajdāth*). The Qur'an appears to show that the idle pursuits continue as nonbelievers are in their graves; when taken into the full context of the Qur'an's consistent portrayal of nonbelievers as dead in their graves (e.g. Qur'an 35:22), as discussed in the previous chapters, then the emergence from these graves is likely a metaphor, as well. The repeated connection of nonbelievers and the grave-bound dead suggests strongly that the portrayal of resurrection is also metaphorical. Accordingly, one would naturally conclude that the Qur'an assumes two types of life and death: the physical and the spiritual, each with its form of resurrection. For the physically dead, the Qur'an frequently uses the analogy that resurrection could be performed the same way it was created the first time (re-creation or rebirth), as discussed in Chapter 5. However, the Qur'an appears to be more concerned with spiritual death, and therefore spiritual resurrection, when the dead soul (*nafs*) emerges from its grave – although that may be the physical grave of the body, which is made of earth.

Chapter 9

THE RED COW AND BRINGING BACK THE DEAD

Amid the vivid portrayals of resurrection in the Qurʾan, another, subtler depiction of bringing back the dead illuminates the theme. It is the ritual of the red cow, in which the Qurʾan alludes to a biblical rite that the Qurʾan describes for its ability to bring back the dead.

The biblical account of the ritual of the red cow is a paradox par excellence.[1] Its absurdity has perplexed Jewish communities throughout history. The ritual is for purification, where those defiled by a dead corpse would be purified. However, the priests and everyone who performs the ritual, themselves being pure, become defiled in the process. The same water that defiled the pure is also used to purify the defiled. While the defilement occurs because of a corpse, another corpse (the sacrificed red cow) reinstates purity. Therefore, if the Qurʾan suggests that the Israelites asked Moses if he is mocking them, could they truly be blamed? 'And when Moses said to his people, "God commands you to slaughter a cow [*baqarah*]," they said, "Do you take us in mockery?" He said, "I seek refuge in God from being among the ignorant"' (Qurʾan 2:67).

Accordingly, this chapter looks closely into how the Qurʾan understands this ritual paradox, especially in the context of resurrection. The Qurʾan frequently uses antithesis as a rhetorical style, including something and its opposite arising from one another. For example, God brings out the dead from the living and the living from the dead (e.g. Qurʾan 6:95, 10:31, 30:19). Other examples include bringing the night from the day and the day from the night (e.g. Qurʾan 22:61, 31:29, 35:13, 57:6) and God is described in the same verse as severe in punishment but yet most merciful (e.g. Qurʾan 5:98). In Arabic rhetoric, this is known as *muqābalah* or *ṭibāq* (antithesis). It appears that much of the logic and reasoning used by Jewish communities has been highly influenced by Greek philosophy, especially in Hellenistic Judaism,[2] after which much rabbinic literature was styled. The same may be said for the flourishing field of Qurʾanic rhetorical studies.[3] Classical Muslims also used Greek philosophy in their theological discourses.[4] Of course, that does not mean that Jewish philosophy is Greek, but that the Hellenistic influence has played a role in reshaping Jewish philosophy throughout history; the Talmudic context has become an amalgamation of both.[5] Nonetheless, Jewish logic and rationale maintained its distinction from Greek logic,[6] but traces do appear and, as Rivka Ulmer describes it, 'This influence may have been so significant that the phenomenon of evolving rabbinic Judaism found its distinctive expression only after it had come into contact with Hellenistic culture.'[7]

The reason that the influence of Greek logic might have been a problem for understanding apparent paradoxes, whether in the Bible, like the ritual of the red cow, or in the Qurʾan, is that when and where a particular ritual was created, Greek logic played no role. Hence, the apparent paradoxes surface when applying Hellenistic methods. There is a possibility that a different kind of logic existed in the Near East, in which these paradoxes would make rational sense. For example, Indian and Buddhist logic contain a concept known as the *catuṣkoṭi*, granting a statement four possibilities: it can be true, it can be false, it can be true and false simultaneously, or it can be neither true nor false concurrently[8] – and, in some variants of this logic in Buddhism, another possibility is none of the above.[9] The Chinese logic of uniting the opposites, as found in Taoism, is also another philosophical alternative.[10] The assumption cannot be that early Judaism or Qurʾanic philosophy during the time of Muḥammad used these specific types of oriental philosophies, but Near Eastern logic could easily have been very different from Hellenistic. Greek logic would not have been and should not be the default logic either tradition had used. Actually, Ernest Horton Jr. has pointed out how Qoheleth's use of opposites and their union is distinct in its logic, being neither Greek nor Far Eastern.[11] Consequently, the apparent paradox in these texts might not have been paradoxical at all in the philosophical logic and reasoning initially intended and applied.

The description of the red cow

The Qurʾanic narrative of the cow appears to have similarities to the red cow in Numbers 19 and the cow whose neck is broken (i.e. Deuteronomy 21). This, however, should not be too surprising, as *Midrash Tanḥuma* also discusses both together, along with the red cow's relationship to the golden calf, which the Qurʾan discusses before the cow narrative.[12]

While the red cow ritual is biblically described to purify a person from being contaminated by a dead corpse, the Qurʾanic narrative situates it with some kind of resurrection, 'We said, "Strike him with part of it [presumably the cow]." Thus does God give life to the dead and show you His signs, that haply you may understand' (Qurʾan 2:73).

In Deut. 21:1–9, the term *ʿeglâ* is used for the atonement of an unsolved murder, a narrative possibly referenced in the Qurʾan by some interpretations. Deuteronomy's narrative is mainly a ritual for the atonement of an unsolved murder,[13] while the Qurʾan's narrative appears to be somewhat unspecific, and the cow with a specific colour may not necessarily be confused with the one required for murder:

> 67 And when Moses said to his people, 'God commands you to slaughter a cow [*baqarah*],' they said, 'Do you take us in mockery?' He said, 'I seek refuge in God from being among the ignorant.' 68 They said, 'Call upon your Lord for us, that He

> may clarify for us what she is.' He said, 'He says she is a cow [*baqarah*] neither old nor young,[14] middling between them: so do what you are commanded.' [69]They said, 'Call upon your Lord for us, that He may clarify for us what her colour is.' He said, 'He says she is a yellow cow [*baqarah*]. Bright is her colour, pleasing the onlookers.' [70]They said, 'Pray for us to your Lord, that He may clarify for us what she is. Cows [*al-baqar*] are much alike to us, and if God will we will surely be guided.' [71]He said, 'He says she is a cow [*baqarah*] not broken to plow the earth or to water the tillage, sound and without blemish.' They said, 'Now you have brought *al-ḥaqq*.' So they slaughtered her, but they almost did not. [72]And when you slew a soul and cast the blame upon one another regarding it – and God is the discloser of what you were concealing – [73]We said, 'Strike him with part of it.' Thus does God give life to the dead and show you His signs, that haply you may understand.
>
> Qur'an 2:67–73

Although Deuteronomy's narrative typically uses *ʿeglâ* for the cow upon first description, it elsewhere uses the term *ʿeglat bāqār*, while the Qur'an uses only *baqarah*. Its root, *b-q-r*, has various meanings, including: to investigate or to seek,[15] which is also attested in Ezekiel:

> As a shepherd[16] seeks out [*baqqārat*] his flock[17] when he is among his scattered sheep, so will I seek out [*ăbaqqēr*] my sheep. I will rescue them from all the places to which they have been scattered on a day of clouds and thick darkness.
>
> Ezek. 34:12

From the same root, the meaning to inquire or to meditate is also attested in other parts of the Hebrew Bible (e.g. Lev. 13:36, 27:33; Ps. 27:4; 2 Kgs. 16:15). The *Theological Dictionary of the Old Testament* (*TDOT*) suggests that this root is distinct from the root that means cattle or herd.[18] Nonetheless, the Arabic root *b-q-r* also has instances where it means 'to investigate' and 'to seek', such as with knowledge.[19] This meaning gives the fifth Shīʿī *imām* his nickname al-Imām Muḥammad al-Bāqir (the knowledgeable).[20] The Arabic term also means 'to dig deep',[21] which perhaps evolved into 'to investigate'. Furthermore, the meaning of cattle or herd, not necessarily specific to a cow, is also used in Hebrew, Aramaic[22] and Arabic.[23] Although Deut. 21:1–9 speaks of a cow to be sacrificed as atonement for an unsolved murder, another cow of a specific red colour is found in the purification laws in Numbers 19.

The descriptions of the cow in Numbers' purification laws and in Deuteronomy's unsolved murder are similar enough to put them in conversation but different enough to note. Numbers adds the colour of the cow as *ʾădummâ* (red), while the Qur'an uses the term *ṣafrāʾ*. Although the term *ṣafrāʾ* is typically understood as yellow, it is not necessarily so. The Arabic term *ṣafrāʾ* is somewhat ambiguous, as it could also mean black.[24] Nonetheless, the colour of gold and saffron is also described as *ṣafrāʾ*,[25] which can be yellowish or reddish for saffron – keep in mind that the etymology of saffron is related to that of the colour, *ṣafrāʾ*. The term *ṣāpār* in Aramaic is also the early morning light,[26] which would be reddish-yellow.

Therefore, the colour descriptions of the cow in Numbers and the Qur'an should not necessarily be seen as distinct from one another.[27]

In Saadia Gaon's (d. 942 CE) Arabic translation of the Bible, he uses the Qur'anic term *ṣafrā'* in his translation of the red cow's colour. Assuming that Saadia should have been able to distinguish between the yellow and red colours in Arabic, David Freidenreich considers his biblical translation to have been influenced by the Qur'anic narrative.[28] Freidenreich quotes Joseph Qafiḥ's argument that Saadia understood the word *ṣafrā'* as the yellowish-brown colour of cows that occurs naturally, as a blood-like red colour is unnatural, and Saadia assumes the commands can only be for naturally occurring things.[29] Freidenreich argues that Saadia's choice of the Arabic term is due to how Muslims understood this term in the Qur'an, putting it on the spectrum between yellowness and blackness, and that the intended meaning that Saadia understood is black,[30] although I find it very unlikely, as it would go against the Mishnaic requirement that if it has as many as two black hairs, it would be rendered unfit.[31] I think it is more likely that Saadia might have understood *ṣafrā'* as brown, instead. If Freidenreich argues that the Arabic terms for yellow and red should be distinct, then the same can be said for yellow and black. The Qur'an uses the root *ḥ-m-r* to mean red only in one verse (i.e. Qur'an 35:27), but the root *ṣ-f-r* appears several times, and is mostly not typically understood as only purely yellow, but also brownish, as it describes dead plants (e.g. Qur'an 39:21, 57:20). Therefore, the Arabic root *ṣ-f-r* indeed describes a variation of colours within the yellowness and blackness spectrum, including reddish and brownish.

There was no distinct word for brown in the earliest Arabic literature, and the Arabic term later used derives from Ethiopic (*bun*), as a reference to the colour of coffee.[32] Accordingly, I feel that the argument over how different the Qur'anic *ṣafrā'* is from the biblical reddish when it comes to the red cow is unnecessary, even though Abraham Geiger (d. 1874 CE) considered it a Qur'anic error.[33] In fact, the Hebrew *'ădummâ* shares the same root as the term for earth, which is also brownish. Table 9.1 summarizes the cow descriptions among the texts.

The cow of Numbers 19 is used for purification purposes,[34] in situations outlined as follows: after touching a dead *nepeš*, for anyone inside a tent where a person dies, for every uncovered vessel, for anyone in the open field who touches a person killed by a sword or touches a dead person, a human bone, or a grave. The purification appears to be highly connected with the dead. The topic of Deuteronomy 21 is atonement for an unsolved murder, which is also evidently related to death.[35]

The cow needs to be without defect or blemish, according to both the Books of Numbers and Qur'anic narratives. This specificity might mean that such a cow is acceptable for sacrifice (e.g. Lev. 22:20–25),[36] a practice that appears to have been generally closely followed for sacrificial animals.[37] However, some Qumran scrolls and rabbinic discourses suggest that a controversy existed during the Second Temple period over whether the red cow was to be considered a sacrifice.[38] The implication is that if it were not considered a sacrifice, laypeople would be able to take part in the ritual.[39]

Table 9.1 Descriptions of the cow

Numbers	**Deuteronomy**	**Qur᾽an**
red		reddish / yellow
cow (*ha-pārâ*)	cow (*ʿeglat bāqār* – female calf of the cattle)	cow (*baqarah*)
without defect / without blemish		without defect / without blemish
never yoked	never yoked / never worked	never ploughed / never irrigated
		not old
		not young
	valley with running water, neither ploughed nor sown	

Only at the end of the Qur᾽anic narrative does it address the issue of murder, which possibly contextualizes it with Deuteronomy. However, the Qur᾽anic verse immediately after the cow narrative describes rocks that gush forth water (i.e. Qur᾽an 2:74), which Numbers 20 also describes immediately after the description of the red cow ritual. Some scholars believe that the Qur᾽an appears to link both Numbers' and Deuteronomy's narratives together and are aware of both.[40] However, the Qur᾽an also appears to portray some kind of discussion between Moses and his people on the cow's description, which appears in neither Numbers 19 nor Deuteronomy 21.

According to the Qur᾽an's formulation of the narrative, Moses tells his people that God commanded them to kill a cow. They are not amused by such a request and think that Moses is making fun of them. He responds that this is not at all his intention. His people appear to continue to ask questions to specify the attributes of the cow. Once satisfied, they tell him, 'Now you have brought *al-ḥaqq*' (Qur᾽an 2:71) and slaughter the cow. The Qur᾽an continues to narrate that they were about not to slaughter it, perhaps even because of the rarity of performing this ritual.

I argue that the term *al-ḥaqq* in Qur᾽an 2:71 should not necessarily be understood as 'truth', which is how it is typically rendered. A cognate to the Hebrew *ḥuqqâ* or the plural *ḥuqqîm*, *al-ḥaqq* should be understood here as a statute, much as it perhaps is in the *Qiblah* passages within the same Qur᾽anic chapter.[41] Numbers 19 calls the red cow a statute (*ḥuqqâ*) three times (i.e. Num. 19:2, 19:10, 19:21), and rabbinic law also makes inferences based on its designation as a statue (*ḥuqqâ*). For example, on the debate whether the ritual of the red cow needs to be done by the High Priest in future generations after Eleazar the priest in Num. 19:3, the hermeneutical marker in the Babylonian Talmud is '*ḥoqâ ḥoqâ*': the use of 'statute' in Num. 19:2 and 'statute' in Lev. 16:34, suggesting that as the service of Yom Kippur is performed by the High Priest, so is the red cow ritual.[42] The Talmudic hermeneutics used here to derive this is the concept of '*gezerah shawah*' (equal or similar rule),[43] which uses analogical reasoning that parallels the concept of '*qiyās*' in Islamic jurisprudence.

Therefore, as it is with the *Qiblah* passages, the term *al-ḥaqq* in the Qur'an pertaining to the cow in question is more likely to mean a statute instead of truth, moving in parallel with the term used for the red cow in Numbers and the Talmud, such that it would resonate with the Jewish Qur'anic audience. The Qur'an shows that the Israelites felt that they are being mocked. When it says that you (Moses) have now come with *al-ḥaqq*, it is very likely that the Qur'an is using the rabbinic interpretation of this term pertaining to the red cow, which simply means that you (Moses) have now come with a suprarational command, which human rationality does not understand, but which is followed because it is divinely ordained.

The description of the cow in the Qur'an is not much different from that found in Numbers and Deuteronomy. However, the Qur'an appears to show that the Israelites were trying to get very detailed descriptions of the cow, which Moses did not initially provide. The Mishnah devotes a whole tractate with the rabbis describing the ritual of the red cow and the majority of the rules, which are extremely stringent and not fully mentioned in Numbers.[44] As if the detailed rules described by the rabbis in the Mishnah were not enough, the Tosefta continues with rabbis explaining these Mishnaic rules.[45] Due to the rarity of this red cow, especially since having as many as two black hairs, would render it unfit, the Mishnah writes that the ritual involving a red cow had been performed only nine times at most – first by Moses, next by Ezra, and either five or seven times after Ezra.[46]

Is it possible that the Qur'an is arguing about the stringent rabbinic rulings regarding the red cow ritual that is not specifically mentioned in Numbers? There is some evidence in its narrative that suggests the Qur'an's possible awareness of the rabbinic rulings concerning the red cow. Neither Numbers nor Deuteronomy gives any detail concerning the age of the cow. Numbers uses the term *pārâ* for the cow, while Deuteronomy uses *'eglâ* and *bāqār*. The age of this heifer or cow is difficult to determine since the terms used to refer to it include almost all ages. However, the Qur'an appears to add the description that the cow should be neither too young nor too old, but somewhere in between. Though the description of the cow's age cannot be determined in either Numbers or Deuteronomy, the first Mishnaic rule concerning the red cow features a debate among the rabbis over the suitable age of the cow: the issue being whether it should be not less than a year old, not less than two years old, or as old as five years.[47] While they quibble, R. Yehoshua suggests three years of age, but uses the unusual term *shelashit*. When asked as to his meaning, he responds that he simply received the tradition as such without explanation,[48] as the rationale behind the red cow ritual is also transmitted through tradition without any real reasoning.[49] The usage of numbers has been argued to be a rhetorical device used in ancient Near Eastern, biblical and rabbinic literature,[50] but its usage in the Mishnah about the age of the red cow might have been an editing device, which is rarely used in the Hebrew Bible.[51]

Additionally, since the Mishnah describes how rabbis disqualified a cow that has as much as two hairs that are not red, Qur'an 2:69 uses the phrase 'He said, "He says she is a yellow cow [*baqarah*]. Bright is her colour, pleasing [*tasurru*] the onlookers."' The term *tasurru* is understood to mean pleasing. Nonetheless, the root *s-r-r* or *š-r-r* has various meanings. Among the meanings this term in Ugaritic, Aramaic, and Ethiopic is 'to ascertain', 'to authenticate' and 'to establish firmly'.[52] The Sumerian *sír-* also has the same meaning.[53] With such a definition found in a wide range of geographical locations surrounding Arabia in all directions, it would not be surprising if it were also understood in Arabia. The Qur'an's use of the term should not be unexpected because it is understood by the rabbinic Jewish community – much as *ḥaqq* is possibly used for statute instead of truth in the cow passage. Thus, the colour of the cow being *tasurru al-nāẓirīn* is more likely to mean ascertained or authenticated by the onlookers. This would align with the rule in the Mishnah that the cow should have no more than one hair of a different colour to qualify for the ritual. To ascertain or to authenticate the colour with such a stringent ruling appears in neither Numbers nor Deuteronomy but it does appear in the Mishnah, Tosefta and the Talmuds. Accordingly, the Qur'an, just like the *Qiblah* passages,[54] is fully aware of such rulings from rabbinic literature, and not only from the Hebrew Bible.[55]

Many of the rules on the red cow in the Mishnah were incorporated within the Jerusalem and Babylonian Talmuds. Since the text about the rules of the red cow does not include any discussion by later rabbis (Amoraim) between the third and sixth centuries CE, it has been suggested that the rituals of the red cow were no longer performed during that period.[56] This is natural, since the rituals required priestly functions, which were suspended after the destruction of the Second Temple.[57] Nonetheless, the Babylonian Talmud refers to the red cow in many other discussions, which means that although the ritual was no longer performed, it still came up in the minds of the Amoraim rabbis, scattered throughout various Talmudic tractates.[58] It appears that rabbinic thought during the time of the Qur'an continued to keep the ritual of the red cow in mind, requiring the Qur'an to engage with it even though it was no longer performed. It has been suggested that the Amoraim rabbis continued to bring up the red cow in their discussions in the Talmud because it was an ambiguous puzzle.[59] Since the Talmudic rabbis are fond of logical deliberations on jurisprudence, the red cow paradox makes a wonderful intellectual exercise to discuss.

The red cow paradox

The ritual concerning the red cow seems to be one of the the most bizarre to Jewish communities, as many *midrashim* attest. The source of its absurdity lies in the irrationality of purifying someone who has been defiled due to contact with a dead corpse by sprinkling them with the ashes of a red cow (itself a dead corpse) mixed with living (running) waters. The absurdity does not stop there: the priests and everyone involved in the process of preparing the red cow ritual are themselves defiled in the ritual. In other words, to prepare the purification material, pure individuals will be defiled so that defiled individuals can become pure. The same water that purifies the defiled is what defiles the pure.

Many scholars have attempted to explain the paradox. Suggesting that the key to unlocking the mystery is the fact that it is a sin offering (*ḥaṭṭāʾt*) (i.e. Num. 19:9).[60] Jacob Milgrom and other recent scholars located the ritual's roots in pre-Israelite rites to purify from corpse contamination.[61] As a purifying rite, the pre-Israelite ritual absorbs the contamination of what it attempts to purify.[62] Albert Baumgarten identifies this as the main flaw in Milgrom's analysis:[63] purification offerings are contaminated *after* they have been used in the purification process, while the red cow's ritual contaminates those involved in it even *before* it is used in the purification process.[64]

Consequently, Baumgarten argues for a different hypothesis, in that those who are involved in the preparation of the red cow become overly sanctified and need to return to normalcy.[65] One pillar of support Baumgarten marshals is that the High Priest needs to bathe before entering the Holy of Holies on the Day of Atonement, and he needs to do so again after completing the sacred ritual and leaving his garments aside (i.e. Lev. 16:23–24).[66] Baumgarten explains that as the High Priest enters the Holy of Holies and performs the ritual, he becomes overly sanctified and, therefore, cannot return to normalcy and face the people in that state. Baumgarten cites Ezek. 44:19, which states that the priests need to take off their garments after serving in the Holy of Holies so as not to transmit sacredness to (*yĕqaddĕšû*) the laity.[67] While the analogy to the Day of Atonement ritual may work, it is a major flaw to assume the same occurs in the ritual of the red cow, for a very simple reason: the text of Numbers 19 is very explicit that those involved in the ritual become impure (*ṭamēʾ*). Neither Leviticus nor Ezekiel use this description for a priest after entering the Holy of Holies. Ezekiel is explicit that they are sanctified, using the root *q-d-š*, and not impure. Accordingly, Numbers 19 would not use the term that everyone involved in the red cow's ritual would become impure simply to mean that one has become overly sanctified. Therefore, while Baumgarten is justified to find Milgrom's explanation flawed, his own explanation is equally problematic.

Other interpretations have been floated: William Gilder suggests that perhaps the red cow ritual conveys a symbolic meaning instead of the effectiveness of its actual act, but that this symbolic meaning itself is absent from the text;[68] Dominic Rudman argues that the ritual has a weak polluting agent purifying a greater impurity,[69] but that still does not solve the paradox.

Numbers (*Bamidbar*) *Rabbah*, a *midrash* dated sometime in the eleventh or twelfth century CE – but from a portion essentially identical to *Midrash Tanḥuma*, dated around the eighth century – states the following concerning the rabbinic commentary on Numbers 19 about the red cow concerning how the pure come out of the impure and calling it a statute (*ḥuqqat*) attempting to make sense of the ritual:

> This is the statute [*ḥuqqat*] – As it is said verse (Job 14:4): Who gave (brought forth) purity to one who is impure?, such as Abraham from Terah, Hezekiah from Aḥaz, etc., Israel from the nations of the world, the world to come from this world. … There we learned (Parah 4:4): those who occupy themselves with the Parah from beginning to end, impurify their clothes, but it makes clothes Pure.

God said: I carved a law (into the fabric of creation), a decree I made, you have no ability to transgress (override) My law!

This is the statute [*ḥuqqat*] of the Torah – (Ps. 12:6) The sayings of God are pure (i.e. they purify). . . . as it is said: And the Lord spoke to Moses and Aaron, saying, This is the ordinance [*ḥuqqat*] of the Torah:
. . . The Holy One blessed be he said to Moses: 'to you I will reveal the reason for the red cow, but for others it will be a decree [*ḥuqqat*] (without reason),' . . .

A gentile asked Rabbi Yochanan ben Zakkai, 'These rituals you do, they seem like witchcraft! You bring a heifer, burn it, crush it up, and take its ashes. [If] one of you is impure by the dead [the highest type impurity], two or three drops are sprinkled on him, and you declare him pure?!' He said to him, 'Has a restless spirit ever entered you?' He said to him, 'No!' 'Have you ever seen a man where a restless spirit entered him?' He said to him, 'Yes!' [Rabbi Yochanan ben Zakkai] said to him, 'And what did you do for him?' He said to him, 'We brought roots and made them smoke beneath him, and pour water and it flees.' He said to him, 'Your ears should hear what leaves from your mouth! The same thing is true for this spirit, the spirit of impurity, as it is written, (Zech. 13:2) 'Even the prophets and the spirit of impurity will I remove from the land.' They sprinkle upon him purifying waters, and it [the spirit of impurity] flees.' After he left, our rabbi's students said, 'You pushed him off with a reed. What will you say to us?' He said to them, 'By your lives, a dead person doesn't make things impure, and the water doesn't make things pure. Rather, God said, "I have instated a statute, I have decreed a decree [*ḥuqqat ḥaqaqti gezera gazarti*], and you have no permission to transgress what I decreed," as it says 'This is a statute [*ḥuqqat*] of the Torah.'[70]

The Qur᾿anic narrative of the cow speaks of hitting the parts of the cow against itself and it is thus that God resurrects the dead. Although the narrative of the red cow in Numbers or the cow whose neck is broken in Deuteronomy is an issue of impurity due to death or atoning for an unsolved murder, it does not specifically raise the topic of resurrection. In the aforementioned *midrash*, however, a question from Job 14:4 arises: 'who gave purity to the impure?' Then the *midrash* gives examples of Abraham (pure) coming out of Terah (impure), Hezekiah (pure) from Ahaz (impure), Israel (pure) from the nations of the world (impure), and the world to come (pure) from this world (impure). The *midrash* is more specific about how the pure emerges from the impure. This is further exemplified in *Numbers Rabbah* 19:4, which in turn is also elaborated upon by the rabbis in *Qoheleth Rabbah* 8:1.5:

R. Mana of Shaab in Galilee said in the name of R. Joshua b. Levi: In connection with every law which the Holy One, blessed be He, communicated to Moses, He expounded to him its uncleanness and purification; but when he reached the chapter, Speak unto the priests (Lev. 21), he [Moses] spoke before Him, 'Lord of the universe, if these [the priests] are defiled wherewith do they regain their state of purity?' He gave no answer, and at that time the face of Moses changed. When,

> however, He reached the chapter of the Red Heifer, the Holy One, blessed be He, said to Moses, 'Moses, when I made to you the statement "Speak unto the priests," and you asked Me, "If they are defiled wherewith do they regain their purity?" I gave you no answer. This is their method of purification, "And for the unclean they shall take of the ashes of the burning of the purification from sin (Num. 19:7)."' He [Moses] spoke before Him, 'Lord of the universe, is this purification [i.e. Moses asked of the Lord the very question that kept puzzling the rabbis through the generations – how can ashes, themselves defiling, remove the defilement caused by contact with the dead]?' And the Holy One, blessed be He, replied, 'Moses, it is a statute (*ḥoq*), and I have made a decree, and nobody can fathom my decree.'[71]

Noticeably, it is as though God brings the pure out of the impure. The Qur'anic narrative, which is not explicit about how the pure comes out of the impure, perhaps instead uses the metaphor of the living coming out of the dead, where the pure is symbolic of the living and the impure symbolic of the dead (as itself is the cause of impurity in Numbers 19). This symbolism is explicit in Qur'an 91:7–10, where a pure soul (*zakiyyah*) is contrasted with a buried soul: '[7]by the soul and the One Who fashioned it [8]and inspired it as to what makes it iniquitous or reverent! [9]Indeed, he prospers who purifies it [*zakkāhā*]. [10]And indeed he fails who buries it [*dassāhā*]'[72] (Qur'an 91:7–10). Therefore, the pure vis-à-vis impure imagery of the red cow ritual midrash parallels how the Qur'an sometimes contrasts purity with death instead.

Additionally, in one of the Qur'anic accounts of the golden calf, the consequence of *al-sāmirī*'s involvement was a dictum against him by Moses saying 'In the life [*al-ḥayāt*][73] it shall be yours to say, "Touch not"' (Qur'an 20:97). Michael Pregill convincingly argued that *al-sāmirī* is an epithet of Aaron,[74] and that the Qur'an is alluding to priestly purity when using the phrase 'touch not'. If that is the case, then here also we would see how the Qur'an is using 'life' as a symbol for 'purity', for when this verse says 'in the life', it would be alluding to purity. In other words, it is as if the Qur'an is saying, 'in purity, you are to so say, "Touch not"'.[75] Noteworthy, the Qur'an recalls an account of the golden calf not very long before the cow narrative further attesting to the possible understanding that the cow ritual is not intending to bring the life back from the dead literally, but as bringing the pure out of the impure.

Given the context, the Qur'anic narrative concerning the cow perhaps is not literally about the physical resurrection of the dead, but a metaphor for how those who are spiritually alive come out of those who are spiritually dead. Note also that the aforementioned *midrash* relates the rabbinic understanding of the term *ḥoq* – as a suprarational decree that is not understood by human reason – with the Qur'anic use of *al-ḥaqq* in the cow narrative, as discussed earlier. The Qur'an seems to be aware of its rabbinic interpretation and for that reason show that the Israelites ultimately tell Moses after his description of the cow that he has brought them *al-ḥaqq*, because his explanation of God's commandment makes no rational sense.

The Qur'anic narrative of the cow is further connected with the red cow of Numbers 19 because immediately after the narrative, the Qur'an discusses the rock that brings forth water, which is itself mentioned in Numbers 20.

> Then your hearts hardened thereafter, being like stones or harder still. For indeed among stones are those from which streams gush forth, and indeed among them are those that split and water issues from them, and indeed among them are those that crash down from the fear of God. And God is not heedless of what you do.
>
> Qur'an 2:74

This Qur'anic passage that comes immediately after the cow's narrative seems to engage with the waters of Meribah, immediately after the red cow's narrative in Numbers:

> [7]and the LORD spoke to Moses, saying, [8]'Take the staff, and assemble the congregation, you and Aaron your brother, and tell the rock before their eyes to yield its water. So you shall bring water out of the rock for them and give drink to the congregation and their cattle.' [9]And Moses took the staff from before the LORD, as he commanded him. [10]Then Moses and Aaron gathered the assembly together before the rock, and he said to them, 'Hear now, you rebels: shall we bring water for you out of this rock?' [11]And Moses lifted up his hand and struck the rock with his staff twice, and water came out abundantly, and the congregation and their livestock drank.
>
> Num. 20:7–11

Numbers Rabbah provides the following commentary on this narrative, which is echoed in the Qur'an's accusation of the Israelite stubbornness when discussing the rock that gushes with water:

> They began to say 'Moses knows the statute [*ḥoq*] of the rock. If he asks, it will bring forth water.' So Moses was uncertain – 'If I listen to them I nullify the words of the Allpresent, and the Holy One (Job 5:13) "takes the wise in their craftiness."' But Moses had been careful for 40 years not to get angry at them, because he was terrified of the oath the Holy One swore: 'Not one of these men will see [the land]. . .' They said to him: 'Here is a rock; just as you want to bring forth water from another rock, bring it forth from this one.' He shouted at them 'Hear now, you rebels [*ha-morîm*]!' 'Rebels [*ha-morîm shyṭîn*]' has many meanings: (1) 'stubborn ones' [*ha-morîm sarbānîm*] (2) 'fools' – in the sea villages they call fools '*morîm*.' (3) 'those who teach their teachers.' (4) 'archers' (In I Sam 30:3 the word '*morîm*' is used to mean 'archers.') . . . Even so, Moses only used the rock that the Holy One told him [to use].[76]

This *midrash* essentially provides several meanings for the term *mōrîm*, one of which is *sarbānîm*, meaning disobediently stubborn. When the Qur'anic passage explains that their hearts were like stone or harder still, it appears also to understand *mōrîm* in the Numbers narrative as stubborn. This might suggest that the Qur'an is aware of some *midrashic* traditions that were later compiled in *Numbers Rabbah*.

Ali Aghaei argues that the Qur'anic narrative might be engaging with the Haftarah reading on the Parashat of the Sabbath of Parah,[77] which includes a reading from Ezek. 36:16–36(38).[78] That passage in Ezekiel discusses how God would purify the Israelites, who had been scattered. God would replace their hearts of stone with a heart of flesh (i.e. Ezek. 36:26), which perhaps is the accusation in Qur'an 2:74: that their hearts are as hard as stone or even harder. Ezek. 36:33–38 shows how God will bring back to life the desolate cities, which has echoes in Qur'an 2:259, as discussed earlier; however, what is more significant on the issue of resurrection is that these passages in Ezekiel immediately precede the resurrection imagery of the valley of dry bones in Ezekiel 37. Since this image of resurrection is understood metaphorically, then the same may be said about the Qur'an, in which its narrative of the cow is related to bringing the dead back to life. The purification of Israel in Ezekiel 36–37 depicts their resurrection by reviving desolate cities and bringing the exile back. Perhaps the Qur'an is not even specifically talking about God's ability to return the exiled Israelites historically, but is also addressing the Jewish Diaspora and, thus, in conversation with Jewish liturgy.

Qoheleth Rabbah, a haggadic commentary to the book of Qoheleth dated between the sixth and eighth centuries CE,[79] fits well into the period of the Qur'anic composition. According to *Qoheleth Rabbah*, King Solomon has the wisdom to understand the various statutes of the Torah, but even after seeking more wisdom, he could not comprehend the red cow ritual.[80] The author of *Qoheleth Rabbah* appears to be saying that even though Solomon was a wiser man than Moses, even he was unable to understand the logic of the red cow ritual. *Midrash Tanḥuma* shares this assessment: 'Solomon said, "All this I have stood, and I have questioned a red cow, and I have asked and searched, and I have said wisdom, and it is far from me".'[81] The paradox of the red cow ritual seems to have been completely incomprehensible, as seen by the Jewish attitudes at least at the time of the *midrash*. Alfred Edersheim stated, 'Without some deeper symbolical meaning attaching to them, the peculiarities of the sin-offering of the red heifer would indeed be well-nigh unintelligible.'[82]

It is perhaps such an attitude that the Qur'an is engaging with when stating that the Jews felt they were being mocked by Moses:

> And when Moses said to his people, 'God commands you to slaughter a cow [*baqarah*],' they said, 'Do you take us in mockery?' He said, 'I seek refuge in God from being among the ignorant.'
>
> Qur'an 2:67

The Qur'an appears to affirm that this *ḥaqq* is not meant as a mockery just because it appears to make no sense. The Qur'an justifies this statute and gives a reason behind it, 'Thus does God give life to the dead and show you His signs, that haply you may understand' (Qur'an 2:73). The purpose of this puzzle, according to the Qur'an, is that God wants to show how the living indeed come out of the dead, or perhaps in the Jewish understanding, the pure come out of the impure.

The notion of God bringing the living out of the dead is reiterated in several passages in the Qur᾽an. Some of these appear to have inner-Qur᾽anic allusions to one another. For example,

> [3]And among humankind are those who dispute concerning God, without knowledge, and follow every rebellious satan [*shayṭānin marīd*], [4]for whom it is decreed that, should anyone take him as a protector, he will cause him to go astray and guide him unto the punishment of the Blaze. [5]O humankind! If you are in doubt [*rayb*] concerning the Resurrection, [remember] We created you from dust, then from a drop, then from a blood clot, then from a lump of flesh, formed and unformed, that We may make clear for you. And We cause what We will to remain in the wombs for a term appointed. Then We bring you forth as an infant, then that you may reach maturity. And some are taken in death, and some are consigned to the most abject life, so that after having known they may know nothing. And you see the earth desiccated, but when We send down water upon it, it stirs and swells and produces every delightful kind. [6]That is because God is *al-ḥaqq*,[83] and because He gives life to the dead, and because He is Powerful over all things, [7]and because the Hour is coming, in which there is no doubt [*lā rayb*], and because God will resurrect whosoever is in the graves. [8]And among humankind are those who dispute concerning God without knowledge, without guidance, and without an illuminating Book.
>
> Qur᾽an 22:3–8

There are five points of intertextuality between these passages and those about the red cow. The first point concerns those who dispute God without knowledge, recalling the Israelites in the waters of Meribah, according to Numbers 20. The second point is the Qur᾽anic passage calling anyone who disputes God without knowledge a rebellious satan (*shayṭānin marīd*) or, in *Numbers Rabbah*, *ha-morim shyṭin*. The third point is the Qur᾽anic use – twice in the preceding passage – of the term *rayb*, which is also used in Num. 20:3 in the narrative of the waters gushing out of the rock in Meribah and is, in fact, the reason the place is called Meribah, according to Num. 20:13. The fourth point is the use of the term *ḥaqq* in Qur᾽an 22:6, which the red cow of Numbers 19 and its Jewish commentary also frequently use, and which is also used in the narrative of the cow in Qur᾽an 2:71. The fifth point of intertextuality is the passage's concern with resurrecting the dead, just as the narrative of the cow in the Qur᾽an. With these five intertextualities, it seems that the passage above is an inner-Qur᾽anic allusion to the cow narrative in the Qur᾽an. Accordingly, the resurrection of the dead in these passages might also be metaphorical, meaning to bring forth the pure from the impure.

Another passage in the Qur᾽an that also discusses the resurrection of the dead also appears to have an inner-Qur᾽anic allusion with the cow narrative and the waters of Meribah:

> [14]They will call unto them, 'Were we not with you?' They reply, 'Indeed! But you tempted yourselves, bided your time, and doubted [*irtabtum*]; and false hopes

> deluded you till the Command of God came, and the Deluder deluded you concerning God. [15]So this day no ransom shall be taken from you, or from those who disbelieved.' Your refuge shall be the Fire; it shall be your master. What an evil journey's end! [16]Has not the time come for those who believe for their hearts to be humbled to the remembrance of God and *al-ḥaqq*[84] that has come down, and to be not like those who were given the Book aforetime? But the span of time was too long for them, such that their hearts hardened and many of them are iniquitous. [17]Know that God revives the earth after its death. We have indeed made the signs clear for you, that haply you may understand.
>
> Qur'an 57:14–17

The consequence of such inner-Qur'anic allusion is that if the resurrection in the cow narrative is understood metaphorically, then this passage, which is typically understood eschatologically, might also be metaphorical. The first point of intertextuality is the use of the term *irtabtum* from the root *rayb* used in Qur'an 22:5 and 22:7 and used in Numbers 20, as discussed earlier. The second point is the above passage's discussion of a ransom, which can be understood as a sacrifice. The sacrifice of the red cow seems a likely interpretation, especially when placed within the context of the remaining intertextualities. The third point is the use of the term *ḥaqq*, as used in the Qur'anic narrative of the cow and the red cow of Numbers 19 and its commentary. The fourth point is the hardening of hearts like those of the People of the Book, which appears to be an inner-Qur'anic allusion to Qur'an 2:74's narration of the waters of Meribah. The resurrection of the dead, as also seen in the Qur'anic narrative of the cow (i.e. Qur'an 2:73) is the fifth point of intertextuality, and the sixth is the statement '*qad bayyannā lakum al-āyāt la'allakum ta'qilūn* [We have indeed made the signs clear for you, that haply you may understand]' (Qur'an 57:17), which parallels '*wa-yurīkum āyātihi la'allakum ta'qilūn* [and show you His signs, that haply you may understand]' (Qur'an 2:73). Given these six points of intertextuality, it seems likely that the resurrection of the dead in Qur'an 57:14–17 is metaphorical, moving in parallel with the passages discussed earlier.

The red cow as an allusion to the golden calf

Some rabbinic traditions link the red cow ritual with the golden calf narrative.[85] The Qur'anic narrative of the reddish/yellowish cow is preceded by that narrative as well (i.e. Qur'an 2:51–54). According to the Talmud, the rabbis suggest that the Israelites were supposed to have everlasting life, because they accepted the Torah and the angel of death would have no authority over them.[86] However, the Israelites were re-subjected to mortality because of the sin of the golden calf.[87]

According to Rashi, the reason the red cow ritual was entrusted to Eleazar instead of his father, Aaron, is due to the latter's role in the golden calf; Aaron essentially became unworthy of performing a role.[88] Rashi interprets the three types of yarn – cedarwood, hyssop, and scarlet – in the ritual to symbolize the

3,000 men who fell by the edge of the sword due to the golden calf.[89] He also explains symbolically, the cedar is lofty while the hyssop is lowly, so that a person who prides themselves on a high position is a sinner, so to receive atonement they need to make themselves as lowly as the hyssop and the worm (in Hebrew, a play on words with scarlet yarn).[90] Rashi also states that, as the golden calf made everyone who took part in it impure, so are those who take part in the ritual of the red cow made impure.[91] Because the Israelites became morally blemished and defective because of the golden calf, the unblemished and without defect red cow would be the cause for their atonement – to regain their perfection.[92] Additionally, the red cow symbolizes the mother of the golden calf, which takes away the sin caused by its child.[93] While Rashi is a medieval commentator, he drew from various prior sources.[94] After all, the relationship between the red cow and the golden calf appears in *Midrash Tanḥuma*, which states, 'Let a heifer come and atone for the incident of the [golden] calf.'[95] While *Midrash Tanḥuma* and Rashi are post-Qur'anic, the relationship between the red cow and the golden calf have traces to earlier traditions of the Amoraic period (around third through fifth century CE).[96]

David Wright argues that Num. 31:19–24 is connected to the red cow ritual in Numbers 19.[97] However, one noteworthy difference in Num. 31:23 is that anything that can go through (withstand) fire, such as gold, needs to be placed first into the fire and then into the water to be purified. If Num. 31:19–24 is connected with the red cow of Numbers 19, as David Wright argues,[98] then it might connect to the golden calf, which also went through fire before being mixed with water and given to the Israelites to drink, as some sort of atonement or, arguably, purification. The golden calf was melted in fire, smashed into fine dust, mixed with streaming water (something that is also necessary with the red cow), and then the Israelites were made to drink it (i.e. Exod. 32:20). All of these features link the golden calf with the red cow ritual in rabbinic literature.

In the scenario of drinking the golden calf, Philippe Guillaume writes, 'What the Israelites drunk and why is entirely unexplained.'[99] Though not itself a paradox, it still is a puzzle in its own right. While the Levites only killed 3,000 of the guilty Israelites, Moses apparently had everyone drink the calf, and Exod. 32:3 explicitly states that all the people were, in fact, guilty of bringing gold to Aaron for the golden calf. Guillaume suggests that perhaps drinking the calf allowed the Levites to determine who was guilty of the sin and who was not, as it is apparent that not everyone was necessarily guilty, especially if the Levites killed only 3,000 and spared the rest.[100] Otherwise, Guillaume remarks that if the Levites were the only ones not guilty, they would have killed all other non-Levites, but that did not happen.[101] Other scholars, such as Christopher Begg, also argued alongside Guillaume that drinking the calf separated the guilty from the nonguilty.[102] While Begg and Guillaume make solid observations about the golden calf narrative, Mark O'Brien is correct that there still is no evidence that the real purpose for everyone to drink the calf was to expose the guilty.[103] O'Brien emphasizes that everyone was guilty, especially in light of Exod. 32:3.[104] Essentially, even after the Levites kill the 3,000 people, Moses addresses the people the next day that they were sinful and says that he will ask God to atone for their sin (i.e. Exod. 32:30).

This suggests that there were still sinful people in his audience. As Moses asks God to forgive the sin of the people, the narrative itself remains inconclusive on whether God has forgiven them or not, because God states that He will blot from His book (the book of life as addressed in Chapter 5) anyone who has sinned against Him (i.e. Exod. 32:33–34). The narrative even continues with God then smiting the Israelites because they made the calf (i.e. Exod. 33:35).

All this suggests that even after the Levites killed the 3,000, the sinners were still among those who remained. Perhaps everyone was indeed guilty, which would make Begg and Guillaume's suggestion that drinking the calf was to expose the sinners for the Levites to kill unlikely. The Levitical killing also appears in the Qur'anic narrative of the golden calf with the specific command by Moses to the Israelites: 'kill yourselves [*f-aqtulū anfusakum*]' (Qur'an 2:54).

After discussing the golden calf and the red cow narratives, the Qur'an returns to the golden calf again. Qur'an 2:92–93 states that the golden calf was drunk by the Israelites due to their sinfulness, but it is ambiguous in the sense that it states that they drank the calf into their hearts instead of into their bellies. Accordingly, it is unknown whether the Qur'an understands the Exodus narrative as something literal or symbolic. While Exodus is not explicit on the reason why the Israelites were given the golden calf to drink, it appears that the Qur'an understands the reason is due to their sin; something understood implicitly in Exodus.

Immediately after the first Qur'anic narrative on the golden calf and the Levitical killing, the Israelites tell Moses that they will only believe in him if they see God plainly (i.e. Qur'an 2:55). As a response, a great cry (*ṣā ʿiqah*) seizes them. Qur'an 2:56 implies that the cry had killed them and God had resurrected them after it. This very specific narrative in the Qur'an is ambiguous in terms of what it corresponds to in the biblical or rabbinic tradition. Actually, Exod. 33:18–23 shows Moses asking to see God's glory while interceding for the Israelites after the golden calf incident. The Qur'an brings up this narrative in Qur'an 7:143, where Moses is taken by a loud cry (*ṣa ʿiqā*) and is then awakened from it. Traditional exegetes such as al-Ṭabarī have read this Moses narrative as implying his death and resurrection.[105] Yet, it appears al-Ṭabarī may somehow have had some knowledge of Jewish tradition, in which he explicitly mentions the Torah, as he states that God informs Moses that nobody sees him and survives,[106] an allusion to Exod. 33:20.

Yet the Qur'anic narrative of Moses asking to see God in Qur'an 7:143 differs somewhat from Exod. 33:18–23. In the Qur'anic narrative, God asks Moses to watch a mountain; when God descends and the mountain remains in its place, Moses will be able to see God. However, when God descends, the mountain is crushed, implying that Moses will not be able to see God – and in fact, Moses is overcome by a great cry and then repents. This implies that Moses had sinned, unless one understands *tubtu ilayk* ('I repent to you') simply by its etymology connoting that Moses is returning to God (perhaps in will, in mind, etc) instead of necessarily a repentance from sin.

To understand the mystery of the red cow, one must first understand the connotations attached to the golden calf.[107] To explain why a golden calf was chosen by the Israelites as an object of worship, Stephen Newman[108] looks to an ancient Egyptian link in the worship of the goddess Hathor (something other scholars also consider).[109] Although this hypothesis is not necessarily fully convincing, it still is interesting to note. Since Hathor was associated in ancient Egypt with life and reproduction, Newman suggests it to be a possible reason why a red cow would have the power to purify those who were in contact with the dead:[110]

> Rabbi Moshe ha-Darshan explains that the rite of burning the Red Heifer was a re-enactment of the destruction of the Golden Calf at the foot of Mount Sinai. Thus, it would also be a symbolic destruction of the cow-goddess Hathor which the Golden Calf represented. This explains why a red cow was needed for the ritual. The association with cleansing from impurity as a result of contact with a dead body is understood, in light of the midrash in TB Avodah Zarah 22b, to mean that the Israelites attained a state of immortality at Mount Sinai, but lost it due to the sin of the Golden Calf. Purification from death thus involves rejection of the Golden Calf, demonstrated by the ashes of the Red Heifer. This is especially powerful considering that Hathor was associated in Egypt with life and reproduction. Seen in this light, the Red Heifer ritual is a total rejection of Egyptian idolatry and its symbols. The ritual includes burning a crimson thread (Num. 19:6), which may likewise be a negation of the magic scarlet ribbon worn by the cow-goddess that was thought capable of binding evil spirits.[111]

So while the red cow represents idolatry, according to biblical (e.g. Gen. 35:2) and Mishnaic accounts,[112] those who are in contact with idols become impure.[113] Accordingly, Newman states, 'The impurity contracted by dealing with the Red Heifer is therefore associated with the idolatry that it represented.'[114] Yet Hathor also had a role in assisting the dead into their journey to the afterlife:[115] she also passes between the realms of the living and the dead,[116] perhaps also associating the red cow with death and resurrection.

Although the golden calf narrative is in Exodus and the ritual of the red cow is in Numbers, the Qur'an does contextualize both into a single narrative on the history of the Israelites saved from Egypt (i.e. Qur'an 2:49–74). While an intertextual analysis is not fully conclusive, it might be possible that the Qur'an is perhaps aware of some Jewish traditions that link the red cow ritual with the golden calf. Since the Qur'an describes the colour of the red cow with *ṣafrā'*, which as described can be reddish or yellowish, it might itself be an allusion to the colour presumed by the Qur'an for the golden calf. Though I find the most convincing alternative is that the Qur'anic colour and that of Numbers 19 simply denote a brownish cow, it does not preclude the Qur'an's use of polysemy and wordplay.

Consider the following: (1) some Jewish traditions make a connection between the golden calf and the red cow; (2) some rabbinic traditions understand that the Israelites were given immortality due to their experience at Sinai, but were resubjected to death due to the golden calf; and (3) the red cow is undoing the sin of the golden calf. From these premises, one might deduce that the red cow purifies the Israelites from the realm of the dead so that they may partake in the realm of the living. Perhaps this deduction means the Qur'an is associating the red cow narrative with death and resurrection, similar to Parashat Parah's reading of Ezek. 36:16–38, which itself is contextualized with death and resurrection found in Ezekiel 37.

Conclusion

The cow narrative in Qur'an 2:67–73 has elements that include the red cow's account in Numbers 19 and Deut. 21:1–9, as well as in rabbinic literature, especially about the cow's age and the description of her needing to be satisfactory of uniform colour. It is, therefore, without doubt that the Qur'an is aware of Jewish tradition and literature about the red cow. The main difference is that the Qur'an places it in the context of resurrection, while the biblical and rabbinic literature do not always do so – at least not directly.

Yet this context should not be surprising. The narratives of the man in the desolate town (i.e. Qur'an 2:259) and Abraham and the birds (i.e. Qur'an 2:260) are, in fact, in the same chapter as the cow narrative in the Qur'an (i.e. Qur'an 2:67–74). While there are debates on structures of Qur'anic chapters using literary theories, such as ring composition theory, we can remain agnostic about them and the fine lines that divide them. Such structural analyses offer the possibility that those narratives are linked not only thematically but also structurally. For example, Raymond Farrin has analysed the structure of Sūrah al-Baqarah (Chapter of the Cow) and developed a ring structure for its style and theme.[117] The narrative of the cow Farrin places as section C of the chapter, which constitutes Qur'an 2:40–103. Farrin argues that this section addresses primarily the Children of Israel, which coheres the main theme of this section. However, he categorizes Qur'an 2:254–284 as section B′, arguing that it mainly addresses believers to remind them of God's knowledge and power paralleling section B (i.e. Qur'an 2:21–39), which discusses the narrative of God creating Adam and Eve. However, I would think that starting section B′ at Qur'an 2:254 might be too early for this section. If Qur'an 2:259–260 alludes to the exile and the covenant, then it might be part of section C′, paralleling the address to the Israelites in section C, where the cow narrative is placed. According to Farrin, section C (i.e. Qur'an 2:40–103) addresses the Children of Israel and discusses Moses as a lawgiver, while C′ (i.e. Qur'an 2:178–253) discusses laws given to the new community. It might be possible that section C′ includes the material at least up to Qur'an 2:260, where its audience is reminded of the relationship with the Israelite exile and covenant.

Using a different approach, Richard Bell had earlier connected Qur'an 2:258–260 with Qur'an 2:243 due to discussing death and resurrection.[118] With such a thematic approach, it might be possible to connect the three together: the narratives of the cow, the man in the desolate town, and Abraham and the birds. Although the Qur'an puts them in the context of death and resurrection while their biblical, extrabiblical and rabbinic accounts do not, it has been shown that the Qur'an understands death and resurrection in those narratives metaphorically, especially with Abraham having children and with his children returning to the land promised. Therefore, it would not be surprising for death and resurrection in the cow narrative also to be understood metaphorically – especially with their possible connection to Ezek. 36:16–38 through Parashat Parah, which discusses the return of Israelite exiles or Diaspora and contextualizes the resurrection scene of Ezekiel 37.

According to both the Bible and the rabbinic tradition, 'death' is the chief source of *ṭum'ah* (impurity).[119] Jacob Milgrom states:

> The bodily impurities enumerated in the Torah focus on four phenomena: death, blood, semen, and scale-disease. Their common denominator is death. Vaginal blood and semen represent the forces of life; their loss – death. In the case of scale-disease, this symbolism is made explicit: Aaron prays for his stricken sister, 'Let her not be like a corpse' (Num. 12:12). Furthermore, scale-disease is powerful enough to contaminate by overhang, and it is no accident that it shares this feature with the corpse (Num. 19:14). The wasting of the body, the common characteristic of all biblically impure skin diseases, symbolizes the death process as much as the loss of blood and semen.[120]

Milgrom continues,

> Of all the diachronic changes that occur in the development of Israel's impurity laws, this clearly is the most significant: the total severance of impurity from the demonic and its reinterpretation as a symbolic system reminding Israel of its imperative to cleave to life and reject death.[121]

The Qur'an might understand resurrection in the cow narrative as purification from *ṭum'ah* or death. Yet this death does not necessarily have to be physical. As the rabbis in the Talmud state, the Israelites became immortal for accepting the Torah but lost this immortality due to the sin of the golden calf. Thus, perhaps the Qur'an even understands this as spiritual death, in which the red cow is undoing the sin of the golden calf that caused such spiritual death.

Many scholars have had different approaches in understanding biblical and rabbinic impurity laws, some emphasizing death and others sin (itself associated with spiritual death). Still others approach it from a hygienic perspective emphasizing the sacredness of the Temple. Vered Noam states:

> From Philo of Alexandria to contemporary scholars, a multitude of approaches to understanding the formative concept of purity and impurity in biblical writings have been proposed, with the numerous explanations reflecting the prevailing circumstances, the accepted norms, and the sentiments of their authors no less than they do the world of the Bible. These approaches can be classified according to their underlying perception of impurity, . . . Some of them derive from the naturalistic perception of impurity as an entity, explaining it variously as a reflection of demonic worlds, an expression of death with all that

> it entails, or a "side effect" of transition states and human crises. A second approach, meanwhile, proposes a symbolic interpretation that views ritual impurity as a reflection of moral values of sin and expiation. And yet a third approach, at the opposite end of the spectrum, represents an absolute reduction of biblical impurity, interpreting it instrumentally as a system that lacks actual existence or inner content but that serves certain social needs, whether religious or secular, such as hygiene, aesthetics, reinforcing the sacredness of the Temple or the distinctiveness of the Jewish people, strengthening the status of the priesthood, or disputing pagan concepts of holiness.[122]

In short, in the narrative of the cow the Qur'an is consistent with its other narratives that have been discussed thus far, in which the concepts of death and resurrection are metaphorical.

Chapter 10

CONCLUSION: DEATH AND RESURRECTION IN THE QUR'AN

The Qur'an's principal and most prominent theme is the Day of Resurrection, and it has typically been assumed that the phenomenon involves physical bodily resurrection. Presuming that outlook, it would seem that the Qur'an is, indeed, very explicit about bodily resurrection, especially as some passages depict it very vividly. However, close analysis shows that many Qur'anic passages explicitly discussing resurrection are perhaps mainly metaphorical. Many of the most intense depictions of bodily resurrection in the Qur'an are rearticulations of biblical, extrabiblical and rabbinic traditions that do not demonstrate physical resurrection in the sense of dead bones leaving their graves. They are, however, physical in the sense of restoring a nation, rebuilding the Temple, or even having physical children. Therefore, one can deduce that many Qur'anic passages about resurrection are metaphorical such that even the physical aspects do not take on the imagery of dead bodies rising from graves.

Since the Qur'an numerously identifies resurrection in a very metaphorical manner, it was essential to understand the concepts of life and death in the Qur'an. These also frequently take on metaphorical layers: there are believers, who are portrayed to be spiritually alive, and there are nonbelievers, who are explicitly described to be spiritually dead. Additionally, the vast majority of the terms that the Qur'an uses to designate nonbelievers have a common denominator in their semantic range dealing with issues about death. In other words, the Qur'an is describing zombies. The zombies of the Qur'an are those who are spiritually dead but appear to be physically alive; they walk, talk and interact physically, but they are dead souls encapsulated in physical bodies, which is nothing other than tombs for their souls.

With so much metaphor at play, there is little doubt that some concepts of life, death and resurrection that are described by the Qur'an may be understood spiritually. This brings to light some Sufi literature, such as that of Ibn ʿArabī, which explicitly interprets the Qur'an in a very spiritual manner, especially on these exact topics of life, death, and resurrection. Throughout history, much of that literature was considered esoteric (*bāṭinī*), and the interpreters sometimes leapt to conclusions when the exoteric meanings appeared more physical than spiritual. However, as is shown in the many examples, the Qur'an explicitly speaks of zombies, those who are spiritually dead. Moreover, the biblical, extrabiblical and rabbinic narratives in their context intertextualized with the Qur'an have nothing to do with physical resurrection in the sense of dead bodies leaving their graves. Accordingly, one might infer that the motive behind the Qur'anic rearticulation seems instead to be its emphasis on a metaphorical understanding of death and resurrection, as well.

The grand question that arises is why Muslims, early in their history, almost always interpreted these passages as referring to physical, not metaphorical or spiritual, resurrection. Why were Muslims very early in their history convinced of the superiority of their Temple, the Ka'bah, taking it to be the real and true focal point for prayer? I have argued in an earlier work that once we intertextualize the *Qiblah* passages with its biblical and rabbinic literature, it becomes clearer that this is not the Qur'an's main argument.[1] Similarly, when much Sufi literature, like that of Ibn 'Arabī, had incessantly argued how *al-Masjid al-Ḥarām* is symbolic of the heart, which many have considered to be an esoteric (*bāṭinī*) interpretation, it was also found that the Qur'an makes that point philologically, which is further validated with its intertextuality.[2] This might suggest that some of those esoteric interpretations may not necessarily be considered without valid linguistic support through intertextuality, and therefore, perhaps should not ineludibly be considered heretical by some traditionalists.

The scenario regarding resurrection seems very similar. Why did Muslims in the early years of their history not interpret the Qur'an more in line with its possible biblical and rabbinic subtext or oral tradition? One most likely reason, but perhaps not the only reason, is that Muslims very early in their history did not engage thoroughly with biblical, extrabiblical and rabbinic literature. Their reasons for not doing so could be many: they were perhaps unaware of that literature or they intentionally did not want to deal with it to show the superiority of their Prophet and his scripture, which they wanted to keep independent from their competition. Reuven Firestone had argued that Muslims used reactive theology early in their history in order to distinguish themselves from other religious communities, perhaps motivated by religious competitiveness.[3]

However, Muslim traditions that appeared to be more esoteric (*bāṭinī*) in their interpretations and viewed by other mainstream Muslims as heretical are not necessarily as esoteric as one assumes. That being the case, much dialogue is possible between various traditions, because a systematic methodology can be established in which the views of various groups may be tested, and intertextual polysemy might provide for a way to such a systematic approach.

Physical resurrection of the kind where people leave their graves does not appear to be the main depiction in the Qur'an. Those passages that appear very explicitly literal (e.g. Qur'an 2:259–260) are perhaps metaphorical, as their intertextualities with biblical literature suggest. Even the Qur'anic portrayal of emergence from the tombs (*ajdāth*) is likely metaphorical, as has been shown.

The Qur'an appears to talk about two deaths and two lives, that of the *nafs* (which might be a disembodied soul) and that of the body. In most cases, the Qur'an is highlighting a metaphorical death. Each kind of death apparently has its resurrection. The body is resurrected perhaps in the same way it was created the first time. This might suggest that it undergoes rebirth or that the rebirth is itself a metaphor for spiritual birth. The resurrection of the *nafs* is perhaps more mystical. Qur'an 6:122 appears to point to resurrection not after the body's death, but while the body is alive, thus referring to the resurrected as still walking among people.

According to the Qur'an, nonbelievers have a dead *nafs*. Even though they appear to be physically alive, they are zombies with a living body but a dead *nafs*. The Qur'an is mostly concerned with the resurrection of the *nafs*, as it seeks to win the faith of nonbelievers.

A word of caution is imperative. If the Qur'an describes zombies with a dead *nafs* entombed in a physical body, then its resurrection could still be demonstrated in a physical sense, as emerging from that physical tomb. As soon as the *nafs* becomes alive, it is alive within the physical body, and not somewhere necessarily in a different, nonphysical realm, which is exemplified in the following Qur'anic passage:

> Is he who was dead, and to whom We give life, making for him a light by which to walk among humankind, like unto one who is in darkness from which he does not emerge? Thus for the disbelievers, what they used to do was made to seem fair unto them.
>
> Qur'an 6:122

The other possibility of resurrection is re-creation. The Qur'an frequently describes resurrection as analogous to re-creation, which might or might not suggest reincarnation. It might even suggest a spiritual and nonphysical birth. If the resurrection of the physical body implies rebirth, then it may counter the statements that those in hell cannot ask to be returned to this life (*dunyā*). However, if some Qur'anic verses are suggesting that this life (*dunyā*) is itself hell, then those who do not believe and do not do good deeds will remain there, and perhaps the Qur'an is implying that they cannot change their history or past deeds.

Later Muslims seem to have argued in favour of a bodily resurrection in many of these passages in the same way that Rabbinic Judaism reinterpreted some depictions of resurrection in the Hebrew Bible. The Muslim eschatology of later generations might have been influenced by the folk eschatology of the communities surrounding them.

Though the Qur'anic eschatology seems different from its interpretation by the later Muslim community, it would be premature to confine it to any certain idea. Perhaps we still do not understand exactly what the Qur'an is trying to portray, or perhaps the Qur'an wants to be intentionally obscure. The Qur'an demands that its audience ponder its meanings. This book is a simple and humble attempt to do so. As an old Muslim adage says, 'And God knows best'.

Many of the hermeneutics of the Qur'anic passages – such as the man in the desolate town, Abraham and the birds, and the case of the red/yellow (brown) cow – show considerable intertextuality between the Qur'anic text and its biblical, extrabiblical and rabbinic literature, more so than actually found in traditional

Muslim commentaries. To further understand how the Qur'an engages with such literature, more research must be done, continuing the intertextual approach. Since the method of intertextual polysemy allows us to understand better these relationships and selective Qur'anic uses of terminologies, more research on this method is also essential for understanding better the message that the Qur'an conveys.

Some of the audience of the Qur'an appears to be well-informed about some biblical and extrabiblical traditions, including rabbinic traditions and Jewish liturgy. This illustrates the kind of communities the Qur'an was engaging with in its early formation. With recent scholarship, it is becoming clearer that the Jewish audience of the Qur'an are rabbinic, who had access to the text of the Torah, who had probably performed rabbinic Jewish liturgy, including the daily *Shema'* recitations and *'Amidah*, who possibly read the weekly Torah portions Parashat and Haftarah, who had known rabbinic traditions from the Mishnah and the Talmud, and who also had known extrabiblical traditions and *midrashim* (rabbinic interpretations). They might have had direct access to other books of the Hebrew Bible or traditions that stemmed from them. After all, rabbinic literature often refer to passages from other books of the Hebrew Bible. It would, therefore, not be unusual if different books of the Hebrew Bible were accessible to the Jewish community at the time of the Qur'an in one form or another (directly or indirectly).

The Qur'an's main theme is resurrection but, as has been argued, in many of the most vivid portrayals, that phenomenon appears to be metaphorical or spiritual. No reading of a text as mysterious as the Qur'an can be fixed, but when we take pains to dissect the material, we may see it afresh and realize that our old interpretations were introduced not by the text or its history but by our own assumptions. Ultimately, the conclusion remains yours to make, as this is only a humble attempt, as some form of *ijtihād* to use an Islamic concept, to unravel some meanings behind the mysterious text of the Qur'an.

NOTES

Notes on Transliteration and Translation

1 Nasr, *Study Quran*.
2 *Holy Bible: New Revised Standard Version*.

Introduction

1 Rahman, *Major Themes of the Qurʾān*.
2 Irving, Ahmad, and Ahsan, *Qurʾan*, 73–84; Abdel Haleem, *Understanding the Qurʾan*; Bijlefeld, 'Eschatology'; Saeed, *Qurʾan*, 72–3; Chittick, 'Muslim Eschatology'; Tesei, '*barzakh*', 31.
3 Rustomji, *Garden and the Fire*, 41–4; Lange, *Locating Hell*.
4 Shopenhauer, *World as Will*, 2: 463.
5 Singh, *Death, Contemplation*, x.
6 Dalferth, *Theology and Philosophy*, vii.
7 Plato, *Phaedo*, 81a.
8 O'Shaughnessy, *Muhammad's Thoughts on Death*.
9 Ibid.
10 Ibid., vii.
11 Smith and Haddad, *Islamic Understanding*.
12 See Wansbrough, *Qurʾanic Studies*; Wansbrough, *Sectarian Milieu*.
13 See Crone and Cook, *Hagarism*; Crone, *Slaves on Horses*.
14 Donner, *Muhammad and the Believers*.
15 Reynolds, *Qurʾān and Its Biblical Subtext*.
16 See also Rippin, *Approaches to the History*.
17 Galadari, '*Taqlīd al-Ijtihād*'.
18 Galadari, '*Qibla*'.
19 Ibid.
20 Crone, 'Quranic *Mushrikūn* . . . (Part I)'; Crone, 'Quranic *Mushrikūn* . . . (Part II)'.
21 Ibid.
22 Ibid.
23 Crone, 'Quranic *Mushrikūn* . . . (Part I)'.
24 Ibid., 448.
25 In some Semitic languages, *nepeš* is cognate to the Arabic *nafs*.
26 Steiner, *Disembodied Souls*.
27 Smith, 'Understanding of *Nafs* and *Rūḥ*'.
28 Fakhry, *Islamic Philosophy*, 98.
29 Sadeqzadeh, 'Ibn Sina's Difficulties'.
30 Corbin, *Cyclical Time*, 47–56; Corbin, *History of Islamic Philosophy*, 131–41.
31 Badakhchani, *Spiritual Resurrection*.

32 Sharifi, Khavaninzadeh and Ansarimanesh, 'Bodily Resurrection'.
33 For more on Haggai Mazuz's arguments, see Mazuz, *Religious and Spiritual Life*.

Chapter 1

1 For more details on the origins of the immortality of the soul and the concept of transmigration of souls in Pythagoreanism, see Bordoy, 'Origin of the Orphic-Pythagorean Notion'.
2 Boyce, *Zoroastrians*, 26–9.
3 For more on life and death in Ancient Egypt along with the notion of the resurrection, read Assmann, *Tod und Jenseits*.
4 See Garland, *Greek Way*. Also see Long, 'Plato's Doctrine of Metempsychosis'.
5 Birkhan, 'Some Remarks on the Druids', 108–9.
6 See Eliade, *Shamanism*. Also see Mills, 'Preliminary Investigation'; Mills, 'Comparison of Wet'suwet'en Cases'; Mills and Slobodin, *Amerindian Rebirth*.
7 Steadman and Palmer, 'Visiting Dead Ancestors'.
8 Zeller, *Die Philosophie der Griechen*, 1: 324–5.
9 Kahn, *Pythagoras and the Pythagoreans*; Segal, *Life after Death*, 220–1.
10 Kahn, *Pythagoras and the Pythagoreans*, 19.
11 Ho, 'Selfhood and Identity'.
12 See Leach, 'Aryan Invasions'. Also see Misra, 'Date of the Rigveda'.
13 Taylor, 'Anattā Doctrine'; Albahari, 'Against No-*Ātman* Theories'; Carlisle, 'Becoming and Un-becoming'; Sugunasiri, '"Asoulity" as Translation of Anattā'.
14 Becker, *Breaking the Circle*, 8.
15 Kalupahana, *Buddhist Philosophy*, 36–8.
16 Arulchelvam, 'Eternal Eva'; Doniger, *On Hinduism*, 509–22.
17 Albahari, 'Against No-*Ātman*'.
18 Carlisle, 'Becoming and Un-becoming'.
19 Ibid.
20 For more information on the path of the *bodhisattva*, see Dayal, *Bodhisattva Doctrine*; Wilson, 'Monk as Bodhisattva'; Samuels, 'Bodhisattva Ideal'.
21 Robert C. Zaehner argued that the doctrine of '*anattā*' was a means to teach selflessness or the denial of the selfish ego; see Zaehner, *Mysticism, Sacred and Profane*. For those opposing such a theory of the '*anattā*' as merely a teaching to deny the selfish ego, see Collins, *Selfless Persons*. For further information of the different interpretations of the 'anatta' see Harvey, *Selfless Mind*, 17–77.
22 For more details on the concept of rebirth in Buddhism, see Harvey, *Selfless Mind*, 89–108.
23 Hick, *Death and Eternal Life*, 332.
24 Hovav-Machboob, 'Ari's Doctrine'. Also see Pinson, *Reincarnation and Judaism*.
25 Haddad, 'Druze of North America'.
26 Walker, *Reincarnation*, 6.
27 Meysami-Azad, 'Reincarnation in Abrahamic Religions'.
28 Smith and Haddad, *Islamic Understanding of Death*, 8.
29 Khalil, 'Which Road to Paradise?'
30 See Jimoh, 'Reincarnation'. Also see Ọsányìnbí and Falana, 'Evaluation of the Akure Yorùbá'.
31 See Nadel, 'Study of Shamanism'. Also see Johnson, 'Reincarnation in an Islamic Society'.

32 Bennett, 'Reincarnation'.
33 Smith and Haddad, *Islamic Understanding*, 8.
34 Hodgson, 'Al-Darazî and Ḥamza'.
35 Crone, *Nativist Prophets*, 232–52.
36 Mazdak (d. 528 CE) is considered a reformer of the Zoroastrian faith.
37 Foltz, 'Buddhism in the Iranian World'; Shams, 'Khurramdīnīyyah or Khurramīyyah'.
38 Crone, *Nativist Prophets*, 232–52.
39 Foltz, 'Buddhism in the Iranian World'; Shams, 'Khurramdīnīyyah or Khurramīyyah'; Rezkhani, 'Mazdakism, Manichaeism and Zoroastrianism'.
40 Al-Fayyūmī, *Tarīkh al-fikr*, 514.
41 Al-Bayḍāwī, *Anwār al-tanzīl*, 5:108; al-Samīn al-Ḥalabī, *al-Durr al-maṣūn*, 8:342; Ibn ʿĀdil al-Ḥanbalī, *al-Lubāb fī ʿulūm al-kitāb*, 14:213.
42 Unlike *TSQ*, I interpret '*ẓann*' as 'delusion' and not 'conjecture'.
43 Crone, 'Quranic *Mushrikūn* . . . (Part I)'.
44 Ibid., 461–3.
45 Ibid.
46 Ibid., 469–70.
47 Al-Ḥillī, *Mukhtaṣar baṣāʾir al-darajāt*, 17–18, 26, 29, 37–8; Buckley, 'Early Shiite Ghulah'; Inloes, 'Authentication of Hadith'.
48 Brody, 'Jewish Reflections'. For more details on the history of resurrection of the dead in Judaism, see Elledge, *Resurrection of the Dead*.
49 See footnote in al-Maʿarrī, *Saqṭ al-zand*, 291.
50 See Homerin, 'Echoes of a Thirsty'.
51 Gasimova, 'Models, Portraits'.
52 Zaehner, *Dawn and Twilight*.
53 Gasimova, 'Models, Portraits'.
54 Brandon, *History, Time and Deity*, 53–6; Böwering, 'Ideas of Time'.
55 Watt, 'Muḥammad's Contribution', 28.
56 See the discussion in Crone, 'Quranic *Mushrikūn* . . . (Part II)', 2–3.
57 Crone, 'Kavād's Heresy', 40.
58 Raman, 'Reincarnation and Personal Identity'.
59 For a comprehensive history of Hinduism and its relationship religions of some early Indo-European tribes, see Bryant and Patton, *Indo-Aryan Controversy*; also see Allen, 'Hero's Five Relationships'; Jackson, 'Light from Distant Asterisks'.
60 Bryant, *Origins of Vedic Culture*; Bryant and Patton, *Indo-Aryan Controversy*; Kristiansen, 'Proto-Indo-European Languages'; Anthony and Ringe, 'Indo-European Homeland'; Haak et al., 'Massive Migration'; Pereltsvaig and Lewis, *Indo-European Controversy*.
61 For a more comprehensive relationship, see McEvilley, *Shape of Ancient Thought*.
62 Smith, 'Transmigration and the Sufis'.
63 Ibid.; Madelung, 'Abū Yaʿqūb al-Sijistānī'; Walker, 'Doctrine of Metempsychosis', 235; Amanat, 'Nuṭqawi Movement', 287; Schmidtke, 'Doctrine of the Transmigration', 238; Bennett, 'Reincarnation'; Friedman, *Nuṣayrī-ʿAlawīs*; Khalil, 'Which Road?'
64 Mettinger, *Riddle of Resurrection*.
65 Frankfort, *Kingship and the Gods*, 4.
66 Ibid.
67 See Ring, 'Christ's Resurrection'. Also see Yamauchi, 'Tammuz and the Bible'. Also see Bostock, 'Osiris and the Resurrection'.
68 Endsjø, 'Immortal Bodies'.

69 Speck, *Naskapi*; Martin, *Keepers of the Game*; Nelson, 'Conservation Ethic and Environment'; Campbell, *Way of Animal Powers*; Guenther, 'Animals in Bushman Thought'; Wenzel, *Animal Rights, Human Rights*; Ingold, 'From Trust to Domination'; Whitley, 'Cognitive Neuroscience'; Winkelman, 'Shamanism as the Original Neurotheology'; Serpell, 'Animals and Religion', 11–12.
70 Taylor, *Death and the Afterlife*, 114–15.
71 This is also the case of the ancient Near East; see El-Khouri, 'Fertility as an Element'; Sumegi, *Understanding Death*.
72 See Childe, 'Urban Revolution'. Also see Weisdorf, 'From Foraging to Farming'. Also see Simmons, *Neolithic Revolution*.
73 Isaac, *Geography of Domestication*, 107.
74 Spooner, *Population Growth*.
75 Pargament, *Psychology of Religion*; Pargament, Ano, and Wachholtz, 'Religious Dimension of Coping'; Ano and Vasconcelles, 'Religious Coping'; Pargament, *Spiritually Integrated Psychotherapy*; Wunn and Klein, 'Evolutionary Processes in Early Religion'.
76 Segal, *Life after Death*, 33, 81–2, 114–18.
77 Richards, *Mapping Time*.
78 Munn, 'Cultural Anthropology of Time'; Gell, 'Time and Social Anthropology'.
79 For the history of calendars, see Judge, *Dance of Time*.
80 Taylor, *Death and the Afterlife*, 28–33.
81 Quirke, 'Creation Stories in Ancient Egypt'.
82 See Wells, 'Mythology of Nut'. Also see Mojsov, 'Ancient Egyptian Underworld'.
83 Wells, 'Origin of the Hour'.
84 Elledge, 'Resurrection of the Dead'.
85 Assmann, *Tod und Jenseits*.
86 For a history of the resurrection of the body in early Judaism and Christianity, see Setzer, *Resurrection of the Body*.
87 Segal, *Life After Death*, 121.
88 Meier, 'Debate on the Resurrection'; Setzer, 'Resurrection of the Dead'.
89 Gillman, *Death of Death*, 96–7; Elledge, *Resurrection of the Dead*, 44–53.
90 Boyce, *History of Zoroastrianism*, 2: 193; Winston, 'Iranian Component', 187–9.
91 Boyce, *History of Zoroastrianism*, 3: 408; Elledge, 'Resurrection of the Dead', 24–6.
92 Boyce, *History of Zoroastrianism*, 3: 412; Finkelstein, *Pharisees*, 1: 148–51.
93 Winston, 'Iranian Component', 186–7, 200–10; Duchesne-Guillemin, *Western Response to Zoroaster*, 90–4; Boyce, *History of Zoroastrianism*, 3: 417–27; Hinnells, 'Zoroastrian Influence', 7–8; Tigchelaar, and Martínez, 'Iranian Influences in Qumran'; Elman, 'Zoroastrianism and Qumran'. Not all scholars, however, agree of the dualistic nature of the Dead Sea Scrolls and any Zoroastrian influence; see Heger, 'Another Look at Dualism', 55–6; Tukasi, 'Dualism and Penitential Prayer', 169–70.
94 Barr, 'Question of Religious Influence'; Lang, 'Street Theatre'; Isbell, 'Zoroastrianism and Biblical Religion'; Routledge, 'Death and Afterlife'.
95 Dexinger, 'Samaritan Eschatology', 281–3; Dexinger, 'After Life'; Dexinger, 'Eschatology', 88; Lehnardt, 'Massekhet Kutim'.
96 Pummer, *Early Christian Authors*, 47, 59, 106, 146, 375; Lehnardt, 'Massekhet Kutim'.
97 As discussed earlier, especially references in the Book of Isaiah, as suggested by Boyce.
98 The Egyptian influence on concepts of resurrection has been argued by some scholars as an alternative historical origin of resurrection in Judaism; see Schipper, 'Egypt and Israel'; Evian, 'Egypt and Israel'; Huddlestun, 'Ancient Egypt and Israel'.

99 There is a debate on the role of Zoroastrianism in influencing Judaism during the exile, see Martin-Achard, *From Death to Life*, 186–9; Hengel, *Judaism and Hellenism*, 1: 196, 2: 130f.; Boyce, *History of Zoroastrianism*; Greenspoon, 'Origin of the Idea of Resurrection', 259–61; Boyce, 'Zoroaster, Zoroastrianism'; Nigosian, *Zoroastrian Faith*; Bremmer, 'Resurrection between Zarathustra', 96–8; Day, 'Development of Belief', 241–57; Griffiths, 'Legacy of Egypt', 1047–8; Davies, *Death, Burial and Rebirth*, 40–6; McDannell and Lang, *Heaven*, 12–14. Examples of those arguing in favour of the Zoroastrian hypothesis see Cohn, *Cosmos, Chaos*. Opponents include Eichrodt, *Theology of the Old Testament*, 1: 516–17; Lacocque, *Book of Daniel*, 243; Barr, 'Question of Religious Influence'; Goldingay, *Daniel*, 286, 318; Collins, *Daniel*, 396. Although earlier scholars considered a higher Persian influence on Judaism during the exile, evidence of such has been debated. See Day, 'Development of Belief', 240–2; Bremmer, 'Resurrection', 99–101; Johnston, *Shades of Sheol*, 234–6.

100 Sheol is a place of darkness where the dead go to, regardless of whether they were righteous or not. The Septuagint translates it as Hades, which is the Greek equivalent of the underworld.

101 Levenson, *Resurrection and the Restoration*.

102 Ibid., 65.

103 Typically understood as chapters 1–39 of the Book of Isaiah.

104 Hays, 'Egyptian Loanword'; Hays, '"My Beloved Son"'; Hays, '"There is Hope"'. For those arguing in favour of the Israelites living in Egypt, see Dever, *Who Were the Early Israelites*.

105 For more details, see Levy and van den Brink, *Egypt and the Levant*; Cohen-Weinberger and Goren, 'Levantine-Egyptian Interactions'; Sparks, 'Canaan in Egypt', 25–54; Killebrew, *Biblical Peoples*, 51–92.

106 For the Amarna letters, see Moran, *Amarna Letters*.

107 For the historical context of Egypt and Israel, see Greifenhagen, *Egypt on the Pentateuch's*.

108 Assmann, *Tod und Jenseits*, 73.

109 For details of Egyptian interaction with Palestine, see Ash, *David, Solomon and Egypt*.

110 Glassman, *Origins of Democracy*, 1: 590–1.

111 Cross, *Canaanite Myth and Hebrew Epic*, 343–7; Martin-Achard, *From Death to Life*, 195–205; Xella, 'Death and the Afterlife'; Day, 'Development of Belief', 245–8; Day, 'Resurrection Imagery'; Mettinger and Hendel, 'Riddle of Resurrection'; Elledge, *Resurrection of the Dead*, 53–7.

112 Wright, *Resurrection of the Son of God*, 126–7.

113 For a comprehensive overview of the roots of Jewish thoughts of the afterlife and its variances throughout history, see Raphael, *Jewish Views*.

114 de Moor, 'Concepts of Afterlife'.

115 Greenspoon, 'Origin of the Idea of Resurrection'.

116 Lévy, *La légende de Pythagore*, 255; Glasson, *Greek Influence in Jewish Eschatology*, 31.

117 Russell, *Method & Message of Jewish Apocalyptic*, 385–90.

118 Bauckham, 'Life, Death, and the Afterlife'; Segal, *Life after Death*, 248–81.

119 Marmorstein, 'Doctrine of the Resurrection'.

120 The *Targums* are interpretations of the Hebrew Bible typically written in Aramaic.

121 Sysling, *Teḥiyyat ha-Metim*.

122 Elledge, 'Future Resurrection of the Dead', 416.

123 von Ehrenkrook, 'Afterlife', 99.

124 For further details on the history of Second Temple Judaism to rabbinic Judaism, see Schiffman, *From Text to Tradition*; Avery-Peck, 'Death and Afterlife'; Neusner, 'Death

and Afterlife'; Schiffman, *Understanding Second Temple*; Sivertsev, *Households, Sects*; Cohn, *Memory of the Temple*; Musano, 'Destruction of the Temple'. On how death rituals evolved in rabbinic Judaism, see Kraemer, *Meanings of Death*; Golbert, 'Judaism and Death'.

125 m. Sotah 9:15; also b. Sotah 11a; j. Shabbat 1:3; also j. Sheqalim 3:3.
126 j. Shebiʾit 4:8; also j. Sanhedrin 10:3.
127 Keller, 'Hebrew Thoughts'.
128 Park, *Conceptions of Afterlife*, 63; Rutgers, 'Death and Afterlife'.
129 m. Sanhedrin 10:1. An Epicurean is one who follows the teaching of Epicurus (d. 270 BCE) who was materialistic and attacked superstition and divine intervention. Also see b. Sanhedrin, 90a–90b; b. ʿAbodah Zarah 17b; j. Peʾah 1:1; j. Sanhedrin 10:1. Also see Grant, 'Resurrection of the Body'; Manuel and Manuel, 'Sketch for a Natural History'; Bastomsky, 'Talmudic View of Epicureanism'; Avery-Peck, 'Death and Afterlife'; Setzer, 'Resurrection of the Dead'; Labendz, '"Know What to Answer the Epicurean"'.
130 von Ehrenkrook, 'Afterlife in Philo and Josephus'.
131 b. Pesaḥim 68a; *Sanhedrin* 91b. Also see Neusner, 'Death and Afterlife'; Flesher, 'Resurrection of the Dead', 322–3; Bronner, 'Resurrection Motif'.
132 A heave-offering was an offering dedicated to God in a ceremony officiated by the priest.
133 Marmorstein, 'Doctrine'; Rubin, 'From Corpse to Corpus'; Neusner, 'Death and Afterlife'.
134 b. Sanhedrin 90b. Also see Neusner, 'Death and Afterlife'.
135 b. Sanhedrin 90b. Also see Neusner, 'Death and Afterlife'.
136 b. Sanhedrin 90b. Also see Neusner, 'Death and Afterlife'; Labendz, 'Know What'.
137 b. Sanhedrin 90b. Also see Neusner, 'Death and Afterlife'.
138 b. Sanhedrin 90b. Also see Neusner, 'Death and Afterlife'.
139 b. Sanhedrin 90b; also see Hullin 12:5; also j. Sanhedrin 10:2. Also see Neusner, 'Death and Afterlife'. Compare with Bar, 'Resurrection or Miraculous Cures?'
140 b. Berakhot 15b.
141 Wright, 'Making a Name for Oneself'.
142 Ibid., 156.
143 Caneday, 'Qoheleth'.
144 b. Shabbat 152b; also j. Shabbat 1:3; also j. Sheqalim 3:3. Also see Neusner, 'Death and Afterlife'.
145 Levenson, *Resurrection and the Restoration*, esp. 156–65.
146 Tuell, 'True Metaphor'.
147 Fensham, 'Curse of the Dry Bones', 59–60; Collins, 'Afterlife in Apocalyptic Literature'.
148 There is a scholarly debate on whether or not the Qumran community believed in a literal physical resurrection doctrine, with the majority arguing that they did not espouse such a belief. See Dimant, 'Resurrection, Restoration'; Hogeterp, 'Resurrection and Biblical Tradition'; Hogeterp, 'Belief in Resurrection'; Popović, 'Bones, Bodies'; Zangenberg, 'Human Body in Death'; Wold, 'Agency and Raising the Dead'; Evans, 'To What Extent'.
149 Pearson, 'Dry Bones'.
150 Wischnitzer-Bernstein, 'Conception of the Resurrection'.
151 Paulien, 'Resurrection and the Old Testament'.
152 b. Pesaḥim 118a. Also see Neusner, 'Death and Afterlife'; Arnow, '*Sh'fokh Ḥamatkha*'.
153 b. Taʿanit 2a; also b. Sanhedrin 113a. Also see Neusner, 'Death and Afterlife'.

154 b. Baba Batra 16a. Also see Silver, *Maimonidean Criticism*; Neusner, 'Death and Afterlife'.
155 b. Niddah 73a; also j. Kilayim 9:3; also j. Ketubot 12:3. Also see Neusner, 'Death and Afterlife'.
156 Levenson, *Resurrection and the Restoration.*
157 On a history about the various forms of Judaism at the time, see Saldarini, *Pharisees, Scribes*; Sanders, *Judaism.*
158 Viviano and Taylor, 'Sadducees, Angels, and Resurrection', 498. Also see Daube, 'On Acts 23'.
159 For more on this debate, see Parker, 'Terms "Angel" and "Spirit"'.
160 Kilgallen, 'Sadducees and Resurrection'.
161 Thiessen, 'Buried Pentateuchal Allusion'.
162 Denaux, 'Controversy between Jesus'.
163 Cohn-Sherbok, 'Jesus' Defense'; Setzer, 'Resurrection of the Dead'; Elledge, *Life after Death.*
164 Setzer, 'Resurrection of the Dead'.
165 Trick, 'Death, Covenants'.
166 Ibid.
167 The understanding that resurrection is the recompense for the suffering of the righteous from within the Maccabean context of martyrdom has been argued by scholars; see Seeligerms, 'Erwägungen zu Hintergrund und Zweck', 189; Bauckham, *Fate of the Dead*, 41. Compare with Enoch 63:10 and Qoh. 12:5; and on the Book of Enoch's perspective, see Elledge, 'Resurrection of the Dead', 32–5. For the Pharisees understanding of only the resurrection of the righteous, see Elledge, 'Resurrection of the Dead', 43.
168 Compare with Pss. Sol. 13.11; 15.10, and the Dead Sea Scrolls.
169 Tromp, 'Can These Bones Live', 63–8.
170 Draper, 'Resurrection and Zechariah 14.5'.
171 The *Didache* is also known as the *Teachings of the Twelve Apostles*, assumed to be written sometime in the second century CE. For an overview of the *Didache*'s origins, see Draper and Jefford, *Didache.*
172 Shepkaru, 'From After Death'.
173 Charlesworth, 'Where Does the Concept of Resurrection Appear'.
174 Lehtipuu, *Debates over the Resurrection*, 65.
175 Segal, *Life After Death*, 394.
176 Ibid., 368.
177 Crone, 'Quranic *Mushrikūn* . . . (Part II)', 3–5.
178 Also compare with Stepaniants, 'Encounter of Zoroastrianism with Islam'.
179 Crone, '"Nothing but Time Destroys Us"'.
180 *TSQ* translates '*asāṭīr*' as fables.
181 Al-Farāhīdī, *al-ʿAyn*, 7: 210–11; Ibn Manẓūr, *Lisān al-ʿarab*, 4: 363–5; henceforth, *Lisān al-ʿarab.*
182 Crone, 'Nothing but Time', 134.
183 Ibid., 135–6.
184 Firestone, 'Qur'ān and the Bible'.
185 Reeves, 'Some Explorations'.
186 Sinai, 'Pharaoh's Submission'.
187 Reynolds, *Qurʾān and Its Biblical Subtext*; Reynolds, *Qurʾān and the Bible.*
188 El-Badawi, *Qurʾān and the Aramaic Gospel Traditions*; El-Badawi, 'Impact of Aramaic'.

189 Zellentin, 'Gentile Purity Law'.
190 Firestone gives a very brief evolution of such scholarship in the West. See Firestone, 'Qur'ān and the Bible', 3.
191 Firestone, 'Qur'ān and the Bible', 2–3.
192 Galadari, *Qur'anic Hermeneutics*.
193 Dormandy, 'Epistemic Humility'.
194 Ibid., 293.
195 Ibid., 296.
196 Dormandy, 'Epistemic Benefits'.
197 Reynolds, *Qur'ān and Its Biblical Subtext*; Reynolds, *Qur'ān and the Bible*.
198 El-Badawi, *Qur'ān and the Aramaic Gospel Traditions*; El-Badawi, 'Impact of Aramaic'.
199 Galadari, *Qur'anic Hermeneutics*, 103–16.
200 Galadari, 'Camel Passing'.
201 Fishbane, *Biblical Interpretation*.
202 Galadari, *Qur'anic Hermeneutics*; Galadari, '*Qibla*'; Galadari, 'Role of Intertextual Polysemy'.
203 Newby, *History of the Jews*, 57–9; Firestone, *Jewish Culture*; Hoyland, 'Jews of the Hijaz'; Galadari, '*Qibla*'; Mazuz, *Religious and Spiritual Life*, 21–3; Graves, 'Upraised Mountain'.
204 Examples of these start with Abraham Geiger (Geiger, *Was hat Mohammed*), and continued with William St. Clair Tisdall (Tisdall, *Original Sources of the Qur'an*), Charles C. Torrey (Torrey, *Jewish Foundation of Islam*), Richard Bell (Bell, *Origin of Islam*), and many others.
205 Wasserstrom, *Between Muslim and Jew*.
206 Graves, 'Apocryphal Elements', 165.
207 Treves, 'Conjectures Concerning the Date'; Gonzalez, 'Zechariah 9–14'; Tiemeyer, *Zechariah's Vision*.
208 Dormandy suggests that epistemic humility translates to 'limitations-owning', when a person understands the limits of their cognitive abilities. Dormandy, 'Epistemic Humility', 298.
209 Iser, *Act of Reading*.
210 While being critical of the existence of such a thing as an ideal standard based on an objectivist theory, Iser states, 'The very fact that this ideality has to be brought out, and indeed conveyed, by interpretation shows that it is not directly given to the reader, and so we can safely say that the relative indeterminacy of a text allows a spectrum of actualizations' (Ibid., 24).
211 Beal, 'Reception History'.
212 Smith, 'Study of Religion'; Smith, *What Is Scripture*.

Chapter 2

1 Rakesh and Ayati, 'Concept of Death'.
2 Hasker, *Emergent Self*; Corcoran, 'Physical Persons'; Corcoran, 'Constitution View'.
3 Brown, 'Nonreductive Physicalism'; Dolan, 'Soul Searching'; Gray, 'Whatever Happened'; Graves, *Mind, Brain*; Preston, Ritter and Helper, 'Neuroscience and the Soul'.
4 Farah and Murphy, 'Neuroscience and the Soul', 1168; Clarke, 'Neuroscience'.
5 Gay, *Neuroscience and Religion*.
6 Gefter, 'Creationists Declare War'; Moreland, *Soul*.

7 Walach, 'Neuroscience, Consciousness, Spirituality'; Corcoran, *Rethinking Human Nature*; Jeeves, *Minds, Brains*; Aymard, 'Neuroscience, Materialism'.
8 Zhuravlev and Avetisov, 'Definition of Life'; Tsokolov, 'Why Is the Definition of Life'; Benner, 'Defining Life'; Bruylants, Bartik and Reisse, 'Is It Useful'; Jagers op Akkerhuis, 'Towards a Hierarchical Definition'; Tirard, Morange and Lazcano, 'Definition of Life'.
9 Machery, 'Why I Stopped'.
10 Ibid.
11 For more details, see Green, *Body, Soul, and Human Life*.
12 Cooper, 'Scripture and Philosophy'; Steiner, *Disembodied Souls*.
13 Cooper, *Body, Soul, and Life Everlasting*, 33; Cooper, 'Scripture and Philosophy'.
14 Davis, 'Ecclesiastes 12:1–8-Death'; also see Pfeiffer, 'Peculiar Skepticism'; Zuck, 'God and Man'; Yerushalmi, *Book of Kohelet*, xii–xiv.
15 Kang, 'Qoheleth versus a Later Editor'.
16 Bream, 'Life without Resurrection'.
17 Lategan, 'Theological Dialectic', 183; Kang, 'Qoheleth'.
18 Even some traditional biblical scholars agree that this passage does not necessarily describe the immortality of the soul; e.g. Schoors, 'Koheleth', 301–2; Kang, 'Qoheleth'.
19 Pfeiffer, 'Peculiar Skepticism'. Some scholars insist that bodily resurrection is still evident in Qoheleth 12:7 (e.g. Hight, 'Berkeley and Bodily Resurrection'), but I find such an argument extremely weak and highly unlikely.
20 Cooper, 'Body-Soul Question'.
21 Frisch and Schiffman, 'Body in Qumran Literature'.
22 Hickman, 'Nature of the Self'.
23 Pryke, '"Spirit" and "Flesh"'.
24 Shihadeh, 'Classical Ashʿarī Anthropology'.
25 Shihadeh, 'Al-Ghazālī and Kalām'.
26 Compare with Loukas, Saad, Tubbs and Shoja, 'Heart and Cardiovascular System'.
27 Cox, 'Origen and the Bestial Soul'; Pun, 'Theology of Progressive Creationism'; Held and Rust, 'Genesis Reconsidered'; Whitekettle, 'All Creatures Great and Small'; Anderson, 'Theological Anthropology'; Auld, 'imago dei'; Kemmerer, 'Jewish Ethics'; Turpin, 'Did Death of Any Kind Exist'.
28 The Talmud is a text of rabbinic discourse that typically interprets Jewish law. The Babylonian Talmud was compiled *c.* sixth century, although it continued to be edited until *c.* eighth century.
29 Efros, 'Textual Notes'.
30 Orel and Stolbova, *Hamito-Semitic*, 278.
31 Marcus, 'Verb "To Live"'.
32 *Theological Dictionary of the Old Testament*, henceforth *TDOT*, 4: 327–30.
33 Al-Farāhīdī, *al-ʿAyn*, 7: 431; Ibn Manẓūr, *Lisān al-ʿarab*, henceforth *Lisān al-ʿarab*, 7: 264
34 Anderson, 'Islamic Spaces'.
35 Liddell and Scott, *Greek-English Lexicon*, 1412; also see Lust, Eynikel, and Hauspie, *Greek-English Lexicon*.
36 York, 'Proto-Indo-European Vocabulary'.
37 Imruʾ-ul-Qays (d. 544) possibly used the root to mean a long period of time (al-Maṣṭāwī, *Dīwān*, 144) and Ṭarafah b. al-ʿAbd al-Bikrī (d. 563) used it to mean a flat paved ground (al-Aʿlam al-Shantamarī, *Dīwān*, 66).
38 It is more common than the root *b-l-ṭ* and is found in many pre-Islamic poetry, some even attributed to the third century as in the poetry attributed to Mālik b. Fahm al-Azdī (d. 231) (ʿUbayd, *Shuʿarāʾ ʿUmān*, 83).

39 Al-Farāhīdī, *al-ʿAyn*, 8: 42–3; *Lisān al-ʿarab*, 3: 94–7.
40 Al-Farāhīdī, *al-ʿAyn*, 2: 137; *Lisān al-ʿarab*, 4: 601–3.
41 The term *maʿmar* for a dwelling and lively place with people is found in the pre-Islamic poetry of Kulayb b. Rabīʿah al-Taghlibī (d. 492) (Abū Zayd, *Shuʿarāʾ Taghlib*, 2: 136).
42 Al-Farāhīdī, *al-ʿAyn*, 2: 137; *Lisān al-ʿarab*, 4: 603–4.
43 Al-Farāhīdī, *al-ʿAyn*, 3: 317–21; *Lisān al-ʿarab*, 14:210–23.
44 The meaning of *ḥayy* as a lively city with people may be seen in pre-Islamic poetry attributed to Mālik b. Fahm al-Azdī (d. 231) (ʿUbayd, *Shuʿarāʾ ʿUmān*, 83) and in various others, such as Zayd b. ʿAmr al-Hamdānī (d. 538) (Abū Yāsīn, *Shiʿr Hamdān*, 257).
45 From Herdner, *Corpus des tablettes*, 17:6:25; as translated in Wyatt, *Religious Texts*, 273.
46 From Herdner, *Corpus des tablettes*, 17:1:37; as translated in Wyatt, *Religious Texts*, 261.
47 *TDOT*, 4: 330–1.
48 Smith, 'Concourse between the Living and the Dead'; Zahir al-Din, 'Man in Search'.
49 *TDOT*, 10: 65–70; Brown-Driver-Briggs, *A Hebrew and English Lexicon of the Old Testament*, henceforth *BDB*, 675.
50 *TDOT*, 9: 497–504.
51 Ibid., 13: 361–5.
52 Walton, *Ancient Near Eastern Thought*, 203–16; Cooper, 'Scripture and Philosophy'.
53 Wright, 'Rûaḥ'; Wiggins, 'Tempestuous Wind'; Lewis, 'ʿAthtartu's Incantations'; Moskala, 'Holy Spirit'; Wilson-Wright, 'Love Conquers All'; van Dyk, 'Spirit of God'.
54 Gier and Petta, 'Hebrew and Buddhist Selves'.
55 Grollman, 'Death in Jewish Thought'; Raphael, *Jewish Views*, xxvii–xxviii; Jerome, 'Detachment as a Prerequisite'.
56 Al-Farāhīdī, *al-ʿAyn*, 7: 270–1; 7: 275.
57 In al-Aghlab al-ʿIjlī's (d. 21/642) poetry, he says, 'separates between the *nafs* and the *nasīm*' and, thus, implying those terms are not synonymous (al-Qaysī, 'al-Aghlab al-ʿIjlī', 126).
58 Finnestad, 'On Transposing Soul and Body'.
59 Ibid.
60 Ibid.
61 Ibid.
62 Ibid.
63 Ibid.
64 Walton, *Ancient Near Eastern Thought*, 210–13. For Israelite understanding of the composition of human beings, see Walton, *Ancient Near Eastern Thought*, 212–15.
65 *The Assyrian Dictionary of the Oriental Institute of the University of Chicago*, henceforth *CAD*, 11.1: 296–305, 11.1: 318.
66 *TDOT*, 9: 500.
67 *CAD*, 14: 117–26.
68 Ibid., 4: 397–401. Also see, Steinert, *Aspekte des Menschseins*, 271–404.
69 Speiser, *Ancient Near Eastern Texts*; Grayson, *Ancient Near Eastern Texts*.
70 Some scholars interpret '*eṭemmu*' as not necessarily the soul of the dead, but also the soul of the living; see Shehata, *Annotierte Bibliographie*, 10.
71 *CAD*, 19: 84–97. The Akkadian root of '*ṭēmu*' is shared with '*ṭamu*', which means to twist and entwine (*CAD*, 19: 45–6). This is similar to the Arabic 'ʿ*aql*', which also means intellect and shares the root with twisting as well.
72 *CAD*, 3: 74–81.

73 Moran, 'Creation of Man'.
74 Cooper, 'Wind and Smoke'; Scurlock, 'Images of Tammuz'.
75 Greenfield, 'Une rite religieux'; Steiner, *Disembodied Souls*, 116–17.
76 Bottéro, *Mésopotamie*; Yamauchi, 'Life, Death, and Afterlife'; Skålvold, 'Images of Death'.
77 This is attested in the *Epic of Atrahasis* (I 208–230); see Steinert, *Aspekte des Menschseins*, 322.
78 Al-Farāhīdī, *al-ʿAyn*, 7: 408–9.
79 Ibid.
80 Orel and Stolbova, *Hamito-Semitic*, 395–6.
81 *CAD*, 11.1: 296.
82 *CAD*, 11.1: 304, 11.1: 318.
83 Ibid, 11.2: 166–70.
84 Ibid, 11.2: 169–70.
85 Ibid, 11.1: 304, 11.2: 170.
86 *Lisān al-ʿarab*, 6: 238, on '*n-f-s*'.
87 *TDOT*, 9: 502.
88 *BDB*, 659–61.
89 *Lisān al-ʿarab*, 6: 238, on '*n-f-s*'.
90 *Lisān al-ʿarab*, 6: 236–237, on '*n-f-s*'.
91 *BDB*, 661.
92 *Genesis Rabbah*, 2:7.
93 *Genesis Rabbah*, 2:7.
94 Robinson, *Christian Doctrine of Man*.
95 Nürnberger, 'Dust of the Ground'; O'Connor, 'Genesis 2:7'.
96 Köhler, *Old Testament Theology*, 142.
97 Compare with Blenkinsopp, 'Saving One's Soul'; Dougherty, *Problem of Animal Pain*, 154–78; Rothenberg, *Rabbi Akiva's Philosophy*, 67–88.
98 Noort, 'Taken from the Soil'.
99 van der Meer, 'Anthropology in the Ancient Greek'; Popović, 'Anthropology, Pneumatology, and Demonology'; Wyss, 'From Cosmogony to Psychology'.
100 Paton, 'Hebrew Idea of the Future Life'; Gillman, *Death of Death*, 76–7.
101 Staples, '"Soul" in the Old Testament'; Crawford, *Battle for the Soul*, 1–23.
102 Moore, 'Prophet as Mentor'.
103 Steiner, *Disembodied Souls*, 81–92.
104 *BDB*, 659–61.
105 Murphy, 'Human Nature', 20–3.
106 Wolff, *Anthropology of the Old Testament*, 13–14.
107 Parpola, *Etymological Dictionary*, 1: 278
108 Schroeder, 'Evolution'.
109 This is debatable, as Daniel Lys disagrees that the Septuagint (LXX) uses the term '*psychē*' as a form of dualism (Lys, 'Israelite Soul'). However, the LXX translators could have used other terms for a dead body, and therefore, using '*psychē*' could have meant something else.
110 I am not aware of much in-depth research in biblical studies of why that is. I presume it is because most biblical scholars dismiss the possibility of a dualistic nature of humans by ancient Israelites, and take it for granted.
111 To see how Ezek. 44:25 references Lev. 21:1, see Zipor, 'Greek Version'; Ganzel, 'Defilement and Desecration'; de Hemmer Gudme, 'How Should We Read'; Lapsley,

'Body Piercings'; Cornelius, 'Motivation and Limits', 1189; Awabdy, 'Yhwh Exegetes Torah'; MacDonald, *Priestly Rule*; Ginsburskaya, 'Purity and Impurity', 17.

112 Many biblical scholars insist that dualism was not part of the Israelite culture (see for example, Cooper, *Body, Soul, and Life*; Block, 'Beyond the Grave'), but as shown, this is not necessarily the case.

113 *Samʾal* is located in modern-day Turkey. It used to be part of the ancient Aramaean kingdom of Samʾal. Its language is closely related to the Northwest Semitic group.

114 Steiner, *Disembodied Souls*, 14.

115 Ibid, 137–40.

116 Ibid., 137.

117 Ibid., 10–22, esp. 17.

118 Edzard, 'Role of South Arabian'.

119 A dream soul is the soul believed to depart the body of a sleeping person. Qurʾan 39:42 might be referring to two kinds of souls (*nafs*), one of which might be the dream soul, which Steiner also suggests (Steiner, *Disembodied Souls*, 47). Steiner also cites rabbinic literature that Ps. 31:5 and Job 12:10 are references to the dream soul (Steiner, *Disembodied Souls*, 47–8). Also see Frazer, *Golden Bough*, 3: 36–42; Ginzberg, *Legends of the Jews*, 5: 74.

120 Steiner, *Disembodied Souls*, 18.

121 Ibid., 18. Also see Scurlock, 'Soul Emplacements', 1.

122 Steiner, *Disembodied Souls*, 20–1.

123 Ibid., 19–20.

124 Ibid., 21.

125 Sedgwick, 'Who Am I Now'.

126 Not all agree that this is spiritual and not bodily death that is being discussed by the psalter. See Simeon, *Horae Homileticae*, 6: 277–9.

127 Augustine of Hippo (d. 430 CE), *Expositions on the Book of Psalms*, 8: 224.

128 See Barré, 'Psalm 116'; compare with Prinsloo, 'Psalm 116'; Potgieter, 'Psalm 56'.

129 Fishbane, *Kiss of God*.

130 Bogue, 'Betrayal of God', 12.

131 *NRSV* uses meat instead of flesh.

132 Al-Farāhīdī, *al-ʿAyn*, 7: 271; *Lisān al-ʿarab*, 6: 238–9.

133 Barr, 'Scope and Problems', 7.

134 Saucy, 'Theology of Human Nature', 31–41; Billauer, 'On Judaism and Genes'.

135 Nelson, 'Life and Living'; Collins, 'Discourse Analysis'.

136 Some scholars would agree to this, but suggest that it can denote a dead body as in the instance of Lev. 19:28 or Num. 5:2, as described earlier.

137 Boyd, 'One's Self-Concept'.

138 Uitti, 'Health and Wholeness', 51.

139 Hogan, 'Exegetical Background'; Schmid, 'Loss of Immortality'; Ladouceur, 'Evolution and Genesis 2–3', 163. Some scholars prefer to use metaphoric death and not spiritual death in this passage precisely for the reason of a monistic view of the body-soul issue; see Gordon, 'Ethics of Eden', 22.

140 Philo, *Legum allegoriae*, 1:105–7.

141 Steiner, *Disembodied Souls*, 69–70.

142 Kilwing, 'נֶפֶשׁ und ΨYXH', 386.

143 Steiner, *Disembodied Souls*, 69–70.

144 Wright, *Man in the Process of Time*; Osei-Bonsu, '2 Cor 5:1–10'; Huang, 'Death in the Hebrew Bible'.

145 Chafer, *Systematic Theology*, 4: 414–15; Walvoord, *Revelation of Jesus Christ*, 134–5; Hoyt, *End Times*, 45–7; Harris, *Raised Immortal*; Edgar, 'Biblical Anthropology . . . Part 1'; Edgar, 'Biblical Anthropology . . . Part 2'.
146 Osei-Bonsu, 'Intermediate State'; Edgar, 'Paul and the Person'.
147 Fryer, 'Intermediate State'; Harrison, 'In Quest of the Third Heaven'; Cooper, 'Scripture and Philosophy'; Cooper, 'Biblical Anthropology'.
148 Schmithals, *Gnosticism in Corinth*, 216–17. Also concurred by Jörg Baumgarten; see Baumgarten, *Paulus und die Apokalyptik*, 142–3.
149 Also highlighted by Dieter Georgi on the forms of non-Gnostic Hellenistic mysticism; see Georgi, *Die Gegner des Paulus*, 179ff, 298; Harrison, 'In Quest of the Third Heaven'.
150 Plevnik, 'Taking Up of the Faithful'; Tabor, 'Returning to the Divinity'; Zwiep, *Ascension of the Messiah*. Also see Vawter, 'Intimations of Immortality'; Tabor, '"Returning to the Divinity"'; Poirier, 'Endtime Return of Elijah'; Snyman, 'Malachi 4:4–6'. On the study of the spirit of Elijah cast upon Elisha, see Rice, 'Elijah's Requirement, 1'; Zucker, 'Elijah and Elisha'. Moses *passim*. (Cohn's index gives nearly 300 references.)
151 Philo, *De Somnii*, 1.36, 1.232.
152 Baumgarten, *Paulus und die Apokalyptik*, 142.
153 Josephus, *On Wars*, 7.8.7.
154 Tesei, '*barzakh*'; Archer, *Place Between Two Places*.
155 Ibn Ḥazm, *al-Faṣl fil-milal*, 5: 55–6; al-Suyūṭī, *Sharḥ al-ṣudūr*. As with most classic and medieval Muslim scholars, most do not differentiate between '*rūḥ*' and '*nafs*' and use them interchangeably. Accordingly, some scholars would speak of a disembodied '*rūḥ*', while others speak of a disembodied '*nafs*', yet they all mean the same to these scholars. For more scholars speaking of the disembodiment, especially at the intermediate state, see Ibn Abī al-ʿIzz, *Sharḥ al-ʿaqīdah al-ṭaḥāwiyyah*, 395.
156 Ibn Qayyim uses the term '*rūḥ*', as he uses it interchangeably with the term '*nafs*'. See Ibn Qayyim al-Jawziyyah, *al-Rūḥ fil-kalām*, 115, 187.
157 *Ṣaḥīḥ al-Bukhārī*, 4: 131 (#3326), 4: 132 (#3327), 8: 50 (#6227); *Ṣaḥīḥ Muslim*, 4: 2179 (#2834), 4: 2183 (#2841); Ibn Ḥanbal, *Musnad*, 7: 15–17 (#7165), 8: 219–20 (#8156); also see Ibn Abī Dawūd, *al-Baʿth*, 57 (#64, #65); Ibn al-Mulaqqin Sirāj al-Dīn, *al-Tawḍīḥ*, 19: 141; al-ʿAsqalānī, *al-Maṭālib*, 18: 721–3 (#4265), 18: 724–7 (#4262); al-Ḥamlāwī, *al-Takhallī*, 184.
158 Al-Ṭabarānī, *al-Muʿjam al-kabīr*, 20: 280 (#663, #664).
159 Cullman, 'Immortality of the Soul'; Williams, *Problems of the Self*, 19–25; van Inwagen, 'Possibility of Resurrection'; Hick, *Death and Eternal Life*; Bynum, *Resurrection of the Body*; Swineburn, *Evolution of the Soul*; Baker, *Persons and Bodies*; Baker, 'Death and the Afterlife'; Baker, 'Persons and the Metaphysics'; Bresnan, *Awakening*.
160 *Lisān al-ʿarab*, 6: 233–4.
161 Smith, 'Understanding of *Nafs*', 152. Also see al-ʿUtaybī, *al-Qiyāmah al-ṣughrā*, 85.
162 Tlili, 'From Breath to Soul'.
163 Al-Ghazālī, *Iḥyāʾ*, 1: 45, 3: 4.
164 Ibid., 1: 54.
165 Al-Khaṭīb, *al-Tafsīr al-Qurʾānī*, 12: 1166.
166 Ibrahīm, 'Nihāyah al-ḥayāh', 3.
167 Ibid.
168 m. Sanhedrin 4:5; b. Sanhedrin 37b
169 Ibid.
170 Ibid.

171 Segal, *Life after Death*, 651.
172 The Septuagint (LXX) in Job 23:13 does not translate '*nepeš*' as '*psychē*' (soul), but as '*autos*' meaning himself. Also, Amos 6:8 significantly departs from the Masoretic Text, and one of its departure is not identifying '*nepeš*' as '*psychē*' (soul), but translates it as '*eautou*', which is simply himself.
173 Marter, 'Hebrew Concept of "Soul"'; Harvey, 'Is Biblical Man'; Lampe, *God as Spirit*.
174 Picken, 'Tazkiyat al-nafs'.
175 Ibid.
176 Ibid., 108.
177 Ibid.
178 Ibid., 108–9.
179 Ibid., 109–10.
180 However, '*ẓann*' may be understood as zeal instead of conjecture; see Galadari, 'Qur'anic Faith'.
181 Picken, 'Tazkiyat al-nafs', 110–12.
182 Ibid., 112–15. Also see Smith and Haddad, *Islamic Understanding*, 16.
183 Picken, 'Tazkiyat al-nafs', 112–17. Also see Smith and Haddad, *Islamic Understanding*, 16.
184 Al-Rāzī, *Mafātīḥ*, (Q. 3:185), 9: 451; al-Rāzī, *Mafātīḥ*, (Q. 21:35), 22: 143.
185 Al-Rāzī, *Mafātīḥ*, (Q. 3:185), 9: 452.
186 Ibid.
187 Ibid.
188 Jaffer, 'Fakhr al-Dīn al-Rāzī'.
189 *TSQ* translates this in the future-tense, but it is very much possible in the present-tense.
190 See Al-Ṭabarī, *Jāmiʿ*, (Q. 39:42), 21: 298. Also see al-Rāzī, *Mafātīḥ*, (Q. 39:42), 26: 455–6.
191 Al-Rāzī, *Mafātīḥ*, (Q. 39:42), 26: 455–6.
192 Al-Ṭabarsī, *Majmaʿ*, (Q. 39:42).
193 Al-Tustarī, *Tafsīr*, (Q. 39:42).
194 Burckhardt, 'Concerning the "Barzakh"'; Smith and Haddad, *Islamic Understanding*, 108–10, 121–5, 183; Akbar, 'Study on the World of Barzakh'.
195 Dakake, 'Soul as Barzakh'; Peerwani, 'Death and the Post-Mortem States'; Stenmark, 'Theories of Human Nature'; Afsaruddin, 'Dying in the Path of God', 169.

Chapter 3

1 Miller and Truog, 'Decapitation'; Shewmon, 'Constructing the Death Elephant'; Thomas, 'Continuing the Definition'; de Georgia, 'History of Brain Death'; Truog and Miller, 'Defining Death'; Truog and Miller, 'Changing the Conversation'; Lewis, Cahn-Fuller, and Caplan, 'Shouldn't Dead Be Dead'.
2 Truog, 'Time to Abandon Brain Death'; Souter and van Norman, 'Ethical Controversies'.
3 Randhawa, 'Death and Organ Donation'; Segal, 'Religious Objections'.
4 Padela, Shanawani and Arozullah, 'Medical Experts'; Padela, Arozullah and Moosa, 'Brain Death'; Rady and Verheijde, 'Brain-Dead Patients'; Miller, 'Opinions on the Legitimacy'; Rady and Verheijde, 'Response to the Legitimacy'; Chamsi-Pasha and Albar, 'Do Not Resuscitate'.

5 Bedir and Aksoy, 'Brain Death Revisited'; Padela and Basser, 'Brain Death'; Qazi, Ewell, Munawar, Asrar, and Khan, 'Degree of Certainty'.

6 This is the case even when different cultures had various definitions of death. For example, the ancient Greeks considered the heart, the muscular organ, to be the first to live and the first to die (Bernat, 'Definition and Criterion of Death'; also see Bradley, Feldman and Johansson, *Oxford Handbook of Philosophy of Death*).

7 Taylor, *Buried Soul*; Solomon, Greenberg, Schimel, Arndt and Pyszczynski, 'Human Awareness'; Davies, *Death, Ritual and Belief*.

8 Steadman and Palmer, 'Visiting Dead Ancestors'.

9 Mortuary rites are not necessarily an indication of some afterlife beliefs. Compare with King, 'Apes, Hominids'; Granger, Gibbon, Kuman, Clarke, Bruxelles and Caffee, 'New Cosmogenic Burial Ages'; Grosman and Munro, 'Natufian Ritual Event'; Sala and Conrad, 'Taphonomic Analysis'; Knuston, 'First Burials', 1–2; Knuston, 'First Recorded Burials', 2–3.

10 Siegel, 'Psychology of Life after Death'.

11 Finkelstein and Silberman, *Bible Unearthed*, 16.

12 Taylor, *Death and the Afterlife*; Ikram, *Death and Burial*.

13 *TDOT*, 187. Also see Allen, *Debate between a Man*, 124–31.

14 Manning, 'Representation of Justice'.

15 Ibid.

16 Ibid.

17 Ancient Semites might have controlled parts of Egypt (such as the controversial Hyksos invasion or the likes) and vice-versa; see Schneider, 'Foreign Egypt'; Sparks, 'Canaan in Egypt'; Assante, 'Inside and Out'; Bader, 'Cultural Mixing'; Mourad, 'Rise of the Hyksos'.

18 Strange, 'Idea of Afterlife'.

19 ben Dor Evian, 'Egypt and the Levant'.

20 Finkelstein and Silberman, *Bible Unearthed*; Bar, Kahn, and Shirley, *Egypt, Canaan and Israel*; Finkelstein, ben Dor Evian, Boaretto and Weiner, 'Reconstructing Ancient Israel'; ben Dor Evian, 'Egypt and Israel'; Lipschits, Gadot, and Adams, *Rethinking Israel*.

21 Scurlock, 'Death and the Afterlife'.

22 Compare with Lesko, 'Death and the Afterlife.'

23 *CAD*, 10.1: 421–7; del Olmo Lete, 'Môtu and Baʕlu'.

24 McAffee, 'Life and Mortality'.

25 Jean and Hoftijzer, *Dictionnaire des inscriptions*.

26 It is attested in Tell el-Amarna tablets; see Rainey, *El-Amarna Correspondence*, 1: 1288.

27 *TDOT*, 8: 190.

28 Erman and Grapow, *Wörterbuch der ägyptischen Sprache*, 2: 165ff.

29 Orel and Stolbova, *Hamito-Semitic*, 380, 391.

30 *TDOT*, 8: 189.

31 *CAD*, 16: 67–70.

32 Smith, 'Concourse between the Living and the Dead'.

33 *TDOT*, 12: 373. Also see al-Farāhīdī, *al-ʿAyn*, 7: 8–10; *Lisān al-ʿarab*, 11: 391–4.

34 *CAD*, 16: 72.

35 *TDOT*, 12: 373.

36 Roman, *Étude de la phonologie*, 1: 162–209; Brown, 'New Data'.

37 Ibn Suhayl al-Naḥawī, *al-Ḍād wal-ẓāʾ*; al-Dānī, *al-Farq bayn al-ḍād wal-ẓāʾ*; al-Ṣiqillī, *Maʾrifah al-ḍād wal-ẓāʾ*; al-Zanjānī, *al-Farq bayn al-ḍād wal-ẓāʾ*; al-Ḥarrānī, *al-Miṣbāḥ*; Ibn al-Ṣābūnī al-Ishbīlī, *Maʿrifah al-farq*; al-Jiyyānī, *al-Iʿtimād*; al-Shaybānī, *al-Farq bayn al-ḍād wal-ẓāʾ*; al-Ḍāmin, *Fāʾit naẓāʾir al-ẓāʾ wal-ḍād*.

38 Brown, 'New Data'.
39 *CAD*, 16: 189–94, 16: 238–43.
40 Leslau, *Comparative Dictionary*, 555–6.
41 Orel and Stolbova, *Hamito-Semitic*, 117–19.
42 *TDOT*, 12: 396–7.
43 *CAD*, 16: 70–1, 16: 73. Also see *CAD*, 16: 77–8. Also see *CAD*, 16: 241.
44 Leslau, *Comparative Dictionary*, 556.
45 Ibid.
46 *TDOT*, 12: 396–7.
47 van Acker, 'צלמות'. Compare with Eybers, 'Root *Ṣ-L*'.
48 Thomas, 'צלמות'.
49 *CAD*, 16: 78–86.
50 *BDB*, 853–4.
51 Some scholars argue otherwise; see Clines, 'Etymology of Hebrew Ṣelem'.
52 *CAD*, 16: 190.
53 Christiansen, 'Dark Koran'.
54 Abdul-Raof, 'Conceptual and Textual Chaining'.
55 *Lisān al-ʿarab*, 12: 377–9.
56 *Lisān al-ʿarab*, 12: 373–7.
57 *BDB*, 378–9; Leslau, *Comparative Dictionary*, 591.
58 Al-Farāhīdī, *al-ʿAyn*, 7: 8–10.
59 *CAD*, 12: 12–16. Also see Foster, 'Letters and Literature'; Steinert, *Aspekte des Menschseins*, 231–56.
60 *TDOT*, 11: 477.
61 Fensham, 'Common Trends'.
62 Al-Farāhīdī, *al-ʿAyn*, 6: 111–12; *Lisān al-ʿarab*, 5: 46–8.
63 *TDOT*, 11: 477.
64 Obermann, 'Votive Inscriptions'; Neiman, 'PGR'; Healey, 'Ugarit and Arabia'.
65 Leslau, *Comparative Dictionary*, 156.
66 *TDOT*, 11: 477.
67 Ibn Hishām, *al-Sīrah*, 1: 170.
68 Al-Fākihī, *Akhbār Makkah*, 5: 165–6; Ibn al-Jawzī, *al-Muntaẓam*, 2: 290–1, 296–8, 311; Ibn al-Athīr, *al-Kāmil fil-tarīkh*, 1: 598–603; al-Samīn al-Ḥalabī, *ʿUmdah al-ḥuffāẓ*, 3: 204.
69 Ibn Hishām, *al-Sīrah*, 1: 170; Al-Fayrūzʾābādī, *al-Qāmūs al-Muḥīṭ*, 455.
70 Ibn al-Jawzī, *al-Muntaẓam*, 2: 311.
71 Ibid.
72 Ibn al-Athīr, *al-Kāmil*, 1: 598–9, 1: 601.
73 Mujāhid, *Tafsīr*, 686.
74 Ibn ʿArabī, *Tafsīr*, (Q. 75: 1–6).
75 Irfatpour, 'Aesthetic Imagery'.
76 *Lisān al-ʿarab*, 4: 52. Compare with *TDOT*, 2: 308–11. Also see Albright, 'Specimens of Late Ugaritic Prose'; Merlini, 'Lexical Field of "Purity"'; Ouro, 'Term ṭᵉhôrâ'.
77 *Lisān al-ʿarab*, 5: 144–51. Also see *TDOT*, 7: 289; *BDB*, 497.
78 Cole, 'Infidel or Paganus'.
79 Ibid., 634.
80 Ibn Kathīr, *al-Bidāyah wal-nihāyah*, 9: 555, 9: 559.
81 Al-Farāhīdī, *al-ʿAyn*, 5: 356–8; *Lisān al-ʿarab*, 5: 150.
82 *Lisān al-ʿarab*, 5: 150.

83 *CAD*, 8: 189–90.
84 Al-Zamakhsharī, *al-Kashshāf* (Q. 57:20), 4: 478–9.
85 Al-Rāzī, *Mafātīḥ* (Q. 57:20), 29: 463–4.
86 Ibn Kathīr, *Tafsīr*, 8: 24–5.
87 *Lisān al-ʿarab*, 5: 146–7.
88 Al-Rāzī, *Mafātīḥ* (Q. 57:20), 29: 463–4.
89 Al-Farāhīdī, *al-ʿAyn*, 5: 356–8.
90 *Lisān al-ʿarab*, 5: 144–51.
91 *CAD*, 8: 178–80.
92 *BDB*, 497–8.
93 The Hebrew term for a nonbeliever is used, for example, in b. Sanhedrin 39a.
94 Al-Farāhīdī, *al-ʿAyn*, 5: 356–8.
95 *Lisān al-ʿarab*, 5: 144–51.
96 Al-Farāhīdī, *al-ʿAyn*, 5: 356–8; *Lisān al-ʿarab*, 5: 150; Alzoubi and al-Qudrah, 'Nabataean Architectural Terminology'.
97 Leslau, *Comparative Dictionary*, 277.
98 Khairy, 'Analytical Study'; Abdelaziz and Rababeh, 'Terminology Used'; Khairy, 'Mada'in Saleh'; Alzoubi and Smadi, 'Nabataean Funerary Inscription'.
99 Schoff, 'Camphor'.
100 O'Connor, 'Arabic Loanwords'; Healey, *Nabataean Tomb Inscriptions*, 69.
101 See Kaufman, *Targum Lexicon*. Also see Bosman, Oosting and Potsma, *Wörterbuch zum Alten Testament*. Compare with Richard, 'HT 31'; Loesov, 'New Attempt'; Mutzafi, *Comparative Lexical Studies*, 35.
102 *Lisān al-ʿarab*, 10: 357–60.
103 *Lisān al-ʿarab*, 10: 358.
104 Leslau, *Comparative Dictionary*, 388–9.
105 In Aramaic, the root '*n-f-q*' is used to mean to leave and to go out. Taking this as an etymological source, the Arabic polysemes that are defined by '*n-f-q*' would have sense. See *Gesenius' Lexicon*, 558.
106 *Lisān al-ʿarab*, 10: 358–9.
107 *Lisān al-ʿarab*, 10: 358–9.
108 *Lisān al-ʿarab*, 10: 357.
109 Ibn Ḥanbal, *Musnad* (al-Risālah), 36: 434–5 (#22122).
110 ʿAbbās, *Dīwān*, 229.
111 Leslau, *Comparative Dictionary*, 389; also see Leslau, 'South-East Semitic'.
112 *CAD*, 11.1: 277–8.
113 Ahmad, 'Qurʾānic Concepts', 33–4.
114 *Lisān al-ʿarab*, 12: 90.
115 *BDB*, 175.
116 Hecker, *Biradical Origin*, 74, 99.
117 Al-Farāhīdī, *al-ʿAyn*, 6: 118; *Lisān al-ʿarab*, 12: 92–3. Also see *BDB*, 175. Compare with Feigin, 'Ḥamôr Gārîm'; Forchheimer, 'Semantic Development'.
118 Cotton et al., *Corpus Inscriptionum*.
119 Al-Farāhīdī, *al-ʿAyn*, 6: 119; *Lisān al-ʿarab*, 12: 91–4.
120 Al-Qawwāl, *Dīwān*, 81.
121 *Lisān al-ʿarab*, 12: 409–12. Also see *TDOT*, 11: 289–303.
122 Al-Qaysī, *Shiʿr Muzāḥim*, 125.
123 Feigin, 'Ḥamôr Gārîm'. Also see Feigin, 'Haggārîm'.
124 Forchheimer, 'Semantic Development'. Compare with Heck, 'Issachar'.

125 Al-Farāhīdī, *al-ʿAyn*, 6: 60; *Lisān al-ʿarab*, 12: 99–100. *BDB*, 177.
126 *BDB*, 177; Koehler and Baumgartner, *HALOT*, 1846.
127 See Levin, *Semitic and Indo-European*, 2: 377. Also see the supplement information of Agmon and Bloch, 'Statistics of Language'.
128 Cases of this specific shift are attested during the Akkadian consonantal shifts, see von Soden, *Grundriss der Akkadischen*, 44 (§35(c)); also see Pentiuc, *West Semitic Vocabulary*, 84.
129 It occurs in Geʿez with the meaning of gentle; see Leslau, *Comparative Dictionary*, 310–12.
130 *CAD*, 9: 38.
131 Al-Ṭabarī, *Jāmiʿ*, (Q. 18:27), 17: 650–2; (Q. 72:22), 23: 669–70.
132 Al-Farāhīdī, *al-ʿAyn*, 3: 182–3.
133 Ibid.; *Lisān al-ʿarab*, 3: 388–90; Samār, *Dirāsāt fil-muʿtaqadāt*, 78–9.
134 Al-Farāhīdī, *al-ʿAyn*, 3: 182–3.
135 Al-Rāzī, *Mafātīḥ*, (Q. 18:27), 21: 454–5; (Q. 72:22), 30: 675.
136 Al-Ṭabarī, *Jāmiʿ*, (Q. 18:27), 17: 650–2.
137 Al-Aʿlam al-Shantamarī, *Dīwān*, 50.
138 Al-Muʿaybid, *Dīwān*, 106.
139 After all, the root '*kh-l-d*' means to penetrate, and for that reason a type of rat or mole that digs into the ground is called '*khuld*' in Arabic (Al-Farāhīdī, *al-ʿAyn*, 4: 232; *BDB*, 317). Also see the root '*kh-l-d*' can mean to dig or to creep in Middle Hebrew, Palestinian Aramaic, and Syriac (Levy, *Wörterbuch über die Talmudim und Midraschim*). This is the etymology of the mole rat in Leviticus 11:29, since it bores a hole in the ground (*nafaq*).

Chapter 4

1 Rakesh and Ayati, 'Concept of Death'.
2 Ibid.
3 Galadari, 'Reincarnation vs. Resurrection'.
4 I chose to translate *bashar* as flesh instead of human being, as is given in *TSQ*, as it is more loyal to the root meaning of the word and important to the argument of this study, which distinguishes *nafs* from *bashar*.
5 O'Shaughnessy, *Muhammad's Thoughts*, 6. The order of the passages are as appears in O'Shaughnessy, which is based on his adopted chronological order of the Qurʾan.
6 Ibid., 14.
7 Ibid., 15.
8 The association between a non-dying person in hell in Qurʾan 87:13 and skins roasted in hell in Qurʾan 4:56 is also noted Ḥāfiẓ al-Ḥakamī (d. 1377/1924) (al-Ḥakamī, Ḥāfiz, *Maʿārij al-qubūl*, 2: 864–5).
9 Al-Ṭabarī, *Jāmiʿ*, (Q. 14:17), 16: 550, (Q. 20:74), 18: 342, (Q. 87:13), 24: 373.
10 Ibn ʿArabī, *Tafsīr*, *op. cit*.
11 O'Shaughnessy, *Muhammad's Thoughts*, 6.
12 Ibid., 9–13.
13 Ibid., 24.
14 Ibid., 14–15, 23–4.
15 Crone, 'Nothing but Time', 137.
16 Smith and Haddad, *Islamic Understanding*, 17.

17 Crone, 'Quranic *Mushrikūn* . . . (Part I)', 448.
18 Golzadeh and Pourebrahim, 'Death Metaphor'.
19 Sardaraz and bin Ali, 'Conceptualisation of Death'.
20 Ibid.
21 Berrada, 'Metaphors of Light'.
22 Ibid., 55.
23 Berrada, 'Metaphors of Light'.
24 Ibid., 58.
25 Ibid., 58–60.
26 Ibid., 60.
27 El-Sharif, 'Metaphors We Believe'.
28 Compare with El-Zeiny, 'Criteria for the Translation'.
29 Al-Ali, El-Sharif, and Alzyoud, 'Functions and Linguistic Analysis'.
30 Al-Zayla'ī, *Tabyīn al-ḥaqā'iq*, 2: 2; Āq Shamsul-Dīn, *Fuṣūl al-badā'i'*, 2: 428; al-Naysābūrī, *Gharā'ib al-Qur'an*, 314; al-Qārī, *Mirqāh al-mafātīḥ*, 8: 3256 (#5200), 8: 3300 (#5274), 8: 3391; al-Muqrī al-Tilmisānī, *Nafḥ al-ṭīb*, 6: 314; Ḥaqqī, *Rūḥ al-bayān*, 1: 73, 1: 161, 1: 288, 2: 139, 2: 178, 3: 230, 9: 519; al-Khādmī, *Barīqah maḥmūdiyyah*, 2: 130; al-Mubarakfūrī, *Tuḥfah al-aḥwadhī*, 6: 515; al-Ithyūbī, *Mashāriq al-anwār*, 3: 248. Nonetheless, Ibn Ḥajar (d. 852/1449), al-Sakhāwī (d. 902/1497), and al-Qārī (d. 1014/1606) suppose this prophetic tradition to be false; see Ibn Ḥajar, *al-Imtā' bil-arba'īn*, 98; al-Sakhāwī, *al-Maqāṣid al-ḥasanah*, 682 (#1213), 761; al-Qārī, *Sharḥ al-shifā*, 2: 461, 2: 522. For modern scholarship on this Sufi notion, see Kugle, 'Die before Dying'; Perreira, 'Die before You Die'; Ahmad, 'Man and His Spiritual Position'; Fahm, 'Brief Analysis'.
31 Sharifi, 'Self-realization'; Shah-Kazemi, 'Wisdom of Gratitude', 70.
32 Sukdaven, Mukhtar, and Fernana, 'Timbuktu Manuscript'.
33 Farīd, *Tazkiyah al-nufūs*; Yusoff et al., 'Purification of Soul'.
34 Al-Ghazālī, *Iḥyā'*, 3: 43, 3: 61. Also see Justin Parrott's engagement with al-Ghazālī's work on arrogance and pride, Parrott, 'Al-Ghazali and the Golden Rule'.
35 Anees, 'From Knowledge to Nihilism'.
36 This discussion is based on that published in Galadari, 'Role of Intertextual Polysemy'.
37 Al-Ṭabarī, *Jāmi'*, (Q. 16:21), 17: 188.
38 Al-Tha'labī, *al-Kashf wal-bayān*, 6: 12–13.
39 Al-Rāzī, *Mafātīḥ*, (Q. 16:21), 20: 192–6.
40 Al-Ṭūsī, *al-Tibyān al-jāmi'*, 6: 370–1.
41 Al-Ṭabarsī, *Majma'*, (Q. 16:21), 6: 147.
42 al-Suhaylī, *al-Rawḍ al-unf*, 3: 99, 3: 190.
43 Ibn Qayyim al-Jawziyyah, *al-Jawāb al-kāfī*, 55.
44 Al-Tustarī, *Tafsīr*, 90.
45 Al-Sulamī, *Ḥaqā'iq al-tafsīr*, 1: 364.
46 Al-Baqlī, *Ḥaqā'iq al-Qur'ān*, 314–5.
47 Ibn al-Ḥāj al-Fāsī, *al-Madkhal*, 3: 56–7.
48 I added 'and' in the beginning of the verse, as it is what the Arabic uses, but for some reason not translated in *TSQ*. I also corrected what seems to be a grammatical mistake in *TSQ*.
49 Al-Afghānī, *Juhūd 'ulamā'*, 1: 501–5; Zaynū, *Majmū'ah rasā'il al-tawjīhāt*, 3: 392–3; Āl al-Shaykh, *Hādhih mafāhimunā*, 47; Āl al-Shaykh, *al-Tamhīd*, 186; al-Ḥaqawī, *al-Tawḍīḥ*, 98–100, 573.
50 Ibid.; Ṣaqr, *Kashf shubuhāt al-ṣūfiyyah*, 42–6.

51 Crone, 'Religion of the Qur'anic Pagans'.
52 Al-Afghānī, *Juhūd ʿulamāʾ*, 2: 846–51; al-Ḥaqawī, *al-Tawḍīḥ*, 102.
53 Al-Ṭabarī, *Jāmiʿ*, (Q. 35:22), 20: 457–8.
54 Al-Ṭabarī, *Jāmiʿ*, (Q. 6:122), 12: 88–93.
55 Al-Rāzī, *Mafātīḥ*, (Q. 6:122), 13: 132–4.
56 Al-Zajjāj, *Maʿānī al-Qurʾān*, 4: 369.
57 Ibn al-Ḥāj al-Fāsī, *al-Madkhal*, 3: 57.
58 Al-Zajjāj, *Maʿānī al-Qurʾān*, 4: 369, *my translation*.
59 Abū ʿAlī al-Fārsī, *al-Ḥujjah lil-qurrāʾ*, 6: 47, *my translation*.
60 Ibn ʿArabī, *Tafsīr al-Qurʾān*, Q. 6:122.
61 Al-Ṭabarī, *Jāmiʿ*, (Q. 2:154), 3: 214–219; al-Rāzī, *Mafātīḥ*, (Q. 2:154), 4: 125–8.
62 Ibn ʿArabī, *Tafsīr al-Qurʾān*, Q. 2:154.
63 Al-Ṭabarī, *Jāmiʿ*, (Q. 36:70), 20: 549–50.
64 Ibn al-Zubayr al-Ghirnāṭī, *al-Burhān*, 205.
65 Al-Ṭabarī, *Jāmiʿ*, (Q. 6:36), 11: 341–342; al-Rāzī, *Mafātīḥ*, (Q. 6:36), 12: 521–2. Also compare with Ibn al-Zubayr al-Ghirnāṭī, *al-Burhān*, 165–6.

Chapter 5

1 The Eighteen Benedictions (now nineteen) is known as the ʿ*Amidah* containing nineteen blessings. They are recited in the daily Jewish prayers with some seasonal variation.
2 m. Berakhot 5:2; b. Berakhot 26b, 29a, 33a; b. Taʿanit 1:1; b. Taʿanit 7a; j. Taʿanit 1:1. See discussion in Kern-Ulmer, 'Consistency and Change'.
3 b. Taʿanit 2a–2b. See Kern-Ulmer, 'Consistency and Change'.
4 b. Taʿanit 2a–2b; j. Berakhot 5:2. See Kern-Ulmer, 'Consistency and Change'.
5 Paul, 'Heavenly Tablets'.
6 Ibid.
7 b. Rosh Hashanah 16b.
8 Paul, 'Heavenly Tablets'.
9 Ibid.
10 Knust and Wasserman, 'Earth Accuses Earth'.
11 *NRSV* uses 'underworld' instead of 'earth'.
12 Ambrose, *Epistle 26*.
13 See *Anchor Yale Bible Commentary*, henceforth *AYBC*, 29: 334. Also see Jeremias, *Parables of Jesus*, 228; Schnackenburg, *Gospel According to St. John*, 2: 166; Whitacre, *John*, 4: 207–8; Keener, *Gospel of John*, 1: 737.
14 For a scholarly review of diverse interpretations of Jesus writing on the ground, see Knust and Wasserman, 'Earth Accuses Earth'.
15 Minear, 'Writing on the Ground'.
16 Knust, 'Early Christian Re-Writing'.
17 Ibid.
18 Wasserman, 'Patmos Family'.
19 Aichele, 'Reading Jesus Writing'.
20 Ibid.; Keith, 'Recent and Previous Research'; Keith, 'Initial Location'; Hughes, 'Lukan Special Material'.
21 Aichele, 'Reading Jesus Writing'.
22 Knust, 'Early Christian Re-Writing'.

23 Carmichael, 'Marriage and the Samaritan Woman'; Ariarajah, 'Water of Life'; Holt, 'Fountain of Living Water'.
24 *NRSV* uses 'feast' instead of 'quench', but the Hebrew term is more connected to drink than food.
25 *AYBC*, 17: 164; Gardner, 'Way to Eternal Life'.
26 Compare with Day, 'Daniel of Ugarit'; Spronk, *Beatific Afterlife*.
27 For more on this Ugaritic text, see Wright, *Ritual in Narrative*.
28 Wyatt, *Religious Texts*, 273–4.
29 McAffee, 'Rephaim, Whisperers'. Compare with l'Heureux, 'Ugaritic and Biblical Rephaim'; de Moor, 'Rāpi'ūma—Rephaim'.
30 The Hebrew term used in the Masoretic text is '*nĕbēlātî*', which means 'my corpse', although most translations use 'their bodies/corpses'. However, although the Hebrew uses the singular 'my corpse', it states that *they* will rise (*yĕqûmûn*). Due to this grammatical mystery, but keeping loyal to the Masoretic text, I translate it as 'my corpse they shall rise'.
31 *NRSV* translates '*rĕpā'îm*' as 'those long dead'. The Hebrew could mean shades (perhaps ghosts).
32 *AYBC*, 19: 371.
33 Ibid.
34 See Scholl, *Die Elenden in Gottes Thronrat*, 141–5; Polaski, *Authorizing an End*, 238–42.
35 For a further analysis of the grammatical interpretation of this passage, see van der Woude, 'Resurrection or Transformation', 143–64.
36 Schmitz, 'Grammar of Resurrection'.
37 Ibid., 148; compare with Hasel, 'Resurrection in the Theology'; van der Woude, 'Resurrection or Transformation?'
38 *BDB*, 614–15; *TDOT*, 9: 151.
39 Compare with Rabbinic use of rain and dew and their references from the Hebrew Bible; see Kern-Ulmer, 'Consistency and Change'.
40 *Genesis Rabbah*, 2:5–6. Also see Kern-Ulmer, 'Consistency and Change'; Neusner, *Confronting Creation*, 65–70.
41 Fox, 'Rhetoric of Ezekiel's Vision'; Charlesworth, 'Where Does the Concept', 2–3; Elledge, 'Resurrection of the Dead', 34–5.
42 Buck, 'רוח in Ezekiel', 55–7.
43 Birkeland, 'Belief in the Resurrection'.
44 *AYBC*, 22a: 749–50.
45 b. Sanhedrin, 92b.
46 Tromp, 'Can These Bone', 61–3.
47 Tuell, 'True Metaphor'.
48 Grassi, 'Ezekiel xxxvii 1–14'; Schenk, *Der Passionsbericht nach Markus*, 78; Senior, 'Death of Jesus'; Troxel, 'Matt 27.51–4 Reconsidered'; Quarles, 'Matthew 27:51–53'.
49 Refer to Waters, 'Matthew 27:52–53'; Weren, 'Human Body'.
50 Neuss, *Das Buch Ezechiel*.
51 Suh, 'Use of Ezekiel 37'.
52 Ibid.
53 Ibid.
54 Ibid.; also see Lohfink, *Does God Need the Church*, 206.
55 Hartman and Di Lella, *Book of Daniel*, 307; Nickelsburg, *Resurrection, Immortality*, 17–18; Lacocque, *Livre de Daniel*, 179; Goldingay, *Daniel*, 285; Bailey, 'Intertextual Relationship'; Dimant, 'Resurrection, Restoration'; Bronner, 'Resurrection Motif'.

56 Preuß, 'Auferstehung', 131–2; Lindenberger, 'Daniel 12:1–4'; Sawyer, 'My Secret Is with Me', 313–15.
57 Gardner, 'Way to Eternal Life'; Rodriguez, 'Heavenly Books of Life'.
58 Duhm, *Das Buch Jesaja*, 172. Joseph Blenkinsopp also supports this argument with various linguistic and thematic affinities between Isaiah and Daniel. Of course, not in the sense that Isaiah did truly author Daniel, but the author of the Book of Daniel attempts to interpret the Book of Isaiah and uses it as its own subtext; see Blenkinsopp, *Opening the Sealed Book*, 14–18, 261–2. Compare with Lester, *Daniel Evokes Isaiah*. Also see Kim, 'Biblical Interpretation', 172–85.
59 I changed the transliteration of this term to conform with the Arabic rendition. *TSQ* keeps it as '*ʿIlliyyūn*'.
60 *Lisān al-ʿarab*, 13: 203–4.
61 *CAD*, 15: 21.
62 *Hebrew and Aramaic Lexicon of the Old Testament*, henceforth *HALOT*, 742.
63 Leslau, *Comparative Dictionary*, 492.
64 *Lisān al-ʿarab*, 2: 295–6.
65 *Targum Lexicon*.
66 *Lisān al-ʿarab*, 2: 295–6.
67 Stewart, 'Poetic License', 241–3.
68 O'Shaughnessy, 'Seven Names for Hell'.
69 Contrast with al-Farāhīdī, *al-ʿAyn*, 6: 56.
70 Ibid.
71 Stewart, 'Poetic License', 241–4.
72 Makkī bin Abī Ṭālib, *al-Hidāyah ilā bulūgh al-nihāyah*, 5: 3448.
73 Al-Qurṭubī, *al-Jāmiʿ*, 9: 82.
74 Al-Suyūṭī, *Muʿtarak al-aqrān*, 3: 222.
75 Beck, *Evolution of the Early Qur'ān*, 16.
76 de Blois, 'Ḥijāratun min sijjīl', 62.
77 Compare with Orel and Stolbova, *Hemito-Semitic*, 471.
78 Compare with al-Farāhīdī, *al-ʿAyn*, 6: 53.
79 van Selms, 'siǧǧīn and siǧǧīl'.
80 Orel and Stolbova, *Hemito-Semitic*, 132.
81 *Lisān al-ʿarab*, 10: 456–7.
82 Al-Ṭabarī, *Jāmiʿ*, 24: 282–5, (Q. 83:7).
83 Ibn ʿArabī, *Tafsīr* (Q. 83:1–11).
84 For more details on the history of the interpretation of this passage by the early churches, see Scharlemann, 'He Descended into Hell'; Dalton, *Christ's Proclamation*, esp. 28–32; Reicke, *Disobedient Spirits*, esp. 19–35; Clark-Soles, *Death and the Afterlife*, 195–211; Campbell and van Rensburg, 'History of the Interpretation'; Du Toit, 'Study of 1 Peter 3:18–4:6'; Pierce, 'Spirits and the Proclamation'; Alfeyev, *Christ the Conqueror*; Pierce, *Spirits and the Proclamation*; Laufer, *Hells' Destruction*; Marcar, 'In the Days of Noah'; Kuryliak, 'Методы интерпретации 1 Петр. 3:18–22'. Wayne Grudem disagrees with most scholars on the correct understanding of the prison in 1 Peter 3:18–20 in that it is not to be described as hell; see Grudem, 'He Did Not Descend'. Compare with Lauber, *Barth on the Descent*.
85 For more on the function of the depictions of rebellious angels in the New Testament and its relationship with Jewish tradition, see Pearson, 'Reminiscence of Classical Myth'; Charles, 'Angels under Reserve'; Billings, 'Angels who Sinned'; De Vivo, *2 Peter 2:4–16*.

86 While the Qur'anic term '*aṣfād*' (sing. *ṣafad*) is typically understood as chains, the term is infrequently used. The possible Semitic cognate is Akkadian '*ṣāpītu*' meaning tower (*CAD*, 16: 97) or '*ṣippatu*', which possibly means a metal or alloy (*CAD*, 16: 203). The replacement of '*t*' with '*d*' may not be too unusual, as the city of Safed (Arabic: Ṣafad) is Zephath (*ṣĕpat*) in the Hebrew Bible (e.g. Judges 1:34), which in itself is related to '*ṣ-p-h*' or '*ṣ-p-y*' meaning to keep watch, spy, or even watchtower (*miṣpe*) (*BDB*, 859–60). The only time the Hebrew Bible uses '*ṣāpad*' is in Lam. 4:8, which means to draw together (*BDB*, 859).

87 Thomassen, 'Islamic Hell'. There is a Muslim tradition sometimes attributed to Ḥasan ibn ʿAlī and sometimes to others that states, 'In Hell, there is [no valley], no room, no cave, no yoke, no bind, and no chain except that the name of its owner written on it before he is created' (Ibn Abī al-Dunyā, *Ṣifah ahl al-nār*, 56; Ibn Baṭṭah, *al-Ibānah al-kubrā*, 4: 284; al-Suyūṭī, *al-Durr al-manthūr*, 5: 238).

88 Al-Ṭabarī, *Jāmiʿ*, 20: 492–4 (Q. 36:8).

89 There are various opinions among Muslim traditions of what is meant being recorded in a clear '*imam*'. Some traditional exegetes consider it as part of 'Umm al-Kitāb' (the Mother of the Book) (al-Ṭabarī, *Jāmiʿ*, 20: 499, (Q. 36:12)) or even perhaps the Preserved Tablet (*al-Lawḥ al-Maḥfūẓ*) (al-Ṭabarsī, *Majmaʿ*, (Q. 36:12); al-Rāzī, *Mafātīḥ*, 26: 258–9, (Q. 36:12)). However, Nizari Ismāʿīlīs interpret this verse as evidence that there needs to be a manifest *imām* instead of a hidden *imām* at all times (Hunzai, *Wise Qur'an*, 9, 47).

90 Gwynne, 'Neglected Sunnah', esp. 456.

91 O'Shaughnessy, 'Seven Names'.

92 Bauer and Leander, *Historische Grammatik*, 61.

93 *TDOT*, 11: 123.

94 Gaster, 'Combat of Death'.

95 *Lisān al-ʿarab*, 14: 271–5.

96 Leslau, *Comparative Dictionary*, 138. In some other Afroasiatic languages, the term means family, which also appears to have a semantic range of nearness (Orel and Stolbova, *Hemito-Semitic*, 149).

97 *BDB*, 1088–9.

98 *BDB*, 1088.

99 Izutsu, *God and Man*, 87.

100 Izutsu, *God and Man*, 88.

101 Margoliouth, 'Origins of Arabic Poetry'; Seidensticker, 'Authenticity of the Poems', 88; Reynolds, *Qur'ān and Its Biblical Subtext*, 30–4; Sinai, 'Religious Poetry'.

102 *CAD*, 1.1: 170.

103 *CAD*, 1.1: 186.

104 *CAD*, 1.1: 188.

105 *CAD*, 1.1: 193–5.

106 Al-Farāhīdī, *ʿAyn*, 4: 303–4.

107 Abdel Haleem, 'Life and Beyond'.

108 Ezek. 38:8 uses the phrase, 'latter years'.

109 See Buchanan, 'Eschatology'; von Rad, *Genesis*, 417; Hoffman, 'Terms *ʾaḥărît ha-yāmîm*'; Hoffman, 'Eschatology'; Sigvartsen, 'Afterlife Views'. Also see Rudolph, *Handbuch zum Alten Testament*, *in loc*. Gerald Klingbeil considers the term '*ʾaḥărît ha-yāmîm*' in the Pentateuch as evidence of its eschatological nature. He is one of the few scholars to make such a stance when compared to most others (Klingbeil, 'Looking at the End'). Compare with Fried and Mills, 'Messiah and the End'.

110 Turner, 'Wealth as an Immortality Symbol'.
111 Abdel Haleem, 'Life and Beyond', 66.
112 Bensaid, Machouche, and Grine, 'Qur'anic Framework'.
113 Al-Ṭabarī, *Jāmi'*, 12: 88–93 (Q. 6:122).
114 Ibn 'Arabī, *Tafsīr* (Q. 6:122).
115 Abdel Haleem, 'Hereafter and Here-and-Now', 118.
116 *TSQ* translates '*al-ḥayawān*' as 'life indeed'. I added the article 'the' prior to life to conform with the Arabic rendition. In addition, due to the argument made, it is more likely an adjective.
117 Sībawayh (d. 180/796) is a very famous early grammarian of Arabic, who was originally Persian.
118 Al-Zajjāj, *Ma'ānī al-Qur'ān*, 4: 173; Abu-l-Baqā' al-'Ukbarī, *al-Tibyān*, 2: 1035; al-Suyūṭī, *Mu'tarak al-aqrān*, 1: 313; Ṣāfī, *al-Jadwal*, 21: 17; Darwīsh, *I'rāb al-Qur'ān*, 7: 456–7.
119 Al-Zarkashī, *al-Burhān*, 2: 505–9.
120 Ibn Jinnī, *al-Khaṣā'iṣ*, 2: 201.
121 Sībawayh, *al-Kitāb*, 3: 204–6, 3: 644–7; al-Istrabādhī, *Sharḥ shāfiyah Ibn al-Ḥājib*, 196–198–201.
122 Crone, 'Quranic *Mushrikūn* . . . (Part I)', 450–1.
123 O'Shaughnessy, *Creation and the Teaching*, 73; Crone, 'Quranic *Mushrikūn* . . . (Part I)', 464–5; Crone, 'Quranic *Mushrikūn* . . . (Part II)'.
124 Hogan, 'Mother Earth'; Flannery, 'Go Ask a Woman's Womb'; de Long, 'Ask a Woman'.
125 Elledge, *Resurrection of the Dead*, 76–7.
126 Ibid., 79.
127 Kutsko, *Between Heaven and Earth*, 129–49; Buck, 'רוח in Ezekiel', 55–7.
128 *Pseudo-Ezekiel* is a text of the Dead Sea Scrolls.
129 Elledge, *Resurrection of the Dead*, 80.
130 Tromp, 'Can These Bones'.
131 Bertaina, 'Bodily Resurrection'.
132 *TSQ* translates '*insān*' as 'man', which I have changed to 'human'.
133 Unlike the *TSQ*, I prefer translating '*insān*' as 'human' instead of 'man'. This standard is done throughout the book.
134 Al-Ṭībī, *al-Kāshif*, 2: 568; al-Fattanī, *Majma' biḥār al-anwār*, 4: 628–9; al-Qārī, *Mirqāh al-mafātīḥ*, 1: 179.
135 Al-Rāghib al-Iṣfahānī, *Tafṣīl al-nash'atayn*, 116.
136 Al-Ghazālī, *Mīzān al-'amal*, 398.
137 Smith and Haddad, *Islamic Understanding*, 21, 31, 105–10, 131–2, 136.
138 Asad, 'Symbolism and Allegory', (appendix).
139 For very brief views of some traditional and Sufi Muslim thought, see Shahraki and Keramatifard, 'Bodily Resurrection'; Al Ghouz, 'Recasting al-Bayḍāwī's'.
140 Al-Ghazālī, *Tahāfut al-falāsifah*, esp. 276, 299–300; Yusuf, 'Discussion between al-Ghazzālī'.
141 Jules Janssens argues that al-Ghazālī's *Tahāfut* though has good knowledge of Ibn Sīnā's works is not necessarily directed to them (Janssens, 'Al-Ghazzali's *Tahafut*'). However, on the issue of bodily resurrection, it is very likely that al-Ghazālī has Ibn Sīnā's discourse on the issue in mind or, at least, that is how the *Tahāfut*'s audience felt. After all, Ibn Rushd felt that al-Ghazālī's *Tahāfut* was directed to Ibn Sīnā's works in some instances, including the issue of resurrection.
142 Yusuf, 'Discussion between al-Ghazzālī'.
143 Ibn Rushd, *Tahāfut al-tahāfut*; Yusuf, 'Discussion between al-Ghazzālī'.

144 Al-Ṭabarī, *Jāmi'*, 1: 418–27, Q. 2:28 and also on Q. 40:11.
145 Al-Darwīsh, *Fatāwī al-lajnah al-dā'imah*, 2: 411.
146 O'Shaughnessy, *Muhammad's Thoughts*, 14–15, 23–4.
147 O'Shaughnessy, *Muhammad's Thoughts*, 15.
148 McNamara, *New Testament and the Palestinian Targum*, 117–25; Bogaert, 'La "seconde mort"'.
149 Gardner and Lieu, *Manichaean Texts*, 202–4.
150 Crone, 'Quranic *Mushrikūn*'; Crone, 'Nothing but Time'.
151 McNamara, *New Testament*, 117–25; *AYBC*, 38: 393–6.
152 Deutsch, 'Transformation of Symbols'; Moyise, *Old Testament in the Book of Revelation*, 55–6, 65–6; Lambrecht, 'Final Judgments'; Hoeck, *Descent of New Jerusalem*, 197–9.
153 Sani and Ruma, 'Concretizing the Abstract'.
154 Mohamed, 'Metaphor of Nature'; Kazemi and Nodoushan, 'Conversation Analytic Perspective'.
155 *TSQ* translates '*al-ḥayawān*' as 'life indeed'. I added the article 'the' prior to life to conform with the Arabic rendition. In addition, due to the argument made, it is more likely an adjective.

Chapter 6

1 Reynolds, *Qur'ān and the Bible*, 101–2.
2 Tesei, '*barzakh*'.
3 Pielow, 'Sleepless in Paradise' 434.
4 Tesei, '*barzakh*', 7–38, 41–2.
5 Tlili, *Animals in the Qur'an*, 196–211.
6 Ibid.
7 Ibid.
8 Ibid.
9 As also argued in Galadari, *Qur'anic Hermeneutics*.
10 Galadari, 'Camel Passing'.
11 Al-Ṭabarī, *Jāmi'*, 5: 438–84, (Q. 2:259).
12 Ibn 'Arabī, *Tafsīr*, (Q. 2: 259).
13 Al-Ṭabarī, *Jāmi'*, 5: 438–84, (Q. 2:259). Mahmoud Ayoub discusses traditional exegetes' identification of Ezra/Jeremiah in this passage; see Ayoub, 'Uzayr in the Qur'an'. Also see Renard, 'Images of Abraham'; El-Khatib, 'Jerusalem in the Qur'an'; Comerro, 'Esdras Est-Il le Fils de Dieu'; Wheeler, 'Arab Prophets'.
14 Ayoub, 'Uzayr'.
15 Reynolds, *Qur'ān and the Bible*, 101–2.
16 More on the naming of Ḥoni the Circle Drawer, see Filipowski, *Sefer Yuchsin haShalem*, 63; Schurer, *History of the Jewish People*, 235; Ron, 'Death of Honi'.
17 b. Ta'anit 23a; j. Ta'anit 23a. Also see Neusner, *Rabbinic Traditions*, 177; Ginzberg, *Legends of the Jews*, 2: 1091.
18 Heller, 'Éléments, parallèles'; Honigmann, 'Stephen of Ephesus'; Herzer, *4 Baruch*, 90; Ron, 'Death of Honi'; Archer, *Place between Two*, 126–9.
19 See Nibley, 'Qumran and "the Companions of the Cave"'; also see Bellamy, 'Al-Raqīm or al-Ruqūd'; Roberts, 'Parable of Blessing'; Netton, 'Towards a Modern Tafsīr'; Griffith, 'Christian Lore'.
20 Hoyland, 'Language of the Qur'an', 30–9.

21 The *Apocryphon Jeremiae de captivitate Babylonis* (*History of the Captivity in Babylon*) is a pseudepigraphical work that provides more details that does not exist in the Hebrew Bible's Book of Jeremiah.
22 Haelewyck, *Clavis Apocryphorum*, 185.
23 Piovanelli, 'Les Paralipomènes de Jérémie'; Piovanelli, 'Praise of "The Default Position"'.
24 Simon-Shoshan, 'Past Continuous'.
25 b. Taʿanit 23a.
26 Hasan-Rokem, *Tales of the Neighborhood*, 86ff, esp. 109–10; Avery-Peck, 'Galilean Charismatic', 155–6.
27 Simon-Shoshan, 'Past Continuous', 8.
28 To understand the difference of the narratives between the Yerushalmi and Bavli Talmuds, see Neusner, *Rabbinic Traditions*, 177.
29 j. Taʿanit 3:9.
30 Simon-Shoshan, 'Past Continuous'.
31 For more on Nehemiah in this context, see Bergren, 'Nehemiah in 2 Maccabees 1:10–2:18'.
32 Simon-Shoshan, 'Past Continuous'.
33 4 Baruch is found in the Greek tradition with an Ethiopian translation, and is considered canonical by the Ethiopian Orthodox Tewahedo Church. There are many similarities between 4 Baruch and 2 Baruch (*Syriac Apocalypse of Baruch*) (Herzer, *4 Baruch*, xvi–xxx). However, dating 4 Baruch cannot be pinpointed, as there are various theories whether 4 Baruch is based on 2 Baruch or vice versa (Kohler, 'Pre-Talmudic Haggada', 408), or that each used a common source (Riaud, 'Paralipomena Jeremiae', 106–25). There is a debate on the dating of 2 Baruch from 63 BCE, when Jerusalem fell to Pompey's army (Hadot, 'Datation de l'Apocalypse') through 135–132 BCE, during the Bar Kokhba revolt (See Schmid, 'Baruch und die ihm zugeschriebene apokryphe'; also see Bogaert, 'Le nom de Baruch'; Murphy, 'Temple in the Syriac Apocalypse'). Parts of 4 Baruch has also been argued to have been Christianized by later authors (Riaud, 'Figure of Jeremiah').
34 Wright, *Baruch ben Neriah*, 62–6.
35 Gowan, *Theology of the Prophetic Books*; Olyan, 'Unnoticed Resonances'; Strong, 'Egypt's Shameful Death'; Tuell, 'True Metaphor'.
36 Allison, *4 Baruch*, 201.
37 Gowan, *Theology of the Prophetic Books*.
38 Ibid.
39 Reynolds, *Qurʾān and the Bible*, 101–2.
40 Wright, *Baruch ben Neriah*, 62–6; Allison, *4 Baruch*, 267.
41 Allison, *4 Baruch*, 323.
42 The English translation of 4 Baruch is taken from Kraft and Purintum (1972) *Paraleipomena Jeremious*, Missoula MT: Scholars Press.
43 Herzer, 'Difficult Time'; Sigvartsen, *Afterlife and Resurrection*, 99. Nonetheless, interpreting an eschatological resurrection of the dead from graves may be associated with the Christianization of 4 Baruch in light of 4 Bar. 9:10–32; see Riaud, 'Puissant t'emportera'; Riaud, 'Figure of Jeremiah'. Compare with Wolff, 'Irdisches'; Herzer, *Paralipomena Jeremiae*. Accordingly, an eschatological interpretation of a literal resurrection of the dead from graves is uncalled for, unless one puts it in the context of the Christian origins of the conclusion. Otherwise, within its Jewish setting, it is more likely that the whole concept of resurrection in 4 Baruch is the re-emerging of the Israelite nation and rebuilding of the Temple in the earthly Jerusalem and not necessarily in a heavenly New Jerusalem.

44 The final section of 4 Baruch appears to have had a Christian redactor contextualizing it with the Christian Messiah (see Riaud, 'Figure of Jeremiah'; Herzer, *4 Baruch*, xxx; Robinson, '4 Baruch'; Sigvartsen, *Afterlife and Resurrection*, 100–1). It has been argued that not only the ending of 4 Baruch is Christianized, but that it may have many Christianized redactions throughout (van der Horst, 'Pious Long-Sleepers').
45 Simon-Shoshan, 'Past Continuous'.
46 Ibid.
47 Ibid., 29.
48 van der Horst, 'Pious Long-Sleepers'.
49 Ibid.
50 Telford, *Barren Temple*, 132–56, 176–204; Kinman, *Jesus' Entry*, 124–32; Heil, 'Narrative Strategy'; Brown, 'Mark 11:1–12:12'; Kloppenborg, 'Evocatio Deorum'; Jindo, *Biblical Metaphor*, 117–18, 151, 164; Gasparro, 'malédiction du figuier'; Miquel, 'Impatient Jesus'.
51 *AYBC*, 21a: 523–4.
52 Rubinger, 'Jeremiah's Epistle'; Seitz, 'Crisis of Interpretation'; Essels, 'Jeremiah 24:1–10'; Kessler, 'Jeremiah 25:1–29'; Millar, 'Psychoanalytic View', 970; Plant, *Good Figs*; Bryan, 'End of Exile'.
53 Young, 'Eagle and the Basket'; Callaway, *Jeremiah Through the Centuries*, 301.
54 Kinman, *Jesus' Entry*, 124.
55 Heil, 'Narrative Strategy', 78.
56 *Lisān al-ʿarab*, 13: 502.
57 *TDOT*, 6: 438–9.
58 Ibid.
59 *TDOT*, 5: 345.
60 *CAD*, 19: 85–97.
61 *BDB*, 380–1.
62 *TDOT*, 5: 345.
63 Makujina, 'Possible Old Persian'. Compare with Gabbay, 'Hebrew Śôm Śekel'; Leuchter, *Levites and the Boundaries*, 239.
64 Galadari, '*Qibla*'.
65 Ibid.
66 Al-Ḥāwī, *Sharḥ dīwān al-Farazdaq*, 2: 33. Also see, *Lisān al-ʿArab*, 12: 366.
67 *Lisān al-ʿArab*, 12: 365.
68 *TDOT*, 5: 345.
69 For more on the debates concerning Ezra-Nehemiah, its composition, authorship, and redaction, see Esler, 'Ezra-Nehemiah'; Min, *Levitical Authorship*; Farisani, 'Composition and Date'; Wright, 'New Model'; Blenkinsopp, *Judaism, The First Phase*; Klingbeil, 'Between the Traditional and the Innovative'; Eskenazi, 'Revisiting the Composition'; Lee, 'Authority and Authorization'; Collins, 'Transformation of the Torah'; Vroom, *Authority of Law*; Amzallag, 'Authorship of Ezra and Nehemiah'.
70 Knowles, 'Pilgrimage Imagery'; Knowles, *Centrality Practiced*, 77–104. Compare with Merrill, 'Pilgrimage and Procession'.
71 *Lisān al-ʿarab*, 2: 226–30.
72 Or *paragraph by paragraph*.
73 Makujina, 'On the Possible'. Compare with Gabbay, 'Hebrew Śôm Śekel'; Leuchter, *Levites*, 239.
74 Graves, 'Public Reading'; Talmon-Heller, 'Reciting the Qurʾan'. Compare with Eskenazi, 'Structure of Ezra-Nehemiah'; Watts, *Reading Law*; Ryan, *Role of the Synagogue*; Wright, *Communal Reading*; Peterson, *Genesis as Torah*, 7.

75 Wheeler, 'Israel and the Torah'.
76 Feldman, '"What Israel Forbade"'.
77 Ibid.
78 Galadari, 'Qibla'.
79 Galadari, *Qur'anic Hermeneutics.*
80 b. Sukkah 20a.
81 Knowles, 'Pilgrimage Imagery'.
82 b. Erubim 54a–54b.
83 b. Berakhot 57a.
84 Knowles, 'Pilgrimage Imagery'.
85 *BDB*, 748–59.
86 Knowles, 'Pilgrimage Imagery'.
87 Ibid., 67–8.
88 Ibid., 71.
89 Ibid., 73.
90 Ibid.
91 Ibid.
92 Meyers, 'Use of *tôrâ*,' 73.
93 Kalimi, 'Land of Moriah'.
94 Hamerton-Kelly, 'Temple'; Eybers, 'Rebuilding'; Petersen, 'Temple in Persian Period'; Clines, 'Haggai's Temple'; Gowan, *Theology of the Prophetic Books*, 162–5; Albertz, *Exilszeit*; Edelman, *Origins of the Second Temple*; Gregory, 'Postexilic Exile'; Assis, 'Composition, Rhetoric'; Baker, *Eschatological Role.*
95 Kim, *Jerusalem in the Achaemenid Period.*
96 Hamerton-Kelly, 'Temple'; Eybers, 'Rebuilding'; Mason, 'Some Echoes'; Petersen, 'Temple in Persian Period'; Marinkovic, 'What Does Zechariah 1–8 Tell Us'; Gowan, *Theology of the Prophetic Books*, 177; Albertz, *Exilszeit*; Edelman, *Origins of the Second Temple*; Gregory, 'Postexilic Exile'; Baker, *Eschatological Role.*
97 Gowan, *Theology of the Prophetic Books*, 181.
98 Ibid., 162–5.
99 Ronald Pierce has argued the relationship between the Books of Haggai, Zechariah, and Malachi (Pierce, 'Literary Connectors').
100 Al-Ṭabarī, *Jāmiʿ*, 6: 19–25, (Q. 3:93).
101 Goettsberger, 'Über das 3. Kapitel.'
102 For the relationship between the term *bōkeh* in Ezra 10:1 and Ps. 84:6–7, see Moretsi, 'Translation Technique.'
103 Or *paragraph by paragraph.*
104 Knowles, 'Pilgrimage Imagery'; Knowles, *Centrality Practiced*, 77–104; Compare with Merrill, 'Pilgrimage and Procession'.
105 Radford, 'Psalm LXXXIV'.
106 Holtz, 'God as Refuge'.
107 Culley, 'Temple in Psalms', 197; Baker, *Eschatological Role*, 231.
108 Miller, 'Korahites'; Smith, 'Psalms as a Book for Pilgrims'; Benedetto, 'Psalm 84'; Adnams, 'Pilgrimage'; Moretsi, 'Translation Technique'.
109 For the Qur'anic allusion of the Sacred Mosque (Sacred House) as the heart, see Galadari, '*Qibla*'.
110 For why the Peshitta's translation uses somewhat a different understanding than the Masoretic text, see Moresti, 'Translation Technique'.
111 *BDB*, 987.

112 Treves, 'Conjectures'; Gonzalez, 'Zechariah 9–14'; Tiemeyer, *Zechariah's Vision*.
113 Halpern, 'Ritual Background'; Chyutin, *New Jerusalem Scroll*, 12; Kline, *Glory in Our Midst*, 50–1; *AYBC*, 25b: 149–61.
114 I translate *al-nās* as 'people', which seems more universal in the Arabic, as opposed to *TSQ*'s translation of 'mankind'. Unlike other situations where I translate this term to humankind, people in the context of this passage might be a specific group and not humankind generally.
115 See Al-Ṭabarī, *Jāmiʿ*, 7: 70–89, (Q. 3:103). Also see al-Ṭabarī, *Jāmiʿ*, 7: 110–18, (Q. 3:112).
116 Hayajneh, 'Usage of Ancient South Arabian', esp. 125, 133.
117 Firestone, 'Is There a Notion', esp. 404.
118 *AYBC*, 25c: 280–1.
119 Cohn-Sherbok, *Judaism*, 44–60; Bodner, *Jeroboam's Royal Drama*; Sergi, 'United Monarchy'.
120 Na'aman, 'Hezekiah and the Kings'; Galil, 'Last Years'; Goldberg, 'Two Assyrian Campaigns'.
121 Miller and Hayes, *History of Ancient Israel*; Na'aman, 'Historical and Chronological Notes'; Lipschits, *Fall and Rise*.
122 Reddit, 'Two Shepherds'.
123 Assis, 'Zechariah's Vision'; Boda, *NIV Application Commentary*, 465; Gan, *Metaphor of the Shepherd*, esp. 61–72.
124 Rubenstein, 'Sukkot'.
125 See note in Schaberg, 'Major Midrashic Traditions', 77; Gowan, *Theology of the Prophetic Books*, 117–20.
126 For a detailed linguistic and theological study on this verse, see Shead, *Mouth Full of Fire*.
127 Aberbach, '*Wʾtn Lhm Yʿbrwm*'; Jindo, *Biblical Metaphor*, 198–200.
128 For the common symbolism, see Frayer-Griggs, *Saved through Fire*, 127, 221; Adamo, 'Burning Bush'.
129 Frayer-Griggs, *Saved through Fire*, 62–3, 202, 221.
130 Ibid., 66–8, 102–3, 207, 225–6, 242.
131 Frayer-Griggs, *Saved through Fire*.
132 *NRSV* uses 'our God', but the Hebrew is 'my God'.
133 Vang, 'Israel in the Iron-Smelting Furnace'.
134 Holm, 'Fiery Furnace'.
135 Ibid. Also see Sawyer, 'Meaning of BARZEL'.
136 For a brief study on the broken covenant in Jeremiah 11, see Mweemba, 'Broken Covenant'.
137 Johnson, 'Fire in God's House'; Meschel, 'Use of the Metal Lead'.
138 *NRSV* transposes 'silver' to the beginning, when the MT has it at the end of the verse.
139 Frayer-Griggs, *Saved through Fire*.
140 Reynolds, 'On the Qurʾanic Accusation'.
141 Ibid.
142 Galadari, *Qurʾanic Hermeneutics*, 68–82.
143 Compare with my article, Galadari, '*Qibla*'.
144 Ibn ʿAsākir, *Tārīkh Dimashq*, 32: 451.
145 Al-Suyūṭī, *al-Durr al-manthūr*, 2: 23.
146 Al-Shaʿrāwī, *al-Khawāṭir*, 19: 11709.
147 Lumbard, 'Covenant and Covenants', 3.

148 Hayajneh, 'Usage of Ancient South Arabian', 125, 133.
149 Firestone, 'Is There a Notion', 404.
150 Frishman, 'And Abraham Had Faith'.
151 Gowan, *Theology of the Prophetic Books*.
152 Avery-Peck, 'Galilean Charismatic', 156.
153 b. ʿAbodah Zarah 5a.

Chapter 7

1 For a detailed study on God's promise and covenant with Abraham portrayed in Genesis 15, see Ha, *Genesis 15*; Williamson, *Abraham, Israel and the Nations*.
2 b. Taanit 23a.
3 Reynolds, *Qurʾān and the Bible*, 102.
4 Cohen, 'Analysis of an Exegetic Tradition'; Stemberger, 'Genesis 15'.
5 Cohen, 'Analysis of an Exegetic Tradition', 15.
6 Ibid.
7 See Moberly, *Bible, Theology, and Faith*, 131. For a detailed study on Paul's emphasis in the faith of Abraham see Minear, *Obedience of Faith*; Watson, *Paul and the Hermeneutics*; Visscher, *Romans 4*; Schliesser, 'Abraham Did Not "Doubt"'; McFarland, 'Whose Promise'; Wright, 'Paul and the Patriarch' (compare with Lambrecht, 'Romans 4'); Hsieh, 'Abraham as Heir'; Burnett, 'So Shall Your Seed Be'; Hoff, 'One Gospel'.
8 Cohen, 'Analysis of an Exegetic Tradition'; Stemberger, 'Genesis 15'.
9 Moberly, *Bible*, 131; see Minear, *Obedience*; Watson, *Paul and the Hermeneutics*; Visscher, *Romans 4*; Schliesser, 'Abraham Did Not "Doubt"'; McFarland, 'Whose Promise'; Wright, 'Paul and the Patriarch'; Lambrecht, 'Romans 4'; Hsieh, 'Abraham as Heir'; Hoff, 'One Gospel'.
10 Tobin, 'What Shall We Say'.
11 Tobin, 'What Shall We Say', 437.
12 Ladd, 'Israel and the Church'.
13 Wright, 'Paul and the Patriarch', 213–14.
14 Schliesser, *Abraham's Faith*, 429–30.
15 Tan, 'Shema', esp. 195–7; Wright, 'Paul and the Patriarch', 215; Woods, 'Jew-Gentile'.
16 Nanos, *Mystery of Romans*, 179–7.
17 Ibid., 187–201.
18 Hirschfeld, *New Researches*, 35; Neuwirth, 'Two Faces'; Neuwirth, 'Qurʾan in the Field'; Sabbath, 'Iterations of One'.
19 Galadari, *Qurʾanic Hermeneutics*, 109.
20 Williams, 'Righteousness of God'.
21 Kister, 'Romans 5:12–21'. Compare with Tobin, 'Jewish Context'.
22 Kister, 'Romans 5:12–21'.
23 Kister, 'Leave the Dead'; Kister, 'Divorce, Reproof'.
24 Kister, 'Romans 5:12–21', 402.
25 Black, 'Pauline Perspectives'.
26 Ibid., 424.
27 Wasserman, *Death of the Soul*, 143.
28 Wasserman, 'Death of the Soul in Romans 7'; Wasserman, *Death of the Soul*.
29 Black, 'Pauline Perspectives'.
30 Origen, *Commentary on the Epistle to the Romans*, 270–1.

31 Ibid., 263–5.
32 Burns, 'Augustine's Role'; Rackett, 'What's Wrong'.
33 Pelagius, *Commentarii in epistolas S. Pauli.*
34 For further details, see Zecher, *Role of Death.*
35 Zecher, *Role of Death.*
36 Ibid., 2.
37 Al-Ṭabarī, *Jāmiʿ*, (Q. 2:258), 5: 432–437.
38 Al-Ṭabarī, *Jāmiʿ*, (Q. 2:258), 5: 432–437.
39 *BDB*, 144.
40 Hasel, 'Meaning'; Miller, 'Sin and Judgment'; Klein, 'Call, Covenant'; Viberg, *Symbols of Law*, 54–69; Klingbeil, *Bridging the Gap*, 184; also see Potter, 'New Covenant'; Freedman, *Divine Commitment*, 1: 171–5; Kaiser, *Promise-Plan*, 59–61, 199–203; Delalay, 'Covenant Ritual', 12–14.
41 Hasel, 'Meaning', 64; Miller, 'Sin and Judgment', 612; Klein, 'Call, Covenant', 123.
42 Wenham, 'Symbolism of the Animal Rite'; Hess, 'Bible and Alalakh'.
43 Stemberger, 'Genesis 15', 146–8.
44 Anbar, 'Genesis 15'; Hong, 'Exegetical Reading', 165–6; Stemberger, 'Genesis 15', 146–8.
45 Anbar, 'Genesis 15'; Hong, 'Exegetical Reading', 165–6.
46 *Genesis Rabbah, in loc*; Begg, 'Rereadings of the "Animal Rite"'; Cairus, 'Protection and Rewards'.
47 Visotzky, 'Genesis in Rabbinic Literature'.
48 Mazuz, 'Northern Arabia'.
49 Visotzky, 'Genesis in Rabbinic Literature', 579–80.
50 Stemberger, 'Genesis 15'.
51 The Midrash translates '*meshulshelet*' as three kinds, which means for three different purposes.
52 *Genesis Rabbah, in loc.*
53 *Genesis Rabbah, in loc.*
54 Ibid.; Stemberger, 'Genesis 15'.
55 This occurs when an individual is in doubt as to whether he committed a transgression that would have required a sin offering.
56 *Genesis Rabbah, in loc.*
57 A burnt offering is a sacrificed animal given as a gift or tribute to God. A sin offering is a sacrificed animal given to atone for sin.
58 m. Zebahim 6:4, 6:5.
59 *Genesis Rabbah, in loc*; Stemberger, 'Genesis 15'.
60 *Genesis Rabbah, in loc.*
61 Ibid.; Stemberger, 'Genesis 15'.
62 *Genesis Rabbah, in loc*; Begg, 'Rereadings'.
63 Mandel, 'Midrashic Exegesis'.
64 Ibid.
65 *Genesis Rabbah, in loc.*
66 Ibid.
67 Emphasis mine.
68 Emphasis mine.
69 b. Sanhedrin 89b.
70 Emphasis mine.
71 *Genesis Rabbah, in loc*; Stemberger, 'Genesis 15'.
72 *Genesis Rabbah, in loc*; Begg, 'Rereadings'; Stemberger, 'Genesis 15'.

73 *Genesis Rabbah*, *in loc*; Begg, 'Rereadings'; Stemberger, 'Genesis 15'.
74 *Genesis Rabbah*, *in loc*.
75 Ibid.
76 Ibid.
77 Ibid.
78 Ibid., 289.
79 *Genesis Rabbah*, *in loc*.
80 Ibid.
81 Ibid. Compare with Ginzberg, 'Some Observations'.
82 *Genesis Rabbah*, *in loc*.
83 Ibid.; Stemberger, 'Genesis 15'.
84 Frymer-Kensky, 'Patriarchal Family'; Spitz, 'Through Her'; Havrelock, 'Myth of Birthing'.
85 *Genesis Rabbah*, *in loc*.
86 The relationship between a womb and a grave is also a motif seen in the Talmud as mentioned earlier, b. ʿAbodah Zarah 5a.
87 b. ʿAbodah Zarah 5a.
88 Finkelstein, 'Development of the Amidah', 1–43; Finkelstein, 'Development of the Amidah', 127–70.
89 For a commentary on the ʿAmidah, see Rosenberg, *Jewish Liturgy*.
90 Kimelman, 'Daily ʿAmidah'.
91 Ibid.
92 Kessler, '"Shield" of Abraham'.
93 Benthal, 'Financial Worship'.
94 b. Baba Batra 10a.
95 Righteousness and charity share the same root, and so it is a wordplay. See Hurvitz, 'Biblical Roots'.
96 b. Baba Batra 10a.
97 Gray, 'Redemptive Almsgiving'; Gray, 'Rabbis and the Poor'.
98 The Talmud's teaching also parallels Tobit 12:8–10, which also emphasizes praying to be made in conjunction with charity. Charity is better than storing gold, and delivers a person from death to life.
99 b. Baba Batra 10b. For further critical details, see Gray, 'People, Not the Peoples'.
100 b. Baba Batra 9b. Also see Poulin, 'Loving-Kindness'.
101 b. Baba Batra 9b–10a.
102 Kimelman, 'Messiah of the Amidah', 320.
103 b. Sanhedrin 91b.
104 Galadari, '*Qibla*'.
105 Kimelman, 'Shemaʿ and Its Rhetoric'.
106 Kimelman, 'Daily ʿAmidah', 175.

Chapter 8

1 *TSQ* translates '*dassāhā*' as 'obscures it'.
2 Al-Farāhīdī, *al-ʿAyn*, 7: 185–6; *Lisān al-ʿarab*, 6: 82–3.
3 *BDB*, 155.
4 *NRSV* uses 'they' instead of 'he' in the MT.
5 Lavrov, 'Meaning of the Word כֶּלַח', 53–4; Hoeck, 'Harvest—Herald—Hero'.

6 *NRSV* uses 'as a shock of grain comes up to the threshing floor' instead of 'like a sheaf comes up'.
7 Al-Farāhīdī, *al-ʿAyn*, 6: 73.
8 *Lisān al-ʿarab*, 2: 128.
9 Ibn Maymūn al-Baghdādī, *Muntahā al-ṭalab*, 93–4.
10 *BDB*, 155.
11 *Lisān al-ʿarab*, 6: 192–3.
12 This is a suggestion according to *BDB*, 155, and I find it a compelling argument. This may not be too surprising, due to consonantal shifts that occurred in Proto-Semitic. In this case, it appears that the *jīm* shifted to *kāf*, while the *thāʾ* shifted to *shīn*, and subsequently *sīn*, which has frequently occurred in various terms.
13 Al-Farāhīdī, *al-ʿAyn*, 7: 256–7; *Lisān al-ʿarab*, 11: 660–1.
14 *BDB*, 675.
15 *Lisān al-ʿarab*, 11: 661–2.
16 This is a concept also discussed in classical Muslim commentaries, where people's souls were created before the physical bodies, interpreting Qurʾan 7:172; see for example, al-Ṭabarī, *Jāmiʿ*, (Q. 7: 172), 13:222–50. Compare with Awn, 'Ethical Concerns'; Zysow, 'Two Unrecognized'; Mohamed, 'Fitrah'.
17 For further details on this concept see my argument on this issue in Galadari, '*Creatio ex Nihilo*'.
18 Ibn ʿArabī, *Tafsīr al-Qurʾān*, (Q. 70:43).
19 Ibn ʿArabī, *Tafsīr al-Qurʾān*, (Q. 2:259–260).
20 Al-Ṭabarī, *Jāmiʿ*, (Q. 2:28), 1: 418–27. Also al-Ṭabarī, *Jāmiʿ*, (Q. 40:11), 21: 360–1.
21 Afsar, 'Literary Critical Approach'; Kakakhel, 'Study on the Qurʾanic Way'.
22 The comparison between *ẓulm* (injustice) and *ẓulumāt* (darkness) with justice (*ʿadl*) and light (*nūr*) has been discussed by various classical Muslim scholars; see al-Bayḍāwī, *Anwār al-tanzīl*, 5: 49; Abū Zahrah, *Zahrah al-tafāsīr*, 3: 1307. Also see a prophetic tradition (*ḥadīth*) making similar comparisons, al-Bukhārī, *Ṣaḥīḥ*, 3: 129 (#2447); Muslim, *Ṣaḥīḥ*, 4: 1996 (#2578); Ibn Ḥanbal, *Musnad*, 9: 474 (#5662), 10: 89 (#5832), 10: 342 (#6210), 10: 479 (#6446), 11: 26 (#6487), 11: 398 (#6792), 11: 429 (#6838), 15: 349–350 (#9569), 22: 352 (#14461); Abū Dawūd (d. 204/889) (1999) *Musnad*, ed. Muḥammad bin ʿAbdul-Muḥsin al-Turkī, Cairo: Hajr, 3: 408 (#2002), 4: 28 (#2386); al-Tirmidhī, *Sunan*, 3: 445 (#2030).
23 Najm-ul-dīn al-Kubrā, *al-Taʾwīlāt al-najmiyyah*, (Q. 46:33).
24 Al-Rāzī, *Mafātīḥ*, (Q. 79:36), 31: 48–9.
25 Ibn ʿArabī, *Tafsīr*, (Q. 79:36).
26 Al-Rāzī, *Mafātīḥ*, (Q. 102:5–7), 32: 272–4.
27 Al-Ghazālī, *Mishkāt al-anwār*, 81–93. Compare with Berrada, 'Metaphors of Light'; Ali, *Faith, Philosophy*, 54–77. Also compare to Parast, 'Thought Barriers'. For further details on this issue in mystical Islam, see Gorjian and Farahanipour, 'Man's Truth'.
28 For Ismāʿīlī interpretation, see ʿAbdān, *Kitāb shajarah al-yaqīn*, 136–7, 150–1. Though the reference used attributes this book to ʿAbdān, it is allegedly attributed to Abū Tammām (d. *c.* fourth/tenth century); see Walker, 'Abū Tammām'. Compare with De Smet, 'Ismaʿili-Shiʿi Visions'. For Ikhwān al-Ṣafāʾ (Brethren of Purity) usage of this passage in their *Risālah al-jāmiʿah*, see Schmidtke, 'Doctrine of the Transmigration'. Compare with Marquet, 'La philosophie des Ikhwan', 599–636. For Ahl-i-Ḥaqq interpretation, see Khismatulin, 'Just a Step Away'.
29 Al-Ṭabarī, *Jāmiʿ*, 22: 88, (Q. 55:35); Ibn Kathīr, *Tafsir*, 7: 273, (Q. 55:35).
30 Homerin, 'Echoes of a Thirsty'; Crone, 'Quranic *Mushrikūn* . . . (Parts I and II)'.

Chapter 9

1 Baumgarten, 'Paradox of the Red Heifer'.
2 Winston, 'Hellenistic Jewish Philosophy'.
3 Ibn al-Mu'tazz, *al-Badī' fil-badī'*, 124–52; al-Zarkashī, *al-Burhān*, 3: 458–4: 19; al-Suyūṭī, *Mu'tarak al-aqrān*, 1: 314–17; Zebiri, 'Towards a Rhetoric Criticism'; Halldén, 'What Is Arab Islamic Rhetoric'; Cuypers, 'Semitic Rhetoric'; De Gifis, *Shaping a Qur'ānic Worldview*, 37–8; Cuypers, *Composition of the Qur'an*, 3–4, 8, 18, 94, 164–165; Stetkevych, 'From *Jāhiliyyah*'; Wan Ahmad et al., 'Method of the Qur'an'.
4 Peters, 'Greek and Syriac Background'; Nasr, *Islamic Philosophy*.
5 Novak, 'Talmud as a Source'.
6 Maccoby, *Philosophy of the Talmud*, esp. 191–202.
7 Ulmer, 'Advancement of Arguments', 48.
8 Gunaratne, 'Logical Form'.
9 Bharadwaja, 'Rationality, Argumentation'; Gunaratne, 'Understanding Nāgārjuna's'; Priest, 'None of the Above'.
10 Cua, 'Opposites as Complements'. Compare with Járos, 'Synergy of Complements'.
11 Horton, 'Koheleth's Concept'.
12 *Midrash Tanḥuma*, Ḥuqqat 6–8.
13 For a detailed study, see Willis, *Elders of the City*. Also see Blech, 'Thematic Linkage'; Robinson, 'Deuteronomy 21:1–9'.
14 *TSQ* translates '*wa-lā bikr*' as without calf. However, it could also be understood as not firstborn or not young (*Lisān al-'arab*, 7: 203–4).
15 *BDB*, 133–4.
16 *NRSV* uses 'shepherds' in the plural, although the MT is singular.
17 *NRSV* uses 'flocks' in the plural, although the MT is singular.
18 *TDOT*, 2: 209.
19 *Lisān al-'arab*, 4: 74.
20 Ibid.
21 Ibid.
22 *BDB*, 133–4.
23 *Lisān al-'arab*, 4: 73–4.
24 Ibid.: 460.
25 Ibid.: 460. Its relationship with Middle Persian '*zarr*' meaning gold, yellow, or to shine is also possible, itself associated with saffron.
26 *BDB*, 861.
27 Reynolds, *Qur'ān and the Bible*, 52.
28 Freidenreich, 'Use of Islamic Sources'.
29 Ibid., 390–2.
30 Ibid., 392.
31 m. Ṭahorot, Parah.
32 The reason I am suggesting possibly an Ethiopic influence in the Arabic term for brown, is that though the root (*b-n*) is Semitic and attested even in Arabic to mean seed or nut, it is usually a specific reference to coffee bean in Ethiopic, and from it the Ethiopic reference to brown.
33 Heschel, 'Philological Uncanny'.
34 Blau, 'Red Heifer'.
35 Junker, 'Disorderly Body'; MacDonald, 'Hermeneutics and Genesis'; Belnap, 'Defining the Ambiguous'.

36 Nolland, 'Sin, Purity'.
37 Greer, 'Cursed Be the Cheat'.
38 Birenboim, '*Tevul Yom*'.
39 Ibid.
40 Aghaei, 'Morphology of the Narrative'. 52–3.
41 See my argument on the term in Galadari, '*Qibla*'.
42 b. Yoma 42b.
43 For more information, see Chernick, *Gezarah Shavah*.
44 m. Ṭahorot, Parah.
45 t. Ṭahorot, Parah.
46 m. Ṭahorot, Parah.
47 m. Ṭahorot, Parah.
48 m. Parah, 1:1.
49 Yadin-Israel, 'For Mark Was Peter's Tanna''.
50 Pasternak and Yona, 'Numerical Sayings'.
51 Pasternak and Yona, 'Use of Numbers'.
52 *TDOT*, 15: 482–3; Leslau, *Comparative Dictionary*, 534–5.
53 Parpola, *Etymological Dictionary*, 312.
54 Galadari, '*Qibla*'.
55 The interaction of the Qur'anic community with Jews who were possible precursors of the rabbinic tradition is very much possible. Compare with Newby, *History of the Jews*, 57–9; Firestone, *Jewish Culture*; Hoyland, 'Jews of the Hijaz'; Galadari, '*Qibla*'; Mazuz, *Religious and Spiritual*; Graves, 'Upraised Mountain'.
56 Blau, 'Red Heifer'.
57 For some debates on the rabbinic rendition of purity laws made obsolete after the destruction of the Second Temple, see Poirier, 'Purity beyond the Temple'; Balberg, *Purity, Body*.
58 Poirier, 'Purity beyond the Temple'; Balberg, *Purity, Body*.
59 Poirier, 'Purity beyond the Temple'; Balberg, *Purity, Body*.
60 Milgrom, 'Paradox of the Red Cow'.
61 Ibid. See also Lev, Ephraim and Lev-Yadun, 'Probable Pagan Origin'.
62 Milgrom, 'Paradox'.
63 Baumgarten, 'Paradox'.
64 Ibid. Emphasis is Baumgarten's.
65 Ibid.
66 Ibid.
67 Ibid., 448.
68 Gilders, 'Why Does Eleazar'.
69 Rudman, 'Water for Impurity'.
70 *Numbers Rabbah*, 19.
71 Blau, 'Red Heifer', 77–8.
72 *TSQ* translates '*dassāhā*' as 'obscures it'.
73 *TSQ* translates '*al-ḥayāt*' as 'this life'. However, the Arabic text only says 'the life' with no explicit mention to 'this life' necessarily.
74 Pregill, *Golden Calf*, 348–58.
75 Ibid., 358–79.
76 *Numbers Rabbah* 19.9.
77 Aghaei, 'Qur'anic Intertextuality'.
78 Some traditions read Ezek. 36:16–36, while others read Ezek. 36:16–38.

79 Kiperwasser, 'Toward a Redaction History'.
80 *Qohelet Rabbah*, 7:23.4.
81 *Midrash Tanḥuma*, Ḥuqqat 6.
82 Edersheim, *Temple*, 351–2.
83 Moving along the previous definition of '*al-ḥaqq*', I keep the original term here instead of translating it to 'truth', as used by the *TSQ*.
84 Moving along the previous definition of '*al-ḥaqq*', I keep the original term here instead of translating it to 'truth', as used by the *TSQ*.
85 Newman, 'Understanding the Mystery'.
86 b. ʿAbodah Zarah 5a.
87 b. ʿAbodah Zarah 5a.
88 Rashi on Num. 19:22.
89 Ibid.
90 Ibid.
91 Ibid.
92 Ibid.
93 Ibid.
94 Newman, 'Understanding the Mystery'; Schoenfeld, *Isaac on Jewish and Christian Altars*, 31–60.
95 *Midrash Tanḥuma*, Ḥuqqat 8
96 From homiletic material found in *Pesiqta de-Rav Kahana*. See Pregill, *Golden Calf*, 131–2, 258.
97 Wright, 'Purification from Corpse-Contamination'.
98 Ibid.
99 Guillaume, 'Drinking Golden Bull', 135.
100 Ibid., 135–47.
101 Ibid., 140.
102 Begg, 'Destruction of the Calf'.
103 O'Brien, 'Dynamics of the Golden Calf'.
104 Ibid.
105 Al-Ṭabarī, *Jāmiʿ*, (Q. 7:143), 13: 92–8.
106 Al-Ṭabarī, *Jāmiʿ*, (Q. 7:143), 13: 90–96.
107 Newman, 'Understanding the Mystery.'
108 Ibid. Compare with Chung, *Sin of the Calf*.
109 Danelius, 'Sins of Jeroboam.'
110 Newman, 'Understanding the Mystery.'
111 Newman, 'Understanding the Mystery', 107. On the scarlet ribbon worn by Hathor, see Harris, *Ancient Egyptian Divination*, 59.
112 m. Shabbat 9:1.
113 Newman, 'Understanding the Mystery', 107.
114 Ibid.
115 Lichtheim, *Ancient Egyptian Literature*, 197–9; Brewer and Teeter, *Egypt and the Egyptians*, 170; McGill, 'Hathor'; Basson, 'Goddess Hathor', 27, 81–5.
116 Graves-Brown, *Dancing for Hathor*, 166–7.
117 Farrin, 'Surat al-Baqara'. Compare with Robinson, *Discovering the Qur'an*; Zahniser, 'Major Transitions'; Klar, 'Text-Critical Approaches . . . Part One'; Klar, 'Text-Critical Approaches . . . Part Two'.
118 Bell, *Commentary on the Qurʾān*.
119 Feldman, 'Death as Estrangement'.

120 Milgrom, 'Rationale for Biblical Impurity', 109–10.
121 Ibid., 110.
122 Noam, 'Ritual Impurity', 67–9.

Chapter 10

1 Galadari, '*Qibla*'.
2 Ibid.
3 Firestone, 'Abraham's Son'.

BIBLIOGRAPHY

ʿAbbās, Iḥsān (ed.). *Sharḥ dīwān Labīd b. Rabīʿah al-ʿĀmrī*, Kuwait: Ministry of Guidance and News, 1962.

Abdel Haleem, Muhammad. 'The Hereafter and Here-and-Now in the Qurʾan'. *Islamic Quarterly* 33, no. 2 (1989): 118.

Abdel Haleem, Muhammad. 'Life and Beyond in the Qurʾan'. In *Beyond Death: Theological and Philosophical Reflections of Life after Death*, edited by Dan Cohn-Sherbok and Christopher Lewis, 66–79. Basingstoke: Palgrave Macmillan, 1995.

Abdel Haleem, Muhammad. *Understanding the Qurʾan: Themes and Style*. London: I.B. Tauris, 1999.

Abdelaziz, Mahdi and Shaher Rababeh. 'The Terminology Used to Describe Tombs in the Nabataean Inscriptions and Its Architectural Context'. *Levant* 40, no. 2 (2008): 177–83.

Abdul-Raof, Hussein. 'Conceptual and Textual Chaining in Qurʾanic Discourse'. *Journal of Qurʾanic Studies* 5, no. 2 (2003): 72–94.

ʿAbdān. *Kitāb shajarah al-yaqīn*, edited by ʿĀrif Tāmir. Beirut: al-Āfāq al-Jadīdah, 1982.

Aberbach, D. '*Wʾtn Lhm Yʿbrwm* (Jeremiah VIII 13): The Problem and Its Solution'. *Vetus Testamentum* 27, no. 1 (1977): 99–101.

Abū ʿAlī al-Fārsī (d. 377/987). *al-Ḥujjah lil-qurrāʾ al-sabʿah*, edited by Badr-ul-Dīn Qahwajī and Bashīr Juwayjābī. Damascus: al-Maʾmūn lil-Turāth, 1933.

Abū Dawūd (d. 204/889). *Musnad*, edited by Muḥammad bin ʿAbdul-Muḥsin al-Turkī. Cairo: Hajr, 1999.

Abū Isḥāq al-Zajjāj (d. 311/923). *Maʿānī al-Qurʾān wa-iʿrābih*, edited by ʿAbdul-Jalīl ʿAbduh Shalabī, Beirut: ʿĀlam al-Kutub, 1988.

Abu-l-Baqāʾ al-ʿUkbarī (d. 616/1219). *al-Tibyān fī iʿrāb al-Qurʾān*, edited by ʿAlī M. Al-Bajawī, Cairo: ʿĪssa al-Bābī al-Ḥalabī, n.d.

Abū Yāsīn, Ḥusayn ʿĪsā (ed.). *Shiʿr Hamdān wa-akhbāruhā*. Riyadh: al-ʿUlūm, 1983.

Abū Zahrah (d. 1394/1974). *Zahrah al-tafāsīr*. al-Fikr al-ʿArabī, n.d.

Abū Zayd, ʿAlī (ed.). *Shuʿarāʾ Taghlib*. Kuwait: al-Majlis al-Waṭanī lil-Thaqāfah wal-Funūn wal-Ādāb, 2000.

Adamo, David T. 'The Burning Bush (Ex 3:1–6): A Study of Natural Phenomena as Manifestation of Divine Presence in the Old Testament and in African Context'. *HTS Theological Studies* 73, no. 3 (2017).

Adnams, E. Louise. 'Pilgrimage: A Paradigm for Spiritual Formation'. *McMaster Journal of Theology and Ministry* 12, (2010–11): 132–65.

Ahmad, Absar. 'Qurʾānic Concepts of Human Psyche'. In *Qurʾānic Concepts of Human Psyche*, edited by Zafar A. Ansari, 15–38. Islamabad: International Institute of Islamic Thought, 1992.

Aghaei, Ali. 'The Morphology of the Narrative Exegesis of the Qur'an: The Case of the Cow of the Banū Isrāʾīl (Q2:67–74)'. In *Reading the Bible in Islamic Context: Qur'anic Conversations*, edited by Daniel J. Crowther, Shirin Shafaie, Ida Glaser, and Shabbir Akhtar, 167–94. Abingdon: Routledge, 2017.

Aghaei, Ali. 'Qur'anic Intertextuality with Jewish-Rabbinic Tradition: The Case of "the Cow" in Q 2:67–74'. *The Centre for Muslim-Christian Studies*, 19 May 2020.

Agmon, Noam and Yigal Bloch. 'Statistics of Language Morphology Change: From Biconsonantal Hunters to Triconsonantal Farmers'. *PLoS ONE* 8, no. 12 (2013): e83780.
Ahmad, Bahrudin. 'Man and His Spiritual Position in Rumi's Doctrine'. *Katha* 8, no. 1 (2012): 47–57.
Aichele, George. 'Reading Jesus Writing'. *Biblical Interpretation* 12, no. 4 (2004): 353–68.
Akbar, Asadalizadeh. 'A Study on the World of Barzakh from the Traditional and Theological Perspective'. *The Islamic Science Quarterly* 4, no. 16 (2015): 31–64.
Afsar, Ayaz. 'A Literary Critical Approach to Qur'ānic Parables'. *Islamic Studies* 44, no. 4 (2005): 481–501.
Afsaruddin, Asma. 'Dying in the Path of God: Reading Martyrdom and Moral Excellence in the Quran'. In *Roads to Paradise: Eschatology and Concepts of the Hereafter in Islam*, edited by Sebastian Günther and Todd Lawson, 162–180. Leiden: Brill, 2017.
Āl al-Shaykh, Ṣāliḥ b. ʿAbdulʿazīz. *Hādhih mafāhimunā*. Riyadh: Idārah al-Masājid wal-Mashārīʿ al-Khayriyyah, 2001.
Āl al-Shaykh, Ṣāliḥ b. ʿAbdulʿazīz. *al-Tamhīd li-sharḥ kitāb al-tawḥīd*. Riyadh: al-Tawḥīd, 2003.
Al Ghouz, Abdelkader. 'Recasting al-Bayḍāwī's Eschatological Concept of Bodily Resurrection: Shams al-Dīn al-Iṣfahānī and Aḥmad al-Ījī in Comparative Perspective'. *Mamlūk Studies Review* 20 (2017): 39–54.
Al-Aʿlam al-Shantamarī (d. 476/1084). *Dīwān Ṭarafah b. al-ʿAbd*, edited by Durriyyah al-Khaṭīb and Luṭfī al-Saqqāl. Beirut: al-ʿArabiyyah lil-Dirāsāt, 2000.
Al-Afghānī, Shams-ul-Dīn b. Muḥammad b. Ashraf b. Qayṣar (d. 1420/2000). *Juhūd ʿulamāʾ al-Ḥanafiyyah fī ibṭāl ʿaqāʾid al-qubūriyyah*. Riyadh: al-Ṣumayʿī, 1996.
Al-Ali, Ali, Ahmad El-Sharif and Mohamed S. Alzyoud. 'The Functions and Linguistic Analysis of Metaphor in the Holy Qurʾan'. *European Scientific Journal* 12, no. 14 (2016): 164–74.
Al-ʿAsqalānī (d. 852/1449). *al-Maṭālib al-ʿulyā bi-zawāʾid al-masānīd al-thamāniyah*, edited by Saʿd ibn Nāṣir al-Shathrī. Riyadh: al-ʿĀṣimah, 2000.
Al-Baqlī, Rūzbihān (d. 606/1209). *Ḥaqāʾiq al-Qurʾān*, edited by Aḥmad Farīd al-Mazīrī. Beirut: al-Kutub al-ʿIlmiyyah, 2008.
Al-Bayḍāwī (d. 685/1286). *Anwār al-tanzīl wa-asrār al-taʾwīl*, edited by Muḥammad ʿAbdulraḥmān al-Marʿashlī. Beirut: Iḥyāʾ al-Turāth al-ʿArabī, 1998.
Al-Bukhārī (d. 256/870). *Ṣaḥīḥ al-Bukhārī*, edited by M.Z.N. Al-Nāṣir. Beirut: Ṭawq al-Najāh, 2002.
Al-Ḍāmin, Ḥātim Ṣ. *Fāʾit naẓāʾir al-ẓāʾ wal-ḍād*. Damascus: al-Bashāʾir, 2003.
Al-Dānī, Abū ʿAmr (d. 444/1053). *al-Farq bayn al-ḍād wal-ẓāʾ fī kitāb Allāh ʿazz wa-jall wa-fi-l-mashhūr min al-kalām*, edited by Ḥātim Ṣ. al-Ḍāmin. Damascus: al-Bashāʾir, 2007.
Al-Darwīsh, Aḥmad ibn ʿAbdulrazzāq (ed.). *Fatāwī al-lajnah al-dāʾimah – Vol. 1*. Riyadh: Riʾāsah Idārah al-Buḥūth al-ʿIlmiyyah wal-Iftāʾ, n.d.
Al-Fākihī (d. 272/886). *Akhbār Makkah fī qadīm al-dahr wa-ḥadīthih*, edited by ʿAbdul-Malik ʿAbdullāh Duhaysh. Beirut: Khiḍr, n.d.
Al-Farāhīdī (d. 170/786). *al-ʿAyn*, edited by Mahdī al-Makhzūmī and Ibrāhīm al-Sāmarrāʾī. Beirut: al-Hilāl, n.d.
Al-Fattanī, Muḥammad (d. 986/1578). *Majmaʿ biḥār al-anwār fī gharāʾib al-tanzīl wa-laṭāʾif al-akhbār*. Hyderabad: Osmania Oriental Publications Bureau, 1967.
Al-Fayrūzʾābādī (d. 813/1414). *al-Qāmūs al-Muḥīṭ*, edited by Muḥammad N. al-ʿArqūsī. Beirut: al-Risālah, 2005.
Al-Fayyūmī, Muḥammad Ibrahīm (d. 1427/2007) *Tarīkh al-fikr al-dīnī al-jāhilī*. Cairo: al-Fikr al-ʿArabī, 1994.

Al-Ghazālī (d. 505/1111). *Iḥyā' 'ulūm al-dīn*. Beirut: al-Ma'rifah, n.d.
Al-Ghazālī (d. 505/1111). *Tahāfut al-falāsifah*, edited by Sulaymān Dunyā. Cairo: al-Ma'ārif, n.d.
Al-Ghazālī (d. 505/1111). *Mishkāt al-anwār*, edited by Abul-'Ala 'Afīfī. Cairo: al-Qawmiyyah, n.d.
Al-Ghazālī (d. 505/1111). *Mīzān al-'amal*, edited by Sulaymān Dunyā. Cairo: al-Ma'ārif, 1964.
Al-Ḥakamī, Ḥāfiz (d. 1377/1924). *Ma'ārij al-qubūl bi-sharḥ sullam al-wuṣūl ila 'ilm al-uṣūl*, edited by 'Umar b. Maḥmūd Abū 'Umar. Dammam: Ibn al-Qayyim, 1990.
Al-Ḥāwī, Īliyyā. *Sharḥ dīwān al-Farazdaq*. Beirut: al-Kitāb al-Lubnānī, 1983.
Al-Ḥamlāwī, 'Umar al-'Arbāwī (d. 1405/1985). *al-Takhallī 'an al-taqlīd wal-taḥallī bil-aṣl al-mufīd*. Ouargla: al-Warrāqah al-'Aṣriyyah, 1984.
Al-Ḥaqawī, Khuldūn b. Maḥmūd b. Naghawī. *al-Tawḍīḥ al-rashīd fī sharḥ al-tawḥīd al-muthayyal bil-tanfīd li-shubuhāt al-'anīd*. Unknown publisher, n.d.
Al-Ḥarrānī, Abul-'Abbās (c. 618/1221). *al-Miṣbāḥ fil-farq bayn al-ḍād wal-ẓā'*, edited by Ḥātim Ṣ. al-Ḍāmin. Damascus: al-Bashā'ir, 2003.
Al-Ḥillī, Ḥasan ibn Sulaymān (d. *c.* 800s/1400s). 1951. *Mukhtaṣar baṣā'ir al-darajāt*. Qom: al-Rasūl al-Muṣaṭafa Publications, n.d. (orig. Najaf: al-Maṭba'ah al-Ḥaydariyyah).
Al-Istrabādhī, Najm al-Dīn (d. 686/1287). *Sharḥ shāfiyah Ibn al-Ḥājib*, edited by Muḥammad Nūr al-Ḥasan, Muḥammad al-Zafzāf and Muḥammad Muḥyī-l-Dīn 'Abdulmajīd. Beirut: al-Kutub al-'Ilmiyyah, 1975.
Al-Ithyūbī, Muḥammad 'Alī Ādam. *Mashāriq al-anwār al-wahhājah wa-maṭāli' al-asrār al-bahhājah fī sharḥ sunan al-imām Ibn Mājah*. Riyadh: al-Mughnī, 2006.
Al-Jiyyānī, Jamāluddīn Ibn Mālik (d. 672/1273). *al-I'timād fī naẓā'ir al-ẓā' wal-ḍād*, edited by Ḥātim Ṣ. al-Ḍāmin. Damascus: al-Bashā'ir, 2003.
Al-Khādmī, Abū Sa'īd (d. 1176/1763). *Barīqah maḥmūdiyyah fī sharḥ ṭarīqah Muḥammadiyyah wa-sharī'ah nabawiyyah fī sīrah Aḥmadiyyah*. Cairo: Maṭba'ah al-Ḥalabī, 1925.
Al-Khaṭīb, 'Abdulkarīm Yūnus (d. 1390/1970). *al-Tafsīr al-Qur'ānī lil-Qur'ān*. Cairo: al-Fikr al-'Arabī, n.d.
Al-Ma'arrī (d. 449/1057). *Saqṭ al-zand*, edited by Aḥmad Shams-al-Dīn. Beirut: al-Kutub al-'Ilmiyyah, n.d.
Al-Maṣṭāwī, 'Abdulraḥmān (ed.). *Dīwān Imru'-ul-Qays*. Beirut: al-Ma'rifah, 2004.
Al-Mu'aybid, Muḥammad Jabbār. *Dīwān 'Adī b. Zayd al-'Ibādī*. Baghdad: Ministry of Culture, 1965.
Al-Mubarakfūrī, 'Abdulraḥmān (d. 1353/1934). *Tuḥfah al-aḥwadhī bi-sharḥ jāmi' al-Tirmidhī*. Beirut: al-Kutub al-'Ilmiyyah, n.d.
Al-Muqrī al-Tilmisānī, Aḥmad (d. 1041/1631). 1968. *Nafḥ al-ṭīb min ghiṣn al-Andalus al-raṭīb – wa-dhikr wazīruhā Lisān al-Dīn bin al-Khaṭīb*, edited by Iḥsān 'Abbās. Beirut: Ṣādir, 1997.
Al-Naysābūrī (d. 850/1446). *Gharā'ib al-Qur'an wa-raghā'ib al-furqān*, edited by Zakariyyā 'Umayrāt. Beirut: al-Kutub al-'Ilmiyyah, 1996.
Al-Qārī, 'Alī (d. 1014/1606). *Sharḥ al-shifā*. Beirut: al-Kutub al-'Ilmiyyah, 2001.
Al-Qārī, 'Alī (d. 1014/1606). *Mirqāh al-mafātīḥ sharḥ mishkāh al-maṣābīḥ*. Beirut: al-Fikr, 2002.
Al-Qawwāl, Anṭwān (ed.). *Dīwān Muhalhal b. Rabī'ah*, Beirut: al-Jīl, 1995.
Al-Qaysī, Nūrī Ḥumūdī (ed.). *Shi'r Muzāḥim al-'Uqaylī*, Baghdad: Ḥātim al-Ḍāmin, 1976.
Al-Qaysī, Nūrī Ḥumūdī (ed.). 'al-Aghlab al-'Ijlī: Ḥayātuh wa-shi'ruh.' *Majallah al-Mujamma' al-'Ilmī al-'Irāqī* 31, no. 3 (1980): 104–44.

Al-Qurṭubī (d. 671/1273). *al-Jāmi' li-aḥkām al-Qur'ān*, edited by Aḥmad al-Bardūnī and Ibrāhīm Iṭfish. Cairo: al-Kutub al-Miṣriyyah, 1964.

Al-Rāghib al-Iṣfahānī (d. 502/1108). *Tafṣīl al-nash'atayn wa-taḥṣīl al-sa'ādatayn*. Beirut: al-Ḥayāh, 1983.

Al-Rāzī (d. 606/1209). *Mafātīḥ al-ghayb*. Beirut: Iḥyā' al-Turāth al-'Arabī, 2000.

Al-Sakhāwī (d. 902/1497). *al-Maqāṣid al-ḥasanah fī bayān kathīr min al-aḥādīth al-mushtaharah 'ala al-alsinah*. Beirut: al-Kitāb al-'Arabī, 1985.

Al-Samīn al-Ḥalabī (d. 756/1355). *al-Durr al-maṣūn fī 'ulūm al-kitāb al-maknūn*, edited by Aḥmad Muḥammad al-Kharrāṭ. Damascus: al-Qalam, n.d.

Al-Samīn al-Ḥalabī (d. 756/1355). *'Umdah al-ḥuffāẓ fī tafsīr ashraf al-alfāẓ*, edited by Muḥammad B. 'Uyūn-al-Sūd. Beirut: al-Kutub al-'Ilmiyyah, 1996.

Al-Sha'rāwī (d. 1419/1998). *al-Khawāṭir*. Cairo: Akhbār al-Yawm, 1997.

Al-Shaybānī, Taqi-ul-dīn (d. 797/1395). *al-Farq bayn al-ḍād wal-ẓā'*, edited by Ḥātim Ṣ. al-Ḍāmin. Damascus: al-Bashā'ir, 2003.

Al-Ṣiqillī, Abul-Ḥasan (d. 450/1058). *Ma'rifah al-ḍād wal-ẓā'*, edited by Ḥātim Ṣ. al-Ḍāmin. Damascus: al-Bashā'ir, 2003.

Al-Suhaylī, Abul-Qāsim (d. 581/1185). *al-Rawḍ al-unf fī sharḥ al-sīrah al-nabawiyyah l-Ibn Hishām*, edited by 'Umar 'Abdulsalām al-Sulāmī. Beirut: Iḥyā' al-Turāth al-'Arabī, 2000.

Al-Sulamī, Abū 'Abdul-Raḥmān (d. 412/1021). *Ḥaqā'iq al-tafsīr*, edited by Sayyid 'Imrān. Beirut: al-Kutub al-'Ilmiyyah, 2001.

Al-Suyūṭī (d. 911/1505). *al-Durr al-manthūr fil-tafsīr bil-ma'thūr*. Beirut: al-Ma'rifah, n.d.

Al-Suyūṭī (d. 911/1505). *Mu'tarak al-aqrān fī i'jāz al-Qur'ān*. Beirut: al-Kutub al-'Ilmiyyah, 1988.

Al-Suyūṭī (d. 911/1505). *Sharḥ al-ṣudūr bi-sharḥ ḥāl al-mawtā wal-qubūr*. Beirut: al-Ma'rifah, 1996.

Al-Ṭabarānī (d. 360/918). *al-Mu'jam al-kabīr*, edited by Ḥamdī ibn 'Abdulmajīd. Cairo: Maktabah Ibn Taymiyyah, 1994.

Al-Ṭabarī (d. 310/923). *Jāmi' al-bayān 'an ta'wīl āy al-Qur'ān*, edited by Aḥmad Muḥammad Shākir. Beirut: al-Risālah, 2000.

Al-Ṭabarsī (d. 548/1153). *Majma' al-bayān fī tafsīr al-Qur'ān*. Beirut: al-A'lamī, 1995.

Al-Tha'labī (d. 427/1035). *al-Kashf wal-bayān 'an tafsīr al-Qur'ān*, edited by Abū Muḥammad 'Āshur. Beirut: Iḥyā' al-Turāth al-'Arabī, 2002.

Al-Ṭībī, Sharaf-ul-Dīn (d. 743/1342). *al-Kāshif 'an ḥaqā'iq al-sunan*, edited by 'Abdulḥamīd Hindawī. Makkah: Nizār Muṣṭafā al-Bāz, 1997.

Al-Tirmidhī (d. 279/892). *Sunan*, edited by Bashshār 'Awwād Ma'rūf. Beirut: al-Gharb al-Islāmī, 1998.

Al-Ṭūsī (d. 460/1067). *al-Tibyān al-jāmi' li-'ulūm al-Qur'ān*, edited by Aḥmad al-'Āmlī. Tehran: al-I'lām al-Islāmī, 1989.

Al-Tustarī (d. 283/896). *Tafsīr al-Qur'ān*, edited by Muḥammad 'Uyūn al-Sūd. Beirut: al-Kutub al-'Ilmiyyah, 2003.

Al-'Utaybī, 'Umar ibn Sulaymān al-Ashqar. *al-Qiyāmah al-ṣughrā*. Kuwait: al-Nafā'is, 1991.

Al-Zamakhsharī (d. 538/1144). *al-Kashshāf 'an ḥaqā'iq ghawāmiḍ al-tanzīl*. Beirut: al-Kitāb al-'Arabī, 1987.

Al-Zanjānī, Abul-Qāsim (d. 471/1078). *al-Farq bayn al-ḍād wal-ẓā'*, edited by Mūsā B. al-'Alīlī. Baghdad: Ministry of Endowment and Religious Affairs, 1983.

Al-Zarkashī (d. 794/1392). *al-Burhān fī 'ulūm al-Qur'ān*, edited by Muḥammad Abū-l-Faḍl Ibrāhīm, Beirut: al-Ma'rifah, 1957.

Al-Zaylaʿī, Fakhr-ul-Dīn (d. 743/1343). *Tabyīn al-ḥaqāʾiq sharḥ kanz al-daqāʾiq wa-ḥashiyah wahạshiyah al-Shilbī* (d. 1021/1612). Cairo: al-Maṭbaʿah al-Kubrā al-Amīriyyah, n.d.

Albahari, Miri. 'Against No-*Ātman* Theories of *Anattā*'. *Asian Philosophy* 12, no. 1 (2002): 5–20.

Albertz, Rainer. *Die Exilszeit*, Stuttgart: W. Kohlhammer, 2001.

Albright, W.F. 'Specimens of Late Ugaritic Prose'. *Bulletin of the American Schools of Oriental Research* 150 (1958): 36–8.

Alfeyev, Ilarion. *Christ the Conqueror of Hell: The Descent into Hades from an Orthodox Perspective*. Yonkers, NY: St. Vladimir's Seminary Press, 2009.

Ali, Zain. *Faith, Philosophy and the Reflective Muslim*. London: Palgrave Macmillan, 2013.

Allen, James P. *The Debate Between a Man and His Soul: A Masterpiece of Ancient Egyptian Literature*. Leiden: Brill, 2011.

Allen, N.J. 'The Hero's Five Relationships: A Proto-Indo-European Story'. In *Myth and Mythmaking: Continuous Evolution in Indian Tradition*, edited by Julia Leslie, 1–20. Richmond: Curzon, 1996.

Allison, Dale C. Jr. *4 Baruch: Paraleipomena Jeremiou*. Berlin: De Gruyter, 2018.

Alzoubi, Mahdi and Hussein al-Qudrah. 'Nabataean Architectural Terminology'. *Mediterranean Archaeology and Archaeometry* 15, no. 2 (2015): 53–61.

Alzoubi, Mahdi and Sahar Smadi. 'A Nabataean Funerary Inscription from Blaihed Museum'. *Arabian Archaeology and Epigraphy* 27, (2016): 79–83.

Amanat, Abbas. 'The Nuṭqawi Movement of Maḥmūd Pisīkhānī and His Persian Cycle of Mystical-Materialism'. In *Medieval Ismaʿili History and Thought*, edited by Farhad Daftary, 281–98. Cambridge: Cambridge University Press, 1996.

Amzallag, Nissim. 'The Authorship of Ezra and Nehemiah in Light of Differences in Their Ideological Background'. *Journal of Biblical Literature* 137, no. 2 (2018): 271–97.

Anbar, Moshe. 'Genesis 15: A Conflation of Two Deuteronomic Narratives'. *Journal of Biblical Literature* 101, no. 1 (1982): 39–55.

Anderson, Glaire D. 'Islamic Spaces and Diplomacy in Constantinople (Tenth to Thirteenth Centuries CE)'. *Medieval Encounters* 15, no. 1 (2009): 86–113.

Anderson, Ray. 'Theological Anthropology'. In *The Blackwell Companion to Modern Theology*, edited by Gareth Jones, 82–94. Malden, MA: Blackwell, 2004.

Anees, Munawar A. 'From Knowledge to Nihilism: Redeeming Humility'. *Journal of Islamic Philosophy* 1, no. 1 (2005): 5–10.

Ano, Gene G. and Erin B. Vasconcelles. 'Religious Coping and Psychological Adjustment to Stress: A Meta-Analysis'. *Journal of Clinical Psychology* 61, (2005): 461–80.

Anthony, David W. and Don Ringe. 'The Indo-European Homeland from Linguistic and Archaeological Perspectives'. *Annual Review of Linguistics* 1 (2015): 199–219.

Āq Shamsul-Dīn (d. 834/1429). *Fuṣūl al-badāʾiʿ fī uṣūl al-sharāʾiʿ*, edited by Muḥammad Ḥussayn Muḥammad Ḥassan Ismāʿīl. Beirut: al-Kutub al-ʿIlmiyyah, 2006.

Archer, George. *A Place Between Two Places: The Qurʾānic Barzakh*. Piscataway, NJ: Gorgias Press, 2017.

Ariarajah, Wesley. 'The Water of Life'. *The Ecumenical Review* 34, no. 3 (1982): 271–9.

Arnow, David. '*Sh'fokh Ḥamatkha* in the Mekhlita of Rabbi Ishmael and the Passover Haggadah: A Search for Origins and Meaning'. *Conservative Judaism* 65, nos. 1–2 (2013): 32–54.

Arulchelvam, Maheswari. 'The Eternal Eva: Matter in Hindu Philosophic Thought'. *The Sri Lanka Journal of the Humanities* 19, nos. 1–2 (1993): 34–45.

Asad, Muhammad. 'Symbolism and Allegory in the Qur'an'. In *The Message of the Qur'an*. Gibraltar: al-Andalus, 1980.

Ash, Paul S. *David, Solomon and Egypt: A Reassessment*. Sheffield: Sheffield Academic, 1999.

Assante, Julia. 'Inside and Out: Extra-Dimensional Aspects of the Mesopotamian Body, with Egyptian Parallels'. In *Religion und Menschenbild*, edited by Manfried Dietrich, Wilhelm Dupre, Ansgar Häußling, Annemarie Mertens, and Rüdiger Schmitt, 3–18. Münster: Ugarit-Verlag, 2010.

Assis, Elie 'Composition, Rhetoric and Theology in Haggai 1:1–11'. *The Journal of Hebrew Scriptures* 7, no. 11 (2007).

Assis, Elie. 'Zechariah's Vision of the Ephah (Zech. 5:5–11)'. *Vetus Testamentum* 60, no. 1 (2010): 15–32.

Assmann, Jan. *Tod und Jenseits im alten Ägypten*. Munich: C.H. Beck, 2001.

Augustine of Hippo (d. 430). *Expositions on the Book of Psalms*, edited by P. Schaff, translated by A.C. Coxe. New York, NY: Christian Literature Company, 1888.

Auld, Graeme. 'imago dei in Genesis: Speaking in the Image of God'. *The Expository Times* 116, no. 8 (2005): 259–62.

Avery-Peck, Alan J. 'Death and Afterlife in the Early Rabbinic Sources: The Mishnah, Tosefta, and Early Midrash Compilations'. In *Judaism in Late Antiquity: Death, Life-After-Death, Resurrection and The World-to-Come in the Judaisms of Antiquity*, edited by Alan J. Avery-Peck and Jacob Neusner, 243–66. Leiden: Brill, 2000.

Avery-Peck, Alan J. 'The Galilean Charismatic and Rabbinic Piety: The Holy Man in the Talmudic Literature'. In *The Historical Jesus in Context*, edited by Amy-Jill Levine, Dale C. Allison Jr. and Dominic Crossan, 149–65. Princeton, NJ: Princeton University Press, 2006.

Awabdy, Mark A. 'Yhwh Exegetes Torah: How Ezekiel 44:7–9 Bars Foreigners from the Sanctuary'. *Journal of Biblical Literature* 131, no. 4 (2014): 685–703.

Awn, Peter J. 'The Ethical Concerns of Classical Sufism'. *The Journal of Religious Ethics* 11, no. 2 (1983): 240–63.

Aymard, Jeremy M. 'Neuroscience, Materialism, and the Soul: Limit Questions'. *Dialogue & Nexus* 4 (2017): 2.

Ayoub, Mahmoud. 'Uzayr in the Qur'an and Muslim Tradition'. In *Studies in Islamic and Judaic Traditions: Papers Presented at the Institute for Islamic-Judaic Studies*, edited by William M. Brinner and Stephen D. Ricks, 3–18. Atlanta, GA: Scholars Press, 1986.

Badakhchani, S. Jalal (ed. and trans.). *Spiritual Resurrection in Shi'i Islam*. London: I.B. Tauris, 2017.

Bader, Bettina. 'Cultural Mixing in Egyptian Archaeology: The "Hyksos" as a Case Study'. *Archaeological Review from Cambridge* 28, no. 1 (2013): 257–86.

Bailey, Daniel P. 'The Intertextual Relationship of Daniel 12:2 and Isaiah 26:19: Evidence from Qumran and the Greek Versions'. *Tyndale Bulletin* 51, no. 2 (2000): 305–8.

Baker, Eric W. *The Eschatological Role of the Jerusalem Temple: An Examination of the Jewish Writings Dating from 586 BCE to 70 CE*. Hamburg: Anchor Academic, 2015.

Baker, Lynne R. *Persons and Bodies: A Constitution View*. Cambridge: Cambridge University Press, 2000.

Baker, Lynne R. 'Death and the Afterlife'. *Oxford Handbook of the Philosophy of Religion*, edited by William J. Wainwright, 366–91. Oxford: Oxford University Press, 2007.

Baker, Lynne R. 'Persons and the Metaphysics of Resurrection'. *Religious Studies* 43, no. 3 (2007): 333–48.

Balberg, Mira. *Purity, Body, and Self in Early Rabbinic Literature*. Berkeley, CA: University of California Press, 2014.

Bar, Shaul. 'Resurrection or Miraculous Cures? The Elijah and Elisha Narrative against Its Ancient Near Eastern Background'. *Old Testament Essays* 24, no. 1 (2011): 9–18.

Bar, S., D. Kahn and J.J. Shirley. *Egypt, Canaan and Israel: History, Imperialism, Ideology and Literature*. Leiden: Brill, 2011.

Barr, James. 'The Question of Religious Influence: The Case of Zoroastrianism, Judaism, and Christianity'. *Journal of the American Academy of Religion* 53, no. 2 (1985): 201–35.

Barr, James. 'Scope and Problems in the Semantics of Classical Hebrew'. *Zeitschrift für Althebraistik* 6, (1933): 3–14.

Barré, Michael L. 'Psalm 116: Its Structure and Its Enigmas'. *Journal of Biblical Literature* 109, no. 1 (1990): 61–78.

Basson, Danielle. 'The Goddess Hathor and the Women of Ancient Egypt'. Master's Thesis. Stellenbosch: University of Stellenbosch, 2012.

Bastomsky, S.J. 'The Talmudic View of Epicureanism'. *Apeiron* 7, no. 1 (1973): 17–20.

Bauckham, Richard B. *The Fate of the Dead: Studies on the Jewish and Christian Apocalypses*. Leiden: Brill, 1998.

Bauckham, Richard B. 'Life, Death, and the Afterlife in Second Temple Judaism'. In *Life in the Face of Death: The Resurrection Message of the New Testament*, edited by Richard N. Longenecker, 80–95. Grand Rapids, MI: Eerdmans, 1998.

Bauer, Hans and Pontus Leander. 1918–1922. *Historische Grammatik der hebräischen Sprache des Alten Testamentes*. Hildesheim: Georg Olms, 1991.

Baumgarten, Albert I. 'The Paradox of the Red Heifer'. *Vetus Testamentum* 43, no. 4 (1993): 442–51.

Baumgarten, Jörg. *Paulus und die Apokalyptik: Die Auslegung apokalyptischer Überlieferung in den echten Paulusbriefen*, Neukirchen-Vluyn: Neukirchener, 1975.

Beal, Timothy. 'Reception History and Beyond: Toward the Cultural History of Scriptures'. *Biblical Interpretation* 19, nos. 4–5 (2011): 357–72.

Beck, Daniel. *Evolution of the Early Qur'ān: From Anonymous Apocalypse to Charismatic Prophet*. New York, NY: Peter Lang, 2018.

Becker, Carl B. *Breaking the Circle: Death and the Afterlife in Buddhism*. Carbondale and Edwardsville, IL: Southern Illinois University Press, 1993.

Bedir, Ahmet and Şahin Aksoy, 'Brain Death Revisited: It Is Not "Complete Death" according to Islamic Sources'. *Global Medical Ethics* 37, no. 5 (2011): 290–4.

Begg, Christopher. 'The Destruction of the Calf (Exod 32,20/Deut 9,21)'. In *Das Deuteronomium: Entstehung, Gestalt und Botschaft (Deuteronomy: Origin, Form and Message),* edited by Norbert Lohfink, 208–51. Leuven: Leuven University Press, 1985.

Begg, Christopher T. 'Rereadings of the "Animal Rite" of Genesis 15 in Early Jewish Narratives'. *Catholic Biblical Quarterly* 50, no. 1 (1988): 36–46.

Bell, Richard. *The Origin of Islam in Its Christian Environment*. London: Frank Cass, 1968.

Bell, Richard. *A Commentary on the Qur'ān. Volume I: Surahs I–XXIV*. Manchester: University of Victoria, 1991.

Bellamy, James A. 'Al-Raqīm or al-Ruqūd? A Note on Surah 18:9'. *Journal of the American Oriental Society* 111, no. 1 (1991): 115–17.

Belnap, Daniel L. 'Defining the Ambiguous, the Unknown, and the Dangerous: The Significance of the Ritual Process in Deuteronomy 21:1–9'. *Zeitschrift für Altorientalische und Biblische Rechtsgeschichte* 23 (2017): 209–21.

ben Dor Evian, Shirly. 'Egypt and the Levant in the Iron Age: The Ceramic Evidence'. *Tel Aviv* 38, (2011): 94–119.

ben Dor Evian, Shirly. 'Egypt and Israel: The Never-Ending Story'. *Near Eastern Archaeology* 80, no. 1 (2017): 30–9.

Benedetto, Robert. 'Psalm 84'. *Interpretation* 51, no. 1 (1997): 57–61.
Benner, Steven A. 'Defining Life'. *Astrobiology* 10, no. 10 (2010): 1021–30.
Bennett, Anne. 'Reincarnation, Sect Unity, and Identity among the Druze'. *Ethnology* 45, no. 2 (2006): 87–104.
Bensaid, Benaouda, Salah T. Machouche and Fadila Grine. 'A Qur'anic Framework for Spiritual Intelligence'. *Religions* 5, no. 1 (2014): 179–98.
Benthal, Jonathan. 'Financial Worship: The Quranic Injunction to Almsgiving'. *The Journal of the Royal Anthropological Institute* 5, no. 1 (1999): 27–42.
Bergren, Theodore A. 'Nehemiah in 2 Maccabees 1:10–2:18'. *Journal for the Study of Judaism in the Persian, Hellenistic, and Roman Period* 28, no. 3 (1997): 249–70.
Bernat, James L. 'The Definition and Criterion of Death'. *Handbook of Clinical Neurology* 118 (2013): 419–35.
Berrada, Khalid. 'Metaphors of Light and Darkness in the Holy Qur'an: A Conceptual Approach'. *Basamat* 1 (2006): 45–64.
Bertaina, David. 'Bodily Resurrection in the Qur'ān and Syriac Anti-Tritheist Debate'. *Journal of the International Qur'anic Studies Association* 3 (2018): 43–78.
Bharadwaja, V.K. 'Rationality, Argumentation and Embarrassment: A Study of Four Logical Alternatives (catuṣkoṭi) in Buddhist Logic'. *Philosophy East and West* 34, no. 3 (1984): 303–19.
Bijlefeld, Willem A. 'Eschatology: Some Muslim and Christian Data'. *Islam and Christian-Muslim Relations* 15, no. 1 (2004): 35–54.
Billauer, Barbara, P. 'On Judaism and Genes: A Response to Paul Root Wolpe'. *Kennedy Institute of Ethics Journal* 9, no. 2 (1999): 159–65.
Billings, Bradly S. '"The Angels who Sinned . . . He Cast into Tartus" (2 Peter 2:4): Its Ancient Meaning and Present Revalence'. *The Expository Times* 119, no. 11 (2008): 532–7.
Birenboim, Hannan. '*Tevul Yom* and the Red Heifer: Pharisaic and Sadducean Halakah'. *Dead Sea Discoveries* 16, no. 2 (2009): 254–73.
Birkeland, H. 'The Belief in the Resurrection of the Dead in the Old Testament'. *Studia Theologica* 3 (1949): 60–78.
Birkhan, Helmut. 'Some Remarks on the Druids'. In *Runica Germanica Mediaevalia*, edited by Willhelm Heizmann and Astrid van Nahl, 108–9. Berlin: De Gruyter, 2003.
Black, C. Clifton II. 'Pauline Perspectives on Death in Romans 5–8'. *Journal of Biblical Literature* 103, no. 3 (1984): 413–33.
Blau, Joseph L. 'The Red Heifer: A Biblical Purification Rite in Rabbinic Literature'. *Numen* 14, no. 1 (1967): 70–8.
Blech, Benjamin. 'Thematic Linkage in Understanding Halakhah'. *Tradition: A Journal of Orthodox Jewish Thought* 24, no. 1 (1988): 59–68.
Blenkinsopp, Joseph. 'On Saving One's Soul'. *Life of the Spirit* 17, no. 199 (1963): 355–67.
Blenkinsopp, Joseph. *Opening the Sealed Book: Interpretations of the Book of Isaiah in Late Antiquity*. Grand Rapids, MI: Eerdmans, 2006.
Blenkinsopp, Joseph. *Judaism, The First Phase: The Place of Ezra and Nehemiah in the Origins of Judaism*. Grand Rapids, MI: Eerdmans, 2009.
Block, Daniel I. 'Beyond the Grave: Ezekiel's Vision of Death and Afterlife'. *Bulletin for Biblical Research* 2, (1992): 113–41.
Boda, Mark J. *The NIV Application Commentary: Haggai, Zechariah*. Grand Rapids, MI: Zondervan, 2004.
Bodner, Keith. *Jeroboam's Royal Drama*. Oxford: Oxford University Press, 2012.

Bogaert, Pierre-Maurice. 'Le nom de Baruch dans la littérature pseudépigraphique: L'Apocalypse syriaque et le livre deutérocanonique'. In *La littérature juive entre Tenach et Mischna*, edited by W.C. van Unnik. Leiden: Brill, 1974.

Bogaert, Pierre-Maurice. 'La "seconde mort" à l'époque des Tannaim'. In *Vie et survie dans les civilisations orientales*, edited by Aristide Théodorides, Paul Naster and Julien Ries, 199–207. Leuven: Peeters, 1983.

Bogue, Ronald. 'The Betrayal of God'. In *Deleuze and Religion*, edited by Mary Bryden, 9–29. London: Routledge, 2001.

Bordoy, Francesc C. 'On the Origin of the Orphic-Pythagorean Notion of the Immortality of the Soul'. In *On Pythagoreanism*, edited by Gabriele Cornelli, Richard McKirahan and Constantinos Macris, 153–76. Berlin: De Gruyter, 2013.

Bosman, H.J., R. Oosting and F. Potsma. *Wörterbuch zum Alten Testament: Hebräisch/Aramäisch-Deutsch und Hebräisch/Aramäisch-Englisch*. Stuttgart: Deutsche Bibelgesellschaft, 2009.

Bostock, D. Gerald. 'Osiris and the Resurrection of Christ'. *The Expository Times* 112, no. 8 (2001): 265–71.

Bottéro, Jean. *Mésopotamie: L'éciture, la raison et les dieux*. Paris: Éditions Gallimard, 1987.

Botterweck, G.J. and H. Ringgren (eds.), J. T. Willis (trans.). *Theological Dictionary of the Old Testament (TDOT) (Revised Edition)*. Grand Rapids, MI: Eerdmans.

Böwering, Gerhard. 'Ideas of Time in Persian Mysticism'. In *The Persian Presence in the Islamic World*, edited by Richard G. Hovannisian and Georges Sabagh, 172–98. Cambridge: Cambridge University Press, 1998.

Boyce, Mary. *A History of Zoroastrianism: Zoroastrianism under Macedonian and Roman Rule*, 3 vols. Leiden: Brill, 1975–1991.

Boyce, Mary. 'Zoroaster, Zoroastrianism'. In *Anchor Bible Dictionary*, edited by D.N. Freedman, New York, NY: Doubleday, 1992.

Boyce, Mary. *Zoroastrians: Their Religious Beliefs and Practices*. London: Routledge, 2001.

Boyd, Jeffrey H. 'One's Self-Concept and Biblical Theology'. *Journal of the Evangelical Theological Society* 40, no. 2 (1997): 207–227.

Bradley, Ben, Fred Feldman, and Jens Johansson. *The Oxford Handbook of Philosophy of Death*, Oxford: Oxford University Press, 2013.

Brandon, Samuel G.F. *History, Time and Deity: A Historical and Comparative Study of the Conception of Time in Religious Thought and Practice*. Manchester: Manchester University Press, 1964.

Bream, Howard N. 'Life without Resurrection: Two Perspectives from Qoheleth'. In *Light unto My Path: Old Testament Studies in Honor of Jacob M. Meyers*, edited by Howard N. Bream, Ralph D. Heim and Carey A. Moore, 49–65. Philadelphia: Temple University Press, 1974.

Bremmer, Jan N. 'The Resurrection between Zarathustra and Jonathan Z. Smith'. *Nederlands Theologisch Tijdschrift* 50 (1996): 89–107.

Bresnan, Patrick S. *Awakening: An Introduction to the History of Eastern Thought*, 6th ed. Abingdon: Routledge, 2018.

Brewer, Douglas J. and Emily Teeter. *Egypt and the Egyptians*. Cambridge: Cambridge University Press, 2007.

Brody, Baruch. 'Jewish Reflections on the Resurrection of the Dead'. *The Torah u-Madda Journal* (2016): 93–122.

Bronner, Leila L. 'The Resurrection Motif in the Hebrew Bible: Allusions or Illusions?' *Jewish Bible Quarterly* 30, no. 3 (2002): 143–54.

Brown, F., S.R. Driver and C. Briggs. *Enhanced Brown-Driver-Briggs Hebrew and English Lexicon of the Old Testament*. Bellingham, WA: Logos Research Systems, 2000.

Brown, Jonathan A.C. 'New Data on the Delateralization of Ḍād and Its Merger with Ẓāʾ in Classical Arabic: Contributions from Old South Arabic and the Earliest Islamic Texts on Ḍ / Ẓ Minimal Pairs'. *Journal of Semitic Studies* 52, no. 2 (2007): 335–68.

Brown, Scott G. 'Mark 11:1-12:12: A Triple Intercalation?' *Catholic Biblical Quarterly* 64, no. 1 (2002): 78–89.

Brown, Warren S. 'Nonreductive Physicalism and Soul: Finding Resonance between Theology and Neuroscience'. *American Behavioral Scientist* 45, no. 12 (2002): 1812–21.

Bruylants, Gilles, Kristin Bartik and Jacques Reisse. 'Is It Useful to Have a Clear-cut Definition of Life? On the Use of Fuzzy Logic in Prebiotic Chemistry'. *Origins of Life and Evolution Biosphere* 40, no. 2 (2010): 137–43.

Bryan, Steven M. 'The End of Exile: The Reception of Jeremiah's Prediction of a Seventy-Year Exile'. *Journal of Biblical Literature* 137, no. 1 (2018): 107–26.

Bryant, Edwin. *The Origins of Vedic Culture: The Indo-Aryan Migration Debate*. Oxford: Oxford University Press, 2001.

Bryant, Edwin F. and Laurie L. Patton (eds.). *The Indo-Aryan Controversy: Evidence and Inference in Indian History*. Abingdon: Routledge, 2005.

Buchanan, George W. 'Eschatology and the "End of Days"'. *Journal of Near Eastern Studies* 20, no. 3 (1961): 188–93.

Buck, Melissa R. 'רוח in Ezekiel 37 and πνευμα in John 3: Allusion, Pun and Typology', Master's Thesis. Edmonton: Concordia University of Edmonton, 2016.

Buckley, R.P. 'The Early Shiite Ghulah'. *Journal of Semitic Studies* 42, no. 2 (1997): 301–26.

Burckhardt, Titus. 'Concerning the "Barzakh"'. *Studies in Comparative Religion* 13, nos. 1–2 (1979): 24–30.

Burnett, David A. '"So Shall Your Seed Be": Paul's Use of Genesis 15:5 in Romans 4:18 in Light of Early Jewish Deification Traditions'. *Journal for the Study of Paul and His Letters* 5, no. 2 (2015): 211–36.

Burns, J. Patout. 'Augustine's Role in the Imperial Action Against Pelagius'. *Journal of Theological Studies* 30, no. 1 (1979): 67–83.

Bynum, Caroline W. *The Resurrection of the Body in Western Christianity*. New York, NY: Columbia University Press, 1995.

Cairus, Aecio E. 'Protection and Rewards: The Significance of Ancient Midrashic Expositions on Genesis 15:1–6'. PhD Dissertation. Berrien Springs, MI: Andrews University, 1989.

Callaway, Mary C. *Jeremiah Through the Centuries*. Hoboken, NJ: Wiley-Blackwell, 2020.

Campbell, D. N. and Fika J. van Rensburg. 'A History of the Interpretation of 1 Peter 3:18–22'. *Acta Patristica et Byzantina* 19, no. 1 (2008): 73–96.

Campbell, Joseph. *The Way of Animal Powers*. London: Times Books, 1984.

Caneday, Ardel B. 'Qoheleth: Enigmatic Pessimist or Godly Sage?' *Grace Theological Journal* 7, no. 1 (1986): 21–56.

Carlisle, Clare. 'Becoming and Un-becoming: The Theory and Practice of *Anatta*'. *Contemporary Buddhism: An Interdisciplinary Journal* 7, no. 1 (2006): 75–89.

Carmichael, Calum M. 'Marriage and the Samaritan Woman'. *New Testament Studies* 26, no. 3 (1980): 332–46.

Chafer, Lewis Sperry. *Systematic Theology*, 8 vols. Dallas, TX: Dallas Seminary Press, 1947–8.

Chamsi-Pasha, Hassan and Mohammed A. Albar. 'Do Not Resuscitate, Brain Death, and Organ Transplantation: Islamic Perspective'. *Avicenna Journal of Medicine* 7, no. 2 (2017): 35–45.

Charles, J. Daryl. 'The Angels under Reserve in 2 Peter and Jude'. *Bulletin for Biblical Research* 15, no. 1 (2005): 39–48.

Charlesworth, James H. 'Where Does the Concept of Resurrection Appear and How Do We Know That?' In *Resurrection: The Origin and Future of a Biblical Doctrine*, edited by James H. Charlesworth, 1–21. London: T&T Clark, 2006.

Chernick, Michael. *Gezarah Shavah: Its Various Forms in Midrashic and Talmudic Sources*. Lod: Haberman Institute for Literary Research, 1994.

Childe, V. Gordon. 'The Urban Revolution'. *The Town Planning Review* 21, no. 1 (1950): 3–17.

Chittick, William C. 'Muslim Eschatology'. In *The Oxford Handbook of Eschatology*, edited by Jerry L. Walls, 133–50. Oxford: Oxford University Press, 2007.

Christiansen, Johanne L. 'The Dark Koran: A Semantic Analysis of the Koranic Darkness (*ẓulumāt*) and Their Metaphorical Usage'. *Arabica* 62, nos. 2–3 (2015): 185–233.

Chung, Youn H. *The Sin of the Calf: The Rise of the Bible's Negative Attitude toward the Golden Calf*. London: T&T Clark, 2010.

Chyutin, Michael. *The New Jerusalem Scroll from Qumran: A Comprehensive Reconstruction*. Sheffield: Sheffield Academic, 1997.

Clark-Soles, Jaime. *Death and the Afterlife in the New Testament*. London: T&T Clark, 2006.

Clarke, Peter G.H. 'Neuroscience, Quantum Indeterminism and the Cartesian Soul'. *Brain and Cognition* 84, no. 1 (2014): 109–17.

Clines, David J.A. 'The Etymology of Hebrew Ṣelem'. *Journal of Northwest Semitic Languages* 3 (1974): 15–22.

Clines, David J.A. 'Haggai's Temple, Constructed, Deconstructed and Reconstructed'. *Scandinavian Journal of the Old Testament* 7, no. 1 (1993): 51–77.

Cohen, Norman J. 'Analysis of an Exegetic Tradition in the "Melkhita de-Rabbi Ishmael": The Meaning of ʾAmanah in the Second and Third Centuries'. *AJS Review* 9, no. 1 (1984): 1–25.

Cohen-Weinberger, Anat and Yuval Goren. 'Levantine-Egyptian Interactions during the 12th to the 15th Dynasties Based on the Petrography of the Canaanite Pottery from Tell El-Dabʿa'. *Ägypten und Levante* 14 (2004): 69–199.

Cohn, Naftali S. *Cosmos, Chaos, and the World to Come*. New Haven, CT: Yale University Press, 1993.

Cohn, Naftali S. *The Memory of the Temple and the Making of the Rabbis*. Philadelphia, PA: University of Pennsylvania Press, 2013.

Cohn-Sherbok, Dan M. 'Jesus' Defence of the Resurrection of the Dead'. *Journal for the Study of the New Testament* 4, no. 11 (1981): 64–73.

Cohn-Sherbok, Dan M. *Judaism: History, Belief and Practice*. Abingdon: Routledge, 2003.

Cole, Juan. 'Infidel or Paganus? The Polysemy of *kafara* in the Quran'. *Journal of the American Oriental Society* 140, no. 3 (2020): 615–36.

Collins, Jack. 'Discourse Analysis and the Interpretation of Gen 2:4–7'. *Westminster Theological Journal* 61, (1999): 269–76.

Collins, John J. *Daniel: A Commentary on the Book of Daniel*. Minneapolis, MN: Fortress, 1993.

Collins, John J. 'The Afterlife in Apocalyptic Literature'. In *Judaism in Late Antiquity: Death, Life-after-Death, Resurrection and the World-to-Come in the Judaisms of Antiquity*, edited by Alan J. Avery-Peck and Jacob Neusner, 119–40, Leiden: Brill, 2000.

Collins, John J. 'The Transformation of the Torah in Second Temple Judaism'. *Journal for the Study of Judaism* 43, nos. 4–5 (2012): 455–74.

Collins, Steven. *Selfless Persons*, Cambridge: Cambridge University Press, 1982.
Comerro, Viviane. 'Esdras Est-Il le Fils de Dieu?' *Arabica* 52, no. 2 (2005): 165–81.
Cooper, Jerrold S. 'Wind and Smoke: Giving Up the Ghost of Enkidu: Comprehending Enkidu's Ghosts'. In *Rethinking Ghosts in World Religions*, edited by Mu-chou Poo, 23–32. Leiden: Brill, 2009.
Cooper, John W. *Body, Soul, and Life Everlasting: Biblical Anthropology and the Monism-Dualism Debate*. Grand Rapids, MI: Eerdmans, 1989.
Cooper, John W. 'Body-Soul Question: Can We Be Both Confessional and Reformational?' *Pro Rege* 20, no. 1 (1991): 1–12.
Cooper, John W. 'Scripture and Philosophy on the Unity of Body and Soul: An Integrative Method for Theological Anthropology'. In *The Ashgate Research Companion to Theological Anthropology*, edited by Joshua R. Farris and Charles Taliaferro, 27–42. Farnham: Ashgate, 2015.
Cooper, John W. 'Biblical Anthropology Is Holistic and Dualistic'. In *The Blackwell Companion to Substance Dualism*, edited by Jonathan J. Loose, Angus, J.L. Mengue, and J.P. Moreland, 411–26. Hoboken, NJ: Wiley, 2018.
Corbin, Henry. *Cyclical Time and Ismaili Gnosis*, trans. Ralph Manheim and James Morris. London: Kegan Paul, 1983.
Corbin, Henry. *History of Islamic Philosophy*, trans. Liadain Sherrard and Philip Sherrard. London: Kegan Paul, 1993.
Corcoran, Kevin J. 'Physical Persons and Post Mortem Survival Without Temporal Gaps'. In *Soul, Body and Survival: Essays on the Metaphysics of Human Persons*, edited by Kevin Corcoran, 201–17. Ithaca, NY: Cornell University Press, 2001.
Corcoran, Kevin J. 'The Constitution View of Persons'. In *In Search of the Soul: Four Views of the Mind-Body Problem*, edited by Joel B. Green, 153–76. Eugene, OR: Wipf & Stock, 2005.
Corcoran, Kevin J. *Rethinking Human Nature: A Christian Materialist Alternative to the Soul*. Grand Rapids, MI: Baker Academic, 2006.
Cornelius, Elma. 'The Motivation and Limits of Compassion'. *HTS Teologiese Studies* 69, no. 1 (2013): 1189.
Cotton, Hannah M., Leah D. Segni, Werner Eck, Benjamin Isaac, Alla Kushnir-Stein, Haggai Misgav, Jonathan Price, Israel Roll and Ada Yardeni (eds.). *Corpus Inscriptionum Iudaeae/Palaestinae*, Vol. 1, Jerusalem, Part 1: 1–704. Berlin: De Gruyter, 2010.
Cox, Patricia. 'Origen and the Bestial Soul'. *Vigiliae Christianae* 36, no. 2 (1982): 115–40.
Crawford, Robert. *The Battle for the Soul: A Comparative Analysis in an Age of Doubt*. New York, NY: Palgrave Macmillan, 2011.
Crone, Patricia and Michael Cook. *Hagarism: The Making of the Islamic World*. Cambridge: Cambridge University Press, 1977.
Crone, Patricia. *Slaves on Horses: The Evolution of the Islamic Polity*. Cambridge: Cambridge University Press, 1980.
Crone, Patricia. 'Kavād's Heresy and Mazdak's Revolt'. *Iran* 29 (1991): 21–42.
Crone, Patricia. 'The Religion of the Qur'anic Pagans: God and the Lesser Deities'. *Arabica* 57, no. 2–3 (2010): 151–200.
Crone, Patricia. *The Nativist Prophets of Early Islamic Iran: Rural Revolt and Local Zoroastrianism*. Cambridge: Cambridge University Press, 2012.
Crone, Patricia. 'The Quranic *Mushrikūn* and the Resurrection (Part I)'. *Bulletin of the School of Oriental and African Studies* 75, no. 3 (2012): 445–72.
Crone, Patricia. 'The Quranic *Mushrikūn* and the Resurrection (Part II)'. *Bulletin of the School of Oriental and African Studies* 76, no. 1 (2013): 1–20.

Crone, Patricia. '"Nothing but Time Destroys Us": The Deniers of Resurrection in the Qur'ān'. *Journal of the International Qur'anic Studies Association* 1 (2016): 127–47.

Cross, Frank M. *Canaanite Myth and Hebrew Epic*. Cambridge, MA: Harvard University Press, 1973.

Cua, Antonio S. 'Opposites as Complements: Reflections on the Significance of Tao'. *Philosophy East and West* 31, no. 2 (1981): 123–40.

Culley, Robert C. 'The Temple in Psalms 84, 63, and 42–43'. In *Où demeures-tu? Jn I,38: La maison depuis le monde biblique: En homage au professeur Guy Couturier à l'occasion de ses soixante-cinq ans*, edited by André Charron, Guy Couturier, André Myre and Jean-Claude Petit, 187–97. Saint-Laurent, QC: Fides, 1994.

Cullman, Oscar. 'Immortality of the Soul or Resurrection of the Dead.' In *Immortality*, edited by Terence Penelhum, 53–85. Belmont: Wadsworth, 1973.

Cuypers, Michel. 'Semitic Rhetoric as a Key to the Question of the *naẓm* of the Qur'anic Text'. *Journal of Qur'anic Studies* 13, no. 1 (2011): 1–24.

Cuypers, Michel. *The Composition of the Qur'an: Rhetorical Analysis*. London: Bloomsbury, 2015.

Dakake, Maria M. 'The Soul as Barzakh: Substantial Motion and Mullā Ṣadrā's Theory of Human Becoming'. *The Muslim World* 94, no. 1 (2004): 107–30.

Dalferth, Ingolf U. 1988. *Theology and Philosophy*. Eugene, OR: Wipf & Stock, 2001.

Dalton, William J. *Christ's Proclamation to the Spirits: A Study of 1 Peter 3:18–4:6*, 2nd ed. Rome: Editrice Pontificio Istituto Biblico, 1989.

Danelius, Eva. 'The Sins of Jeroboam ben-Nabat'. *Jewish Quarterly Review* 58 (1967): 95–114.

Darwīsh, Muḥyī-l-Dīn (d. 1403/1983). *I'rāb al-Qur'ān wa-bayānuh*. Homs: al-Irshād lil-Shu'ūn al-Jāmi'iyyah, 1995.

Daube, David. 'On Acts 23: Sadducees and Angels'. *Journal of Biblical Literature*. 109, no. 3 (1990): 493–7.

Davies, Douglas. *Death, Ritual and Belief: The Rhetoric of Funerary Rites*, 3rd ed. London: Bloomsbury Academic, 2017.

Davies, Jon. *Death, Burial and Rebirth in the Religions of Antiquity*. London: Routledge, 1999.

Davis, Barry C. 'Ecclesiastes 12:1–8-Death: An Impetus for Life'. *Bibliotheca Sacra* 148, (1991): 298–317.

Day, John. 'The Daniel of Ugarit and Ezekiel and the Hero of the Book of Daniel'. *Vetus Testamentum* 30, no. 2 (1980): 174–85.

Day, John. 'The Development of Belief in Life after Death in Ancient Israel'. In *After the Exile: Essays in Honour of Rex Mason*, edited by J. Barton and D.J. Reimer, 231–57. Macon, GA: Mercer University Press, 1996.

Day, John. 'Resurrection Imagery from Baal to the Book of Daniel'. In *Congress Volume, Cambridge 1995*, edited by J.A. Emerton, *Vetus Testamentum Supplements*, 66: 125–33. Leiden: Brill, 1997.

Dayal, Hal. 1932. *The Bodhisattva Doctrine in Buddhist Sanskrit Literature*, Delhi: Motilal Banarsidass, 1999.

de Blois, François. 'Ḥijāratun min sijjīl'. *Acta Orientalia* 60 (1999): 58–71.

de Georgia, Michael A. 'History of Brain Death as Death: 1968 to the Present'. *Journal of Critical Care* 29, no. 4 (2014): 673–8.

de Gifis, Vanessa. *Shaping a Qur'ānic Worldview: Scriptural Hermeneutics and the Rhetoric of Moral Reform in the Caliphate of al-Ma'mūn*. Abingdon: Routledge, 2014.

de Hemmer Gudme, Anne K. 'How Should We Read Hebrew Bible Ritual Texts? A Ritualistic Reading of the Law of the Nazirite (Num 6,1–21)'. *Scandinavian Journal of the Old Testament* 23, no. 1 (2009): 64–84.
de Long, Kindalee P. '"Ask a Woman": Childbearing and Ezra's Transformation in *4 Ezra*'. *Journal for the Study of the Pseudepigrapha* 22, no. 2 (2012): 114–45.
de Moor, Johannes C. 'Rāpi'ūma—Rephaim'. *Zeitscrift für die alttestamentliche Wissenschaft* 88, no. 3 (1976): 323–45.
de Moor, Johannes C. 'Concepts of Afterlife in Canaan'. *Ugarit-Forschungen* 45 (2014): 373–88.
de Smet, Daniel. 'Isma'ili-Shi'i Visions of Hell: From the "Spiritual" Torment of the Fāṭimids to the Ṭayyibī Rock of Sijjīn'. In *Locating Hell in Islamic Traditions*, edited by Christian Lange, 241–67. Leiden: Brill, 2015.
de Vivo, Jenny. '2 Peter 2:4–16: The Redaction of the Biblical and Intertestamental References Dependent on Jude 5–11 and Their Overall Significance for the Document'. PhD Dissertation. Chicago, IL: Loyola University, 2014.
del Olmo Lete, Gregorio. 'Môtu and Baʕlu at Work: Two Lexicographical Notes on KTU 1.82:5–6'. *Aula Orientalis* 32, no. 1 (2014): 165–76.
Delalay, Marc-André. 'The Covenant Ritual in Genesis 15: Examining the Nature of the Covenant in Light of Its Cultural and Literary Context'. Master's Thesis. Montreal, QC: Concordia University, 2009.
Denaux, Adelbert. 'The Controversy between Jesus and the Sadducees about the Resurrection (Matt 22:23–33) in the Context of Early Jewish Eschatology'. In *Life beyond Death in Matthew's Gospel Religious Metaphor or Bodily Reality?* Ed. Wim Weren, Huub van de Sandt and Joseph Verheyden, 129–51. Leuven: Peeters, 2011.
Deutsch, Celia. 'Transformation of Symbols: The New Jerusalem in Rv 21 1–22 5'. *Zeitschrift für die neutestamentliche Wissenschaft* 78, no. 1–2 (1987): 106–26.
Dever, William G. *Who Were the Early Israelites and Where Did They Come From?* Grand Rapids, MI: Eerdmans, 2003.
Dexinger, Ferdinand. 'Samaritan Eschatology'. In *The Samaritans*, edited by Alan D. Crown, 266–92. Tübingen: Mohr Siebeck, 1989.
Dexinger, Ferdinand. 'After Life'. In *A Companion to Samaritan Studies*, edited by Alan D. Crown and Reinhard Pummer, 9–10. Tübingen: Mohr Siebeck, 1993.
Dexinger, Ferdinand. 'Eschatology'. In *A Companion to Samaritan Studies*, edited by Alan D. Crown and Reinhard Pummer, 86–90. Tübingen: Mohr Siebeck, 1993.
Dimant, Devorah. 'Resurrection, Restoration, and Time-Curtailing in Qumran, Early Judaism, and Christianity'. *Revue de Qumrân* 19, no. 4 (2000): 527–48.
Dolan, Brian. 'Soul Searching: A Brief History of the Mind/Body Debate in the Neurosciences'. *Neurosurgical Focus* 23, no. 1 (2007): E2.
Doniger, Wendy. *On Hinduism*. Oxford: Oxford University Press, 2014.
Donner, Fred. *Muhammad and the Believers: At the Origins of Islam*. Cambridge, MA: Harvard University Press: Harvard University Press, 2010.
Dormandy, Katherine. 'Does Epistemic Humility Threaten Religious Beliefs?' *Journal of Psychology and Theology* 46, no. 4 (2018): 292–304.
Dormandy, Katherine. 'The Epistemic Benefits of Religious Disagreement'. *Religious Studies* 56, no. 3 (2020): 390–408.
Dougherty, Trent. *The Problem of Animal Pain: A Theodicy for All Creatures Great and Small*. Basingstoke: Palgrave Macmillan, 2014.
Draper, Jonathan A. 'Resurrection and Zechariah 14.5 in the Didache Apocalypse'. *Journal of Early Christian Studies* 5, no. 2 (1997): 155–79.

Draper, Jonathan A. and Clayton N. Jefford (eds.). *The Didache: A Missing Piece of the Puzzle in Early Christianity*. Atlanta, GA: Society of Biblical Literature, 2015.
du Toit, Marietjie (2008). 'A Study of 1 Peter 3:18–4:6: An Investigation into the Historical Background of the Doctrine of Christ's Descent into Hades'. Master's Thesis. Pretoria: University of Pretoria, 2008.
Duchesne-Guillemin, Jacques. *The Western Response to Zoroaster*. Oxford: Clarendon Press, 1958.
Duhm, Bernhard. *Das Buch Jesaja*, 2nd ed. Göttingen: Vandenhoeck & Ruprecht, 1922.
Edelman, Diana V. *The Origins of the Second Temple: Persian Imperial Policy and the Rebuilding of Jerusalem*. Abingdon: Routledge, 2005.
Edersheim, Alfred. *The Temple: Its Ministry and Services as They Were at the Time of Jesus Christ*. London: James Clarke & Co, 1959.
Edgar, Brian G. 'Paul and the Person'. *Science and Christian Belief* 12, no. 2 (2000): 151–64.
Edgar, Brian. 'Biblical Anthropology and the Intermediate State, Part 1'. *Evangelical Quarterly* 74, no. 1 (2002): 27–45.
Edgar, Brian. 'Biblical Anthropology and the Intermediate State, Part 2'. *Evangelical Quarterly* 74, no. 2 (2002): 109–21.
Edzard, Lutz. 'On the Role of South Arabian and Ethio-Semitic within a Comparative Semitic Lexicographical Project'. *Oslo Studies in Language* 8, no. 1 (2016): 219–42.
Eichrodt, Walther. *Theology of the Old Testament*. London: Westminster Press, 1961–7.
Efros, Israel. 'Textual Notes on the Hebrew Bible'. *Journal of the American Oriental Society* 45 (1925): 152–4.
El-Badawi, Emran. *The Qur'ān and the Aramaic Gospel Traditions*. Abingdon: Routledge, 2013.
El-Badawi, Emran. 'The Impact of Aramaic (especially Syriac) on the Qur'an'. *Religion Compass* 8, no. 7 (2014): 220–8.
El-Khatib, Abdallah. 'Jerusalem in the Qur'an'. *British Journal of Middle Eastern Studies* 28, no. 1 (2001): 25–53.
El-Khouri, Lamia. 'Fertility as an Element in Late Nabataean Beliefs: The Archaeological Evidence Considered'. *Levant: The Journal of the Council for British Research in the Levant* 39, no. 1 (2007): 81–90.
El-Sharif, Ahmad. 'Metaphors We Believe by: Islamic Doctrine as Evoked by the Prophet Muhammad's Metaphors'. *Critical Discourse Studies* 9, no. 3 (2012): 231–45.
El-Zeiny, Iman. 'Criteria for the Translation and Assessment of Qur'anic Metaphor: A Contrastive Analytic Approach'. *Babel* 57, no. 3 (2011): 247–68.
Eliade, Mircea. *Shamanism: Archaic Techniques of Ecstasy*, trans. Willard R. Trask. Princeton, NJ: Princeton University Press, 1964.
Elledge, Casey D. *Life after Death in Early Judaism: The Evidence of Josephus*. Tübingen: Mohr Siebeck, 2006.
Elledge, Casey D. 'Resurrection of the Dead: Exploring Our Earliest Evidence Today'. In *Resurrection: The Origin and Future of a Biblical Doctrine*, 27–52. London: T&T Clark, 2006.
Elledge, Casey D. 'Future Resurrection of the Dead in Early Judaism: Social Dynamics, Contested Evidence'. *Currents in Biblical Research* 9, no. 3 (2011): 394–421.
Elledge, Casey D. *Resurrection of the Dead in Early Judaism, 200 BCE–CE 200* Oxford: Oxford University Press, 2017.
Elman, Yaakov. 'Zoroastrianism and Qumran'. In *The Dead Sea Scrolls at 60*, edited by Lawrence Schiffman and Shani Tzoref, 91–8. Leiden: Brill, 2010.

Endsjø, Dag Ø. 'Immortal Bodies, before Christ: Bodily Continuity in Ancient Greece and 1 Corinthians'. *Journal for the Study of the New Testament* 30, no. 4 (2008): 417–36.

Erman, A. and H. Grapow. 1926–31. *Wörterbuch der ägyptischen Sprache,* Leipzig: J.C. Hinrichs, 1963.

Eskenazi, Tamara C. 'The Structure of Ezra-Nehemiah and the Integrity of the Book'. *Journal of Biblical Literature* 107, no. 4 (1988): 641–56.

Eskenazi, Tamara C. 'Revisiting the Composition of Ezra-Nehemiah: A Prolegomenon'. In *Foster Biblical Scholarship: Essays in Honor of Kent Harold Richards,* edited by Frank R. Ames and Charles W. Miller, 215–34. Atlanta, GA: Society of Biblical Literature, 2010.

Esler, Philip F. 'Ezra-Nehemiah as a Narrative of (Re-Invented) Israelite Identity'. *Biblical Interpretation* 11, no. 3 (2003): 413–26.

Essels, Willie J. 'Jeremiah 24:1–10 as a Pronouncement of Hope?' *Old Testament Essays* 4, (1991): 397–407.

Evans, Annette. 'To What Extent Is *Ezekiel* the Source of Resurrection of the Dead in 4Q385 *Pseudo-Ezekiel* and Targum Ezekiel?' *Old Testament Essays* 28, no. 1 (2015): 70–85.

Evian, Shirly B.-D. 'Egypt and Israel: The Never-Ending Story'. *Near Eastern Archaeology* 80, no. 1 (2017): 30–9.

Eybers, Ian H. 'The Root *Ṣ-L* in Hebrew Words', *Journal of Northwest Semitic Languages* 2, (1972): 23–36.

Eybers, Ian H. 'The Rebuilding of the Temple according to Haggai and Zechariah'. In *Studies in Old Testament Prophecy*, edited by W.C. van Wyk, 15–26, Potchefstroom: Pro Rege, 1975.

Fahm, Abdulgafar O. 'Brief Analysis of the Meditation on Death in Sufism: With Reference to al-Ghazālī and Rūmī'. *International Journal of Religion & Spirituality in Society* 4, no. 3 (2014): 7–14.

Fakhry, Majid. *Islamic Philosophy, Theology and Mysticism: A Short Introduction*, 2nd ed. Oxford: Oneworld, 2000.

Farah, Martha J. and Nancey Murphy. 'Neuroscience and the Soul'. *Science* 323, no. 5918 (2009): 1168.

Farīd, Aḥmad. *Tazkiyah al-nufūs wa-tarbiyatuhā*, edited by Mājid b. Abī al-Layl. Beirut: al-Qalam, 1985.

Farisani, Elelwani. 'The Composition and Date of Ezra-Nehemiah'. *Old Testament Essays* 17, no. 2 (2004): 208–30.

Farrin, Raymond K. 'Surat al-Baqara: A Structural Analysis'. *The Muslim World* 100, no. 1 (2010): 17–32.

Feigin, Samuel I. 'Ḥamôr Gārîm: "Castrated Ass"'. *Journal of Near Eastern Studies* 5, no. 3 (1946): 230–3.

Feigin, Samuel I. 'Haggārîm: "The Castrated One"'. *Hebrew Union College Annual* 21, (1948): 355–64.

Feldman, Emanuel. 'Death as Estrangement: The Halakhah of Mourning'. *Judaism* 21, no. 1 (1972): 59–66.

Feldman, Noah. '"What Israel Forbade to Himself": A Case of Biblical Exegesis in the Qur'an?' *Diné Israel* 24, (2007): 217–25.

Fensham, F. Charles. 'Common Trends in Curses of the Near Eastern Treaties and Kudurru-Inscriptions Compared with Maledictions of Amos and Isaiah'. *Zeitschrift für die Alttestamentliche Wissenschaft* 75, no. 2 (1963): 155–75.

Fensham, Frank C. 'The Curse of the Dry Bones in Ezekiel 37:1–14 Changed to a Blessing of Resurrection'. *Journal of Northwest Semitic Languages* 13 (1987): 59–60.

Filipowski, Herschell. *Sefer Yuchsin haShalem*, edited by Abraham Zacuto, London: Chevrat Meorerei Yeshenim, 1858.

Finkelstein, Israel and Neil A. Silberman. *The Bible Unearthed: Archaeology's New Vision of Ancient Israel and the Origin of Its Sacred Texts*. New York, NY: The Free Press, 2001.

Finkelstein, Israel, Shirly ben Dor Evian, Elisabetta Boaretto and Steve Weiner. 'Reconstructing Ancient Israel: Integrating Macro- and Micro-archaeology'. *Hebrew Bible and Ancient Israel* 1, no. 1 (2012): 133–50.

Finkelstein, Louis. 'The Development of the Amidah'. *The Jewish Quarterly Review* 16, no. 1 (1925): 1–43.

Finkelstein, Louis. 'The Development of the Amidah'. *The Jewish Quarterly Review* 16, no. 2 (1925): 127–70.

Finkelstein, Louis. *The Pharisees: The Sociological Background of Their Faith*. Philadelphia, PA: Jewish Publication Society, 1938.

Finnestad, Ragnhild B. 'On Transposing Soul and Body into a Monistic Conception of Being: An Example from Ancient Egypt'. *Religion* 16, no. 4 (1986): 359–73.

Firestone, Reuven. 'Abraham's Son as the Intended Sacrifice (Al-Dhabih, Qur᾽an 37:99–113): Issues in Qur᾽anic Exegesis'. *Journal of Semitic Studies* 34, no. 1 (1989): 95–131.

Firestone, Reuven. *Jewish Culture in the Formative Period of Islam*. New York, NY: Schocken Books, 2002.

Firestone, Reuven. 'The Qur'ān and the Bible: Some Modern Studies of Their Relationship'. In *Bible and Qur'ān: Essays in Scriptural Intertextuality*, edited by John C. Reeves, 1–22. Atlanta, GA: Society of Biblical Literature, 2003.

Firestone, Reuven 'Is There a Notion of "Divine Election" in the Qur᾽ān?' in *New Perspectives on the Qur᾽ān: The Qur᾽ān in Its Historical Context 2*, edited by Gabriel S. Reynolds, 393–410. Abingdon: Routledge, 2011.

Fishbane, Michael. *Biblical Interpretation in Ancient Israel*. Oxford: Oxford University Press, 1985.

Fishbane, Michael. *The Kiss of God: Spiritual and Mystical Death in Judaism*. Seattle, WA: University of Washington Press, 1994.

Flannery, Frances. '"Go Ask a Woman's Womb": Birth and the Maternal Body as Sources of Revelation and Wisdom in *4 Ezra*'. *Journal for the Study of the Pseudepigrapha* 21, no. 3 (2012): 243–58.

Flesher, Paul V.M. 'The Resurrection of the Dead and the Sources of the Palestinian Targums to the Pentateuch'. In *Judaism in Late Antiquity: Death, Life-after-Death, Resurrection and the World-to-Come in the Judaisms of Antiquity*, edited by Alan J. Avery-Peck and Jacob Neusner, 311–32, Leiden: Brill, 2000.

Foltz, Richard. 'Buddhism in the Iranian World'. *The Muslim World* 100, nos. 2–3 (2010): 204–14.

Forchheimer, Paul. 'The Semantic Development of Hebrew Gerem'. *Word* 4, no. 3 (1948): 209–11.

Foster, Benjamin R. 'Letters and Literature: A Ghost's Entreaty'. In *Before the Muses*. Baltimore, MD: University of Maryland Press, 1993.

Fox, Michael V. 'The Rhetoric of Ezekiel's Vision of the Valley of the Bones'. *Hebrew Union College Annual* 51, (1980): 1–15.

Frankfort, Henri. *Kingship and the Gods: A Study of Ancient Near Eastern Religion as the Integration of Society & Nature*. Chicago, IL: University of Chicago Press, 1948.

Frayer-Griggs, Daniel. *Saved through Fire: The Fiery Ordeal in New Testament Eschatology*. Eugene, OR: Pickwick, 2016.

Frazer, James G. *The Golden Bough: A Study in Magic and Religion*. New York, NY: Macmillan, 1935–7.

Freedman, Noel D. *Divine Commitment and Human Obligation*. Grand Rapids, MI: Eerdmans, 1997.

Freidenreich, David M. 'The Use of Islamic Sources in Saadiah Gaon's Tafsir of the Torah'. *The Jewish Quarterly Review* 93, nos. 3–4 (2003): 353–95.

Fried, Lisbeth S. and Edward J. Mills III. 'The Messiah and the "End of Days" in the Book of Isaiah and in the Deuterocanonical Literature'. In *The Early Reception of the Book of Isaiah*, edited by Kristin de Troyer and Barbara Schmitz, 51–66. Berlin: De Gruyter, 2019.

Friedman, Yaron. *The Nuṣayrī-ʿAlawīs: An Introduction to the Religion, History and Identity of the Leading Minority in Syria*. Leiden: Brill, 2010.

Frisch, Alexandria and Lawrence H. Schiffman. 'The Body in Qumran Literature: Flesh and Spirit, Purity and Impurity in the Dead Sea Scrolls'. *Dead Sea Discoveries* 23, no. 2 (2016): 155–82.

Frishman, Judith '"And Abraham Had Faith": But in What? Ephrem and the Rabbis on Abraham and God's Blessings'. In *The Exegetical Encounter between Jews and Christians in Late Antiquity*, edited by Emmanouela Grypeou and Helen Spurling, 163–80. Leiden: Brill, 2009.

Frymer-Kensky, Tikva. 'Patriarchal Family Relationships and Near Eastern Law'. *The Biblical Archaeologist* 44, no. 4 (1981): 209–14.

Fryer, N.S.L. 'The Intermediate State in Paul'. *HTS Teologiese Studies* 43, no. 3 (1987): 448–84.

Gabbay, Uri. 'Hebrew Śôm Śekel (Neh. 8:8) in Light of Aramaic and Akkadian'. *Journal of Semitic Studies* 59, no. 1 (2014): 47–51.

Galadari, Abdulla. 'Reincarnation vs. Resurrection: The Debate Ends'. *Proceedings of the Asian Conference on Ethics, Religion and Philosophy*, (2012): 9–26.

Galadari, Abdulla. 'The *Qibla*: An Allusion to the *Shema*ʿ'. *Comparative Islamic Studies* 9, no. 2 (2013): 165–94.

Galadari, Abdulla. 'The Role of Intertextual Polysemy in Qurʾanic Exegesis'. *Quranica: International Journal on Quranic Research* 3, no. 4 (2013): 35–56.

Galadari, Abdulla. 'The *Taqlīd al-Ijtihād* Paradox: Challenges to Qurʾanic Hermeneutics'. *Al-Bayān: Journal of Qurʾān and Ḥadīth Studies* 13, (2015): 145–67.

Galadari, Abdulla. '*Creatio ex Nihilo* and the Literal Qurʾan'. *Intellectual Discourse* 25, no. 2 (2017): 381–408.

Galadari, Abdulla. 'The Camel Passing through the Eye of the Needle: A Qurʾanic Interpretation of the Gospels'. *Ancient Near Eastern Studies* 55, (2018): 77–89.

Galadari, Abdulla. *Qurʾanic Hermeneutics: Between Science, History, and the Bible*. London: Bloomsbury Academic, 2018.

Galadari, Abdulla. 'Qur'anic Faith and Reason: An Epistemic Comparison with the Kālāma Sutta'. *Studies in Interreligious Dialogue* 30, no. 1 (2020): 45–67.

Galil, Gershon. 'The Last Years of the Kingdom of Israel and the Fall of Samaria'. *Catholic Biblical Quarterly* 57, no. 1 (1995): 52–65.

Gan, Jonathan. 'The Metaphor of the Shepherd in Zechariah 11:4–17'. Master's Thesis. Pretoria: University of South Africa, 2010.

Ganzel, Tova. 'The Defilement and Desecration of the Temple in Ezekiel'. *Biblica* 89, no. 3 (2008): 369–79.

Gardner, Anne E. 'The Way to Eternal Life in Dan 12:1e-2 or How to Reverse the Death Curse of Genesis 3'. *Australian Biblical Review* 40 (1992): 1–19.
Gardner, Iain and Samuel N.C. Lieu (eds.). *Manichaean Texts from the Roman Empire*. Cambridge: Cambridge University Press, 2004.
Garland, Robert. *The Greek Way of Death*. Ithaca, NY: Cornell University Press, 1985.
Gasimova, Aida. 'Models, Portraits, and Signs of Fate in Ancient Arabian Tradition'. *Journal of Near Eastern Studies* 73, no. 2 (2014): 319–40.
Gasparro, Lorenzo. 'La "malédiction du figuier" (Mc 11, 12-25) et la dimension symbolique de l'Évangile de Marc'. *Revue Biblique* 121, no. 3 (2014): 375–91.
Gaster, Theodor Herzl. 'The Combat of Death and the Most High: A Proto-Hebrew Epic from Ras-Samra'. *The Journal of the Royal Asiatic Society of Great Britain and Ireland* 64, no. 4 (1932): 856–96.
Gay, Volney P. (ed.). *Neuroscience and Religion: Brain, Mind, Self, and Soul*. Lanham, MD: Lexington Books, 2009.
Gefter, Amanda. 'Creationists Declare War over the Brain'. *New Scientist* 200, no. 2679 (2008): 46–7.
Geiger, Abraham. *Was hat Mohammed aus dem Judenthume aufgenommen?* Bonn: F. Baaden, 1833.
Gell, Alfred. 'Time and Social Anthropology'. In *Time in Contemporary Intellectual Thought*, edited by Patrick J.N. Baert, 2: 251–68. Amsterdam: Elsevier, 2000.
Georgi, Dieter. *Die Gegner des Paulus im 2. Korintherbrief: Studien zur religiösen Propaganda in der Spätantike*. Neukirchen-Vluyn: Neukirchener, 1964.
Gesenius, William. 1846. *Gesenius' Hebrew-Chaldee Lexicon to the Old Testament*. Bellingham, WA: Logos Bible Software, 2003.
Gier, Nicholas F. and Johnson Petta. 'Hebrew and Buddhist Selves: A Constructive Postmodern Study'. *Asian Philosophy* 17, no. 1 (2007): 47–64.
Gilders, William K. 'Why Does Eleazar Sprinkle the Red Cow Blood? Making Sense of a Biblical Ritual'. *The Journal of Hebrew Scriptures* 6, no. 9 (2006): 1–16.
Gillman, Neil. 1997. *The Death of Death: Resurrection and Immortality in Jewish Thought*. Woodstock, VT: Jewish Lights, 2015.
Ginsburskaya, Mila. 'Purity and Impurity in the Hebrew Bible'. In *Purity: Essays in Bible and Theology*, edited by Andrew B. Latz and Arseny Ermakov, 3–29. Cambridge: James Clark, 2017.
Ginzberg, Louis. 'Some Observations on the Attitude of the Synagogue towards the Apocalyptic-Eschatological Writings'. *Journal of Biblical Literature* 41, no. 1–2 (1922): 115–36.
Ginzberg, Louis. *The Legends of the Jews*, trans. Henrietta Szold. Philadelphia, PA: Jewish Public Society, 1909–8.
Ginzberg, Louis. *Legends of the Jews*. Philadelphia, PA: Jewish Publication Society, 2003.
Glassman, Ronald M. *The Origins of Democracy in Tribes, City-States and Nation-States*. Berlin: Springer, 2017.
Glasson, T. Francis. *Greek Influence in Jewish Eschatology: With Special Reference to the Apocalypses and Pseudepigrapha*. London: Society for Promoting Christian Knowledge, 1961.
Goettsberger, J. 'Über das 3. Kapitel des Esrabuchs'. *Journal of the Society of Oriental Research* 10 (1926): 270–80.
Golbert, Rebecca. 'Judaism and Death: Finding Meaning in Ritual'. In *Death and Religion in a Changing World*, edited by Kathleen Garces-Foley, 45–68. Armonk, NY: M.E. Sharpe, 2006.

Goldberg, Jeremy. 'Two Assyrian Campaigns against Hezekiah and Later Eighth Century Biblical Chronology'. *Biblica* 80, no. 3 (1999): 360–90.

Goldingay, John E. *Daniel, World Biblical Commentary*, Vol. 30. Dallas, TX: Word Books, 1989.

Golzadeh, Ferdows A. and Shirin Pourebrahim. 'Death Metaphor in Religious Texts: A Cognitive Semantics Approach'. *International Journal of the Humanities* 20, no. 4 (2013): 61–78.

Gonzalez, Hervé. 'Zechariah 9-14 and the Continuation of Zechariah during the Ptolemaic Period'. *Journal of Hebrew Scriptures* 13, no. 9 (2013).

Gordon, Robert P. 'The Ethics of Eden: Truth-Telling in Genesis 2–3'. In *Ethical and Unethical in the Old Testament: God and Humans in Dialogue*, edited by Katherine J. Dell, 11–33. New York, NY: T&T Clark, 2010.

Gorjian, Mahdi and Farzaneh Farahanipour. 'Man's Truth and Perfectionism Mohammad'. *Pazhuhishnamih Irfan* 3, no. 5 (2012): 159–79.

Gowan, Donald E. *Theology of the Prophetic Books: The Death and Resurrection of Israel.* Louisville, KY: Westminster John Knox, 1998.

Granger, Darryl E., Ryan J. Gibbon, Kathleen Kuman, Ronald J. Clarke, Laurent Bruxelles and Marc W. Caffee. 'New Cosmogenic Burial Ages for Sterkfontein Member 2 Australopithecus and Member 5 Oldowan'. *Nature* 522, (2015): 85–8.

Grant, Robert M. 'The Resurrection of the Body'. *The Journal of Religion* 28, no. 2 (1948): 120–30.

Grassi, J. 'Ezekiel xxxvii 1–14 and the New Testament'. *New Testament Studies* 11, (1965): 162–4.

Graves, Mark. *Mind, Brain and the Elusive Soul: Human Systems of Cognitive Science and Religion*. Abingdon: Routledge, 2013.

Graves, Michael. 'The Public Reading of Scripture in Early Judaism'. *Journal of the Evangelical Theological Society* 50, no. 3 (2007): 467–87.

Graves, Michael. 'Apocryphal Elements in the New Testament and Qur'ān'. *Journal of Ecumenical Studies* 47, no. 2 (2012): 152–66.

Graves, Michael W. 'The Upraised Mountain and Israel's Election in the Qur'an and Talmud'. *Comparative Islamic Studies* 11, no. 2 (2015): 141–77.

Graves-Brown, Carolyn. *Dancing for Hathor: Women in Ancient Egypt*. London: Continuum Books, 2010.

Gray, Alison J. 'Whatever Happened to the Soul? Some Theological Implications of Neuroscience'. *Mental Health, Religion & Culture* 13, no. 6 (2010): 637–48.

Gray, Alyssa M. 'Redemptive Almsgiving and the Rabbis of Late Antiquity'. *Jewish Studies Quarterly* 18, no. 2 (2011): 144–84.

Gray, Alyssa M. 'The People, Not the Peoples: The Talmud Bavli's "Charitable" Contribution to the Jewish-Christian Conversation in Mesopotamia'. *Review of Rabbinic Judaism* 20, no. 2 (2017): 137–67.

Gray, Alyssa M. 'Rabbis and the Poor in Palestinian Amoraic Literature and the Bayblonian Talmud'. In *A Companion to Late Ancient Jews and Judaism: Third Century BCE to Seventh Century CE*, edited by Naomi Koltun-Fromm and Gwynn Kessler, 217–28. Hoboken, NJ: Wiley, 2020.

Grayson, A.K. (trans.) *The Ancient Near Eastern Texts Relating to the Old Testament*, edited by J.B. Pritchard, 3rd ed., 512–14. Princeton, NJ: Princeton University Press, 1969.

Green, Joel B. *Body, Soul, and Human Life: The Nature of Humanity in the Bible*. Grand Rapids, MI: Baker Academic, 2008.

Greenfield, Jonas C. 'Une rite religieux arameén et ses parallèles'. *Revue Biblique* 80, no. 1 (1973): 46–52.

Greenspoon, Leonard J. 'The Origin of the Idea of Resurrection'. In *Traditions in Transformation: Turning Points in Biblical Faith*, edited by Baruch Halpern and Jon D. Levenson, 247–321. Winona Lake, IN: Eisenbrauns, 1981.

Greer, Jonathan S. '"Cursed Be the Cheat Who Offers a Blemished Animal!" A Broken Tibia from a Sacrificial Deposit at Tel Dan and Its Implications for Understanding Israelite Religious Practice'. In *The Wide Lens of Archaeology: Honoring Brian Hesse's Contributions to Anthropological Archaeology*, edited by Justin Lev-Tov, Paula Hesse and Allan Gilbert, 193–201. Atlanta, GA: Lockwood Press, 2017.

Gregory, Bradley C. 'The Postexilic Exile in Third Isaiah: Isaiah 61:1–3 in Light of Second Temple Hermeneutics'. *Journal of Biblical Literature* 126, no. 3 (2007): 475–96.

Greifenhagen, F.V. *Egypt on the Pentateuch's Ideological Map: Constructing Biblical Israel's Identity*. Sheffield: Sheffield Academic, 2002.

Griffith, Sidney. 'Christian Lore and the Arabic Qur'ān: "Companions of the Cave" in *Sūrat al-Kahf* and in Syriac Christian Tradition'. In *The Qur'ān and Its Historical Context*, edited by Gabriel S. Reynolds, 109–37. Abingdon: Routledge, 2008.

Griffiths, J.G. 'The Legacy of Egypt in Judaism'. In *The Cambridge History of Judaism*, edited by William Horbury, W.D. Davies, and John Sturdy, Vol. 3, *The Roman Period*, 1025–51. Cambridge: Cambridge University Press, 1999.

Grollman, Earl A. 'Death in Jewish Thought'. In *Death and Spirituality*, edited by Kenneth J. Doka and John D. Morgan, 26–31. Abingdon: Routledge, 2017.

Grosman, Leore and Natalie D. Munro. 'A Natufian Ritual Event'. *Current Anthropology* 57, no. 3 (2016): 311–31.

Grudem, Wayne. 'He Did Not Descend into Hell: A Plea for Following Scripture Instead of the Apostle's Creed'. *Journal of the Evangelical Theological Society* 34, no. 1 (1991): 103–13.

Guenther, Mathias. 'Animals in Bushman Thought, Myth, and Art'. In *Hunters and Gatherers 2: Property, Power and Ideology*, edited by Tim Ingold, David Riches, and James Woodburn, 192–202. Oxford: Berg, 1988.

Guillaume, Philippe. 'Drinking Golden Bull: The Erased Ordeal in Exodus 32'. In *Studies on Magic and Divination in the Biblical World*, edited by Helen R. Jacobus, Anne K. de Hemmer Gudme and Philippe Guillaume, 135–47. Piscataway, NJ: Gorgias Press, 2013.

Gunaratne, R.D. 'The Logical Form of Catuṣkoṭi: A New Solution'. *Philosophy East and West* 30, no. 2 (1980): 211–39.

Gunaratne, R.D. 'Understanding Nāgārjuna's Catuṣkoṭi'. *Philosophy East and West* 36, no. 3 (1986): 213–34.

Gwynne, Rosalind W. 'The Neglected Sunnah: Sunnat Allāh (The Sunnah of God)'. *American Journal of Islamic Social Sciences* 10, no. 4 (1993): 455–63.

Ha, John. *Genesis 15: A Theological Compendium of Pentateuchal History*. Berlin: De Gruyter, 1989.

Haak, Wolfgang, Iosif Lazaridis, Nick Patterson, Nadin Rohland, Swapan Mallick, Bastien Llamas, Guido Brandt, Susanne Nordenfelt, Eadaoin Harney, Kristin Stewardson, Qiaomei Fu, Alissa Mittnik, Eszter Bánffy, Christos Economou, Michael Francken, Susanne Friedrich, Rafael Garrido Pena, Fredrik Hallgren, Valery Khartanovich, Aleksandr Kokhlov, Michael Kunst, Pavel Kuznetsov, Harald Meller, Oleg Mochalov, Vayacheslav Moiseyev, Nicole Nicklisch, Sandra L. Pichler, Roberto Risch, Manuel A. Rojo Guerra, Christina Roth, Anna Szécsényi-Nagy, Joachim Wahl, Matthias Meyer, Johannes Krause, Dorcas Brown, David Anthony, Alan Cooper, Kurt W. Alt and David Reich. 'Massive Migration from the Steppe Was a Source for Indo-European Languages in Europe'. *Nature* 522, (2015): 207–11.

Haddad, Yvonne Y. 'The Druze of North America'. *The Muslim World* 81, no. 2 (1991): 111–32.
Hadot, Jean. 'La Datation de l'Apocalypse Syriaque de Baruch'. *Semitica* 15 (1965): 79–5.
Haelewyck, J.-C. *Clavis Apocryphorum Veteris Testamenti*. Turnhout: Brepols, 1998.
Halldén, Philip. 'What Is Arab Islamic Rhetoric? Rethinking the History of Muslim Oratory Art and Homiletics'. *International Journal of Middle East Studies* 37, no. 1 (2005): 19–38.
Halpern, Baruch. 'The Ritual Background of Zechariah's Temple Song'. *Catholic Biblical Quarterly* 40, no. 2 (1978): 167–90.
Hamerton-Kelly, Robert G. 'The Temple and the Origins of Jewish Apocalyptic'. *Vetus Testamentum* 20, no. 1 (1970): 1–15.
Ḥaqqī, Ismāʿīl (d. 1127/1725). *Rūḥ al-bayān*. Beirut: al-Fikr, n.d.
Harris, Eleanor L. *Ancient Egyptian Divination and Magic*. Boston, MA: Red Wheel/ Weiser, 1998.
Harris, Murray J. *Raised Immortal: Resurrection and Immortality in the New Testament*. Grand Rapids, MI: Eerdmans, 1983.
Harrison, J.R. 'In Quest of the Third Heaven: Paul & His Apocalyptic Imitators'. *Vigiliae Christinae* 58, no. 1 (2004): 24–55.
Hartman, Louis F. and Alexander A. Di Lella. *The Book of Daniel*. New York, NY: Doubleday, 1971.
Harvey, Julien. 'Is Biblical Man Still Alive?' *Biblical Theology Bulletin* 3, no.2 (1973): 167–93.
Harvey, Paul. 1995. *The Selfless Mind: Personality, Consciousness and Nirvana in Early Buddhism*. Abingdon: Routledge, 2012.
Hasan-Rokem, Galit. *Tales of the Neighborhood: Jewish Narrative Dialogues in Late Antiquity*. Berkley, CA: University of California Press, 2003.
Hasel, Gerhard F. 'Resurrection in the Theology of Old Testament Apocalyptic'. *Zeitschrift für die alttestamentliche Wissenschaft* 92, no. 2 (1980): 267–84.
Hasel, Gerhard F. 'The Meaning of the Animal Rite in Genesis 15'. *Journal for the Study of the Old Testament* 6, no. 19 (1981): 61–78.
Hasker, William. *The Emergent Self*. Ithaca, NY: Cornell University Press, 1999.
Havrelock, Rachel. 'The Myth of Birthing the Hero: Heroic Barrenness in the Hebrew Bible'. *Biblical Interpretation* 16, no. 2 (2008): 154–78.
Hayajneh, Hani. 'The Usage of Ancient South Arabian and Other Arabian Languages as an Etymological Source for Qurʾānic Vocabulary'. In *New Perspectives on the Qurʾān: The Qurʾān in Its Historical Context 2*, edited by Gabriel S. Reynolds, 117–46. Abingdon: Routledge, 2011.
Hays, Christopher B. 'An Egyptian Loanword in the Book of Isaiah and the Deir 'Alla Inscription'. *Journal of Ancient Egyptian Interconnection* 4, no. 2 (2012): 17–23.
Hays, Christopher B. '"My Beloved Son, Come and Rest in Me": Job's Return to His Mother's Womb (Job 1:21a) in Light of Egyptian Mythology'. *Vetus Testamentum* 62, no. 4 (2012): 607–21.
Hays, Christopher B. '"There is Hope for a Tree": Job's Hope for the Afterlife in the Light of Egyptian Tree Imagery'. *Catholic Biblical Quarterly* 77 (2015): 42–68.
Healey, John F. 'Ugarit and Arabia: A Balance Sheet'. *Proceedings of the Twenty-Fourth Seminar for Arabian Studies Held at Oxford on 24th–26th July 1990*: 69–78, 1991.
Healey, John F. *The Nabataean Tomb Inscriptions of Mada'in Salih*. Oxford: Oxford University Press, 1993.
Heck, Joel F. 'Issachar: Slave or Freeman? (Gen 49:14–15)'. *Journal of the Evangelical Theological Society* 29, no. 4 (1986): 385–96.

Hecker, Bernice V. *The Biradical Origin of Semitic Roots*. Austin: University of Texas, 2007.
Heger, Paul. 'Another Look at Dualism in Qumran Writings'. In *Dualism in Qumran*, edited by Géza G. Xeravits, 39–101. London: T&T Clark, 2010.
Heil, John P. 'The Narrative Strategy and Pragmatics of the Temple Theme in Mark'. *Catholic Biblical Quarterly* 59, no. 1 (1997): 76–100.
Held, Armin and Peter Rust. 'Genesis Reconsidered'. *Perspectives on Science and Christian Faith* 51, no. 4 (1999): 231–43.
Heller, Bernard. 'Éléments, parallèles et origines de la légende des sept dormants'. *Revue des etudes juives*, 49 (1904): 190–218.
Hengel, Martin. *Judaism and Hellenism: Studies in Their Encounter in Palestine during the Early Hellenistic Period*. Philadelphia, PA: Fortress, 1974.
Herdner, A. *Corpus des tablettes en cunéiformes alphabétiques découvertes à Ras Shamra-Ugarit de 1929 à 1939*. Paris: Imprimerie nationale, Geuthner, 1963.
Herzer, Jens. *Die Paralipomena Jeremiae*. Tübingen: Mohr Siebeck, 1993.
Herzer, Jens. 'Difficult Time: How God Is Understood in the Paralipomena Jeremiae'. *Journal for the Study of the Pseudepigrapha* 11, no. 22 (2000): 9–30.
Herzer, Jens. *4 Baruch (Paraleipomena Jeremiou)*. Atlanta, GA: SBL Press, 2005.
Heschel, Susannah. 'The Philological Uncanny: Nineteenth-Century Jewish Readings of the Qur᾽an'. *Journal of Qur᾽anic Studies* 20, no. 3 (2018): 193–213.
Hess, Richard S. 'The Bible and Alalakh'. In *Mesopotamia and the Bible*, edited by Mark W. Chavalas and K. Lawson Younger, Jr., 208–20. London: T&T Clark, 2003.
Hick, John. 1976. *Death and Eternal Life*, Louisville: Westminster/John Knox, 1994 (orig. London: Collins).
Hickman, Louise. 'The Nature of the Self and the Contemplative of Nature: Ecotheology and the History of the Soul'. In *The Concept of the Soul: Scientific and Religious Perspectives*, edited by Michael Fuller, 5–28. Newcastle: Cambridge Scholars Publishing, 2014.
Hight, Marc A. 'Berkeley and Bodily Resurrection'. *Journal of the History of Philosophy* 45, no. 3 (2007): 443–58.
Hinnells, J.R. 'Zoroastrian Influence on the Judeo-Christian Tradition'. *Journal of the K.R. Cama Oriental Institute* 45, (1976): 1–23.
Hirschfeld, Hartwig. *New Researches into the Composition and Exegesis of the Qoran*. London: Royal Asiatic Society, 1902.
Ho, David Y.F. 'Selfhood and Identity in Confucianism, Taoism, Buddhism, and Hinduism: Contrasts with the West'. *Journal for the Theory of Social Behavior* 25, no. 2 (1995): 121–2.
Hodgson, Marshall G.S. 'Al-Darazî and Ḥamza in the Origin of the Druze Religion'. *Journal of the American Oriental Society* 82, no. 1 (1962): 5–20.
Hoeck, Andreas. *The Descent of New Jerusalem: A Discourse Analysis of Rev 21:1–22:25*. Bern: Peter Lang, 2003.
Hoeck, Andreas. 'Harvest – Herald – Hero: Stephen's Burial and the Church's Early Hermeneutics of Martyrdom'. *Scripta Fulgentina* 26, nos. 51–2 (2016): 7–27.
Hoff, Nathan N. 'One Gospel: Paul's Use of the Abraham Story in Romans 4:1–25'. PhD Dissertation. Dallas, TX: Dallas Theological Seminary, 2018.
Hoffman, Yair. 'The Terms *᾽aḥărît ha-yāmîm* and *ba-yôm ha-hû᾽a* as Eschatological Terms'. *Beth Mikra* 71, (1978): 43544. [Hebrew]
Hoffman, Yair. 'Eschatology in the Book of Jeremiah'. In *Eschatology in the Bible and in Jewish and Christian Tradition*, edited by Hanning G. Reventlow, 75–97. Sheffield: Sheffield Academic, 1997.

Hogan, Karina M. 'The Exegetical Background of the "Ambiguity of Death" in the Wisdom of Solomon'. *Journal for the Study of Judaism in the Persian, Hellenistic, and Roman Period* 30, no. 1 (1999): 1–24.

Hogan, Karina M. 'Mother Earth as a Conceptual Metaphor in 4 Ezra'. *Catholic Biblical Quarterly* 73, no. 1 (2011): 72–91.

Hogeterp, Albert L.A. 'Resurrection and Biblical Tradition: Pseudo-Ezekiel Reconsidered'. *Biblica* 89, no. 1 (2008): 59–69.

Hogeterp, Albert L.A. 'Belief in Resurrection and Its Religious Settings in Qumran and the New Testament'. In *Echoes from the Caves: Qumran and the New Testament*, edited by Florentino G. Martínez, 299–320. Leiden: Brill, 2009.

Holm, Tawny L. 'The Fiery Furnace in the Book of Daniel and the Ancient Near East'. *Journal of the American Oriental Society* 128, no. 1 (2008): 85–104.

Holt, Else K. 'The Fountain of Living Water and the Deceitful Brook'. In *Metaphor in the Hebrew Bible*, edited by Pierre van Hecke, 99–117. Leuven: Peeters, 2005.

Holtz, Shalom E. 'God as Refuge and Temple as Refuge in the Psalms'. In *The Temple of Jerusalem: From Moses to the Messiah: In Honor of Professor Louis H. Feldman*, edited by Steven Fine, 17–26. Leiden: Brill, 2011.

Homerin, Emil. 'Echoes of a Thirsty Owl: Death and Afterlife in Pre-Islamic Arabic Poetry'. *Journal of Near Eastern Studies* 44, no. 3 (1985): 165–84.

Hong, Kyu S. 'An Exegetical Reading of the Abraham Narrative in Genesis: Semantic, Textuality and Theology'. PhD Dissertation. Pretoria: University of Pretoria, 2007.

Honigmann, Ernst. 'Stephen of Ephesus and the Legend of the Seven Sleepers'. In *Patristic Studies*, Ernst Honigmann, 125–68. Vatican City: Biblioteca Apostolica Vaticana, 1953.

Horton, Ernest Jr. 'Koheleth's Concept of Opposites: As Compared to Samples of Greek Philosophy and Near and Far Eastern Wisdom Classics'. *Numen* 19, no. 1 (1972): 1–21.

Hovav-Machboob, Lea. 'The Ari's Doctrine of Reincarnation'. Dissertation. The Jewish Theological Seminary of America, 1983. [Hebrew]

Hoyland, Robert G. 'The Jews of the Hijaz in the Qurʾan and in Their Inscriptions'. In *New Perspectives on the Qurʾan: The Qurʾan in Its Historical Context 2*, 91–116. Abingdon: Routledge, 2011.

Hoyland, Robert. 'The Language of the Qur'an and a Near Eastern Rip van Winkle'. In *A Life with the Prophet? Examining Hadith, Sira and Qur'an: In Honor of Wim Raven*, edited by Albrecht Fuess and Stefan Weninger, 17–44. Berlin: EB-Verlag, 2017.

Hoyt, Herman A. *The End Times*. Chicago, IL: Moody, 1969.

Hsieh, Nelson S. 'Abraham as "Heir of the World": Does Romans 4:13 Expand the Old Testament Abrahamic Land Promises?' *The Master's Seminary Journal* 26, no. 1 (2015): 95–110.

Huang, Wei. 'Death in the Hebrew Bible'. *Journal of Sino-Western Communications* 2, no. 1 (2010): 138–53.

Huddlestun, John R. 'Ancient Egypt and Israel: History, Culture, and the Biblical Text'. In *The Wiley Blackwell Companion to Ancient Israel*, edited by Susan Niditch, 47–66. Malden, MA: Wiley Blackwell, 2016.

Hughes, Kyle R. 'The Lukan Special Material and the Tradition History of the *Pericope Adulterae*'. *Novum Testamentum* 55, no. 3 (2013): 232–51.

Hunzai, Naṣīr al-Dīn Naṣīr. *The Wise Qurʾan and the World of Humanity*. Karachi: Dānishgāh-i Khānah-i Ḥikmat, 2003.

Hurvitz, Avi. 'The Biblical Roots of a Talmudic Term: The Early History of the Concept *ṣedaqah*'. *Language Studies*, no. 2–3 (1987): 155–60. [Hebrew]

Ibn Abī al-Dunyā (d. 281/894). *Ṣifah ahl al-nār*, edited by Muḥammad Khayr Ramaḍān Yūsuf, Beirut: Ibn Ḥazm, 1997.
Ibn Abī al-ʿIzz (d. 792/1390). *Sharḥ al-ʿaqīdah al-ṭaḥāwiyyah*, edited by Aḥmad Shākir. Riyadh: Ministry of Islamic Affairs, 1998.
Ibn Abī Dawūd (d. 316/928). *al-Baʿth*, edited by Muḥammad Zaghlūl. Beirut: al-Kutub al-ʿIlmiyyah, 1987.
Ibn ʿĀdil al-Ḥanbalī (d. 880/1475). *al-Lubāb fī ʿulūm al-kitāb*, edited by ʿĀdil Aḥmad ʿAbdulmawjūd and ʿAlī Muḥammad Miʿwaḍ. Beirut: al-Kutub al-ʿIlmiyyah, 1998.
Ibn al-Athīr (d. 630/1232). *al-Kāmil fil-tarīkh*, edited by ʿUmar ʿAbdulsalām Tudmurī. Beirut: al-Kitāb al-ʿArabī, 1997.
Ibn al-Ḥāj al-Fāsī (d. 737/1336). *al-Madkhal*. Cairo: al-Turāth, n.d.
Ibn al-Jawzī (d. 597/1201). *al-Muntaẓam fī tarīkh al-umam wal-mulūk*, Muḥammad ʿAbdul-Qādir ʿAṭā and Muṣṭafa ʿAbdul-Qādir ʿAṭā. Beirut: al-Kutub al-ʿIlmiyyah, 1992.
Ibn al-Muʿtazz, ʿAbdullāh (d. 296/909). *al-Badīʿ fil-badīʿ*. Beirut: al-Jīl, 1990.
Ibn al-Mulaqqin Sirāj al-Dīn (d. 804/1402). *al-Tawḍīḥ li-sharḥ al-jāmiʿ al-ṣaḥīḥ*. Damascus: al-Nawādir, 2008.
Ibn al-Ṣābūnī al-Ishbīlī (634/1236). *Maʿrifah al-farq bayn al-ḍād wal-ẓāʾ*, edited by Ḥātim Ṣ. al-Ḍāmin. Damascus: Naynawā, 2005.
Ibn al-Zubayr al-Ghirnāṭī (d. 708/1308). *al-Burhān fī tanāsub suwar al-Qurʾān*, edited by Muḥammad Shaʿbānī. Rabat: Ministry of Endowments and Islamic Affairs, 1990.
Ibn ʿArabī (d. 638/1240). *Tafsīr al-Qurʾān*. Beirut: Ṣādir, 2007.
Ibn ʿAsākir (d. 571/1176). *Tārīkh Dimashq*, edited by ʿAmr bin Gharāmeh al-ʿAmrawī. Damascus: al-Fikr, 1995.
Ibn Baṭṭah (d. 387/997). *al-Ibānah al-kubrā*, edited by Riḍā Muʿṭī, ʿUthmān al-Ithyūbī, Yūsuf al-Wābil, al-Walīd b. Sayf al-Naṣr, and Ḥamad al-Tuwayjrī. Riyadh: al-Rāyah, n.d.
Ibn Ḥajar (d. 852/1449). *al-Imtāʿ bil-arbaʿīn al-mutabāyinah al-samāʿ*. Beirut: al-Kutub al-ʿIlmiyyah, 1997.
Ibn Ḥanbal (d. 241/855). *Musnad*, edited by Aḥmad Muḥammad Shākir. Cairo: al-Ḥadīth, 1995.
Ibn Ḥanbal (d. 241/855). *Musnad*, edited by Shuʿayb al-Arnaʿūṭ, ʿĀdil Murshid et al. Beirut: al-Risālah, 2001.
Ibn Ḥazm (d. 456/1064). *al-Faṣl fil-milal wal-ahwāʾ wal-niḥal*. Cairo: al-Khānjī, n.d.
Ibn Hishām (d. 218/833). *al-Sīrah al-Nabawiyyah*, edited by ṬaHa ʿAbdul-Raʾūf Saʿd. Cairo: al-Ṭibāʿah al-Fanniyyah al-Muttaḥidah, n.d.
Ibn Jinnī (d. 392/1002). *al-Khaṣāʾiṣ*. Cairo: al-Hayʾah al-Miṣriyyah al-ʿĀmmah lil-Kitāb, n.d.
Ibn Kathīr (d. 774/1373). *Tafsīr al-Qurʾān al-karīm*, edited by Sāmī Muḥammad Salāmah. Riyadh: Ṭībah, 1999.
Ibn Kathīr (d. 774/1373). *al-Bidāyah wal-nihāyah*, edited by ʿAbdullāh b. ʿAbdulmuḥsin al-Turkī. Cairo: Hajr, 2003.
Ibn Manẓūr (d. 711/1311). *Lisān al-ʿarab*. Beirut: Ṣādir, 1994.
Ibn Maymūn al-Baghdādī (d. 589/1193). *Muntahā al-ṭalab min ashʿār al-ʿArab*, edited by Muḥammad Nabīl Ṭurayfī. Beirut: Ṣādir, 1999.
Ibn Qayyim al-Jawziyyah (d. 751/1350). *al-Rūḥ fil-kalām ʿala arwāḥ al-amwāt wal-aḥyāʾ bil-dalāʾil min al-kitāb wal-sunnah*. Beirut: al-Kutub al-ʿIlmiyyah, n.d.
Ibn Qayyim al-Jawziyyah (d. 751/1350). *al-Jawāb al-kāfī li-man saʾal ʿan dawāʾ al-shāfī aw al-dāʾ wal-dawāʾ*. Casablanca: al-Maʿrifah, 1997.

Ibn Rushd (d. 595/1195). *Tahāfut al-tahāfut*, edited by Aḥmad Shams-ul-Dīn. Beirut: al-Kutub al-ʿIlmiyyah, 2001.
Ibn Suhayl al-Naḥawī (d. 420/1029). *al-Ḍād wal-ẓāʾ*, edited by Ḥātim Ṣ. al-Ḍāmin. Damascus: al-Bashāʾir, 2005.
Ibrahīm, Aḥmad Shawqī. 'Nihāyah al-ḥayāh al-bashariyyah'. *Majjalah mujammaʿ al-fiqh al-islamī*. Jeddah: Organization of Islamic Conference, 1986.
Ikram, Salima. *Death and Burial in Ancient Egypt*. Cairo: American University in Cairo Press, 2015.
Ingold, Tim. 'From Trust to Domination: An Alternative History of Human-Animal Relations'. In *Animals & Human Society: Changing Perspectives*, edited by Aubrey Manning and James A. Serpell, 1–22. London: Routledge, 1994.
Inloes, Amina. 'Authentication of Hadith on the Raj'ah'. MA Dissertation. London: Islamic College for Advanced Studies, in collaboration with Middlesex University, 2009.
Irfatpour, Z. 'Aesthetic Imagery of Abrar and Their Hereafter Place in the Ensan Sura'. *Journal of the Iranian Association of Arabic Language and Literature* 9, no. 26 (2013): 44–72.
Irving, Thomas B., Khurshid Ahmad and Muhammad M. Ahsan. 1979. *The Qurʾan: Basic Teachings*. Leicester: The Islamic Foundation, 2004.
Isaac, Erich. *Geography of Domestication*. Englewood Cliffs, NJ: Prentice Hall, 1970.
Isbell, Charles D. 'Zoroastrianism and Biblical Religion'. *Jewish Bible Quarterly* 34, no. 3 (2006): 143–54.
Iser, Wolfgang. *The Act of Reading: A Theory of Aesthetic Response*. Baltimore, MD: Johns Hopkins University Press, 1978.
Izutsu, Toshihiko. 1981. *God and Man in the Qur'an: Semantics of the Qur'anic Weltanschauung*. Kuala Lumpur: Islamic Book Trust, 2005 (orig. The Hague: Martinus Nijhoff).
Jackson, Peter. 'Light from Distant Asterisks towards a Description of the Indo-European Religious Heritage'. *Numen* 49, no. 1 (2002): 61–102.
Jaffer, Tariq. 'Fakhr al-Dīn al-Rāzī on the Soul (*al-nafs*) and Spirit (*al-rūḥ*): An Investigation into the Eclectic Ideas of *Mafātīḥ al-ghayb*'. *Journal of Qurʾanic Studies* 16, no. 1 (2014): 93–119.
Jagers op Akkerhuis, Gerard A.J.M. 'Towards a Hierarchical Definition of Life, the Organism, and Death'. *Foundations of Science* 15, no. 3 (2010): 245–62.
Janssens, Jules. 'Al-Ghazzali's *Tahafut*: Is It Really a Rejection of Ibn Sina's Philosophy?' *Journal of Islamic Studies* 12, no. 1 (2001): 1–17.
Járos, György G. 'Synergy of Complements and the Exclusivity of Opposites'. *World Futures: The Journal of New Paradigm Research* 56, no. 1 (2000): 1–19.
Jean, C.F. and J. Hoftijzer (ed.). *Dictionnaire des inscriptions sémitiques de l'ouest*. Leiden: Brill, 1965.
Jeeves, Malcolm A. *Minds, Brains, Souls and Gods: A Conversation on Faith, Psychology and Neuroscience*. Westmont, IL: InterVarsity Press, 2013.
Jeremias, Joachim. *The Parables of Jesus*, (2nd rev. edited by), New York, NY: Scribner, 1972.
Jerome, Obiorah M. 'Detachment as a Prerequisite for a Happy Family: A Study of Genesis 2:24'. *Mediterranean Journal of Social Sciences* 7, no. 4 (2016): 526–32.
Jimoh, Shaykh Luqman. 'Reincarnation: Re-Appraising the Belief of Yoruba Muslims within the Context of Islamic Orthodoxy'. *Ilorin Journal of Religious Studies* 2, no. 1 (2012): 81–96.
Jindo, Job Y. *Biblical Metaphor Reconsidered: A Cognitive Approach to Poetic Prophecy in Jeremiah 1–24*. Winona Lake, IN: Eisenbrauns, 2010.

Johnson, Daniel. 'Reincarnation in an Islamic Society: Buton, Indonesia'. *Melanesian Journal of Theology* 20, no. 1 (2004): 43–56.
Johnson, Dennis E. 'Fire in God's House: Imagery from Malachi 3 in Peter's Theology of Suffering (1 Pet 4:12–19)'. *The Journal of the Evangelical Theological Society* 29, no. 3 (1986): 285–94.
Johnston, P.S. *Shades of Sheol: Death and Afterlife in the Old Testament*. Leicester: Apollos, 2002.
Judge, Michael. *The Dance of Time – The Origins of the Calendar: A Miscellany of History and Myth, Religion and Astronomy, Festival and Feast Days*. New York, NY: Arcade Publishing, 2004.
Junker, Sandra. 'The Disorderly Body: Considerations of the Book of Numbers, 19 and Ritual Impurity after Contact with a Corpse'. *Scripta Instituti Donneriani Aboensis* 23, no. 1 (2011): 197–205.
Kahn, Charles H. *Pythagoras and the Pythagoreans: A Brief History*. Indianapolis, IN: Hackett Publishing, 2001.
Kaiser, Walter C. Jr. *The Promise-Plan of God: A Biblical Theology of the Old and New Testaments*. Grand Rapids, MI: Zondervan, 2008.
Kakakhel, Syed S.R. 'A Study on the Qur'anic Way of Coding Parables'. *The Dialogue* 5, no. 2 (2010): 126–35.
Kalimi, Isaac. 'The Land of Moriah, Mount Moriah, and the Site of Solomon's Temple in Biblical Historiography'. *Harvard Theological Review* 83, no. 4 (1990): 345–62.
Kalupahana, David J. *Buddhist Philosophy: A Historical Analysis*. Honolulu, HI: University of Hawaii Press, 1976.
Kang, Seung Il. 'Qoheleth versus a Later Editor: The Origin and Function of Eschatological Elements in Ecclesiastes 12:1–8'. *The Expository Times* 127, no. 7 (2016): 329–37.
Kaufman, Stephen A. (ed.). *Targum Lexicon: A Lexicon to the Aramaic Version of the Hebrew Scriptures from the Files of the Comprehensive Aramaic Lexicon Project (CAL)*. Cincinnati, OH: Hebrew Union College.
Kazemi, Ali and Mohammad A.S. Nodoushan. 'A Conversation Analytic Perspective on Quranic Verses and Chapters'. *Studies in English Language and Education* 5, no. 1 (2018): 1–11.
Keener, Craig S. *The Gospel of John: A Commentary*. Grand Rapids, MI: Baker Academic, 2012.
Keith, Chris. 'Recent and Previous Research on the Pericope Adulterae *(John 7.53–8.11)*'. *Currents in Biblical Research* 6, no. 3 (2008): 377–404.
Keith, Chris. 'The Initial Location of the *Pericope Adulterae* in Fourfold Tradition'. *Novum Testamentum* 51, no. 1 (2009): 1–23.
Keller, Edmund B. 'Hebrew Thoughts on Immortality and Resurrection'. *International Journal for Philosophy of Religion* 5, no. 1 (1974): 16–44.
Kemmerer, Lisa. 'Jewish Ethics and Nonhuman Animals'. *Journal for Critical Animal Studies* 5, no. 2 (2007).
Kern-Ulmer, Brigitte. 'Consistency and Change in Rabbinic Literature as Reflected in the Terms Rain and Dew'. *Journal for the Study of Judaism in the Persian, Hellenistic, and Roman Period* 26, no. 1 (1995): 55–75.
Kessler, Martin. 'Jeremiah 25,1–29: Text and Context. A Synchronic Study'. *Zeitschrift für die alttestamentliche Wissenschaft* 109, no. 1 (1997): 44–70.
Kessler, Martin. 'The "Shield" of Abraham?' *Vetus Testamentum* 63, no. 10 (2013): 32–5.
Khairy, Nabil I. 'An Analytical Study of the Nabataean Monumental Inscriptions at Madā'in Ṣāleḥ'. *Zeitschrift des Deutschen Palästina-Vereins* 96, no. 2 (1980): 163–8.

Khairy, Nabil I. 'The Mada'in Saleh Monuments and the Function Date of the Khazneh in Petra'. *Palestine Exploration Quarterly* 143, no. 3 (2011): 167–75.

Khalil, Mohammad H. 'Which Road to Paradise? The Controversy of Reincarnation in Islamic Thought'. In *Roads to Paradise: Eschatology and Concepts of the Hereafter in Islam*, edited by Sebastian Günther and Todd Lawson, 735–54. Leiden: Brill, 2016.

Khismatulin, Alexey A. 'Just a Step Away from Paradise: *Barzakh* in the Ahl-i-Ḥaqq Teachings'. In *Roads to Paradise: Eschatology and Concepts of the Hereafter in Islam*, edited by Sebastian Günther and Todd Lawson, 689–700. Leiden: Brill, 2017.

Kilgallen, John J. 'The Sadducees and Resurrection from the Dead: Luke 20,27-40'. *Biblica* 67, no. 4 (1986): 478–95.

Killebrew, Ann E. *Biblical Peoples and Ethnicity: An Archaeological Study of Egyptians, Canaanites, Philistines, and Early Israel, 1300–1100 B.C.E.* Atlanta, GA: Society of Biblical Literature, 2005.

Kilwing, Norbert. 'נֶפֶשׁ und ΨYXH: Gemeinsames und Unterscheidendes im hebräischen und griechischen Seelenverständnis'. In *Studien zu Psalmen und Propheten: Festschrift für Hubert Irsigler*. Freiburg: Herder, 2010.

Kim, Daewoong. 'Biblical Interpretation in the Book of Daniel: Literary Allusions in Daniel to Genesis and Ezekiel'. PhD Dissertation. Houston, TX: Rice University, 2013.

Kim, Jieun. *Jerusalem in the Achaemenid Period: The Relationship between Temple and Agriculture in the Book of Haggai*. Bern: Peter Lang, 2016.

Kimelman, Reuven. 'The Daily ʿAmidah and the Rhetoric of Redemption'. *The Jewish Quarterly Review* 79, nos. 2–3 (1988): 165–97.

Kimelman, Reuven. 'The Shemaʿ and Its Rhetoric: The Case for the Shemaʿ Being More than Creation, Revelation, and Redemption'. *The Journal of Jewish Thought and Philosophy* 2 (1992): 111–56.

Kimelman, Reuven. 'The Messiah of the Amidah: A Study in Comparative Messianism'. *Journal of Biblical Literature* 116, no. 2 (1997): 313–20.

King, Barbara J. 'Apes, Hominids, and the Roots of Religion'. *General Anthropology* 16, no. 2 (2009): 1–8.

Kinman, Brent. *Jesus' Entry into Jerusalem: In the Context of Lukan Theology and the Politics of His Day*. Leiden: Brill, 1995.

Kiperwasser, Reuevn. 'Toward a Redaction History of Kohelet Rabbah: A Study in the Composition and Redaction of Kohelet Rabbah 7:7'. *Journal of Jewish Studies* 61, no. 2 (2010): 257–77.

Kister, Menahem. 'Leave the Dead to Bury Their Own Dead'. In *Studies in Ancient Midrash*, edited by James L. Kugel, 43–56. Cambridge, MA: Harvard University Press, 2001.

Kister, Menahem. 'Romans 5:12–21 against the Background of Torah-Theology and Hebrew Usage'. *Harvard Theological Review* 100, no. 4 (2007): 391–424.

Kister, Menahem. 'Divorce, Reproof, and Other Sayings in the Synoptic Gospels: Jesus Traditions in the Context of "Qumranic" and Other Texts'. In *Text, Thought, and Practice in Qumran and Early Christianity*, edited by Ruth A. Clements and Daniel R. Schwartz, 195–230. Leiden: Brill, 2009.

Klar, Marianna. 'Text-Critical Approaches to Sura Structure: Combining Synchronicity with Diachronicity in *Sūrat al-Baqara*. Part One'. *Journal of Qur'anic Studies* 19, no. 1 (2017): 1–38.

Klar, Marianna. 'Text-Critical Approaches to Sura Structure: Combining Synchronicity with Diachronicity in *Sūrat al-Baqara*. Part Two'. *Journal of Qur'anic Studies* 19, no. 2 (2017): 64–105.

Klein, Ralph W. 'Call, Covenant, and Community: The Story of Abraham and Sarah'. *Currents in Theology and Mission* 15 (1988): 120–7.

Kline, Meredith G. *Glory in Our Midst: A Biblical-Theological Reading of Zechariah's Night Visions*. Eugene, OR: Wipf and Stock, 2001.

Klingbeil, Gerald A. 'Looking at the End from the Beginning: Studying Eschatological Concepts in the Pentateuch'. *Journal of the Adventist Theological Society* 11, nos. 1–2 (2000): 174–87.

Klingbeil, Gerald A. *Bridging the Gap: Ritual and Ritual Texts in the Bible*. Winona Lake, IN: Eisenbrauns, 2007.

Klingbeil, Gerald A. 'Between the Traditional and the Innovative: Ezra-Nehemiah in Current Research'. *Religion Compass* 3, no. 2 (2009): 182–99.

Kloppenborg, John S. 'Evocatio Deorum and the Date of Mark'. *Journal of Biblical Literature* 124, no. 3 (2005): 419–50.

Knowles, Melody D. 'Pilgrimage Imagery in the Returns in Ezra'. *Journal of Biblical Literature* 123, no. 1 (2004): 57–74.

Knowles, Melody D. *Centrality Practiced: Jerusalem in the Religious Practice of Yehud and the Diaspora in the Persian Period*. Atlanta, GA: Society of Biblical Literature, 2006.

Knust, Jennifer W. 'Early Christian Re-Writing and the History of the Pericope Adulterae'. *Journal of Early Christian Studies* 14, no. 4 (2006): 485–536.

Knust, Jennifer and Tommy Wasserman. 'Earth Accuses Earth: Tracing What Jesus Wrote on the Ground'. *Harvard Theological Review* 103, no. 4 (2010): 407–46.

Knuston, Jennifer C. 'First Burials Revealing the Beliefs in the Afterlife at Shanidar Cave, Iraq (CA. 60,000 BC)'. In *Great Events in Religion: An Encyclopedia of Pivotal Events in Religious History*, edited by Florin Curta and Andrew Holt, 1: 1–2. Santa Barbara, CA: ABC-CLIO, 2017.

Knuston, Jennifer C. 'First Recorded Burials of Homo Neanderthalensis at La Chapelle-Aux Saints, France (CA. 60,000 BC)'. In *Great Events in Religion: An Encyclopedia of Pivotal Events in Religious History*, edited by Florin Curta and Andrew Holt, 1: 2–3. Santa Barbara, CA: ABC-CLIO, 2017.

Koehler, Ludwig and Walter Baumgartner. *The Hebrew and Aramaic Lexicon of the Old Testament* (*HALOT*). Leiden: Brill, 1994–2000.

Kohler, Kaufmann. 'Pre-Talmudic Haggada: B – The Second Baruch of Rather the Jeremiah Apocalypse'. *Jewish Quarterly Review* 5 (1893): 407–19.

Köhler, Ludwig. *Old Testament Theology*, translated by A.S. Todd. Philadelphia, PA: Westminister Press, 1957.

Kraemer, David. *The Meanings of Death in Rabbinic Judaism*. Abingdon: Routledge, 1999.

Kraft, Robert and Ann E. Purintun. *Paraleipomena Jeremiou*. Missoula, MT: Scholars Press, 1972.

Kristiansen, K. 'Proto-Indo-European Languages and Institutions – An Archaeological Approach'. In *Departure from the Homeland: Indo-Europeans and Archaeology*, edited by M. Vander Linden and K. Jones-Bley, 11–140. Washington, DC: Institute for the Study of Man, 2009.

Kugle, Scott. 'Die before Dying: Activism and Passivity in Sufi Ethics'. *Journal for Islamic Studies* 26, (2006): 113–55.

Kuryliak, Bohdan. 'Методы интерпретации 1 Петр. 3:18–22 в исторической ретроспективе'. *Theological Reflections: Euro-Asian Journal of Theology* 21, (2018): 31–42.

Kutsko, John F. *Between Heaven and Earth: Divine Presence and Absence in the Book of Ezekiel*. Winona Lake, IL: Eisenbrauns, 2000.

l'Heureux, Conrad. 'The Ugaritic and Biblical Rephaim'. *Harvard Theological Review* 67, no. 3 (1974): 265–74.

Labendz, Jenny R. '"Know What to Answer the Epicurean": A Diachronic Study of the 'Apiqoros in Rabbinic Literature'. *Hebrew Union College Annual* 74, (2003): 175–214.

Lacocque, André. *Livre de Daniel*. Paris: Delachaux et Niestle, 1976.

Lacocque, André. *The Book of Daniel*, London: Society for Promoting Christian Knowledge, 1979.

Ladd, George E. 'Israel and the Church'. *Evangelical Quarterly* 36, no. 4 (1964): 206–13.

Ladouceur, Paul. 'Evolution and Genesis 2–3: The Decline and Fall of Adam and Eve'. *St. Vladimir's Theological Quarterly* 57, no. 1 (2013): 135–76.

Lambrecht, Jan. 'Final Judgments and Ultimate Blessings: The Climatic Visions of Revelation 20,11–21,8'. *Biblica* 81, no. 3 (2000): 362–85.

Lambrecht, Jan. 'Romans 4: A Critique of N. T. Wright'. *Journal for the Study of the New Testament* 36, no. 2 (2013): 189–94.

Lampe, Geoffrey W.H. *God as Spirit*. Oxford: Oxford University Press, 1977.

Lang, Bernard. 'Street Theatre, Raising the Dead, and the Zoroastrian Connection in Ezekiel's Prophecy'. In *Ezekiel and His Book: Textual and Literary Criticism and Their Interrelation*, edited by Johan Lust, 297–316. Leuven: Peeters, 1986.

Lange, Christian (ed.). *Locating Hell in Islamic Tradition*. Leiden: Brill, 2015.

Lapsley, Jacqueline E. 'Body Piercings: The Priestly Body and the "Body" of the Temple in Ezekiel'. *Hebrew Bible and Ancient Israel* 1, no. 2 (2012): 231–45.

Lategan, Werner A. 'The Theological Dialectic of Creation and Death in Hebrew Bible Wisdom Traditions'. PhD Dissertation. Groningen: University of Groningen, 2009.

Lauber, David. *Barth on the Descent into Hell: God, Atonement, and the Christian Life*. Abingdon: Routledge, 2004.

Laufer, Catherine E. *Hells' Destruction: An Exploration of Christ's Descent to the Dead*. Abingdon: Routledge, 2013.

Lavrov, Dmitry. 'The Meaning of the Word כֶּלַח in Job 5:26 and 30:2: Textual and Philological Analysis'. *Theological Reflections* 7, (2006): 51–63.

Leach, Edmund. 'Aryan Invasions over Four Millennia'. In *Culture through Time: Anthropological Approaches*, edited by Emiko Ohnuki-Tierney, 227–45. Stanford, CA: Stanford University Press, 1990.

Lee, Kyong-Jin. 'The Authority and Authorization of the Torah in the Persian Period'. PhD Dissertation. New Haven, CT: Yale University, 2010.

Lehnardt, Andreas. 'Massekhet Kutim and the Resurrection of the Dead'. In *Samaritans: Past and Present – Current Studies*, edited by Menachem Mor and Friedrich V. Reiterer, 175–92. Berlin: De Gruyter, 2010.

Lehtipuu, Outi. *Debates over the Resurrection of the Dead: Constructing Early Christian Identity*. Oxford: Oxford University Press, 2015.

Lesko, Leonard H. 'Death and the Afterlife in Ancient Egyptian Thought'. In *Civilizations of the Ancient Near East*, edited by Jack M. Sasson, 3: 1763–74. New York, NY: Simon and Schuster Macmillan, 1995.

Leslau, Wolf. 'South-East Semitic (Ethiopic and South-Arabic)'. *Journal of the American Oriental Society* 63, no. 1 (1943): 4–14.

Leslau, Wolf. *Comparative Dictionary of Ge'ez*. Wiesbaden: Otto Harrassowitz, 2006.

Lester, G. Brooke. *Daniel Evokes Isaiah: Allusive Characterization of Foreign Rule in the Hebrew-Aramaic Book of Daniel*. London: T&T Clark, 2015.

Leuchter, Mark. *The Levites and the Boundaries of Israelite Identity*. Oxford: Oxford University Press, 2017.

Lev, Ephraim and Simcha Lev-Yadun. 'The Probable Pagan Origin of an Ancient Jewish Custom: Purification with Red Heifer's Ashes'. *Advances in Anthropology* 6, no. 4 (2016): 122–6.

Levenson, Jon D. *Resurrection and the Restoration of Israel: The Ultimate Victory of the God of Life*. New Haven, CT: Yale University Press, 2006.

Levin, Saul. *Semitic and Indo-European, Volume II: Comparative Morphology, Syntax and Phonetics*. Amsterdam: John Benjamins, 2002.

Lévy, Isidore. *La légende de Pythagore de Grèce en Palestine*. Paris: Champion, 1927.

Levy, Jacob. 1883. *Wörterbuch über die Talmudim und Midraschim,* Leipzig: F.A. Brockhaus, 1963.

Levy, Thomas and Edwin C.M. van den Brink (eds.). *Egypt and the Levant: Interrelations from the 4th through the Early 3rd Millennium B.C.E.* London: Bloomsbury, 2002.

Lewis, A., K. Cahn-Fuller and A. Caplan. 'Shouldn't Dead Be Dead? The Search for a Uniform Definition of Death'. *The Journal of Law, Medicine & Ethics* 45, no. 1 (2017): 112–28.

Lewis, Theodore J. ''Athtartu's Incantations and the Use of Divine Names as Weapons'. *Journal of Near Eastern Studies* 70, no. 2 (2011): 207–27.

Lichtheim, Miriam. *Ancient Egyptian Literature 2: The New Kingdom*. Berkeley, CA: University of California Press, 1976.

Liddell, Henry G. and Robert Scott. *A Greek-English Lexicon*. Oxford: Clarendon Press, 1996.

Lindenberger, James M. 'Daniel 12:1–4'. *Interpretation: A Journal of Bible and Theology* 39, no. 2 (1985): 181–6.

Lipschits, Oded. *The Fall and Rise of Jerusalem: Judah under Babylonian Rule*. Winona Lake, IN: Eisenbrauns, 2005.

Lipschits, Oded, Yuval Gadot, and Mathew J. Adams (eds.). *Rethinking Israel: Studies in the History and Archaeology of Ancient Israel in Honor of Israel Finkelstein*. University Park, PA: Eisenbrauns, 2017.

Loesov, Sergey. 'New Attempt at Reconstructing Proto-Aramaic (Part I)'. *Babel und Bibel* 6, (2012): 421–56.

Lohfink, Gerhard. *Does God Need the Church? Toward a Theology of the People of God*, trans. Linda M. Maloney. Collegeville, MN: Liturgical Press, 1999.

Long, Herbert S. 'Plato's Doctrine of Metempsychosis and Its Source'. *The Classical Weekly* 41, no. 10 (1948): 149–55.

Loukas, Marios, Yousuf Saad, R. Shane Tubbs and Mohamadali M. Shoja. 'The Heart and Cardiovascular System in the *Qur'an* and *Hadeeth*'. *International Journal of Cardiology* 140, no. 1 (2010): 19–23.

Lumbard, Joseph E.B. 'Covenant and Covenants in the Qur'an'. *Journal of Qur'anic Studies* 17, no. 2 (2015): 1–23.

Lust, Johan, Erik Eynikel and Katrin Hauspie. *A Greek-English Lexicon of the Septuagint*. Stuttgart: Deutsche Bibelgesellschaft, 2003.

Lys, Daniel. 'The Israelite Soul according to the LXX'. *Vetus Testamentum* 16, no. 2 (1966): 181–228.

Maccoby, Hyam. *The Philosophy of the Talmud*. Abingdon: Routledge, 2002.

MacDonald, Nathan. 'The Hermeneutics and Genesis of the Red Cow Ritual'. *Harvard Theological Review* 105, no. 3 (2012): 351–71.

MacDonald, Nathan. *Priestly Rule: Polemic and Biblical Interpretation in Ezekiel 44*. Berlin: De Gruyter, 2015.

Machery, Edouard. 'Why I Stopped Worrying about the Definition of Life . . . and Why You Should as Well'. *Synthese* 185, no. 1 (2012): 145–64.

Madelung, Wilfred. 'Abū Ya'qūb al-Sijistānī and Metempsychosis'. In *Iranica Varia: Papers in Honor of Professor Ehsan Yarshater*, edited by D. Amin, M. Kasheff, Alireza Sh. Shahbazi, 131–43. Leiden: Brill, 1990.
Makkī bin Abī Ṭālib (d. 437/1045). *al-Hidāyah ilā bulūgh al-nihāyah fī 'ilm ma'ānī al-Qur'ān wa-tafsīrih wa-aḥkāmih wa-jumal min funūn 'ulūmih*, edited by al-Shāhid al-Bushaykhī. Sharjah: University of Sharjah, 2008.
Makujina, John. 'On the Possible Old Persian Origin of the Aramaic שים טעם, "to Issue a Decree"' *Hebrew Union College Annual* 68, (1997): 1–9.
Mandel, Paul. 'Midrashic Exegesis and Its Precedents in the Dead Sea Scrolls'. *Dead Sea Discoveries* 8, no. 2 (2001): 149–68.
Manning, J.G. 'The Representation of Justice in Ancient Egypt'. *Yale Journal of Law and the Humanities* 24, no. 1 (2012): 111–18.
Manuel, Frank E. and Fritzie P. Manuel. 'Sketch for a Natural History of Paradise'. *Daedalus* 101, no. 1 (1972): 83–128.
Marcar, Katie. 'In the Days of Noah: Urzeit/Endzeit Correspondence and the Flood Tradition in 1 Peter 3–4'. *New Testament Studies* 63, no. 4 (2017): 550–66.
Marcus, David. 'The Verb "To Live" in Ugaritic'. *Journal of Semitic Studies* 17, no. 1 (1972): 76–82.
Margoliouth, David S. 'The Origins of Arabic Poetry'. *Journal of the Royal Asiatic Society* 3, no. 3 (1925): 415–49.
Marinkovic, Peter. 'What Does Zechariah 1–8 Tell Us about the Second Temple?' In *Second Temple Studies: Temple and Community in the Persian Period*, edited by Tamara C. Eskenazi and Kent H. Richards, 88–105. Sheffield: Sheffield Academic, 1994.
Marmorstein, Arthur. 'The Doctrine of the Resurrection of the Dead in Rabbinic Theology'. *The American Journal of Theology* 19, no. 4 (1915): 577–91.
Marquet, Yves. 'La philosophie des Ikhwan al-Safa de Dieu à l'homme'. PhD Dissertation. Paris: Université de Paris, 1971.
Marter, E.W. 'The Hebrew Concept of "Soul" in Pre-Exilic Writings'. *Andrews University Seminary Studies* 2, (1964): 97–108.
Martin, Calvin. *Keepers of the Game: Indian-Animal Relationships and the Fur Trade*. Berkley, CA: University of California Press, 1978.
Martin-Achard, R. *From Death to Life: A Study of the Development of the Resurrection in the Old Testament*. Edinburgh: Oliver and Boyd, 1960.
Mason, Rex. 'Some Echoes of the Preaching in the Second Temple? Tradition Elements in Zechariah 1 – 8'. *Zeitschrift für die alttestamentliche Wissenschaft* 96, no. 2 (1984): 221–35.
Mazuz, Haggai. *The Religious and Spiritual Life of the Jews of Medina*. Leiden: Brill, 2014.
Mazuz, Haggai. 'Northern Arabia and Its Jewry in Early Rabbinic Sources: More Than Meets the Eye'. *Antiguo Oriente* 13, (2015): 149–68.
McAffee, Matthew. 'Life and Mortality in Ugaritic: A Lexical, Literary, and Comparative Analysis'. PhD Dissertation. Chicago, IL: University of Chicago, 2015.
McAffee, Matthew 'Rephaim, Whisperers, and the Dead in Isaiah 26:13–19: A Ugaritic Parallel'. *Journal of Biblical Literature* 135, no. 1 (2016): 77–94.
McDannell, Colleen and Bernhard Lang. 1988. *Heaven: A History*, 2nd ed. New Haven, CT: Yale University Press, 2001.
McEvilley, Thomas. *The Shape of Ancient Thought: Comparative Studies in Greek and Indian Philosophies*. New York, NY: Allworth Press, 2002.
McFarland, Orrey. 'Whose Promise, Which Promise? Genesis 15.6 in Philo's *De Virtutibus* and Romans 4'. *Journal for the Study of the New Testament* 35, no. 2 (2012): 107–29.

McGill, B.G. 'Hathor in the Context of the Coffin Texts'. *Studia Antiqua* 6, no. 1 (2008): 27–32.

McNamara, Martin. *The New Testament and the Palestinian Targum to the Pentateuch*. Rome: Pontifical Biblical Institute, 1966.

Meier, John P. 'The Debate on the Resurrection of the Dead: An Incident from the Ministry of the Historical Jesus?' *Journal for the Study of the New Testament* 22, no. 77 (2000): 3–23.

Merlini, Carola G. 'The Lexical Field of "Purity" Verbs in Ancient Hebrew'. *Revue Européenne des Études Hébraïques* 5, (2001): 145–52.

Merrill, Eugene H. 'Pilgrimage and Procession: Motifs of Israel's Return'. In *Israel's Apostasy and Restoration: Essays in Honor of Roland K. Harrison*, edited by Avraham Gileadi, 261–72. Grand Rapids, MI: Baker Academic, 1988.

Meschel, Susan V. 'The Use of the Metal Lead in the Bible'. *Jewish Bible Quarterly* 44, no. 1 (2016): 53–7.

Mettinger, Tryggve N.D. *The Riddle of Resurrection: 'Dying and Rising Gods' in the Ancient Near East*. Stockholm: Almqvist & Wiksell, 2001.

Meyers, Eric M. 'The Use of *tôrâ* in Haggai 2:11 and the Role of the Prophet in the Restoration Community'. In *The Word of the Lord Shall Go Forth: Essays in Honor of David Noel Freedman in Celebration of His Sixtieth Birthday*, edited by Carol L. Meyers and M. O'Connor, 69–76. Winona Lake, IN: Eisenbrauns, 1983.

Meysami-Azad, Shahin. 'Reincarnation in Abrahamic Religions', Master's Thesis, Leiden: University of Leiden, 2017.

Milgrom, Jacob. 'The Paradox of the Red Cow (Num. XIX)'. *Vetus Testamentum* 31, no. 1 (1981): 62–72.

Milgrom, Jacob. 'The Rationale for Biblical Impurity'. *Journal of the Ancient Near Eastern Society* 22 (1993): 107–11.

Millar, David. 'A Psychoanalytic View of Biblical Myth'. *The International Journal of Psychoanalysis* 82, no. 5 (2001): 965–79.

Miller, Andrew C. 'Opinions on the Legitimacy of Brain Death among Sunni and Shi'a Scholars'. *Journal of Religion and Health* 55, no. 2 (2016): 394–402.

Miller, Franklin G. and Robert D. Truog. 'Decapitation and the Definition of Death'. *Journal of Medical Ethics* 36, no. 10 (2010): 632–4.

Miller, J. Maxwell. 'The Korahites of Southern Judah'. *Catholic Biblical Quarterly* 32, no. 1 (1970): 58–68.

Miller, J. Maxwell and John H. Hayes. *A History of Ancient Israel and Judah*. Lousiville, KY: Westminster John Knox, 1986.

Miller, Patrick D. 'Sin and Judgment in Jeremiah 34:17–19'. *Journal of Biblical Literature* 103, no. 4 (1984): 611–13.

Mills, Antonia. 'A Preliminary Investigation of Cases of Reincarnation among the Beaver and Gitksan Indians'. *Anthropologica* 30, no. 1 (1988): 23–59.

Mills, Antonia. 'A Comparison of Wet'suwet'en Cases of the Reincarnation Type with Gitksan and Beaver'. *Journal of Anthropological Research* 44, no. 4 (1988): 385–415.

Mills, Antonia and Richard Slobodin. *Amerindian Rebirth: Reincarnation Belief among North American Indians and Inuit*. Toronto: University of Toronto Press, 1994.

Min, Kyung-jin. *The Levitical Authorship of Ezra-Nehemiah*. London: T&T Clark, 2004.

Minear, Paul S. 'Writing on the Ground: The Puzzle in John 8:1–11'. *Horizons in Biblical Theology* 13, no. 1 (1991): 23–37.

Minear, Paul S. *The Obedience of Faith: The Purposes of Paul in the Epistle to the Romans*. Eugene, OR: Wipf & Stock, 2003.

Miquel, Esther. 'The Impatient Jesus and the Fig Tree: Marcan Disguised Discourse against the Temple'. *Biblical Theology Bulletin* 45, no. 3 (2015): 144–54.
Misra, Satya S. 'The Date of the Rigveda and the Aryan Migration: Fresh Linguistic Evidence'. In *The Indo-Aryan Controversy: Evidence and Inference in Indian History*, Edwin F. Bryant and Laurie L. Patton (eds.), 181–233. Abingdon: Routledge, 2005.
Moberly, R. Walter L. *The Bible, Theology, and Faith: A Study of Abraham and Jesus*. Cambridge: Cambridge University Press, 2000.
Mohamed, Mostapha T. 'The Metaphor of Nature in the Holy Quran: A Critical Metaphor Analysis'. *Journal of Arabic and Human Sciences* 7, no. 3 (2014): 83–100.
Mohamed, Yasien. '"Fitrah" and Its Bearing on Islamic Psychology'. *American Journal of Islamic Social Sciences* 12, no. 1 (1995): 1–18.
Mojsov, Bojana. 'The Ancient Egyptian Underworld in the Tomb of Sety I: Sacred Books of Eternal Life'. *The Massachusetts Review* 42, no. 2 (2001): 489–506.
Moore, Rickie D. 'The Prophet as Mentor: A Crucial Facet of the Biblical Presentations of Moses, Elijah, and Isaiah'. *Journal of Pentecostal Theology* 15, no. 2 (2007): 155–72.
Moran, William L. 'The Creation of Man in Atrahasis I 192–248'. *Bulletin of the American Schools of Oriental Research*, 200, Anniversary Issue in Honor of William F. Albright (1970): 48–56.
Moran, William L. (trans.) *The Amarna Letters*. Baltimore, MD: Johns Hopkins University Press, 1992.
Moreland, J.P. *The Soul: How We Know It's Real and Why It Matters*. Chicago: Moody, 2014.
Moretsi, Lekgetho H. 'The Translation Technique and the Translation of Verbal Forms in Psalm 84 of the Masoretic Text as Employed by the Peshitta'. *In die Skriflig* 51, no. 1 (2017): a2193.
Moskala, Jiří. 'The Holy Spirit in the Hebrew Scriptures'. *Journal of the Adventist Theological Society* 24, no. 2 (2013): 18–58.
Mourad, Anna-Latifa. 'Rise of the Hyksos: Egypt and the Levant from the Middle Kingdom to the Early Second Intermediate Period'. PhD Thesis. Sydney: Macquarie University, 2014.
Moyise, Steve. *The Old Testament in the Book of Revelation*. Sheffield: Sheffield Academic, 1995.
Mujāhid (d. 104/722). *Tafsīr*, edited by Muḥammad Abul-Nīl. Cairo: al-Fikr al-Islāmī al-Ḥadīth, 1989.
Munn, Nancy D. 'The Cultural Anthropology of Time: A Critical Essay'. *Annual Review of Anthropology* 21, (1992): 93–123.
Murphy, Frederick J. 'The Temple in the Syriac Apocalypse of Baruch'. *Journal of Biblical Literature* 106, (1987): 671–83.
Murphy, Nancey. 'Human Nature: Historical, Scientific, and Religious Issues'. In *Whatever Happened to the Soul? Scientific and Theological Portraits of Human Nature*, edited by Warren S. Brown, Nancey Murphy, and H. Newton Malony, 1–29, Minneapolis, MN: Fortress, 1998.
Musano, Ferdinando. 'The Destruction of the Temple in 70 CE: Rabbinic Judaism as a New Religious Movement'. Master's Thesis. Montréal: Concordia University Press, 2017.
Muslim (d. 261/875). *Ṣaḥīḥ Muslim*, edited by M.F. ʿAbdul-Bāqī. Beirut: Iḥyāʾ al-Turāth al-ʿArabī, n.d.
Mutzafi, Hezy. *Comparative Lexical Studies in Neo-Mandaic*. Leiden: Brill, 2014.
Mweemba, Gift. 'The Broken Covenant in Jeremiah 11: A Dissertation of Limited Scope'. Master's Thesis. Pretoria: University of South Africa, 2006.

Na'aman, Nadav. 'Historical and Chronological Notes on the Kingdoms of Israel and Judah in the Eighth Century B.C.' *Vetus Testamentum* 36, no. 1 (1986): 71–92.

Na'aman, Nadav. 'Hezekiah and the Kings of Assyria'. *Tel Aviv* 21, no. 2 (1994): 235–54.

Nadel, S.F. 'A Study of Shamanism in the Nuba Mountains'. *The Journal of the Royal Anthropological Institute of Great Britain and Ireland* 76, no. 1 (1946): 25–37.

Najm-ul-dīn al-Kubrā (Aḥmad bin ʿUmar) (d. 618/1221). *al-Taʾwīlāt al-najmiyyah fil-tafsīr al-ishārī al-ṣūfī*. Beirut: al-Kutub al-ʿIlmiyyah, 2009.

Nanos, Mark D. *The Mystery of Romans: The Jewish Context of Paul's Letter*, Minneapolis, MN: Fortress, 1996.

Nasr, Seyyed Hossein. *Islamic Philosophy from Its Origin to the Present: Philosophy in the Land of Prophecy*. Albany, NY: State University of New York Press, 2006.

Nasr, Seyyed Hossein (ed.). *The Study Quran*. New York, NY: HarperOne, 2015.

Neiman, David. 'PGR: A Canaanite Cult-Object in the Old Testament'. *Journal of Biblical Literature* 67, no. 1 (1948): 55–60.

Nelson, J. Robert. 'On Life and Living: The Semitic Insight'. *The Journal of Medicine and Philosophy* 3, no. 2 (1978): 129–43.

Nelson, Richard K. 'A Conservation Ethic and Environment: The Koyukon of Alaska'. In *Resource Managers: North American and Australian Hunter-Gatherers*, edited by Nancy M. Williams and Eugene S. Hunn, 211–28. New York, NY: American Association for the Advancement of Science, 1982.

Netton, Ian R. 'Towards a Modern Tafsīr of Sūrat al-Kahf: Structure and Semiotics'. *Journal of Qurʾanic Studies* 2, no. 1 (2000): 67–87.

Neusner, Jacob (trans.). *The Mishnah: A New Translation*. New Haven, CT: Yale University Press, 1988.

Neusner, Jacob. *The Rabbinic Traditions about the Pharisees before 70*. Leiden: Brill, 1971.

Neusner, Jacob. 'Death and Afterlife in the Later Rabbinic Sources: The Two Talmuds and Associated Midrash-Compilations'. In *Judaism in Late Antiquity: Death, Life-after-Death, Resurrection and The World-to-Come in the Judaisms of Antiquity*, edited by Alan J. Avery-Peck and Jacob Neusner, 267–91. Leiden: Brill, 2000.

Neusner, Jacob. 1991. *Confronting Creation: How Judaism Reads Genesis: An Anthology of Genesis Rabbah*, Eugene, OR: Wipf & Stock, 2004 (orig. Columbia, SC: University of South Carolina Press).

Neusner, Jacob (trans.). *The Jerusalem Talmud: A Translation and Commentary*, Peabody, MA: Hendrickson Publishers, 2008.

Neusner, Jacob (trans.). *The Babylonian Talmud: A Translation and Commentary*, Peabody, MA: Hendrickson Publishers, 2011.

Neuss, W. *Das Buch Ezechiel in Theologies und Kunst bis zum Ende des XII. Jahrhunderts*. Münster: Aschendorff, 1912.

Neuwirth, Angelika. 'Two Faces of the Qurʾān: *Qurʾān* and *Muṣḥaf*. *Oral Tradition* 25, no. 1 (2010): 141–56.

Neuwirth, Angelika. 'The Qurʾan in the Field of Conflict between the Interpretative Communities: An Attempt to Cope with the Crisis of Qurʾanic Studies'. In *Fundamentalism and Gender: Scripture–Body–Community*, edited by Ulrike Auga, Christina von Braun, Claudia Bruns and Jana Husmann. Eugene, OR: Pickwick, 2013.

Newby, Gordon. *A History of the Jews of Arabia: From Ancient Times to Their Eclipse Under Islam*. Columbia, SC: University of South Carolina Press, 1988.

Newman, Stephen. 'Understanding the Mystery of the Red Heifer Ritual'. *Jewish Bible Quarterly* 43, no. 2 (2015): 106–8.

Nibley, Hugh. 'Qumran and "the Companions of the Cave"'. *Revue de Qumrân* 5, no. 2 (1965): 177–98.

Nigosian, S.A. *The Zoroastrian Faith: Tradition and Modern Research*. Montreal: McGill-Queen's University Press, 1993.

Nickelsburg, George. *Resurrection, Immortality and Eternal Life in Intertestamental Judaism*. Cambridge, MA: Harvard University Press, 1972.

Noam, Vered. 'Ritual Impurity in Tannaitic Literature: Two Opposing Perspectives'. *Journal of Ancient Judaism* 1, (2010): 65–103.

Nolland, John. 'Sin, Purity and the חטאת Offering'. *Vetus Testamentum* 65, no. 4 (2015): 606–20.

Noort, Ed. 'Taken from the Soil, Gifted with the Breath of Life: The Anthropology of Gen 2:7 in Context'. In *Dust of the Ground and Breath of Life (Gen 2:7): The Problem of a Dualistic Anthropology in Early Judaism and Christianity*, edited by Jacques T.A.G.M. van Ruiten and Geurt H. van Kooten, 1–15. Leiden: Brill, 2016.

Novak, David. 'The Talmud as a Source for Philosophical Reflection'. In *History of Jewish Philosophy*, edited by Daniel H. Frank and Oliver Leaman, 49–71. London: Routledge, 1997.

Nürnberger, Klaus. 'Dust of the Ground and Breath of Life (Gen 2:7): The Notion of "life" in Ancient Israel and Emergence Theory'. In *Issues in Science and Theology: What is Life?* edited by Dirk Evers, Michael Fuller, Antje Jackelén, and Knut-Willy Sæther, 101–6. Cham: Springer, 2015.

O'Brien, Mark A. 'The Dynamics of the Golden Calf Story (Exodus 32–34)'. *Australian Biblical Review* 60, (2012): 18–31.

O'Connor, M. 'The Arabic Loanwords in Nabatean Aramaic'. *Journal of Near Eastern Studies* 45, (1986): 213–29.

O'Connor, M. John-Patrick. 'Genesis 2:7 in Conversation: The Exegesis of Paul, Philo, and the Hodayot'. *Zeitschrift für die neutestamentliche Wissenschaft* 110, no. 1 (2019): 84–103.

O'Shaughnessy, Thomas J. 'The Seven Names for Hell in the Qurʾān'. *Bulletin of the School of Oriental and African Studies* 24, no. 3 (1961): 444–69.

O'Shaughnessy, Thomas J. *Muhammad's Thoughts on Death: A Thematic Study of the Qurʾanic Data*. Leiden: Brill, 1969.

O'Shaughnessy, Thomas J. *Creation and the Teaching of the Qurʾān*. Rome: Biblical Institute Press, 1985.

Obermann, Julian. 'Votive Inscriptions from Ras Shamra'. *Journal of the American Oriental Society* 61, no. 1 (1941): 31–45.

Olyan, Saul M. 'Unnoticed Resonances of Tomb Opening and Transportation of the Remains of the Dead in Ezekiel 37:12–14'. *Journal of Biblical Literature* 128, no. 3 (2009): 491–501.

Oppenheim, A. Leo (ed.). *The Assyrian Dictionary*, (*Chicago Assyrian Dictionary* (*CAD*)). Chicago, IL: The Oriental Institute, 1965–98.

Orel, Vladimir E. and Olga V. Stolbova. *Hamito-Semitic Etymological Dictionary: Materials for a Reconstruction*. Leiden: Brill, 1995.

Origen. *Commentary on the Epistle to the Romans, Books 1–5*, translated by Thomas P. Sheck. Washington, DC: Catholic University of America Press, 2001.

Ọsányìnbí, Ọladotun B. and Kehinde Falana. 'An Evaluation of the Akure Yorùbá Traditional Belief in Reincarnation'. *Open Journal of Philosophy* 6, no. 1 (2016): 59–67.

Osei-Bonsu, Joseph. 'Does 2 Cor 5:1–10 Teach the Reception of the Resurrection Body at the Moment of Death?' *Journal for the Study of the New Testament* 9, no. 28 (1986): 81–101.

Osei-Bonsu, Joseph. 'The Intermediate State in the New Testament'. *Scottish Journal of Theology* 44, no. 2 (1991): 169–94.
Ouro, Roberto. 'The Term ṭᵉhôrâ in Genesis 7:2: A Linguistic Study'. *Journal of the Adventist Theological Society* 16, nos. 1–2 (2005): 21–9.
Padela, Aasim I., Hasan Shanawani and Ahsan Arozullah. 'Medical Experts & Islamic Scholars Deliberating over Brain Death: Gaps in the Applied Islamic Bioethics Discourse'. *The Muslim World* 101, no. 1 (2011): 53–72.
Padela, Aasim I. and Taha A. Basser. 'Brain Death: The Challenges of Translating Medical Science into Islamic Bioethical Discourse'. *Medicine and Law* 31, (2012): 433–50.
Padela, Aasim I., Ahsan Arozullah and Ebrahim Moosa. 'Brain Death in Islamic Ethico-Legal Deliberation: Challenges for Applied Islamic Bioethics'. *Bioethics* 27, no. 3 (2013): 132–9.
Parast, Shoja J. 'The Thought Barriers in View of Holy Qur'an'. *International Journal of Biology, Pharmacy and Allied Sciences* 4, no. 10 (2015): 724–32.
Pargament, Kenneth I. *The Psychology of Religion and Coping: Theory, Research, Practice*. New York, NY: Guilford, 1997.
Pargament, Kenneth I., Gene G. Ano and Amy B. Wachholtz. 'The Religious Dimension of Coping: Advances in Theory, Research, and Practice'. In *Handbook of the Psychology of Religion and Spirituality*, edited by Raymond F. Paloutzian and Crystal L. Park, 479–95. New York, NY: Guilford, 2005.
Pargament, Kenneth I. *Spiritually Integrated Psychotherapy: Understanding and Addressing the Sacred*. New York, NY: Guilford, 2007.
Park, Joseph S. *Conceptions of Afterlife in Jewish Inscriptions: With Special Reference to Pauline Literature*. Tübingen: Mohr Siebeck, 2000.
Parker, Floyd. 'The Terms "Angel" and "Spirit" in Acts 23,8'. *Biblica* 84, no. 3 (2003): 344–65.
Parpola, Sima. *Etymological Dictionary of the Sumerian Language*. Winona Lake, IN: Eisenbrauns, 2016.
Parrott, Justin. 'Al-Ghazali and the Golden Rule: Ethics of Reciprocity in the Works of a Muslim Sage'. *Journal of Religious & Theological Information* 16, no. 2 (2017): 68–78.
Pasternak, Ariel R. and Shamir Yona. 'Numerical Sayings in the Literature of the Ancient Near East, in the Bible, in the Book of Ben-Sira and in Rabbinic Literature'. *Review of Rabbinic Judaism* 19, no. 2 (2016): 202–44.
Pasternak, Ariel R. and Shamir Yona. 'The Use of Numbers as an Editing Device in Rabbinic Literature'. *Review of Rabbinic Judaism* 20, no. 2 (2017): 193–234.
Paton, Lewis B. 'The Hebrew Idea of the Future Life: IV. Yahweh's Relation to the Dead in the Earliest Hebrew Religion'. *The Biblical World* 35, no. 4 (1910): 246–58.
Paul, Shalom M. 'Heavenly Tablets and the Book of Life'. *Journal of Ancient Near Eastern Society* 5, no. 1 (1973): 345–54.
Paulien, Jon. 'The Resurrection and the Old Testament: A Fresh Look in Light of Recent Research'. *Journal of the Adventist Theological Society* 24, no. 1 (2013): 3–24.
Pearson, Birger A. 'A Reminiscence of Classical Myth at *II Peter* 2.4'. *Greek, Roman and Byzantine Studies* 10, no. 1 (1969): 71–80.
Pearson, Brook W.R. 'Dry Bones in the Judean Desert: The Messiah of Ephraim, Ezekiel 37, and the Post-Revolutionary Followers of Bar Kokhba'. *Journal for the Study of Judaism* 29, no. 2 (1998): 192–201.
Peerwani, Latimah-Parvin. 'Death and the Post-Mortem States of the Soul: A Comparison of Mulla Sadra with Swedenborg'. *Journal of Shi'a Islamic Studies* 2, no. 4 (2009): 387–400.

Pentiuc, Eugen J. *West Semitic Vocabulary in the Akkadian Texts from Emar*. Winona Lake, IL: Eisenbrauns, 2001.
Pereltsvaig, Asya and Martin W. Lewis. *The Indo-European Controversy: Facts and Fallacies in Historical Linguistics*. Cambridge: Cambridge University Press, 2015.
Perreira, Todd L. '"Die before You Die": Death Meditation as Spiritual Technology of the Self in Islam and Buddhism'. *The Muslim World* 100, nos. 2–3 (2010): 247–67.
Peters, F.E. 'The Greek and Syriac Background'. In *History of Islamic Philosophy*, edited by Seyyed Hossein Nasr and Oliver Leaman, 1: 40–51. London: Routledge, 1996.
Petersen, David L. 'The Temple in Persian Period Prophetic Texts'. *Biblical Theology Bulletin* 21, no. 3 (1991): 88–96.
Peterson, Brian N. *Genesis as Torah: Reading Narrative as Legal Instruction*. Eugene, OR: Cascade Books, 2018.
Pfeiffer, Robert H. 'The Peculiar Skepticism of Qoheleth'. *Journal of Biblical Literature* 53, no. 2 (1934): 100–9.
Philo (d. 50 CE). *The Works of Philo: Complete and Unabridged*, translated by C.D. Yonge. Peabody, MA: Hendrickson, 1995.
Picken, Gavin. 'Tazkiyat al-nafs: The Qur'anic Paradigm'. *Journal of Qur'anic Studies* 7, no. 2 (2005): 101–27.
Pielow, Dorothee. 'Sleepless in Paradise: Lying in State between This World and the Next'. In *Roads to Paradise: Eschatology and Concepts of the Hereafter in Islam*, edited by Sebastian Günther and Todd Lawson, 428–44. Leiden: Brill, 2017.
Pierce, Chad T. 'Spirits and the Proclamation of Christ: 1 Peter 3:18–22 in Its Tradition-Historical and Literary Context'. PhD Thesis. Durham: University of Durham, 2009.
Pierce, Chad T. *Spirits and the Proclamation of Christ: 1 Peter 3:18–22 in Light of Sin and Punishment Traditions in Early Jewish and Christian Literature*. Tübingen: Mohr Siebeck, 2011.
Pierce, Ronald. 'Literary Connectors and a Haggai/Zechariah/Malachi Corpus'. *Journal of the Evangelical Theological Society* 27, no. 3 (1984): 277–89.
Pinson, DovBer. *Reincarnation and Judaism: The Journey of the Soul*. Lanham, MD: Rowman & Littlefield, 1999.
Piovanelli, Pierluigi. 'Les Paralipomènes de Jérémie dépendant-ils de l'Histoire de la captivité babylonienne?' *Bulletin de l'AELAC* 7, (1997): 10–14.
Piovanelli, Pierluigi. 'In Praise of "The Default Position", or Reassessing the Christian Reception of the Jewish Pseudepigraphic Heritage'. *Nederlands theologisch tijdschrift* 61, (2007): 233–50.
Plant, Robin J.R. *Good Figs, Bad Figs: Judicial Differentiation in the Book of Jeremiah*. London: T&T Clark, 2008.
Plevnik, Joseph. 'The Taking Up of the Faithful and the Resurrection of the Dead in 1 Thessalonians 4:13–18'. *Catholic Bible Quarterly* 46, no. 2 (1984): 274–83.
Poirier, John C. '"The Endtime Return of Elijah and Moses at Qumran'. *Dead Sea Discoveries* 10, no. 2 (2003): 221–42.
Poirier, John C. 'Purity beyond the Temple in the Second Temple Era'. *Journal of Biblical Literature* 122, no. 2 (2003): 247–65.
Polaski, Donald C. *Authorizing an End: The Isaiah Apocalypse and Intertextuality*. Leiden: Brill, 2001.
Popović, Mladen. 'Bones, Bodies and Resurrection in the Dead Sea Scrolls'. *Deuterocanonical and Cognate Literature Yearbook*, 221–42. Berlin: De Gruyter, 2009.
Popović, Mladen. 'Anthropology, Pneumatology, and Demonology in Early Judaism: The *Two Spirits Treatise* (1QS III, 12–IV, 26) and Other Texts from the Dead Sea Scrolls'. In

Dust of the Ground and Breath of Life (Gen 2:7): The Problem of a Dualistic Anthropology in Early Judaism and Christianity, edited by Jacques T.A.G.M. van Ruiten and Geurt H. van Kooten, 58–98. Leiden: Brill, 2016.

Potgieter, J. Henk. 'Psalm 56 Read within Its Literary Context in the Psalter and Its Connections with King David'. *Old Testament Essays* 28, no. 3 (2015).

Potter, H.D. 'The New Covenant in Jeremiah XXXI 31–34'. *Vetus Testamentum* 33, no. 3 (1983): 347–57.

Poulin, Joan. 'Loving-Kindness towards Gentiles according to the Early Jewish Sages'. *Theologiques* 11, nos. 1–2 (2003): 89–112.

Pregill, Michael. *The Golden Calf between Bible and Qur'an: Scripture, Polemic, and Exegesis from Late Antiquity to Islam*. Oxford: Oxford University Press, 2020.

Preston, Jesse L., Ryan S. Ritter and Justin Helper. 'Neuroscience and the Soul: Competing Explanations for the Human Experience'. *Cognition* 127, no. 1 (2013): 31–7.

Preuß, Horst Dietrich. '"Auferstehung" in Texten alttestamentlicher Apokalyptik (Jes 26, 7-19; Dan 12, 1–4)'. In *Linguistische Theologie: Bibliche Texte, christliche Verkündigung und theologische Sprachtheorie*, edited by Uwe Gerber und Erhardt Güttgemanns, 131–2. Bonn: Linguistica Biblica, 1972.

Priest, Graham. 'None of the Above: The Catuṣkoṭi in Indian Buddhist Logic'. In *New Directions in Paraconsistent Logic*, edited by Jean-Yves Beziau, Mihir Chakraborty and Soma Dutta, 517–27. New Delhi: Springer, 2015.

Prinsloo, W.S. 'Psalm 116: Disconnected Text or Symmetrical Whole?' *Biblica* 74, no. 1 (1993): 71–82.

Pryke, John. '"Spirit" and "Flesh" in the Qumran Documents and Some New Testament Texts'. *Revue de Qumrân* 5, no. 3 (1965): 345–60.

Pummer, Reinhard. *Early Christian Authors on Samaritans and Samaritanism: Texts, Translations and Commentary*. Tübingen: Mohr Siebeck, 2002.

Pun, Pattle P.T. 'A Theology of Progressive Creationism'. *Perspectives on Science and Christian Faith* 39, (1987): 9–19.

Qazi, Faisal, Joshua C. Ewell, Ayla Munawar, Usman Asrar and Nadir Khan. 'The Degree of Certainty in Brain Death: Probability in Clinical and Islamic Legal Discourse'. *Theoretical Medicine and Bioethics* 34, no. 2 (2013): 117–31.

Quarles, Charles L. 'Matthew 27:51–53: Meaning, Genre, Intertextuality, Theology, and Reception History'. *Journal of the Evangelical Theological Society* 59, no. 2 (2016): 271–86.

Quirke, Stephen. 'Creation Stories in Ancient Egypt'. In *Imagining Creation*, edited by Markham Geller and Mineke Schipper, 61–86. Leiden: Brill, 2007.

Rackett, Michael R. 'What's Wrong with Pelagianism? Augustine and Jerome on the Dangers of Pelagius and His Followers'. *Augustinian Studies* 33, no. 2 (2002): 223–37.

Radford, Lewis B. 'Psalm LXXXIV: A Study in the History of Biblical Interpretation'. *The Expository Times* 42, no. 12 (1931): 556–62.

Rady, Mohamed Y. and Joseph L. Verheijde. 'Brain-Dead Patients Are Not Cadavers: The Need to Revise the Definition of Death in Muslim Communities'. *HEC Forum* 25, no. 1 (2013): 25–45.

Rady, Mohamed Y. and Joseph L. Verheijde. 'A Response to the Legitimacy of Brain Death in Islam'. *Journal of Religion and Health* 55, no. 4 (2013): 1198–205.

Rahman, Fazlur. *Major Themes of the Qur'ān*. Beirut: Bibliotheca Islamica, 1980.

Rainey, Anson F. *The El-Amarna Correspondence: A New Edition of the Cuneiform Letters from the Site of El-Amarna Based on Collations of All Extant Tablets*. Leiden: Brill, 2015.

Rakesh, Mohammad and Ayati, S.M.R. 'The Concept of Death: A Religio-philosophical Analysis'. *Islam and Christian-Muslim Relations* 18, no. 3 (2007): 377–89.

Raphael, Simcha P. *Jewish Views of the Afterlife*. London: Rowman & Littlefield, 1994.

Raman, N.S.S. 'Reincarnation and Personal Identity: The Circle and the End of History in Hinduism'. In *Progress, Apocalypse, and Completion of History and Life after Death of the Human Person in the World Religions*, edited by Peter Koslowski, 8–21. Dordrecht: Kluwer Academic, 2002.

Randhawa, G. 'Death and Organ Donation: Meeting the Needs of Multiethnic and Multifaith Populations'. *British Journal of Anaesthesia* 108, no. S1 (2012): i88–i91.

Reddit, Paul L. 'The Two Shepherds in Zechariah 11:4–17'. *Catholic Biblical Quarterly* 55, no. 4 (1993): 676–86.

Reeves, John C. 'Some Explorations of the Intertwining of Bible and Qur'ān'. In *Bible and Qur'ān: Essays in Scriptural Intertextuality*, edited by John C. Reeves, 43–60. Atlanta, GA: Society of Biblical Literature, 2003.

Reicke, Bo. *The Disobedient Spirits and Christian Baptism: A Study of 1 Peter III.19 and Its Context*. Eugene, OR: Wipf & Stock, 2005.

Renard, John. 'Images of Abraham in the Writings of Jalāl ad-Dīn Rūmī'. *Journal of the American Oriental Society* 106, no. 4 (1986): 633–40.

Reynolds, Gabriel S. *The Qur'ān and Its Biblical Subtext*. Abingdon: Routledge, 2010.

Reynolds, Gabriel S. 'On the Qur'anic Accusation of Scriptural Falsification (*taḥrīf*) and Christian Anti-Jewish Polemic'. *Journal of the American Oriental Society* 130, no. 2 (2010): 189–202.

Reynolds, Gabriel S. *The Qur'ān and the Bible: Text and Commentary*. New Haven, CT: Yale University Press, 2018.

Rezakhani, Khodadad. 'Mazdakism, Manichaeism and Zoroastrianism: In Search of Orthodoxy and Heterodoxy in Late Antique Iran'. *Iranian Studies* 48, no. 1 (2015): 55–70.

Riaud, Jean. 'Les Paralipomena Jeremiae dépendent-ils de 2 Baruch?' *Sileno* 9, (1983): 105–28.

Riaud, Jean. 'Le Puissant t'emportera dans ta tente: La destinée ultime du Juste selon les Paralipomena Jeremiae Prophetae'. In *Hellenica et Judaica: hommage à Valentin Nikiprowetzky*, edited by André Caquot, Hadas-Lebel, Mireille and Riaud, Jean, 257–65. Leuven: Peeters, 1986.

Riaud, Jean. 'The Figure of Jeremiah in the *Paralipomena Jeremiae Prophetae*: His Originality; His "Christianization" by the Christian Author of the Conclusion (9.10–32)'. *Journal for the Study of the Pseudepigrapha* 11, no. 22 (2000): 31–44.

Rice, Gene. 'Elijah's Requirement for Prophetic Leadership (2 Kings 2:1–18)'. *Journal of Religious Thought* 59, no. 1 (2006): 1.

Richard, Roberta J. 'HT 31: An Interpretation'. *Kadmos* 13, no. 1 (1974): 6–8.

Richards, Edward G. *Mapping Time: The Calendar and Its History*. Oxford: Oxford University Press, 1999.

Ring, George C. 'Christ's Resurrection and the Dying and Rising Gods'. *Catholic Biblical Quarterly* 6, no. 2 (1944): 216–29.

Rippin, Andrew (ed.). *Approaches to the History of the Interpretation of the Qur'ān*. Oxford: Clarendon Press, 1988.

Roberts, Nancy N. 'A Parable of Blessing: The Significance and Message of the Qur'anic Account of "The Companions of the Cave"'. *The Muslim World* 83, nos. 3–4 (1993): 295–317.

Robinson, A.G. 'Deuteronomy 21:1–9 a Programmatic Anamoly? A Thematic and Programmatic Analysis of Deuteronomy 21:1–9 within the Context of the Deuteronomist's Agenda'. MTh Thesis. Stellenbosch: Stellenbosch University, 2016.

Robinson, H. Wheeler. *The Christian Doctrine of Man*. Edinburgh: T&T Clark, 1911.

Robinson, Neal. *Discovering the Qur'an: A Contemporary Approach to a Veiled Text*, London: SCM, 1996.

Robinson, S.E. '4 Baruch: A New Translation and Introduction'. In *The Old Testament Pseudepigrapha and the New Testament: Expansions of the 'Old Testament' and Legends, Wisdom, and Philosophical Literature, Prayers, Psalms and Odes, Fragments of Lost Judeo-Hellenistic Works*, edited by James H. Charlesworth, 2: 415–16. New Haven, CT: Yale University Press, 1985.

Rodriguez, Angel M. 'The Heavenly Books of Life and of Human Deeds'. *Journal of the Adventist Theological Society* 13, no. 1 (2002): 10–26.

Roman, André. *Étude de la phonologie et de la morphologie de la koinè arabe*. Aix en Provence: Diffusion, 1983.

Ron, Zvi. 'The Death of Honi the Circle Maker'. *Review of Rabbinic Judaism* 20, no. 2 (2017): 235–50.

Rosenberg, Arnold S. *Jewish Liturgy as a Spiritual System: A Prayer-by-Prayer Explanation of the Nature and Meaning of Jewish Worship*. Lanham, MD: Rowman & Littlefield, 2004.

Rothenberg, Naftali. *Rabbi Akiva's Philosophy of Love*. Basingstoke: Palgrave Macmillan, 2017.

Routledge, Robin L. 'Death and Afterlife in the Old Testament'. *Journal of European Baptist Studies* 9, no. 1 (2008): 22–39.

Rubenstein, Jeffrey L. 'Sukkot, Eschatology and Zechariah 14'. *Revue Biblique* 103, no. 2 (1996): 161–95.

Rubin, Nissan. 'From Corpse to Corpus: The Body as a Text in Talmudic Literature'. In *Self, Soul, and Body in Religious Experience*, edited by Albert I. Baumgarten, Jan Assmann and Guy G. Stroumsa, 171–83. Leiden: Brill, 1998.

Rubinger, Naphtali J. 'Jeremiah's Epistle to the Exiles and the Field in Anathoth'. *Judaism* 26, no. 1 (1977): 84–91.

Rudman, Dominic. 'Water for Impurity or Water of Impurity? The Red Cow of Numbers 19 Revisited'. *Old Testament Essays* 16, no. 1 (2003): 73–8.

Rudolph, Wilhelm *Handbuch zum Alten Testament*, edited by O. Eissfeldt. Tübingen: Mohr Siebeck, 1968.

Russell, David S. *The Method & Message of Jewish Apocalyptic, 200* BC–AD *100*. London: SCM, 1964.

Rustomji, Nerina. *The Garden and the Fire: Heaven and Hell in Islamic Culture*. New York, NY: Columbia University Press, 2008.

Rutgers, L.V. 'Death and Afterlife: The Inscriptional Evidence'. In *Judaism in Late Antiquity: Death, Life-after-Death, Resurrection and the World-to-Come in the Judaisms of Antiquity*, edited by Alan J. Avery-Peck and Jacob Neusner, 293–310. Leiden: Brill, 2000.

Ryan, Jordan J. *The Role of the Synagogue in the Aims of Jesus*. Minneapolis, MN: Fortress, 2017.

Sabbath, Roberta. 'Iterations of One: The Shema as Polemical Trope in the Synoptic Gospels and Qur'an'. *Biblical Theology Bulletin* 48, no. 3 (2018): 133–47.

Sadeqzadeh, Fatemeh. 'Ibn Sina's Difficulties on the Adoption or Rejection of Bodily Resurrection'. *Philosophy of Religion Research* 13, no. 1 (2015): 89–110.

Saeed, Abdullah. *The Qur'an: An Introduction*. Abingdon: Routledge, 2008.

Ṣāfī, Maḥmūd (d. 1376/1957) *al-Jadwal fī iʿrāb al-Qurʾān al-karīm*. Damascus: al-Rashīd, 1998.

Saldarini, Anthony J. *Pharisees, Scribes and Sadducees in Palestinian Society: A Sociological Approach*. Grand Rapids, MI: Eerdmans, 2001.

Sala, Nohemi and Nicholas Conrad. 'Taphonomic Analysis of the Hominin Remains from Swabian Jura and Their Implications for the Mortuary Practices during Upper Paleolithic'. *Quaternary Science Review* 150, no. 15 (2016): 278–300.

Samār, Saʿd ʿA. *Dirāsāt fil-muʿtaqadāt al-ijtimāʿiyyah ʿind al-ʿarab qabl al-Islām*. Damascus: Tamūz, 2014.

Samuels, Jeffrey. 'The Bodhisattva Ideal in Theravāda Buddhist Theory and Practice: A Reevaluation of the Bodhisattva-Śrāvaka Opposition'. *Philosophy East & West* 47, no. 3 (1997): 399–415.

Sanders, E.P. *Judaism: Practice and Belief, 63 BCE–66 CE*, Minneapolis: Fortress, 2016.

Sani, Iro and Mustapha B. Ruma. 'Concretizing the Abstract: Conceptual Metaphors in the Holy Qurʾan'. *European Academic Research* 2, no. 8 (2014).

Ṣaqr, Shiḥātah Muḥammad. *Kashf shubuhāt al-ṣūfiyyah*. Beheira: al-ʿUlūm, n.d.

Sardaraz, Khan and Roslan bin Ali. 'Conceptualisation of Death and Resurrection in the Holy Quran: A Cognitive-Semantic Approach'. *Journal of Nusantara Studies* 1, no. 2 (2016): 11–24.

Saucy, Robert L. 'Theology of Human Nature'. In *Christian Perspectives on Being Human: A Multidisciplinary Approach to Integration*, edited by J.P. Moreland and David M. Ciocchi, 17–54. Eugene, OR: Wipf & Stock, 1993.

Sawyer, John F.A. 'The Meaning of BARZEL in the Biblical Expressions "Chariots of Iron", "Yoke of Iron", etc.'. In *Midian, Moab and Edom: The History and Archaeology of Late Bronze and Iron Age Jordan and North-West Arabia*, edited by John F.A. Sawyer and David J.A. Clines, 129–34. Sheffield: Journal for the Study of the Old Testament Press, 1983.

Sawyer, John F.A. '"My Secret Is with Me" (Isaiah 24,16): Some Semantic Links between Isaiah 24-27 and Daniel'. In *Understanding Poets and Prophets: Essays in Honour of George Wishart Anderson*, edited by A. Graeme Auld, 307–17. Sheffield: Sheffield Academic, 1993.

Schaberg, Jane. 'Major Midrashic Traditions in Wisdom 1, 1–6, 25'. *Journal for the Study of Judaism* 13, no. 1 (1982): 75–101.

Scharlemann, Martin H. '"He Descended into Hell" An Interpretation of 1 Peter 3:18–20'. *Concordia Theological Monthly* 27, no. 2 (1956): 81–94.

Schenk, Wolfgang. *Der Passionsbericht nach Markus: Untersuchungen zur Überlieferungsgeschichte der Passionstraditionen*. Gütersloh: Gütersloher, 1974.

Schiffman, Lawrence H. *From Text to Tradition: A History of Second Temple and Rabbinic Judaism*. Hoboken, NJ: Ktav, 1991.

Schiffman, Lawrence H. *Understanding Second Temple and Rabbinic Judaism*, edited by Jon Bloomberg and Samuel Kapustin. Hoboken, NJ: Ktav, 2003.

Schipper, Bernd U. 'Egypt and Israel: The Ways of Cultural Contacts in the Late Bronze Age and Iron Age (20th–26th Dynasty)'. *Journal of Ancient Egyptian Interconnections* 4, no. 3 (2012): 30–47.

Schliesser, Benjamin. *Abraham's Faith in Romans 4: Paul's Concept of Faith in Light of the History Reception of Genesis 15:6*. Tübingen: Mohr Siebeck, 2007.

Schliesser, Benjamin. '"Abraham Did Not 'Doubt' in Unbelief" (Rom. 4:20): Faith, Doubt, and Dispute in Paul's Letter to the Romans'. *The Journal for Theological Studies* 63, no. 2 (2012): 492–522.

Schmid, Herbert. 'Baruch und die ihm zugeschriebene apokryphe und pseudepigraphische Literatu'. *Judaica* 30, (1974): 54–70.

Schmid, Konrad. 'Loss of Immortality? Hermeneutical Aspects of Genesis 2–3 and Its Early Receptions'. In *Beyond Eden: The Biblical Story of Paradise and Its Reception History*, edited by Konrad Schmid and Christoph Riedweg, 58–78. Tübingen: Mohr Siebeck, 2008.

Schmidtke, Sabine. 'The Doctrine of the Transmigration of Soul according to Shihāb al-Dīn al-Suhrawardī (killed 587/1191) and His Followers'. *Studia Iranica* 28, no. 2 (1999): 237–54.

Schmithals, Walter. *Gnosticism in Corinth: An Investigation of the Letters to the Corinthians.* Nashville, TN: Abingdon, 1971.

Schmitz, Philip C. 'The Grammar of Resurrection in Isaiah 26:19a-c'. *Journal of Biblical Literature* 122, no. 1 (2003): 145–9.

Schnackenburg, Rudolf. *The Gospel According to St. John.* New York, NY: Seabury, 1980.

Schneider, Thomas. 'Foreign Egypt: Egyptology and the Concept of Cultural Appropriation'. *Ägypten und Levante* 13, (2003): 155–61.

Schoenfeld, Devorah. *Isaac on Jewish and Christian Altars: Polemic and Exegesis in Rashi and the Glossa Ordinaria.* New York, NY: Fordham University Press, 2013.

Schoff, Wilfred H. 'Camphor'. *Journal of the American Oriental Society* 42, (1922): 355–70.

Scholl, Reinhard. *Die Elenden in Gottes Thronrat: stilistisch-kompositorische Untersuchungen zu Jesaja 24–27.* Berlin: De Gruyter, 2000.

Schoors, Antoon. 'Koheleth: A Perspective of Life after Death?' *Ephemerides theologicae Lovanienses: commentarii de re theological et canonica* 61 (1985): 301–2.

Schroeder, Gerald L. 'Evolution: The Biblical Account of Life's Development'. In *Origin(s) of Design in Nature: A Fresh, Interdisciplinary Look at How Design Emerges in Complex Systems, Especially Life*, edited by Liz Swan, Richard Gordon and Joseph Seckbach, 287–97. Dordrecht: Springer, 2012.

Schurer, Emil. *The History of the Jewish People in the Age of Jesus Christ.* London: T&T Clark, 2014.

Scurlock, JoAnn. 'Death and the Afterlife in Ancient Mesopotamian Thought'. In *Civilizations of the Ancient Near East*, edited by Jack M. Sasson, 3: 1883–93. New York, NY: Simon and Schuster Macmillan, 1995.

Scurlock, JoAnn. 'Soul Emplacements in Ancient Mesopotamian Funerary Rituals'. In *Magic and Divination in the Ancient World*, edited by Leda Ciraolo and Jonathan Seidel; Ancient Magic and Divination 2. Leiden: Brill, 2002.

Scurlock, JoAnn. 'Images of Tammuz: The Intersection of Death, Divinity, and Royal Authority in Ancient Mesopotamia'. In *Experiencing Power, Generating Authority: Cosmos, Politics, and the Ideology, of Kingship in Ancient Egypt and Mesopotamia*, edited by Jane A. Hill, Philip Jones and Antonio J. Morales, 151–84. Philadelphia, PA: University of Pennsylvania Press, 2013.

Sedgwick, Peter. 'Who Am I Now? Theology and Self-Identity'. *Theology* 104, no. 819 (2001): 196–203.

Seeligerms, Hans R. 'Erwägungen zu Hintergrund und Zweck des apokalyptischen Schlusskapitels der *Didache*'. In *Studia Patristica: Second Century, Tertullian to Nicaea in the West, Clement of Alexandria and Origen, Athanasius*, edited by Elizabeth A. Livingstone, vol. 21, 184–93. Leuven: Peeters, 1989.

Segal, Alan. *Life after Death: A History of the Afterlife in Western Religion.* New York, NY: Doubleday, 2010.

Segal, Eran. 'Religious Objections to Brain Death'. *Journal of Critical Care* 29, no. 5 (2014): 875–7.

Seidensticker, Tilman. 'The Authenticity of the Poems Ascribed to Umayya bin Abī al-Ṣalt'. In *Tradition and Modernity in Arabic Language and Literature*, edited by Jack R. Smart, 87–101. London: Curzon, 1996.

Seitz, Christopher R. 'The Crisis of Interpretation over the Meaning and Purpose of the Exile: A Redactional Study of Jeremiah XXI–XLIII'. *Vetus Testamentum* 35, no. 1 (1985): 78–97.

Senior, Donald. 'The Death of Jesus and the Resurrection of the Holy Ones (Mt 27:51–53)'. *Catholic Biblical Quarterly* 38, no. 3 (1976): 312–29.

Sergi, Omer. 'The United Monarchy and the Kingdom of Jeroboam II in the Story of Absalom and Sheba's Revolts (2 Samuel 15–20)'. *Hebrew Bible and Ancient Israel* 6, no. 3 (2017): 329–53.

Serpell, James A. 'Animals and Religion: Towards a Unifying Theory'. In *The Human-Animal Relationship: Forever and a Day*, edited by Francien de Jonge and Ruud van den Bos, 9–22. Assen: Royal Van Gorcum, 2005.

Setzer, Claudia. 'Resurrection of the Dead as Symbol and Strategy'. *Journal of the American Academy of Religion* 69, no. 1 (2001): 65–102.

Setzer, Claudia. *Resurrection of the Body in Early Judaism and Eary Christianity: Doctrine, Community, and Self-Definition*. Leiden: Brill, 2004.

Shah-Kazemi, Reza. 'The Wisdom of Gratitude in Islam'. In *The World's Greatest Wisdom: Timeless Teachings from Religions and Philosophies*, edited by Roger Walsh, 55–86. Albany, NY: State University of New York Press, 2014.

Shahraki, Habiballah D. and Mahin Keramatifard. 'Bodily Resurrection from Sadrol Motalehin Point of View and Its Evaluation with Chapters of Quran'. *The Social Sciences* 11, no. 6 (2016): 804–9.

Sharifi, Enayatollah, Mohammad H. Khavaninzadeh, and Alireza Ansarimanesh. 'Bodily Resurrection in the Quran and the Bible'. *Āfāq-i Dīn* 6, no. 21 (2015): 7–41.

Sharifi, Hadi. 'Self-realization in the Domain of Islamic Gnosis'. *Islamic Quarterly* 30, no. 4 (1986): 221–36.

Shams, M.J. 'Khurramdīnīyyah or Khurramīyyah'. *Journal of Religious Studies* 3, no. 6 (2010): 55–80.

Shead, Andrew G. *A Mouth Full of Fire: The Word of God in the Words of Jeremiah*. Downers Grove, IL: InterVarsity Press, 2012.

Shehata, Dahlia. *Annotierte Bibliographie zum altbabylonischen Atramḫasīs-Mythos Inūma ilū awīlum*. Göttingen: Seminar für Keilschriftforschung der Universität Göttinegen, 2001.

Shepkaru, Shmuel. 'From After Death to Afterlife: Martyrdom and Its Recompense'. *AJS Review* 24, no. 1 (1999): 1–44.

Shewmon, D. Alan. 'Constructing the Death Elephant: A Synthetic Paradigm Shift for the Definition, Criteria, and Tests for Death'. *The Journal of Medicine and Philosophy* 3, no. 1 (2010): 256–98.

Shihadeh, Ayman. 'Classical Ashʿarī Anthropology: Body, Life, and Spirit'. *The Muslim World* 102, nos. 3–4 (2012): 433–77.

Shihadeh, Ayman. 'Al-Ghazālī and Kalām: The Conundrum of His Body-Soul Dualism'. In *Islam and Rationality: The Impact of al-Ghazali. Papers Collected on His 900th Anniversary, Vol. 2*, edited by Frank Griffel, 113–41. Leiden: Brill, 2016.

Shopenhauer, Arthur. *The World as Will and Representation*, translated by E.F.J. Payne. New York, NY: Dover, 1966.

Sībawayh (d. 180/796). *al-Kitāb*, edited by ʿAbdulsalām Muḥammad Hārūn. Cairo: Maktabah al-Khānjī, 1988.

Siegel, Ronald K. 'The Psychology of Life after Death'. *American Psychologist* 35, no. 10 (1980): 911–31.
Sigvartsen, Jan A. 'The Afterlife Views and the Use of the TaNaKh in Support of the Resurrection Concept in the Literature of Second Temple Period Judaism: The Apocrypha and the Pseudepigrapha'. PhD Dissertation. Berrien Springs, MI: Andrews University, 2016.
Sigvartsen, Jan A. *Afterlife and Resurrection Beliefs in the Pseudepigrapha*. London: T&T Clark, 2019.
Silver, Daniel J. *Maimonidean Criticism and the Maimonidean Controversy 1180–1240*. Leiden: Brill, 1965.
Simeon, C. *Horae Homileticae: Psalms, LXXIII–CL*. London: Samuel Holdsworth, 1836.
Simmons, Alan H. *The Neolithic Revolution in the Near East: Transforming the Human Landscape*. Tucson, AZ: University of Arizona Press, 2007.
Simon-Shoshan, Moshe. 'Past Continuous: The Yerushalmi's Account of Honi's Long Sleep and Its Roots in Second Temple Era Literature'. *Journal for the Study of Judaism* 51, no. 3 (2020): 398–431.
Sinai, Nicolai. 'Religious Poetry from the Quranic Milieu: Umayya b. Abī l-Ṣalt on the Fate of the Thamūd'. *Bulletin of the School of Oriental and African Studies* 74, no. 3 (2011): 397–416.
Sinai, Nicolai. 'Pharaoh's Submission to God in the Qur'an and in Rabbinic Literature: A case Study in Qur'anic Intertextuality'. In *The Qur'an's Reformation of Judaism and Christianity: Return to the Origins*, edited by Holger M. Zellentin, 235–60. Abingdon: Routledge, 2019.
Singh, R. Raj. *Death, Contemplation, and Schopenhauer*. Aldershot: Ashgate, 2007.
Sivertsev, Alexei. *Households, Sects, and the Origins of Rabbinic Judaism*. Leiden: Brill, 2005.
Skålvold, Maja L. 'Images of Death in the Song of Hezekiah and the Conceptual World of the Ancient Near East: The Role of the Comparison in Interpretation of Biblical Texts'. Cand. Theol. Thesis. Oslo: MF Norwegian School of Theology, 2013.
Smith, Jane I. 'The Understanding of *Nafs* and *Rūḥ* in Contemporary Muslim Considerations of the Nature of Sleep and Death'. *The Muslim World* 68, no. 3 (1979): 151–61.
Smith, Jane I. 'Concourse between the Living and the Dead in Islamic Eschatological Literature'. *History of Religions* 19, no. 3 (1980): 224–36.
Smith, Jane I. and Haddad, Yvonne Y. 1981. *The Islamic Understanding of Death and Resurrection*. Oxford: Oxford University Press, 2002.
Smith, Margaret. 'Transmigration and the Sufis'. *The Muslim World* 30, no. 4 (1940): 351–7.
Smith, Mark S. 'The Psalms as a Book for Pilgrims'. *Interpretation* 46, no. 2 (1992): 156–66.
Smith, Wilfred C. 'The Study of Religion and the Study of the Bible'. *Journal of the American Academy of Religion* 39 (1971): 131–40.
Smith, Wilfred C. *What Is Scripture?: A Comparative Approach*, Minneapolis, MN: Fortress, 1993.
Snyman, S.D. 'Malachi 4:4–6 (Heb 3:22–24) as a Point of Convergence in the Old Testament or Hebrew Bible: A Consideration of the Intra and Intertextual Relationships'. *HTS Theological Studies* 68, no. 1 (2012): 1–6.
Solomon, Sheldon, Jeff Greenberg, Jeff Schimel, Jamie Arndt and Tom Pyszczynski. 'Human Awareness of Mortality and the Evolution of Culture'. In *The Psychological Foundations of Culture*, edited by Mark Schaller and Christian S. Crandall, 15–40. Mahwah, NJ: Lawrence Erlbaum, 2004.

Souter, Michael and Gail van Norman. 'Ethical Controversies at End of Life after Traumatic Brain Injury. Defining Death and Organ Donation'. *Critical Care Medicine* 38, no. 9 (2010): S502–S509.

Sparks, Rachael T. 'Canaan in Egypt: Archaeological Evidence for a Social Phenomenon'. In *Invention and Innovation: The Social Context of Technological Change 2: Egypt, the Aegean and the Near East, 1650–1150* BC, edited by Janine Bourriau and Jacke Phillips. Oxford: Oxbow Books, 2004.

Speck, Frank G. *Naskapi: The Savage Hunters of the Labrador Peninsula*. Norman: University of Oklahoma Press, 1977.

Speiser, E.A. (trans.). *The Ancient Near Eastern Texts Relating to the Old Testament*, edited by James B. Pritchard, 3rd ed., 104–7. Princeton, NJ: Princeton University Press, 1969.

Spitz, Elie. '"Through Her I Too Shall Bear a Child": Birth Surrogates in Jewish Law'. *The Journal of Religious Ethics* 24, no. 1 (1996): 65–97.

Spooner, Brian. *Population Growth: Anthropological Implications*. Cambridge, MA: MIT Press, 1972.

Spronk, Klaas. *Beatific Afterlife in Ancient Israel and in the Ancient Near East*. Kevelaer: Butzon & Bercker, 1986.

Staples, W.E. 'The "Soul" in the Old Testament'. *The American Journal of Semitic Languages and Literatures* 44, no. 3 (1928): 145–76.

Steadman, Lyle B. and Craig T. Palmer. 'Visiting Dead Ancestors: Shamans as Interpreters of Religious Traditions'. *Zygon: Journal of Religion and Science* 29, no. 2 (1994): 173–89.

Steiner, Richard C. *Disembodied Souls: The Nefesh in Israel and Kindred Spirits in the Ancient Near East*. Atlanta: SBL Press, 2015.

Steinert, Ulrike. *Aspekte des Menschseins im Alten Mesopotamien*. Leiden: Brill, 2012.

Stemberger, Günter. 'Genesis 15 in Rabbinic and Patristic Interpretation'. In *The Exegetical Encounter between Jews and Christians in Late Antiquity*, edited by Emmanouela Grypeou and Helen Spurling, 143–62. Leiden: Brill, 2009.

Stenmark, Mikael. 'Theories of Human Nature: Key Issues'. *Philosophy Compass* 7, no. 8 (2012): 543–58.

Stepaniants, Marietta. 'The Encounter of Zoroastrianism with Islam'. *Philosophy East and West* 52, no. 2 (2002): 159–72.

Stetkevych, Suzanne P. 'From *Jāhiliyyah* to *Badī'iyyah*: Orality, Literacy, and the Transformations of Rhetoric in Arabic Poetry'. *Oral Tradition* 25, no. 1 (2010): 211–30.

Stewart, Devin. 'Poetic License and the Qur'anic Names of Hell: The Treatment of Cognate Substitution in al-Rāghib al-Iṣfahānī's Qur'anic License'. In *The Meaning of the Word: Lexicology and Qur'anic Exegesis*, edited by Stephen R. Burge, 195–253. Oxford: Oxford University Press, 2015.

Strange, John. 'The Idea of Afterlife in Ancient Israel: Some Remarks on the Iconography in Solomon's Temple'. *Palestine Exploration Quarterly* 117, no. 1 (1985): 35–40.

Strong, John T. 'Egypt's Shameful Death and the House of Israel's Exodus from Sheol (Ezekiel 32.17–32 and 37.1–14)'. *Journal for the Study of the Old Testament* 34, no. 4 (2010): 475–504.

Sugunasiri, Suwanda H.J. '"Asoulity" as Translation of Anattā: Absence, Not Negation'. *Canadian Journal of Buddhist Studies* 7 (2011): 101–34.

Suh, Robert H. 'The Use of Ezekiel 37 in Ephesians'. *Journal of the Evangelical Theological Society* 50, no. 4 (2007): 715–33.

Sukdaven, Maniraj, Asgher Mukhtar and Hamid Fernana. 'A Timbuktu Manuscript Expressing the Mystical Thoughts of Yusuf-ibn-Said'. *Journal for the Study of Religion* 28, no. 2 (2015): 181–201.

Sumegi, Angela. *Understanding Death: An Introduction to Ideas of Self and the Afterlife in World Religions*. Chichester: Wiley, 2014.

Swineburn, Richard. *The Evolution of the Soul*. Oxford: Oxford University Press, 1997.

Sysling, Harry. *Teḥiyyat ha-Metim: The Resurrection of the Dead in the Palestinian Targums of the Pentateuch and Parallel Traditions in Classical Rabbinic Literature*. Tübingen: Mohr Siebeck, 1996.

Tabor, James D. '"Returning to the Divinity": Josephus's Portrayal of the Disappearance of Enoch, Elijah, and Moses'. *Journal of Biblical Literature* 108, no. 2 (1989): 225–38.

Talmon-Heller, Daniella. 'Reciting the Qur'an and Reading the Torah: Muslim and Jewish Attitudes and Practices in a Comparative Historical Perspective'. *Religion Compass* 6, no. 8 (2012): 369–80.

Tan, Kim H. 'The Shema and Early Christianity'. *Tyndale Bulletin* 59, no. 2 (2008): 181–206.

Taylor, John H. *Death and the Afterlife in Ancient Egypt*. Chicago, IL: University of Chicago Press, 2001.

Taylor, Richard. 'The Anattā Doctrine and Personal Identity'. *Philosophy East and West* 19, no. 4 (1969): 359–66.

Taylor, Timothy. *The Buried Soul: How Humans Invented Death*, Boston, MA: Beacon, 2002.

Telford, William R. *The Barren Temple and the Withered Tree: A Redaction-Critical Analysis of the Cursing of the Fig-Tree Pericope in Mark's Gospel and Its Relation to the Cleansing of the Temple Tradition*. Sheffield: Sheffield Academic, 1980.

Tesei, Tommaso. 'The *barzakh* and the Intermediate State of the Dead in the Quran'. In *Locating Hell in Islamic Traditions*, edited by Christian Lange, 29–55. Leiden: Brill, 2015.

The Holy Bible: New Revised Standard Version. Nashville, TN: Thomas Nelson, 1989.

Thiessen, Matthew. 'A Buried Pentateuchal Allusion to the Resurrection in Mark 12:25'. *Catholic Biblical Quarterly* 76, no. 2 (2014): 273–90.

Thomas, Albert G. 'Continuing the Definition of Death Debate: The Report of the President's Council on Bioethics on Controversies in the Determination of Death'. *Bioethics* 26, no. 2 (2012): 101–7.

Thomas, D. Winston. 'צלמות in the Old Testament'. *Journal of Semitic Studies* 7, no. 2 (1962): 191–200.

Thomassen, Einar. 'Islamic Hell'. *Numen* 56, no. 2 (2009): 401–16.

Tiemeyer, Lena-Sofia. *Zechariah's Vision Report and Its Earliest Interpreters: A Redaction-Critical Study of Zechariah 1–8*. London: T&T Clark, 2016.

Tigchelaar, E.J.C. and García Martínez. 'Iranian Influences in Qumran?' *Qumranica Minora I: Qumran Origins and Apocalypticism*, edited by E.J.C. Tigchelaar and García Martínez, 227–42. Leiden: Brill, 2007.

Tirard, Stephane, Michel Morange, and Antonio Lazcano. 'The Definition of Life: A Brief History of an Elusive Scientific Endeavor'. *Astrobiology* 10, no. 10 (2010): 1003–9.

Tisdall, William St. Clair. *The Original Sources of the Qur'an: Its Origin in Pagan Legends and Mythology*. London: Society for Promoting Christian Knowledge, 1905.

Tlili, Sarra. *Animals in the Qur'an*. Cambridge: Cambridge University Press, 2012.

Tlili, Sarra. 'From Breath to Soul: The Quranic Word Ruh and Its (Mis)interpretations'. In *Arabic Humanities, Islamic Thought: Essays in Honor of Everett K. Rowson*, edited by Joseph Lowry and Shawkat Toorawa, 1–21. Leiden: Brill, 2017.

Tobin, Thomas H. 'What Shall We Say that Abraham Found? The Controversy behind Romans 4'. *Harvard Theological Review* 88, no. 4 (1995): 437–52.

Tobin, Thomas H. 'The Jewish Context of Rom 5:12–14'. *Studia Philonica Annual* 13, (2001): 159–75.
Torrey, Charles C. *The Jewish Foundation of Islam*. New York, NY: Jewish Institute of Religion Press, 1933.
Treves, Marco. 'Conjectures Concerning the Date and Authorship of Zechariah IX-XIV'. *Vetus Testamentum* 13, no. 1 (1963): 196–207.
Trick, Bradley R. 'Death, Covenants, and the Proof of Resurrection in Mark 12:18–27'. *Novum Testamentum* 49, no. 3 (2007): 232–56.
Tromp, Johannes. 'Can These Bones Live? Ezekiel 37:1–14 and Eschatological Resurrection'. In *The Book of Ezekiel and Its Influence*, edited by Henk J. Jonge and Johannes Tromp, 61–78. Aldershot: Ashgate, 2007.
Troxel, Ronald L. 'Matt 27.51–4 Reconsidered: Its Role in the Passion Narrative, Meaning and Origin'. *New Testament Studies* 48 (2002): 30–47.
Truog, Robert D. 2006. 'Is It Time to Abandon Brain Death?' In *Organ and Tissue Transplantation*, edited by David Price, 3–12. Abingdon: Routledge, 2016 (orig. Farnham: Ashgate).
Truog, Robert D. and Franklin G. Miller. 'Defining Death: The Importance of Scientific Candor and Transparency'. *Intensive Care Medicine* 40, no. 6 (2014): 885–7.
Truog, Robert D. and Franklin G. Miller. 'Changing the Conversation about Brain Death'. *The American Journal of Bioethics* 14, no. 8 (2014): 9–14.
Tsokolov, Serhiy A. 'Why Is the Definition of Life So Elusive? Epistemological Considerations'. *Astrobiology* 9, no. 4 (2009): 401–12.
Tuell, Steven S. 'True Metaphor: Insights into Reading Scripture from the Rabbis'. *Theology Today* 67, no. 4 (2011): 467–75.
Tukasi, Emmanuel O. 'Dualism and Penitential Prayer in the Rule of the Community (1QS)'. In *Dualism in Qumran*, edited by Géza G. Xeravits, 166–88. London: T&T Clark, 2010.
Turner, Colin. 'Wealth as an Immortality Symbol in the Qur'an: A Reconsideration of the *māl*/*amwāl* Verses'. *Journal of Qur'anic Studies* 8, no. 1 (2006): 58–83.
Turpin, Simon. 'Did Death of Any Kind Exist before the Fall? What the Bible Says about the Origin of Death and Suffering'. *Answers Research Journal* 6, (2013): 99–116.
ʿUbayd, Aḥmad Muḥammad (ed.). *Shuʿarāʾ ʿUmān*. Abu Dhabi: al-Mujammaʿ al-Thaqāfī, 2000.
Uitti, Roger W. 'Health and Wholeness in the Old Testament'. *Consensus* 17, no. 2 (1991): 47–62.
Ulmer, Rivka. 'The Advancement of Arguments in Exegetical Midrash Compared to that of the Greek ΔΙΑΤΡΙΒΗ'. *Journal for the Study of Judaism in the Persian, Hellenistic, and Roman Period* 28, no. 1 (1997): 48–91.
van Acker, David. 'צלמות: An Etymological and Semantic Reconsideration'. *Journal of Northwest Semitic Languages* 43, no. 2 (2017): 97–123.
van der Horst, Pieter W. 'Pious Long-Sleepers in Greek, Jewish, and Christian Antiquity'. In *Tradition, Transmission, and Transformation from Second Temple Literature through Judaism and Christianity in Late Antiquity*, edited by Menahem Kister, Hillel Newman, Michael Segal and Ruth Clements, 93–111. Leiden: Brill, 2015.
van der Meer, Michaël N. 'Anthropology in the Ancient Greek Versions of Gen 2:7'. In *Dust of the Ground and Breath of Life (Gen 2:7): The Problem of a Dualistic Anthropology in Early Judaism and Christianity*, edited by Jacques T.A.G.M. van Ruiten and Geurt H. van Kooten, 36–57. Leiden: Brill, 2016.
van der Woude, Annemarieke. 'Resurrection or Transformation? Concepts of Death in Isaiah 24–27'. In *Formation and Intertextuality in Isaiah 24–27*, edited by J. Todd

Hibbard and Hyun C. P. Kim, 143–64. Atlanta, GA: Society of Biblical Literature, 2013.

van Dyk, Petrus J. 'The Spirit of God, or Is It?' *HTS Theological Studies* 73, no. 3 (2017).

van Inwagen, Peter. 'The Possibility of Resurrection'. *International Journal for Philosophy of Religion* 9, no. 2 (1978): 114–21.

van Selms, Adriaan (1977) 'siğğīn and siğğīl in the Qur'ān'. *Die Welt des Orients* 9, no. 1 (1977): 99–103.

Vang, Carsten. 'Israel in the Iron-Smelting Furnace? Towards a New Understanding of the כּוּר הַבַּרְזֶל in Deut 4:20'. *HIPHIL Novum* 1, no. 1 (2014): 25–34.

Vawter, Bruce. 'Intimations of Immortality and the Old Testament'. *Journal of Biblical Literature* 91, no. 2 (1972): 158–71.

Viberg, Åke. *Symbols of Law: A Contextual Analysis of Legal Symbolic Acts in the Old Testament*. Uppsala: Almqvist & Wiksell, 1992.

Visotzky, Burton L. 'Genesis in Rabbinic Literature'. In *The Book of Genesis*, edited by Thomas Dozeman, Craig A. Evans and Joel N. Lohr, 579–606. Leiden: Brill, 2012.

Visscher, Gerhard H. *Romans 4 and the New Perspective on Paul: Faith Embraces the Promise*. Bern: Peter Lang, 2009.

Viviano, Benedict T. and Justin Taylor. 'Sadducees, Angels, and Resurrection (Acts 12:8–9)'. *Journal of Biblical Literature* 111, no. 3 (1992): 496–8.

von Ehrenkrook, Jason. 'The Afterlife in Philo and Josephus'. In *Heaven, Hell, and the Afterlife: Eternity in Judaism, Christianity, and Islam*, edited by J. Harold Ellens, 97–118. Santa Barbara, CA: Praeger, 2013.

von Rad, Gerhard. *Genesis, The Old Testament Library*, trans. John H. Marks. Philadelphia, PA: Westminster, 1961.

von Soden, Wolfram. 1952. *Grundriss der Akkadischen Grammatik*, Rome: Editrice Pontificio Istituto Biblico, 1995.

Vroom, Jonathan. *The Authority of Law in the Hebrew Bible and Early Judaism: Tracing the Origins of Legal Obligation from Ezra to Qumran*. Leiden: Brill, 2018.

Walach, Harald. 'Neuroscience, Consciousness, Spirituality: Questions, Problems and Potential Solutions: An Introductory Essay'. In *Neuroscience, Consciousness and Spirituality*, edited by Harald Walach, Stefan Schmidt and Wayne B. Jonas, 1–21. Berlin: Springer, 2011.

Walker, E.D. *Reincarnation: A Study of Forgotten Truth*. Whitefish, MT: Kessinger, 2003.

Walker, Paul E. 'The Doctrine of Metempsychosis in Islam'. In *Islamic Studies Presented to Charles J. Adams*, edited by Wael B. Hallaq and Donald P. Little. Leiden: Brill, 1991.

Walker, Paul E. 'Abū Tammām and His *Kitāb al-Shajara*: A New Ismaili Treatise from Tenth-Century Khurasan'. *Journal of the American Oriental Society* 114, no. 3 (1994): 343–52.

Walton, John H. *Ancient Near Eastern Thought and the Old Testament: Introducing the Conceptual World of the Hebrew Bible*. Grand Rapids, MI: Baker Academic, 2006.

Walvoord, John F. *The Revelation of Jesus Christ*. Chicago, IL: Moody, 1966.

Wan Azura Wan Ahmad, Adnan Yusof, Hisyamuddin Ahmad, Rabiatul Adawiyah Muhamad, Ahmad S. Azmi, Zaini Zakaria and Zati Adlin Mat Jalil. 'The Method of the Qur'an and Its Acoustical Miraculous in Kawniyyat Verses: An Analytical Study through the Antithesis (Al-Tibaq) in the Part (Juz' of Amma)'. *Quranica: International Journal of Quranic Research* 10, no. 2 (2018): 125–38.

Wansbrough, John E. *Qur'anic Studies: Sources and Methods of Scriptural Interpretation*. Oxford: Oxford University Press, 1977.

Wansbrough, John. *The Sectarian Milieu: Content and Composition of Islamic Salvation History*. Oxford: Oxford University Press, 1978.

Wasserman, Emma. 'The Death of the Soul in Romans 7: Revisiting Paul's Anthropology in Light of Hellenistic Moral Psychology'. *Journal of Biblical Literature* 126, no. 4 (2007): 793–816.

Wasserman, Emma. *The Death of the Soul in Romans 7: Sin, Death, and the Law in Light of Hellenistic Moral Psychology*. Tübingen: Mohr Siebeck, 2008.

Wasserman, Tommy. 'The Patmos Family of the New Testament MSS and Its Allies in the Pericope of the Adulteress and Beyond'. *TC: A Journal of Biblical Textual Criticism* 7 (2002).

Wasserstrom, Steven M. *Between Muslim and Jew: The Problem of Symbiosis Under Early Islam*. Princeton, NJ: Princeton University Press, 1995.

Waters, Kenneth L. 'Matthew 27:52–53 as Apocalyptic Apostrophe: Temporal-Spatial Collapse in the Gospel of Matthew'. *Journal of Biblical Literature* 122, no. 3 (2003): 489–515.

Watson, Francis. *Paul and the Hermeneutics of Faith*. London: T&T Clark, 2004.

Watt, W. Montgomery. 'Muḥammad's Contribution in the Field of Ultimate Reality and Meaning'. *Ultimate Reality and Meaning* 5, no. 1 (1982): 26–38.

Watts, James W. *Reading Law: The Rhetorical Shaping of the Pentateuch*. Sheffield: Sheffield Academic, 1999.

Weisdorf, Jacob L. 'From Foraging to Farming: Explaining the Neolithic Revolution'. *Journal of Economic Surveys* 19, no. 4 (2005): 561–86.

Wells, Ronald A. 'The Mythology of Nut and the Birth of Ra'. *Studien zur Altägyptischen Kultur* 19 (1992): 305–21.

Wells, Ronald A. 'Origin of the Hour and the Gates of the Duat'. *Studien zur Altägyptischen Kultur* 20 (1993): 305–26.

Wenham, G.J. 'The Symbolism of the Animal Rite in Genesis 15: A Response to G.F. Hasel, JSOT 19 (1981) 61–78'. *Journal for the Study of the Old Testament* 7, no. 22 (1982): 134–7.

Wenzel, George W. *Animal Rights, Human Rights: Ecology, Economy and Ideology in the Canadian Arctic*. Toronto: University of Toronto Press, 1991.

Weren, Wim J.C. 'The Human Body and Life Beyond Death in Matthew's Gospel'. *Deuterocanonical and Cognate Literature Yearbook* (2009): 267–84.

Wheeler, Brannon. 'Israel and the Torah of Muḥammad'. In *Bible and Qur'ān: Essays in Scriptural Intertextuality*, edited by John C. Reeves, 61–85. Atlanta, GA: Society of Biblical Literature, 2003.

Wheeler, Brannon. 'Arab Prophets of the Qur'an and Bible'. *Journal of Qur'anic Studies* 8, no. 2 (2006): 24–57.

Whitacre, Rodney A. *John*. Downers Grove, IL: InterVarsity Press, 1999.

Whitekettle, Richard. 'All Creatures Great and Small Intermediate Level Taxa in Israelite Zoological Thought'. *Scandinavian Journal of the Old Testament* 16, no. 2 (2002): 163–83.

Whitley, David S. 'Cognitive Neuroscience, Shamanism and the Rock Art of Native California'. *Anthropology of Consciousness* 9, no. 1 (1998): 22–37.

Wiggins, Steve A. 'Tempestuous Wind Doing Yhwh's Will: Perceptions of the Wind in the Psalms'. *Scandinavian Journal of the Old Testament* 13, no. 1 (1999): 3–23.

Williams, Bernard. *Problems of the Self*. Cambridge: Cambridge University Press, 1973.

Williams, Sam K. 'The "Righteousness of God" in Romans'. *Journal of Biblical Literature* 99, no. 2 (1980): 241–90.

Williamson, Paul R. *Abraham, Israel and the Nations: The Patriarchal Promise and Its Covenantal Development in Genesis*. Sheffield: Sheffield Academic, 2000.

Willis, Timothy M. *The Elders of the City: A Study of the Elders-Laws in Deuteronomy*. Atlanta, GA: Society of Biblical Literature Press, 2001.

Wilson, Joe B. 'The Monk as Bodhisattva: A Tibetan Integration of Buddhist Moral Points of View'. *Journal of Religious Ethics* 24, no. 2 (1996): 377–402.

Wilson-Wright, Aren M. 'Love Conquers All: Song of Songs 8:6b–7a as a Reflex of the Northwest Semitic Combat Myth'. *Journal of Biblical Studies* 134, no. 2 (2015): 333–45.

Winkelman, Michael. 'Shamanism as the Original Neurotheology'. *Zygon: Journal of Religion and Science* 39, no. 1 (2004): 193–217.

Winston, David. 'The Iranian Component in the Bible, the Apocrypha, and Qumran: A Review of the Evidence'. *History of Religions* 5, no. 2 (1966): 183–216.

Winston, David. 'Hellenistic Jewish Philosophy'. In *History of Jewish Philosophy*, edited by Daniel H. Frank and Oliver Leaman, 30–48. London: Routledge, 1997.

Wischnitzer-Bernstein, Rachel. 'The Conception of the Resurrection in the Ezekiel Panel of Dura Synagogue'. *Journal of Biblical Literature*, 60, no. 1 (1941): 43–55.

Wold, Benjamin. 'Agency and Raising the Dead in 4QPseudo-Ezekiel and 4Q521 2ii'. *Zeitschrift für die neutestamentliche Wissenschaft* 103, no. 1 (2012): 1–19.

Wolff, Christian. 'Irdisches und himmlisches Jerusalem – Die Heilshoffnung in den Paralipomena Jeremiae'. *Zeitschrift für die neutestamentliche Wissenschaft* 82, nos. 3–4 (1991): 147–58.

Wolff, Hans Walter. *Anthropology of the Old Testament*. Philadelphia, PA: Fortress, 1974.

Woods, David B. 'Jew-Gentile Distinction in the One New Man of Ephesians 2:15'. *Conspectus: The Journal of the South African Theological Seminary* 18, no. 9 (2014): 95–135.

Wright, Brian J. *Communal Reading in the Times of Jesus: A Windows into Early Christian Reading Practices*. Minneapolis, MN: Fortress, 2017.

Wright, David P. *Ritual in Narrative: The Dynamics of Feasting, Mourning, and Retaliation Rites in the Ugaritic Tale of Aqhat*. Winona Lake, IL: Eisenbrauns, 2001.

Wright, David P. 'Purification from Corpse-Contamination in Numbers XXXI 19–24'. *Vetus Testamentum* 35, no. 2 (1985): 213–23.

Wright, J. Edward. *Baruch ben Neriah: From Biblical Scribe to Apocalyptic Seer*. Columbia, SC: University of South Carolina Press, 2003.

Wright, J. Stafford. *Man in the Process of Time: An Assessment of the Powers and Functions of Human Personality*. Grand Rapids, MI: Eerdmans, 1956.

Wright, Jacob L. 'A New Model for the Composition of Ezra-Nehemiah'. In *Judah and the Judeans in the Fourth Century B.C.E.*, edited by Oded Lipschitz, Gary N. Knoppers and Rainer Albertz, 333–48. Winona Lake, IN: Eisenbrauns, 2007.

Wright, Jacob L. 'Making a Name for Oneself: Martial Valor, Heroic Death, and Procreation in the Hebrew Bible'. *Journal for the Study of the Old Testament* 36, no. 2 (2011): 131–162.

Wright, John. 'Rûaḥ: A Survey'. In *Prudentia*, edited by David W. Dockrill and Ronald G. Tanner, 5–25. Auckland: University of Auckland, 1985.

Wright, Nicholas T. *The Resurrection of the Son of God*. Minneapolis, MN: Fortress, 2003.

Wright, Nicholas T. 'Paul and the Patriarch: The Role of Abraham in Romans 4'. *Journal for the Study of the New Testament* 35, no. 3 (2013): 207–41.

Wunn, Ina and Constantin Klein. 'Evolutionary Processes in Early Religion: The Psychological Interpretation of the Earliest Indicators of a Religious Sentiment'. *Braunschweiger Naturkundliche Schriften* 11, no. 1 (2012): 127–138.

Wyatt, Nicolas. *Religious Texts from Ugarit* (2nd ed.). London: Sheffield Academic, 2002.

Wyss, Beatrice. 'From Cosmogony to Psychology: Philo's Interpretation of Gen 2:7'. In *De opificio mundi*, *Quaestiones et solutions in Genesin* and *Legum allegoriae*'. In *Dust of the Ground and Breath of Life (Gen 2:7): The Problem of a Dualistic Anthropology in Early Judaism and Christianity*, edited by Jacques T.A.G.M. van Ruiten and Geurt H. van Kooten, 99–116. Leiden: Brill, 2016.

Xella, P. 'Death and the Afterlife in Canaanite and Hebrew Thought'. In *Civilisations of the Ancient Near East*, edited by J. M. Sasson, J. Baines, G. Beckman and K.S. Rubinson, 2059–70. New York, NY: Macmillan, 1995.

Yadin-Israel, Azzan. '"For Mark Was Peter's Tanna ͗": Tradition and Transmission in Papias and the Early Rabbis'. *Journal of Early Christian Studies* 23, no. 3 (2015): 337–62.

Yamauchi, Edwin M. 'Tammuz and the Bible'. *Journal of Biblical Literature* 84, no. 3 (1965): 283–90.

Yamauchi, Edwin M. 'Life, Death, and Afterlife in the Ancient Near East'. In *Life in the Face of Death: The Resurrection Message of the New Testament*, edited by Richard N. Longenecker, 21–50. Grand Rapids, MI: Eerdmans, 1998.

Yerushalmi, Shmuel. *The Book of Kohelet, MeAm Lo ͑ez: Torah Anthology on the Book of Qoheleth*, translated by Zvi Faier. New York, NY: Maznaim, 1988.

York, Michael. 'Toward a Proto-Indo-European Vocabulary of the Sacred'. *Word* 44, no. 2 (1993): 239.

Young, Robin D. 'The Eagle and the Basket of Figs in 4 Baruch: A Response to Jens Herzer'. In *Jeremiah's Scriptures: Production, Reception, Interaction, and Transformation*, edited by Hindy Najman and Konrad Schmid, 392–7. Leiden: Brill, 2017.

Yusoff, Adnan M., Ahmad S. Azmi, Hishomudin Ahmad, Robiatul-Adawiyah Mohd-Amat and Wan A.W. Ahmad. 'Purification of Soul (Islah al-nafs) in the Quran: An Analysis of Al-Ghazali's Method'. *Advanced Science Letters* 24, no. 4 (2018): 2848–50.

Yusuf, Imtiyaz. 'Discussion between al-Ghazzālī and Ibn Rushd about the Nature of Resurrection'. *Islamic Studies* 25, no. 2 (1986): 181–95.

Zaehner, Robert C. *Mysticism, Sacred and Profane: An Inquiry into Some Varieties of Praeternatural Experience*. Oxford: Clarendon Press, 1957.

Zaehner, Robert C. *The Dawn and Twilight of Zoroastrianism*. New York, NY: Putnam, 1961.

Zahir al-Din, M.S. 'Man in Search of His Identity: A Discussion on the Mystical Soul *(Nafs)* and Spirit *(Ruh)*'. *Islamic Quarterly* 24, no. 3 (1980): 96–105.

Zahniser, A.H. Mathias 'Major Transitions and Thematic Borders in Two Long Sūras: al-Baqara and al-Nisā ͗'. In *Literary Structures of Religious Meaning in the Qur ͗ān*, edited by Issa J. Boullata, 26–55. Richmond: Curzon, 2000.

Zangenberg, Jürgen. 'The Human Body in Death and Resurrection'. *Journal for the Study of Judaism* 42, no. 3 (2011): 420–1.

Zaynū, Muḥammad b. Jamīl. *Majmū ͑ah rasā ͗il al-tawjīhāt al-Islāmiyyah li-iṣlāḥ al-fard wal-mujtama ͑*. Riyadh: al-Ṣumay ͑ī, 1997.

Zebiri, Kate. 'Towards a Rhetoric Criticism of the Qur ͗an'. *Journal of Qur ͗anic Studies* 5, no. 2 (2003): 95–120.

Zecher, Jonathan L. *The Role of Death in the Ladder of Divine Ascent and the Greek Ascetic Tradition*. Oxford: Oxford University Press, 2015.

Zellentin, Holger M. 'Gentile Purity Law from the Bible to the Qur'an: The Case of Sexual Purity and Illicit Intercourse'. In *The Qur'an's Reformation of Judaism and Christianity: Return to the Origins*, edited by Holger M. Zellentin, 115–215. Abingdon: Routledge, 2019.

Zeller, Edouard. *Die Philosophie der Griechen in ihrer geschichtlichen Entwicklung*. Leipzig: Fues's, 1869.
Zhuravlev, Y.N. and V.A. Avetisov. 'The Definition of Life in the Context of Its Origin'. *Biogeosciences* 3, no. 3 (2006): 281–291.
Zipor, Moshe A. 'The Greek Version of Leviticus'. *Biblica* 79, no. 4 (1998): 551–62.
Zuck, Roy B. 'God and Man in Qoheleth'. *Bibliotheca Sacra* 148 (1991): 46–56.
Zucker, David J. 'Elijah and Elisha: Part I Moses and Joshua'. *Jewish Bible Quarterly* 40, no. 4 (2012): 225–30.
Zwiep, Arie W. *The Ascension of the Messiah in Lukan Christology*. Leiden: Brill, 1997.
Zysow, Aron. 'Two Unrecognized Karrāmī Texts'. *Journal of the American Oriental Society* 108, no. 4 (1988): 577–87.

INDEX OF BIBLICAL AND QUR'ANIC VERSES

Apocrypha (Deutero-Canonical Books)

Sirach
50 79

2 Maccabees
1:18–2:18 79
7:22–29 68

Hebrew Bible

Genesis
1:20 25, 26
1:20–21 26
1:24 26
1:30 26
2:5–6 59
2:7 26, 28, 31, 32, 60
2:17 31–2
4:10 34
7:22 26
12:1–17:27 108
15 99–100, 101, 102, 104, 105–7, 108–10, 116
15:1–6 106, 112
15:5 106
15:6 100, 102
15:7–21 106
15:8 100
15:9–10 106
15:11 40
15:12 106, 111
15:14 109
15:18 110
16:2 110
17:17 108, 109
18:1–22:24 108
21:8 108
22 108
22:1 108
22:2 88
25:25 58
30:1 97, 110, 111
32:32 86
35:2 143
35:18 32
49:1 65
49:14 43

Exodus
4:19 111
6:4 14
22:6 120
31:17 28
32:3 141
32:20 141
32:30 141
32:32–33 56
32:33–34 142
33:18–23 142
33:35 142
34:16 90
34:24 88

Leviticus
4:13–21 107
4:27–31 107
4:32 107
5:15 107
13 111
13:36 129
14:24 107
16:23–24 134
16:34 131
17:11 31
19:21 107
21 135
21:1 30
21:11 25
22:20–25 130
26:11 34
26:30 34, 40
27:33 129

Numbers
6:6 29
6:12 107
11:17 29
12:12 111, 145
14:29 40
14:32 40
15:31 14
18:28 14
19 128, 129, 130, 131, 134, 136, 139, 140, 144
19:2 131
19:3 131
19:6 143
19:7 136
19:9 134
19:10 131
19:14 145
19:21 131
20 131, 136, 139, 140
20:3 139
20:7–11 137
20:13 139
24:14 65
31:19–24 141
31:23 141

Deuteronomy
4:20 94
4:30 65
6:4 102, 103

7:1 121
7:3 90
7:22 121
12:23 31
20:16 26
21 128, 130, 131
21:1–9 107, 128, 129, 144
30 109
31:29 65
32:39 10, 14

Joshua
2:13 29

Judges
15:5 120

1 Samuel
2:6 10, 14
2:35 34
12:17 55
30:3 137

2 Samuel
22:16 26

1 Kings
8:51 95
17:21–22 32

2 Kings
2:9 29
4:1–4:37 108
5:7 10
16:6 121
16:15 129

Isaiah
1:14 34
2:22 26
24–27 61
26:19 12, 58, 59, 60–1, 68
34:3 40
38 83
40:27–41:16 108
41:8–9 108
42:1 34
48:10 94
56:1 113

Jeremiah
2:13 57
5:14 94
5:15–18 94
5:17 94
8:13 82, 83, 94
11 95
11:4 95
16:18 59
17:13 56
22:29–30 57
23:20 65
24 83
24:1–10 82–3
31:14 34
34:18–22 106
41:9 40
49:39 65
51:39 14

Ezekiel
6:5 40
22:17–22 95
34:12 129
34:25–28 91
36–37 138
36:16–36(38) 138
36:16–38 144, 145
36:26 138
36:33–38 138
37 16–17, 21–2, 28, 60, 61, 68, 80, 138, 144, 145
37:1–10 60
37: 1–14 12, 15, 59–60
37:11 15
37:12 60
37:15–28 93
38:8 65
44:19 134
44:25 29

Hosea
9:10 82

Amos
6:8 34
8:3 40

Jonah
4:3 30

Micah
7:1 82

Zephaniah
1:15 113
1:18 113

Haggai
2:9 88
2:19 82

Zechariah
2 92
2:1–5 92
6:13 88
11:7 94
11:10 94
11:14 93
12:1–3 94
12:6 94
13:2 135
13:8–9 94
14:5 16

Malachi
3:2–3 94

Psalms
12:6 135
17:15 113
18:15 26
21:4 58
23:4 38
27:4 129
33:19 29
36:8–9 58, 64
44:19 38
46:4–5 64
56:8 56

56:13 29, 30
66:10–12 94
69:28 56, 58
84 91
84:4–7 91
84:5 92
84:6 91
107:10 38
107:14 38
116:8–9 30
116:9 15
126:1 78–9
128:6 97
136:13 110
139:16 56

Proverbs
10:2 113
11:4 113
19:17 113
20:27 26
21:21 114
27:18 87
30:15–16 14

Job
4:9 26
5:13 137
5:25–26 119, 120
7:9 15
10:21–22 38
14:4 134, 135
21:32 119
23:13 34
27:3 26
32:8 26
33:4 26
37:10 26

Lamentations
3:6 111

Qoheleth
12:7 15, 24, 28, 121

Daniel
3:27–28 43
5:23 26
6:24 43
8:4 107
8:20–21 107
10:17 26
12:1 56
12:1–2 60–1
12:1–13 12
12:2 60–1

Ezra
1:3 88
1:5 88
1:11 88
3–6 88
3:1–4 88
3:12–13 90
5:8 89
5:11 87
6:1 86
6:3 86, 90
6:8 86
6:11–12 86
6:14 88, 89
6:18 86
6:19–22 88
8:32–5 88
9:8 88
10:1 90

Nehemiah
8 90, 91
8:1–8 86
8:6–9 91
8:9–18 87
8:13–18 88
9:6 115

2 Chronicles
3:1 88

New Testament

Matthew
22:23–33 16
27:51–53 60

Mark
5:21–43 17
11:12–25 83
12:18–27 16

Luke
10:20 56, 57
20:27–38 16

John
3:1–15 67
4:10 57
4:14 57
7:38 57
8 57
8:6–8 57

Acts
23:8 16

Romans
3–4 102
3:30 102, 103
4 100, 101, 103, 105–6, 116
4:1–8 101
4:5 102
4:9–12 101, 102
4:11–12 101
4:13–17a 101
4:13–25 101
4:16 101
4:16–17 101
4:17 102, 110
4:19 108, 110, 116
5 103
5–8 104
5:12 103
5:12–21 103–4
5:14 103
5:17–21 103
6:1–14 103
6:7 104
6:13 103
8 104
8:10–11 104

2 Corinthians
12:2 32

Ephesians
2:1–10 60

Philippians
4:3 56

Colossians
3:5 104

Hebrews
12:23 56

1 Peter
3:18–19 62

2 Peter
2:4 62

Jude
6 62

Revelation
2:11 71
3:5 56
20:1–4 62
20:12–15 71

Pseudepigrapha

1 Enoch
69:28 62

2 Baruch
56:13 62

4 Baruch
3:12–13 79
3:14 79
4:12 79, 81
5:1–35 77, 80
6:2 80
6:6–10 80
6:14 81
6:15–18 81
6:19–25 96
7:7 81
7:12 81
7:13–14 81
7:15–19 81
9:7 81
9:10–32 176 n. 33
9:11–12 81
9:14 81

4 Ezra
4:40–42 68

Pseudo-Philo
19:2 76
19:6 76
28:10 76
29:4 76
33:6 76
35:3 76

Qur'an

2:3 42
2:8–10 42
2:10 42
2:16 39
2:21–39 144
2:28 70, 71, 122
2:34 49
2:40–103 144
2:49–74 143
2:51–54 140
2:54 142
2:55 142
2:56 142
2:67 127, 138
2:67–73 21, 129, 144
2:67–74 144
2:69 132
2:71 131, 139
2:73 128, 138, 140
2:74 131, 137, 140
2:86 64
2:92–93 142
2:96 26, 64
2:109 35
2:133 45
2:154 26, 52
2:175 39
2:178–253 144
2:179 64
2:180 45
2:205 120
2:215 42
2:243 144
2:245 113
2:254 112, 113, 144
2:254–284 144
2:255 63, 83, 103, 106, 114
2:255–260 105
2:256 96, 103, 108
2:256–260 97
2:257 39
2:258 86, 105, 108, 114, 115
2:258–260 105, 112, 144
2:259 20, 75–7, 80, 82, 83–4, 87, 91, 96, 97–8, 99, 100, 102, 103, 105, 107, 108, 111, 112, 116, 121, 122, 138, 144
2:259–260 73, 75–6, 100, 107, 110, 111, 113, 114, 115, 117, 119, 122, 124, 144, 148
2:260 21, 98, 99–100, 102, 103, 104, 106, 108, 112, 116, 120, 121, 124, 144

2:261–274	112	6:25	44, 121	16:21	26, 49–50,
2:262–264	114	6:33–36	53		51, 52,
2:263	114	6:35	42		59
2:264	113, 114	6:36	53	16:59	119
2:269	114	6:38	76	16:60–64	72
2:271	114	6:39	44, 53	16:65	72
2:274	114	6:93	34	16:70	26
2:284	35	6:95	127	16:75	42
2:284–286	111	6:122	45, 50,	16:97	64
2:286	35		51–2, 53,	16:103	43
3	95		66, 123,	17:46	44, 121
3:14	65		149	17:71	61
3:65–67	85	6:125	51	17:71–72	63
3:89–90	89	7:12–13	49	17:72	63
3:91–92	112, 113	7:30	39	17:75	64
3:93	85, 86–7,	7:143	142	17:85	33
	92, 96, 100	7:176–180	44	18:18	84
3:93–95	101, 102	7:180	43	18:19	75
3:93–97	86, 98, 100	7:205	34	18:27	43
3:93–103	96, 97–8	8:3	42	18:28	35
3:93–115	112	8:8	42	18:57	44, 121
3:95	85, 100	8:49	42	19:38	39
3:96	91	9:17–18	26	20:41	34
3:96–97	85, 87, 91	9:68	42	20:55	71
3:97	88, 91	9:118	35	20:67–68	35
3:103	93, 94, 96	9:125	42	20:74	46, 47
3:112	93, 96	10:4	69	20:96	35
3:113–15	90	10:16	26	20:97	64, 136
3:116–117	112, 113	10:31	127	21:34	46
3:154	35	10:34	69	21:34–35	45
3:169	26, 45, 52	10:41–46	123	21:35	34
3:184	50, 53	10:42–46	123	21:44	26
3:185	26, 34, 45,	10:44	123	21:102	34
	50	10:45	123	21:104	69, 125
4:56	125	11:61	26	22:3–8	139
4:61	42	12	61	22:5	3, 26, 140
4:63	35	12:18	35	22:5–7	70
4:65	35	12:25	61	22:6	139
4:128	35	12:53	35	22:7	140
5:16	39	12:68	34	22:17	17
5:30	35	12:77	34	22:46	48
5:32	34	14:16–17	46	22:61	127
5:45	41	14:49	62	22:62	63
5:52	42	14:51	35	23:12–16	70
5:52–54	42	15:58	42	23:14	73
5:89	41	15:99	124	23:37	9
5:95	41	16	49	23:68	18
5:98	127	16:7	26, 34	23:79–85	18
5:116	34	16:20–22	49	23:99	9

23:113 123
25:3 64
25:21 35
26:18 26
27:14 34
27:64 69
27:80–81 39, 51, 123
28:39 3
28:45 26
28:85 39
29:11 42
29:19–20 69
29:57 26, 34, 45
29:63–64 72
29:64 66
30:9 26
30:11 69
30:19 127
30:24–25 56
30:27 69
30:52–53 39, 51, 123
31:7 121
31:11 39
31:22 96
31:28 34
31:29 127
31:30 63
31:34 26, 35
32:7–9 121
32:7–22 121
32:8 120
32:11 121
32:13 121
32:17 121
33:1 42
33:12 42
33:60 42
34:7 67
34:21 3
34:23 63
34:24 39
35:8 35
35:11 26
35:13 127
35:14–26 72
35:19 63
35:19–22 44, 48, 121, 123
35:19–24 63
35:22 26, 50–1, 52, 53, 121, 126
35:22–24 63
35:25 50, 53
35:27 130
35:36–37 46
35:37 26
36:6–12 63
36:12 63
36:49–54 120
36:51 120
36:68 26
36:69–70 51, 52
36:70 42, 52, 53, 68
36:77–79 68
36:77–81 70
37:51–55 125
37:53 125
38:28 39
38:73–78 49
39:21 130
39:22 39
39:30 35
39:36–37 36
39:41 36
39:41–42 35, 51
39:42 30, 36, 38
39:56 35
40:11 71, 121
40:12 63
40:71 62
41:5 44, 121
41:39–40 72
41:40 43
41:44 121
42:4 63
43:11 55
43:40 39
43:74 42
43:83 122
45:24 9, 10, 125, 126
45:34–35 126
46:17 18
46:25 124
46:25–35 124
46:27 124
46:28 124
46:32 124
46:33 124
46:35 123
47:20–34 42
47:36 65
50:16 34, 35
53:8 64
54:4–8 120
54:56 47
56:7–10 56
56:17 66
57:6 127
57:14–17 140
57:17 140
57:20 65, 130
63:3 42
67:2 64
68:1 18
69:19 61
69:23 64
69:25 61
70:42–44 120, 122, 126
71:24 39
71:27 39, 41
72:22 43
75:1–2 35
75:1–6 40
75:2 34
76:4 62
76:14 64
77:26 26
79:11–14 125
79:34 27
79:35 124
79:36 124
79:36–39 124
79:37–41 34
79:38–39 124
79:40–41 34
79:46 123, 124
81:5 76
82:13–14 40
82:14 39
83:1 62
83:4–28 61
83:4–36 56
83:7 39, 40, 61

83:7–9 63
83:8–9 62
83:18 40
83:18–20 63
83:26 28
84:7 61
84:10 61
87:12–13 46
87:13 47
89:27–30 35
90:1–2 26
91:7–10 119, 136
102:5–7 124
112:1 103

2 Aqhat
6:26–29 26
6:26–32 58

Parah
4:4 134

Numbers Rabbah
19:4 135

Qoheleth Rabbah
8:1.5 135

GENERAL INDEX

Abdel Haleem, Muhammad 65
Abimelech 77, 79–81, 82–3
Abraham 99, 107–10
 birds, and the 100–6, 107, 108
 children 99, 100, 104, 109, 110–11
 faith 100–2
 Genesis Rabbah, ritual in 106–11
Abraham's Faith in Romans 4 (Schliesser, Benjamin) 102
ʿ*adl* (justice) 183 n. 22
afterlife 4, 24, 37 *see also* reincarnation *and* resurrection
 Crone, Patricia 3, 9
 Egypt 7, 13, 37–8
 Elledge, Casey 13
 Israelites 12, 13
 Judaism 13–14, 16
 rejection of 13
 Sadducees 16
agriculture 11
ʾ*aḥăwâ* (brotherhood) 93
Aichele, George 57
ajdāth (graves) 119, 120, 121
ākhirah (later world) 64, 65, 66, 67
Akkadian 25, 27, 28, 38, 39
Allison, Dale, Jr. 80
ʿ*amara; ma* ʿ*mar; ma* ʿ*mūrah* (place where people live) 26
Ambrose, Saint 57
ʿAmidah prayer 111–15, 150
anattā (non-self) 8
animals 75–6, 106, 107–9 *see also* red cow, ritual of the
  golden calf 136, 140–4
  sacrifice 130
anti-Jewishness 95
antithesis 127
Apocryphon Jeremiae de captivitate Babylonis (*History of the Captivity in Babylon*) 77
Arabic 25–7, 28, 38
ʿ*Arā* ʾ*is al-bayān fī ḥaqā* ʾ*iq al-Qur* ʾ*ān* (Baqlī, Rūzbihān) 50
Aramaic 28
arrogance 49
aṣlaḥū (reform) 89
audience 5, 84
Augustine, Saint 30, 57

b-l-d root 26
b-l-ṭ root 25–6
b-q-r root 129
ba (soul) 27
bakkah (weeping) 90–1
balāṭu (life) 25
baqarah (cow) 129
Baqlī, Rūzbihān
  ʿ*Arā* ʾ*is al-bayān fī ḥaqā* ʾ*iq al-Qur* ʾ*ān* 50
Baruch 79–81
barzakh (intermediate state) 36
bashar (flesh) 46
Baumgarten, Albert 134
Begg, Christopher 141, 142
Ben Sira 79
Berrada, Khaled 48
Bertaina, David 68
Bible, the. *See* Hebrew Bible *and* New Testament
Biblical Interpretation in Ancient Israel (Fishbane, Michael) 20
birth 69–70, 97 *see also* children *and* re-creation
 rebirth 70, 149
Black, C. Clifton, II 104
blackness 38–9
blessings 91
blmt (immortality) 26
bodhisattvas 8
bodily resurrection 4–5, 47, 67–73, 147–8
 animals 75–6
 definition 4

Elledge, Casey 13
ibn Sīnā 4
nepeš 29
body, the *see also* bodily resurrection
soul, relationship with 23–5, 27, 28–33
Book of Daniel 60–1
book of deeds 56, 63
Book of Deuteronomy 127–33
Book of Exodus 56
Book of Ezekiel 59–60, 138
Book of Ezra-Nehemiah 86, 88, 89–91
Book of Genesis 25, 26–8, 31–2, 99–100, 102, 105–6, 108 see also *Genesis Rabba* and *Parashat Lech-Lecha*
Book of Haggai 88–9
Book of Isaiah 58, 61
book of life 56, 58, 61, 63, 64, 71
Book of Numbers 129–33, 134–7
Book of Psalms 58
Book of Zechariah 92, 93–4
Boyce, Mary 12
brotherhood 93, 94
Brown-Driver-Briggs Lexicon (*BDB*) 120
Buddhism 7–8

Cain and Abel 34
Canaanites, the 13
catuṣkoṭi (logic statement) 128
charity 112–14
Charlesworth, James H. 16–17
children 97, 99, 100, 104, 109, 110–11
descendants 120–1
progeny 121
Christian Doctrine of Man, The (Robinson, H. Wheeler) 28
Christianity 32, 68, 81, 104–5 *see also* New Testament
Didache 16
Climacus, John 104
Ladder of Divine Ascent, The 104–5
Cohen, Norman 100
Cole, Juan 40–1
colours 130, 143
community 5
agricultural 11
Companions of the Cave (Sleepers) 75, 77, 84
covenants 92–3, 94, 99, 108
animals 106
divine 96–7*f*
creation 69–70 *see also* re-creation
Crone, Patricia 2–3, 17, 18
bodily resurrection 47, 67
death 47
nonbelievers 9–10, 50
reincarnation 9–10
second death 71

ḍ-l-l root 38, 39
d-n-y root 64
dahr (time) 10
Dalferth, Ingolf U. 1
al-dār al-ākhirah (other abode) 66, 67
darkness 38–9, 66, 123
darkness/light metaphors 48, 51, 66, 123
day of wrath 117
deafness 121, 123
death 31–2, 45, 66–7, 70–1, 148–9
arrogance, relationship with 49
Berrada, Khaled 48
books of 63
Christianity 104–5
classifications of 47
Climacus, John 104–5
darkness and 38–9, 66
defilement 127, 130
defining 37–8
definition in the Qurʿan 45–53
ego-death 49
first death 46, 71, 72, 122
hearing 121–2
impure symbolism 136
impurity 145 *see also* defilement
living 46
metaphorical 45, 46, 47–9, 51, 97, 102
non-dying 46–7 *see also* zombies
nonbelievers, terms associated with 37–44
O'Shaughnessy, Thomas 46, 47
physical 45, 46, 71, 77, 125, 126
Romans 103–6
second death 46, 47, 71, 122
shadow of 38–9
sleep and 38, 75–6, 97
of the soul 35–6
spiritual 35–6, 49–53, 103–4, 122–6, 145, 147–8
terminologies 37–44

Death of the Soul in Romans 7, The (Wasserman, Emma) 104
defilement 127, 130, 133–6, 141, 143
descendants 120–1 *see also* children
Didache 16
divine covenant 96–7*f*
Dormandy, Katherine 19
doubt 2–3 *see also* nonbelievers
Draper, Jonathan 16
dream soul 162 n. 119
dream state 78
Druze, the 8, 9
dunyā (current world) 64–5, 67, 149
Dura-Europos synagogue paintings 15
dying-and-rising gods 11, 13

ʿeglâ (atonement of unsolved murder) 128–9
ego-death 49
Egypt 7, 13, 38
  afterlife 7, 13, 37–8
  agriculture 11
  Hathor 143
  life, concept of 27
  resurrection 11–12, 13
  Sun-god Ra 11
Eighteen Benedictions 55
Elledge, Casey 13
ʿelyôn (Most High [God]) 63–4
Epic of Atrahasis 27
Epic of Gilgamesh 15
Epicureans 156 n. 129
epistemic humility 19
Epistle to the Ephesians 60
Epistle to the Romans 100–6
eṭemmu (human soul) 27, 30
evildoers 39–40
exile 77–80, 83–5, 111–15 *see also* Jewish Diaspora
  exile and restoration in the Qurʾan 111–15
  return from 60, 88–9, 91, 99, 105
Ezra 77

faith 100–2
al-Farāhīdī, al-Khalil b. Aḥmad 27
  Kitāb al-ʿayn 41, 120
Farrin, Raymond 144
Feldman, Noah 86
fiery furnace 94–6, 109 *see also* hellfire
figs 80–1, 82–3, 87–8, 94, 98
first death 46, 71, 72, 122
first house 85, 90–1
first life 71, 122
Fishbane, Michael
  Biblical Interpretation in Ancient Israel 20
food 82, 84–5, 86–8 *see also* figs
fountain of life 56–8, 64
4 Baruch (*Paraleipomena Jeremiou*) 77, 79–82, 83, 96, 97
Freidenreich, David 130
fujjār (evildoers; nonbelievers) 37, 39–40
al-Fulānī, Yūsuf b. Saʿīd 49

g-r-m root 43
gādîs (sheaf) 119–20
Galadari, Abdulla
  Qurʾanic Hermeneutics: Between Science, History, and the Bible 19
Genesis Rabbah 21, 28, 59, 106–11
al-Ghazālī, Abū Ḥāmid 49
  Mishkāt al-anwār (*The Niche of Lights*) 125
  Tahāfut al-falāsifah 70
goats 107
God
  as redeemer 114
  breath of 26, 28, 121
  niʿmatih (God's favour) 94
  oneness of (*Shemaʿ*) 102
  power of 114–15
  wrath of 94, 95, 96
golden calf 136, 140–4
Gospel of John 57
graves 41–2, 119–20, 121, 126
Greek philosophy 3, 127–8
grief 11
guidance 51–2
Guillaume, Philippe 141, 142
guilt 141–2

ḥ-w-y root 25
ḥ-y-h root 25, 26
ḥ-y-y root 25, 26
ḥabl (covenant; rope) 92–3, 94, 96
Haft bāb (Kātib, Ḥassan-i Maḥmūd-i) 4
ḥajj (pilgrimage) 87

Ḥaqā'iq al-tafsīr (al-Sulamī, Abū ʿAbdulraḥmān) 50
al-ḥaqq (decree; statute; truth) 84, 131–2, 136
Hathor 143
ḥayāh (life) 64, 65, 66
al-ḥayāt al-dunyā (nearer life; this) 64, 65, 66
ḥayawān (life) 66–7
ḥayy; *ḥayyâ* (living) 25, 26 see also *nišmat ḥayyîm*
health 11
hearing 121–2
heart 25
heaven 56–7
ḥebel (measuring line) 92–3
Hebrew 27, 28, 38
Hebrew Bible 12–13, 14–15, 21, 29 *see also* Talmuds, the *and* New Testament
  afterlife 12, 13, 15, 16
  anti-Jewishness 95
  Book of Daniel 60–1
  Book of Deuteronomy 127–33
  Book of Exodus 56
  Book of Ezekiel 59–60, 138
  Book of Ezra-Nehemiah 86, 88, 89–91
  Book of Genesis 25, 26–8, 31–2, 99–100, 102, 105–6 see also *Genesis Rabba* and *Parashat Lech-Lecha*
  Book of Haggai 88–9
  Book of Isaiah 58, 61
  Book of Numbers 129–33, 134–7
  Book of Psalms 58
  Book of Zechariah 92, 93–4
  figs as metaphor 82
  Genesis Rabbah 21, 28, 59, 106–11, 59
  nafs 24
  nepeš 25, 29
  něšāmâ; nišmat 26
  nonbelievers 9–10
  procreation 15
  resurrection 58
  rûaḥ 29
  Septuagint 29
  shadow of death 38–9
  symbolism 80
  targumim, the 13
Hebrewism 28, 29 *see also* Judaism
heifers 107
hell 46–7, 125–6
  Abraham 109
  imprisonment in 61–3
hellfire 124–6
Hinduism 8, 10
Ḥoni ha-Mʿagel (the Circle-Drawer) 77–9, 81, 97
ḥyh (life) 26
ḥym (life) 26
hypocrites 42

Ibn ʿArabī 122, 124
Ibn al-Ḥāj al-Fāsī
  Madkhal 12
Ibn Qayyim al-Jawziyyah 50
Ibn Rushd 70
ibn Sīnā 4
  Kitāb al-najāh 4
  Kitāb al-shifā' 4
  Risālah fil-adwiyah al-qalbiyah 4
Ibrahīm, Aḥmad Shawqī 34
ikhwānā (brotherhood) 93, 94
ʿilliyyīn; *ʿilliyyūn* (book of the living; Most High [God]) 63–4
imām (book) 63
impermanence 8
imprisonment 61–3
impurity 145–6 *see also* defilement
incline 43
intertextual polysemy 20
intertextuality 18–20, 97, 111–16, 139–40, 148–50 *see also* red cow, ritual of the
  book of death 63
  Book of Ezra-Nehemiah 86, 90–2, 97
  Book of Genesis 105–6, 116
  Book of Haggai 89, 92, 97
  book of life 63
  Book of Zechariah 88, 89, 92, 94, 97
  Epistle to the Romans 102–6, 116
  4 Baruch 77, 79–82, 96, 97
  Genesis Rabbah 106–11
  Hebrew Bible covenant 93, 97
  Talmuds, the 77–9, 81–2, 97
intratextuality 20
Islam
  nafs 33–6
  reincarnation 8–9, 10, 47

Islamic Understanding of Death and Resurrection, The (Smith, Jane I. and Haddad, Yvonne, Y.) 2
Israel; Israelites, the 12–13, 88, 99 *see also* Judaism
  bird symbolism 107
  diet 86–7
  exile. *See* exile
  fiery furnace 94–6
  figs as metaphor 82, 83
  Jewish Diaspora 106, 107
  Judah and 93
  purification 138
Izutsu, Toshihiko 64–5

j-d-th root 120
j-r-m root 42–3
j-s-m root 43
al-jaḥīm (hellfire) 124–6
Jeremiah 77, 79, 81, 82–3
Jerome, Saint 57
Jerusalem 83, 88–9
  destruction of 78–80, 83, 97, 105
  God's wrath against 94
  Temple 79–80, 83, 86, 88–91
Jewish Diaspora 107, 108, 109–10
Judah 93
Judaism 150 *see also* Hebrewism *and* Israel; Israelites
  anti-Jewishness 95
  Dura-Europos synagogue paintings 15
  Jewish Diaspora 107, 108, 109–10
  Mishnah, the 13–14
  rabbinic Jews. *See* rabbinic traditions
  mockery 138
  prayer 111–12
  resurrection 12–16
  soul, the 32–3
  Talmuds, the. *See* Talmuds, the
  Talmudic-Rabbinic community 5, 14–15
jurum (body; cut; imperfection; sin) 42

k-f-r root 40, 42
k-p-r root 41
ka (energy) 27
kāfir (farmers; nonbelievers) 40–2
karma 126–7
Kātib, Ḥassan-i Maḥmūd-i
  Haft bāb 4
ʾ-kh-r root 65
Kinman, Brent 83
Kister, Menahem 103–4
Kitāb al-ʿayn (al-Farāhīdī, al-Khalil b. Aḥmad) 41, 120
Kitāb al-najāh (ibn Sīnā) 4
Kitāb al-shifāʾ (ibn Sīnā) 4
Köhler, Ludwig 28
al-Kubrā, Najm-ul-dīn (Ahmad b. ʿUmar)
  al-Taʾwīlāt al-najmiyyah fil-tafsīr al-ishārī al-ṣūfī 124
kuffār (farmers; nonbelievers) 37, 40–2
kuffārah (forgive sins; purify) 41

l-ḥ-d root 43
Ladder of Divine Ascent, The (Climacus, John) 104–5
Lehtipuu, Outi 17
Levenson, Jon
  Resurrection and the Restoration of Israel 13
Levitical killing, the 141–2
liberation 8
life 25–6, 70–1
  book of 56, 58, 61, 63, 64, 71
  definition 23–4
  definition in the Qurʿan 52, 55
  first life 71, 122
  fountain of 56–8, 64
  language comparison 25–33
  metaphors 48–9, 51
  pure symbolism 136
  rain analogy 55–6, 59, 72
  Romans 103–6
  second life 71, 122
  spiritual life 68, 147–8
  worldly 64–7
light/darkness metaphors 48, 51, 66, 123
Lisān al-ʿarab (Ibn Manzur) 33, 41, 120
living death 46
logic 127–8

m-w-t root 38
Machery, Edward 23–4
Madkhal (Ibn al-Ḥāj al-Fāsī) 12
maqām (place) 88
martyrdom 16, 52
mātu (to die) 38
Mazuz, Haggai 5

measuring line (*ḥebel*) 92–3
Mesopotamia 38
metempsychosis 8, 125
methodology 18–22
midrash works 21 *see also* rabbinic traditions/writings
Milgrom, Jacob 134, 145
misguidance 39, 51–2
Mishkāt al-anwār (*The Niche of Lights*) (al-Ghazālī, Abū Ḥāmid) 125
Mishnah, the 13–14, 55, 132–3
mōrîm (stubborn) 137
Moses 131, 135–6, 137, 141–2
Muhammad's Thoughts on Death: A Thematic Study of the Qur'anic Data (O'Shaughnessy, Thomas) 1–2
mujrimūn (nonbelievers; sinners) 37, 42–3
munāfasah (competition) 28
munāfiqūn (hypocrites; nonbelievers) 37, 42
Muslim tradition 2

n-b-l root 58–9
n-b-š 30
n-f-q root 42
n-f-s root 28, 30
n-p-q root 42
n-p-š 30
n-s-l root 120–1
Nabatean 41
nafīs (desired; rare; valued) 28
nafs (self; soul) 3, 4, 5, 23, 30, 33–6, 121
  attributes 35
  buried in a grave 119–20
  death of 35–6, 45–6, 49, 50, 52, 53, 149
  killing 34
  meanings 34–5, 36
  monism/dualism 23–5, 27
  resurrection 4, 5, 149
napishtu; *napshu* (breath; carded wool; life; person; self; throat) 27, 28
natural power 72–3
nĕbēlātî (my corpse) 58
Neolithic Revolution 11
nepeš (appetite; desire; life; self; soul) 25–33, 34
nepeš ḥayyâ (living breath; soul) 25, 27
nepeshtu; *nepeshu* (construction; performance; ritual) 28
nepishu (package of gold/silver) 28
nĕšāmâ; nišmat (breath; wind) 26, 28
New Testament
  Epistle to the Ephesians 60
  Epistle to the Romans 100–6
  fountain of life 56–7
  Gospel of John 57
Newman, Stephen 142–3
nifās (blood) 31
ni'matih (God's favour) 94
nirvana 8
nišmat ḥayyîm (breath of life) 26, 28
nišmat rûaḥ (wrathful breath) 26
Noam, Vered 145
non-dying 46–7 *see also* zombies
non-self, doctrine of 8
nonbelievers 2–3, 37, 49, 149 *see also* doubt
  blindness 123, 124–5
  bodily resurrection 67–8, 72
  Crone, Patricia 9–10
  deafness 121, 123
  al-jaḥīm (hellfire) 124–5
  imprisonment 63
  spiritual death 50–1, 123
  terminologies 37–44
Noort, Ed 28
Numbers (*Bamidbar*) *Rabbah* 134–5, 137

O'Brien, Mark 141
Origen of Alexandria 104
O'Shaughnessy, Thomas 46, 47, 62, 71
  Muhammad's Thoughts on Death: A Thematic Study of the Qur'anic Data 1–2

pagru (body; corpse; person; self) 39
Parashat Lech-Lecha 108
Paul, Saint 32
peš root 29
Pharisees, the 16
Philo 31–2
philosophy 1
  Greek 3, 127–8
  logic 127–8
Picken, Gavin 34
pilgrimage 87, 88, 91
Plato 1
power 70, 72–3, 114–15
prayer 111–15, 150

Pregill, Michael 135
progeny 121 *see also* children
Pseudo-Ezekiel 68
Pseudo-Philo 76
psychē (soul) 29
purification 127, 130, 133–6, 138, 141, 143, 145
Pythagoras 7

q-b-r root 41
Qiblah passages
Qoheleth Rabbah 135–6, 138
Qumran community 156 n. 148
Qur'an 18–22
golden calf narrative 142
Moses narrative 142
red cow, ritual of the. *See* red cow, ritual of the
structure 144
Qur'an 2:259 75–6, 97–8, 107–8, 115–17
divine covenant 96–7
man in desolate town 76–82
measuring line (*ḥebel*) and fiery furnace 92–6
structure 144
ṭaʿām (food; commandment) 82–92, 98
Qur'an 2:260 75–6, 99, 115–17
Abraham and the birds 100–6
Abraham's ritual in *Genesis Rabbah* 106–7
Israelite exile and restoration 111–5
structure 144
Qur'anic Hermeneutics: Between Science, History, and the Bible (Galadari, Abdulla) 19

Ra (Sun-god) 11
rabbinic traditions/writings 16, 20–1, 143, 150 see also *midrash* works *and* Talmuds, the
Abraham 100
charity 112–13
Eighteen Benedictions 55
exilic imagery 111
Genesis Rabbah 21, 28, 59, 106–11
Greek philosophy 127, 128
Midrash Tanḥuma 128, 138, 141
Mishnah, the 13–14, 55, 132–3
Numbers (*Bamidbar*) *Rabbah* 134–6, 137
Qoheleth Rabbah 135–6, 138
red cow, ritual of the 130, 132–8, 140, 143
Shemaʿ 102–3, 112, 115, 150
Sifra 103
ʿAmidah prayer 111–15, 150
raḥmān (God) 66
rain analogy 55–6, 59, 72
rajʿah (the return) 9, 10
Rakesh, Mohammad and Ayati, S.M.R. 23, 45
ramānu (self) 27
rams 107
Rashi 140–1
al-Rāzī, Fakhr al-Dīn 35–6, 41, 49, 51
re-creation 33, 67–73, 149
rebirth 70, 149
red cow, ritual of the 127–8, 144–6
descriptions 128–33
golden calf, allusion to 140–4
paradox 127, 133–140
reincarnation 3, 7–10
Druze, the 8, 9
Islam 8–9, 10, 33
rajʿah 9, 10
religious competitiveness 148
repentance 89
resurrection 3, 11–18, 148–9 *see also* bodily resurrection
nafs 4, 5, 149
as re-creation 67–73
Resurrection and the Restoration of Israel (Levenson, Jon) 13
Reynolds, Gabriel 95
rhetoric 127
Risālah fil-adwiyah al-qalbiyah (ibn Sīnā) 4
Robinson, H. Wheeler
Christian Doctrine of Man, The 28
rock that brings forth water 136–7
rope 92–3
rûaḥ; *rūḥ* (spirit) 26, 28, 29, 33–4

s-j-n root 61–2
ṣ-l-l (Hebrew term) 38
ṣ-l-l root 38
s-n-h root 83–4
s-r-r/*š-r-r* root 133
Saadia Gaon 130
sabīlā (way) 91–2

sacrifice 130
Sadducees, the 12, 16
ṣafrā' (yellow) 129–30
saints 50
ṣalālu; ṣalīlu (cover; fall asleep) 38
ṣalāmu; ṣalmu 39 (darkness; image)
ṣalmāwet (shadow of death) 38–9
Sam'alian 30
Samaritans, the 12
Schliesser, Benjamin
  Abraham's Faith in Romans 4 102
Schmitz, Philip 58
Schopenhauer, Arthur 1
science 23–4
second death 46, 47, 71, 122
second life 71, 122
sek- root 62
Semites, the 3, 26–33
Septuagint 29
Shema' (oneness of God) 102–3, 112, 115, 150
Sheol 13
Sifra 103
sigillum (seal) 62
signum (sign) 62
sijjīl (register of deeds) 62
sijjīn (hell as eternal punishment; book of register) 61–2, 64
ṣillu (cover; shade) 38
Simeon b. Abba 109
Simon-Shoshan, Moshe 78, 79, 81
Singh, R. Raj 1
sinners 42–3, 141–2
sleep 38, 75–9, 83–4, 97, 111
Smith, Jane 8
Smith, Jane I. and Haddad, Yvonne, Y.
  Islamic Understanding of Death and Resurrection, The 2
society
  farming 11
Socrates 1
soul, the 3 see also *nafs* and *nepeš*
  body, relationship with 23–5, 27, 28–33
  Buddhism 7–8
  Christianity 32
  death of 35–6, 104
  dream soul 162 n. 119
  dualism/monism 23–5, 27, 28
  Elledge, Casey 13
  Hebrewism 28–29
  Hinduism 8
  Judaism 32–3
  al-Ṭabarī, Tafsīr 47
spirit 29 see also *rûaḥ*
  spiritual darkness 123
  spiritual death 35–6, 49–53, 103–4, 122–6, 145, 147–8
  spiritual life 68, 147–8
  spiritual resurrection 4, 5, 149
  spiritually blind 123, 124–5
  spiritually deaf 121, 123, 124
staffs 94
Steiner, Richard 30, 32
Stewart, Devin 61–2
Sufi literature 147–8
al-Sulamī, Abū 'Abdulraḥmān
  Ḥaqā'iq al-tafsīr 50
sun, the 11
Sun-god Ra 11
supernatural power 72–3
al-Suyūṭī 62

ṭ-m-m root 27
ṭa'ām (commandment; decree; food) 84–7, 92, 98
al-Ṭabarī, Tafsīr 47, 49, 51, 142
tābū (repent; return) 89
Tafsīr (al-Tustarī, Sahl) 50
Tahāfut al-falāsifah (al-Ghazālī, Abū Ḥāmid) 70
Talmuds, the 14–15, 34, 115, 159 n. 28
  charity 112–14
  Ḥoni ha-M'agel (the Circle-Drawer) 77–9, 81, 97
  prayer 112–13
  rain analogy 55–6
  red cow ritual 133
tanaffas (relieved) 28
targumim, the 13
tasurra (pleasing) 132–3
al-Ta'wīlāt al-najmiyyah fil-tafsīr al-ishārī al-ṣūfī (al-Kubrā, Najm-ul-dīn [b. 'Umar, Ahmad]) 124
Tesei, Tommaso 75
Theological Dictionary of the Old Testament (*TDOT*) 39, 40, 84, 129
time 10, 11

Tlili, Sarra 76
Trick, Bradley 16
al-Tustarī, Sahl
    Tafsīr 50
2 Maccabees 79

Ugaritic 25, 26, 28
ʿ*umur* (life; lifespan) 26
al-ʿurwah al-wuthqā (unfailing handhold) 96

war 40
Wasserman, Emma
    Death of the Soul in Romans 7, The 104
weeping 90–1
Western Semetic 25–6
wrath of God 94, 95
Wright, David 141
Wright, Nicholas T. 102
writing 56–7

yafjur (person asking when Day of Resurrection is) 40
yatanāfasūn (competing; craving) 28
yatanaffasūn (breathing) 28
yatasannah (spoiled) 83–4
Yoruba Muslims 8–9
yulḥidūn (distort; incline) 37, 43

ẓ-l-l (Arabic term) 38
ẓ-l-m root 39
ʿ-ẓ-m root 43
al-Zajjāj, Abū Isḥāq Ibrāhīm ibn Muḥammad ibn al-Sarī 52
zaqīqu (dream soul) 30
Zecher, Jonathan 105
zombies 4, 47, 50, 147–9
Zoroastrianism 9, 12, 17
ẓulm (darken; injustice; wrong) 123, 183 n. 22
ẓulumāt (darkness) 39, 66, 123
Zurvanism 10

www.ingramcontent.com/pod-product-compliance
Lightning Source LLC
Chambersburg PA
CBHW062128300426
44115CB00012BA/1852